PENGUIN BOOKS

HOW IRELAND REALLY WENT BUST

Matt Cooper is the No. 1 bestselling author of *Who Really Runs Ireland?*, which was shortlisted for an Irish Book Award for non-fiction. In over twenty years as a reporter (*Business & Finance*, *Sunday Business Post*, *Irish Independent*) and editor (*Sunday Tribune*), and now as a radio presenter (Today FM) and newspaper opinion columnist (*Sunday Times*, *Irish Examiner*), he has enjoyed proximity and access to the most significant people in Irish politics and business, hearing from them and hearing about them from a variety of sources. His depth of experience means he is in an unrivalled position to assess and interpret the actions of the powerful and their implications for us all.

Praise for *Who Really Runs Ireland?*

'Shocking, hilarious, but ultimately depressing . . . as an overview of what went on this is by far the most readable of the various books now on the shelves . . . hugely entertaining as well as instructive book' *Irish Independent*

'Impressive and eminently readable' *The Irish Times*

'The detail is riveting . . . and a lot of it illumination on the predicament the country finds itself in' *Irish Examiner*

'I am disgusted at how well written it is and its insights about the social partners and the tribunals . . . my heart sinks when it becomes clear that this is a readable view of some of Ireland's insiders' Shane Ross, *Sunday Independent*

'A superbly readable and insightful study of power in contemporary Irish politics and business . . . a must-have' *Irish Mail on Sunday*

'Highly accessible and there is a nice pace to the book, akin to a good thriller . . . fascinating . . . compelling' *Sunday Tribune*

'His snappy writing and anecdotal style give new life to events . . . a lively yet informative insight into Irish society during the Celtic Tiger era' *Evening Echo*

'The scale of Cooper's research is highly impressive . . . an in-depth reference guide to the folly and hubris that brought the country to its current state' *Sunday Business Post*

How Ireland Really Went Bust

MATT COOPER

PENGUIN BOOKS

PENGUIN BOOKS

Published by the Penguin Group
Penguin Books Ltd, 80 Strand, London WC2R ORL, England
Penguin Group (USA) Inc., 375 Hudson Street, New York, New York 10014, USA
Penguin Group (Canada), 90 Eglinton Avenue East, Suite 700, Toronto, Ontario, Canada M4P 2Y3
(a division of Pearson Penguin Canada Inc.)
Penguin Ireland, 25 St Stephen's Green, Dublin 2, Ireland (a division of Penguin Books Ltd)
Penguin Group (Australia), 250 Camberwell Road, Camberwell, Victoria 3124, Australia
(a division of Pearson Australia Group Pty Ltd)
Penguin Books India Pvt Ltd, 11 Community Centre, Panchsheel Park, New Delhi – 110 017, India
Penguin Group (NZ), 67 Apollo Drive, Rosedale, Auckland 0632, New Zealand
(a division of Pearson New Zealand Ltd)
Penguin Books (South Africa) (Pty) Ltd, Block D, Rosebank Office Park, 181 Jan Smuts Avenue,
Parktown North, Gauteng 2193, South Africa

Penguin Books Ltd, Registered Offices: 80 Strand, London WC2R ORL, England

www.penguin.com

First published by Penguin Ireland 2011
Published in Penguin Books 2012
001

Copyright © Matt Cooper, 2011
All rights reserved

The moral right of the author has been asserted

Typeset by Jouve (UK), Milton Keynes
Printed in England by Clays Ltd, St Ives plc

ISBN: 978–1–844–88169–7

www.greenpenguin.co.uk

ALWAYS LEARNING   PEARSON

To the memory of my late parents, Matty and Kathleen

Contents

Prologue: Thursday, 18 November 2010

Taoiseach Brian Cowen was furious. The governor of the Central Bank, Patrick Honohan, had conducted a morning interview on national radio, without first telling him that he would be doing so or what he would be saying. He had pulled the rug from under Cowen's feet, flattening and embarrassing him.

An unwanted agenda of action was being imposed on our government, despite its best efforts to keep a lid on the Irish financial version of Pandora's Box. It had been known that representatives of the International Monetary Fund (IMF) were arriving in Dublin that day, Thursday, 18 November, but the government had been trying to downplay the significance of their arrival, to the mounting disbelief and anger of the public. Everyone had to wake up and smell the coffee, as Honohan used his breakfast-time interview on *Morning Ireland* to set the record straight, to let the people of Ireland know what was happening, that the game was up.

Honohan was in Frankfurt, where the real decisions were being made, at a meeting of the European Central Bank's governing council, of which he was a member. He outlined the reason why the IMF officials were arriving in Dublin: it was to work out the details of giving our state 'a very substantial loan', in conjunction with the special rescue fund set up earlier that year by the European Union to deal with members in financial distress. Why else, he asked rhetorically, would they be in Ireland?

This was a cataclysmic event. For the first time in history we were turning to what was effectively the lender of last resort. It was likely that the terms and conditions set by the IMF in return for a loan would be brutal. Even after a couple of years of successive harsh budgets that had reduced living standards, more austerity would be imposed: taxes would be hiked even more, public-sector wages and jobs would be slashed further and services reduced accordingly.

Those were the practical realities, but the state would also have to deal with the issue of how we would now be viewed in a larger sense, both by ourselves and by others: we had become indigent and could not look after ourselves. We were at the mercy of what one prescient economist had described as 'the kindness of strangers'.

Honohan had undermined almost completely whatever vestiges of Cowen's authority and standing remained. Cowen had been made to look foolish at best, delusional at worst, and, even if he thought he was acting in the public interest by not conceding until he absolutely had to, he would still be regarded as untrustworthy because he hadn't given the people he represented the truth about our situation. All week he and government ministers had sought to reassure the public that things were not as bad as they seemed and that, specifically, the country had enough resources to negate any perceived need to turn to the IMF and the EU for help. Only the previous day Cowen had told the Dáil that it was not in the national interest for him to indicate the government's negotiating position before talks began with officials of the IMF. He maintained that the government's main objective was to ensure, as quickly as possible, that the country retained a banking system that could access funds on the open market at reasonable and affordable prices. 'There has been no question, as has been stated all over the weekend, of a negotiation for a bailout,' he added.

Now Honohan was confirming that our emperor had no clothes. His decision to take to the national airwaves at such a crucial time was pointed. Nobody could ever have imagined any of his eight predecessors – unlike him, all loyal time-serving civil servants – being as brave. 'I think this is the way forward,' said Honohan, the externally appointed academic, selected for his independence by the minister for finance, Brian Lenihan. 'Market conditions have not allowed us to go ahead without seeking the support of our international collaborators.'

To anyone listening the impact was electrifying. Cowen bridled at Honohan's intervention. 'The governor gave his view,' he told the Dáil later that day. 'He is entitled to give his view. I am entitled to give the view about the decision the government will take when the necessary discussions are over.'

Cowen drew attention to Honohan's dual position: he was our Central Bank governor and also a director of the European Central Bank (ECB). 'The governor is part of the governing council of the ECB, and it is a matter of public knowledge what the ECB general view has been,' he said. 'We understand all that. At the end of the day, we have to determine what is the best option for our country and for our people at the time. At the moment we are in the process of working out what the best options are and I think that is what people would expect of a government that is working to protect the interests of the taxpayer,' he said. At that stage the public didn't care about any possible conflict of interest on Honohan's part. They just wanted the truth, and Honohan, unlike their elected politicians, seemed to be the one who was giving it to them. Confidence in Cowen and his government had evaporated.

Honohan was in a somewhat less difficult position than Cowen because he did not have to worry personally about domestic political repercussions. He was not being blamed for the crisis – having only taken his role in 2009 – and he did not have to account publicly for his actions to the electorate. His job was safe. He had sussed the reality, and therefore the inevitability, of the situation long before then. He had feared the worst from the time of the Greek financial crisis in May that year and worried about how Europe had dealt with setting up a controversial rescue package. He knew instinctively that Ireland would have problems securing new loans on the international bond markets, as investor concerns would force the yield demanded on Irish bonds to ever higher levels. As the year went on, he could see deposits leaving Irish banks; he was being told regularly by the ECB that this could not be allowed to continue. By the first week of November he had decided it was inevitable that Ireland would have to seek a bailout. Tellingly, it seems that his views were shared by his deputy, the tough Englishman Matthew Elderfield, who had been recruited as financial regulator; by Kevin Cardiff, the man who was promoted to secretary general at the Department of Finance, despite having overseen the banks prior to the disastrous September 2008 blanket government guarantee to honour all the Irish banking system's debts to depositors and bondholders (the institutions that lent money to the banks to top up the amount they could lend in turn); and by John Corrigan, who had been promoted in 2009 to run the National Treasury Management Agency (NTMA), which manages Ireland's assets and liabilities.

Honohan had developed a very strong working relationship with Lenihan, who had broken convention by appointing him – an acknowledged international expert on banking – as governor of the Central Bank; and Lenihan continued to support him strongly. But, while he had bonded with Lenihan – with whom he shared something of an air of academic eccentricity born of their keen intellects – he was nowhere near as close to Cowen, and therefore unable to convince the Taoiseach about the reality of the situation they were facing.

Honohan was also worried about Cowen's mental strength after the worst two and a half years imaginable, as the latter dealt with an avalanche of economic and political crises. He was not alone in this concern. The public had lost confidence in Cowen's ability to lead and communicate long ago, but many of those closest to him had come to share those fears. They were worried also about both the quality and the timing of his decision-making; and they despaired at the mood swings, which resulted in some public performances that showed strength of character and ambition but too many others that showed a lack of self-belief and a lack of genuine confidence that Ireland's problems could be confronted and overcome.

Cowen had much on his mind. As well as trying to cope with the present and the future, he was dealing with enormous amounts of guilt about his failures in the past. He could never admit it, but the blanket guarantee of bank deposits and bonds that he had authorized and then foisted upon his government in the early hours of 30 September 2008 had not merely failed but made things far worse. His prior record as minister for finance had been eviscerated by the critics because his actions were tantamount to throwing fuel on to the fire of an out-of-control economy. He tried then to put out that fire, though he moved to do so far too late. Unemployment had reached record levels. Forced emigration had returned. Incomes were collapsing. People were struggling to cope with excessive debts. The national mood was grim.

He had since tried to take tough remedial action, authorizing spending cuts and tax increases that were anathema as much to his political instincts as to his economic ones, but he was only accused of making things worse. There were times when he was brave but other times when, for political reasons, he pulled back on certain things that he knew, for economic reasons, he should have done. Cowen loved the Fianna Fáil Party he led; it was arguably as important to him as his country, although some of his critics felt that he regarded the two as almost indistinguishable. He knew that he was being held responsible for wrecking both. He had come to power citing his admiration for his visionary predecessor, Sean Lemass, but would get nowhere near him in the history books of party or state. It was a heavy burden for him to bear. Lenihan's naturally more optimistic nature meant that he soldiered more bravely, remarkably so for a man who had been told in December 2009 that he was suffering from inoperable, and therefore almost certainly terminal, pancreatic cancer, to which he succumbed eventually in June 2011.

Cowen had been so damaged politically by the events of the previous two years that he knew his days as Taoiseach were numbered; he was facing into an electoral disaster of epic proportions that he wanted to defer for as long as possible. He hung on to power tenaciously with a wafer-thin Dáil majority, maintained partly by an unwillingness to hold by-elections in which his opponents would have strengthened their numbers and brought down the government. His critics said that he did this for selfish political reasons and that he was motivated partly by a desire to try to do something, anything, that might minimize losses for Fianna Fáil – but Cowen thought that it was his responsibility to bear these burdens and that it would be cowardly to pass them on to anyone else. He dismissed the argument that his government had performed so poorly that anybody else could do better, and he was contemptuous of what he regarded as empty posturing by some of the most prominent figures on the opposition benches.

But now things had taken a much worse turn than he had expected. He had refused to believe that it had become impossible for Ireland to return to borrowing on international financial markets from 2011, no

matter what his experts were telling him. He had been persuaded by
the experts around him that introducing yet another savage budget –
one that would cut spending and increase taxes by at least €4.5 billion
in 2011 – might help to restore international confidence, at least more
so than anything else, and by mid November the government had
conceded that it would have to do even more, increasing that budgetary adjustment to €6 billion. He had believed the problems at the
banks would not get any worse, but now it was all unravelling. Honohan's public comments had put the tin hat on a brutal week for
Cowen and Lenihan, and they weren't helped by the fact that they
knew it was only going to get worse – for Ireland, for Fianna Fáil and
for them. Having done everything that could have been expected of
them, they believed, at great personal and political cost, they found
that the result of all their efforts was to be punishment rather than
reward.

There was much that Cowen couldn't say publicly, including the
fact that the IMF wasn't necessarily the most important actor in this
unfolding horror story. It was the European Central Bank that had
put a loaded gun to the Irish government's head, prompted by even
more significant political forces from across the Atlantic.

On the previous Friday, frustrated that the Irish government
would not do as they demanded, members of the governing council
of the ECB had decided to brief the international media as to what
they felt should happen to Ireland. It was unattributed stuff from
'sources close to the ECB', but everyone who was involved knew
where it was coming from and why. It was cynical behaviour, designed
to back a sovereign nation into a corner, and seemed worse because
Ireland had done almost everything that had been asked of it by the
European Commission and the ECB, had suffered a great drop in living standards because of its compliance, and had acted with more
transparency and honesty than any other country in similar circumstances. The implied threat that the ECB would withdraw liquidity
support from our banks – which it actually was not entitled to do –
was highly dangerous too, because it accelerated the flight of deposits
from the Irish banks.

But what was going on behind the scenes, at the international political level, was possibly even worse. The previous day the G20 summit of leading industrial nations had started a regular meeting at Seoul in South Korea. The Irish situation came to the top of the agenda unexpectedly because of its importance to the stability of the euro; the fear was that an unmanaged collapse of the Irish State's finances would create a tidal wave of bank losses across Europe and economic panic. Ireland was not represented at the meeting at which its future was discussed other than by the European Commission. The US government's secretary of the treasury, Tim Geithner, took a particularly strong stand. He wanted Ireland's finances forced into the control of the IMF, and also to avail of the specially established European emergency borrowing fund. The ECB was delighted. The bank felt that it had done what it could in providing emergency funding to the Irish banks to replace deposits as they fled, but it now had well more than €100 billion at risk that it wanted back. In any event, its concern was not Ireland but the wider seventeen member states of the euro. The ECB conveniently forgot its own enormous failings in dealing with the crisis, as well as its responsibilities.

European Commission President José Manuel Barroso rang Cowen after the G20 meeting in Seoul to explain that the game was changing. This news came as a considerable shock to Cowen. He and Lenihan had been telling the truth earlier in the month when they'd said that they had not been put under pressure by the commission to get loans from the IMF or the emergency European funds. Lenihan received an official letter from ECB chairman Jean-Claude Trichet that brought up 'the question about whether Ireland would be participating in a programme at that stage', and an angry telephone call between the two followed. Lenihan's department officials ran into an unexpected firestorm at a meeting in Brussels when details of how they would deal with a bailout were demanded of them.

In the face of this unrelenting pressure, Cowen and Lenihan met privately on Saturday for hours to decide on strategy. Lenihan emphasized the views of his officials, Honohan, Corrigan and Cardiff, but bowed to Cowen's superior position and his right to make the ultimate call as to strategy. Cowen was not prepared to give up without a fight. They decided that they could not show weakness – that is, acknowledge the possibility of surrender – and to trust very few people with the reality of the situation, even their cabinet colleagues, for fear that loose tongues would cause unwanted damage.

On Monday, 15 November, Cowen went on RTÉ news to emphasize that Ireland would not be making any aid application to the EU or the IMF 'for the funding of the state' because the country was already funded right up to the middle of next year. The following day he went into the Dáil to repeat this message – condemning what he called 'ill-informed and inaccurate' speculation about the government seeking a bailout – but he conceded that intensive discussions with our European partners were taking place about the banks and the public finances. 'What we need are calm heads and cool consideration of all the issues. These are complicated matters that are not easily understood,' he said. 'This is not an insurmountable challenge and, through working together with our partners in a calm and rational manner, we can resolve these issues and underpin financial stability in the medium and longer term. It is in all of our interests that we find a credible, efficient and above all workable solution that will provide assurance to the markets and thereby restore confidence and stability.'

Yet he was aware too – although it was not disclosed to the public until later – that Lenihan had been put under shocking pressure, at a meeting of European finance ministers in Brussels, to make an immediate announcement that Ireland was seeking an IMF/EU/ECB bailout. An indication of what Lenihan would face had come in the hours before the meeting, from the European Council president, Herman Van Rompuy. 'We're in a survival crisis,' he'd said publicly. 'We all have to work together in order to survive with the eurozone, because if we don't survive with the eurozone, we will not survive with the European Union.'

Lenihan made a valiant defence, refusing to do something that he did not have the authority to do, but he had to make arrangements for the arrival of the IMF and the EU in the coming days. 'Clearly it's important that those who wish to help us and those that wish to work with us should find out all the facts on the ground in Dublin and that will be arranged for them,' Lenihan told reporters after the meeting. 'There's no decision and the government did not commit to enter a facility but there are serious market disturbances. They jeopardize not just Ireland, they threaten the eurozone, so it is essential that we address those structural problems and that we deal with them.'

The public pressure continued. Jean-Claude Juncker, the Luxembourg prime minister, who was also chair of the eurozone finance ministers, said he expected 'within the coming days' a definitive decision on whether Ireland would seek a bailout. Cowen continued to insist that 'there has been no dictation from anybody. What we're involved in here is working with colleagues in respect of currency problems and euro-issue problems that are affecting Ireland, they're affecting other countries. They're particularly affecting Ireland at the moment.' Cowen, in a phrase that was thrown back at him many times afterwards, insisted that 'I don't believe there's any reason for Irish people to be ashamed and humiliated.' He maintained that position even after Honohan spoke on *Morning Ireland*. There began an extraordinary period in which many Irish people felt very ashamed and very humiliated by the manner in which our economic sovereignty was removed and we were bludgeoned into accepting loans on terms that would be ruinous to the country's economic recovery.

Many months later, not long before his death, Lenihan, who was usually very careful to be positive in his public utterances and wonderfully informative in private conversations with journalists, gave a rare on-the-record insight into the trauma he had suffered. In an interview for a BBC radio documentary he described his feelings as the deal with what came to be known as 'the troika' – the IMF, the European Union and the ECB – neared its conclusion. 'I've a very vivid memory of going to Brussels on the final Monday to sign the agreement and being on my own at the airport and looking at the snow gradually thawing and thinking to myself, this is terrible. No Irish minister has ever had to do this before. I had fought for two and a half years to avoid this conclusion. I believed I had fought the good fight and taken every measure possible to delay such an eventuality. And now hell was at the gates.'

This is the story of how we arrived at that hell.

PART ONE

The End of an Era

1. Greece is the Word

Minister for Finance Brian Lenihan and Central Bank Governor Patrick Honohan were at odds over what the international financial rescue of Greece in May 2010 meant to Ireland. Greece had gone bust effectively, its debts of over €350 billion too much for it to bear. It needed rescue by the IMF and the EU, and it would have to make savage cuts to its public budget, to the horror of the Greek people. The ever optimistic Lenihan took solace from the Greek tragedy when he publicly claimed that it somehow emphasized Ireland's strength, that the budgetary measures we were taking were the correct ones and would allow us to escape Greece's fate; we would remain in favour with the international lenders who supplied the money to run the country. Honohan, though, feared that events meant not just that we were vulnerable but that the escape was temporary and that our fate was inevitable: we were heading for the Greek experience of requiring rescue. He feared that loans to the country would become more expensive, then prohibitively so, which would mean they'd dry up and we would be left holding out the begging bowl to the IMF and the EU. They would provide, but they would do so expensively and with onerous terms and conditions.

Greece had much bigger debts than Ireland and far less means of paying them. In April 2010 Greece succumbed to the pressure of the markets, and then the EU, and asked for help. As yields on its two-year bonds went as high as 15.3 per cent, meaning it was impossible to borrow, Greece agreed to 'accept' a rescue package of over €110 billion in new loans but on terms that led to rioting on the streets as Greeks realized that their lifestyles would be changed dramatically and not for the better. The EU and the IMF had stipulated very specific measures as part of the deal: these included adverse changes to the retirement age, pension arrangements for public-sector workers and taxes.

Greece got into trouble on the financial markets because it had lied about its true economic position and lost the trust and confidence of lenders. Even when times were good, Greece had run up very high borrowings and engaged in accounting tricks to hide the true ratios between its debts and its economic activity. It managed to hide the actual figures in the returns it sent to Brussels. A new government, elected in October 2009, admitted that its predecessor had been cooking the books. The European Commission attacked its 'exceptional combination . . . of lax fiscal policy, inadequate reaction to mounting imbalances, structural weaknesses and statistical misreporting'.

The ratings agency Standard & Poor's slashed Greece's credit rating to 'junk' status, which indicated a high risk of default, or non-repayment. In such circumstances, investors demand much higher interest rates if they are going to hold a country's debt, if they hold it at all. The market effectively stopped lending to Greece, forcing it to call in the IMF and the EU to help it find a way to cope with its debts; about €135 billion was owed to European banks, with two thirds of that owed to German and French banks alone.

It threatened to be the sovereign equivalent of the 2008 subprime mortgage banking crisis. Greece became the sovereign version of Bear Stearns, the Wall Street brokerage saved in March 2008 (by contrast with Lehman Brothers, which collapsed the following September).

A senior official from the Organisation for Economic Co-operation and Development (OECD) publicly compared what was happening to Greece to getting the ebola virus and then unhelpfully added that if you have a virus in your leg you cut the leg off. If Greece were to be evicted from the euro, the pressure to do the same to the other members of the so-called PIIGS (Portugal, Italy, Ireland, Greece and Spain) would have become enormous, irrespective of the size of the Spanish and Italian economies, because of perceived weakness in their national balance sheets and their inability to repay debts.

Other European countries, most particularly the Germans, took some persuading that Greece was worthy of saving. They did not want to bail out the indigent, especially when they reckoned that the swift plummeting of the euro – down almost 20 per cent against the dollar in six months – could be blamed on the fiscal incontinence of the Greeks and other eurozone member states. The currency decline was hitting the Germans hard, as their valuable non-EU exports were no longer as profitable as they could have been. People in Germany were speculating that they should expel others from the single currency or leave themselves. Instead, they were being asked to lend Greece more money that they might not get back.

There were the usual rants about speculators, the same investors who apparently had ruined the banks, although they would argue that they had merely taken logical advantage of the self-inflicted weaknesses of those institutions. European Commission President José Manuel Barroso laid the blame for the eurozone's travails at the feet of 'speculators'. These speculators were the same institutions which had bought bonds from governments previously and which had been called investors then for doing so. When they had acted to safeguard or to increase their money – according to their assessment of the information available to them – they were renamed 'speculators' and spat upon, irrespective of the fact that they often had clients' interests to represent.

Most of the buyers of this so-called sovereign debt were long-term investors, looking for security or definite repayment. These are typically pension funds and other investment products looking for stable, long-term investment returns to match their liabilities: the pensions or investment returns they must pay to their customers.

Their continued involvement in the markets, to provide money to countries, was needed. A euro country had never defaulted and lenders to such countries did not expect to lose their money. The practicalities of ensuring that the European banks that had lent to Greece got their money back overcame the moral hazard of rescuing the Greeks from whatever they might have deserved.

With Germany leading the way it was decided that Greece was to get more than €110 billion over three years at an interest rate of just over 5 per cent, compared to the 7.3 per cent that had been demanded of it on the ten-year money markets in previous weeks. Bizarrely, given our financial situation, Ireland was forced to provide €1.3 billion towards the cost of the loan to Greece. Lenihan said the loan would be repaid, with interest, as Greece's economy improved and would not be included in our own overall deficit statistic because 'it is classified as a financial transaction.'

Lenihan exuded his customary confidence in denying that Ireland was at 'great risk' from fallout from the Greek debt crisis. 'The risk of contagion in my view does not extend to Ireland,' he declared. 'Over the last eighteen months we have taken many of the measures that the Greeks are only beginning to take . . . One of the reasons markets are critical of countries other than Greece is because some don't just have public debt problems, they also have structural problems with their economies . . . We're not a country that has the severe structural problems that some of the other Mediterranean countries have shown and the markets have tended to differentiate Ireland out from these countries.'

Honohan, however, knew what ECB President Jean-Claude Trichet was saying about the implications of Greece's situation. Trichet persuaded Germany that it had to act to save Greece by telling one crisis meeting of European leaders that 'this isn't only a problem for one country. It's several countries. It's global. It's a situation that is deteriorating with extreme rapidity and intensity.'

Brian Lenihan was in an incredibly optimistic frame of mind for a man who was suffering from a form of inoperable cancer and who had been given relatively little chance of more than short-term survival.

Lenihan was diagnosed with pancreatic cancer in December 2009, shortly after he had delivered that year's budget. He had told a select group of people his diagnosis before Christmas and word leaked out. A television report broadcast the news before he had made his official statement. When that came in early January, he emphasized that he would continue in his job for as long as he could.

It was a big decision for Lenihan to make personally – would he be able to have the necessary medical treatment while continuing to perform properly in an incredibly arduous role that would require him to have all his wits about him? Once he had indicated to Cowen that he wanted to stay, it was a big decision for An Taoiseach to endorse. Lenihan's aggressive medical treatment would be time-consuming and physically very draining. There was the potential for it to interfere with his judgement. Was Lenihan going to be available at all times when required and would he be impaired in the performance of his duties?

Cowen reckoned that he needed him, almost no matter what. Communication was Lenihan's forte, much as it was one of Cowen's greatest weaknesses. Lenihan was articulate, seemingly plausible and likeable to many, notwithstanding the bad news about the economy and the measures he was imposing to fight the collapse. All are important attributes for a politician. He was the most popular member of a very unpopular government – possibly the only one – even before the revelation of his cancer. But this standing was enhanced by the attitude he displayed towards fighting his illness. There was no trace of self-pity, no hint of evasion of his responsibilities. Indeed, it seemed to invigorate him, and friends speculated that his need to discharge his public duties, and the adrenalin coursing through him, assisted him in prolonging his fight against the spread of the cancer.

That didn't mean the issue of his continued holding of the ministry was closed to reassessment, however. There were times in March and April 2010 when some of Cowen's closest advisers wondered if a mistake was being made, especially as Lenihan took decisions with which they disagreed. It was known in government circles that he did slump during periods of intensive treatment, although this was masked well from the public, and it was appreciated that this was understandable. But there were people close to Cowen who did wonder if they should challenge the consensus about keeping Lenihan in place or if he should perhaps be asked to step aside temporarily. It was a complex dilemma: without the job Lenihan might lose much of what drove him to confront the cancer, but could the country indulge his need to keep a job that might better have been given to someone else?

Lenihan was not flawless in his communication either. He had more than a touch of his late father, a former Tánaiste, and an approach that caused many to remember Brian senior's 'no problem' mantra. He could be almost naive in believing that some of his comments would not offend.

It is likely that a speech that he made at the Irish League of Credit

Unions conference in Killarney in late April 2010 would have caused ructions had it been made by anyone else. Lenihan said other European governments would not have been able to impose the kind of pain on their people that the Irish government had. There would have been 'riots' in France had the pension levy on public servants been introduced in that country. 'The steps taken had impressed our partners in Europe, who are amazed at our capacity to take pain,' he said. What was impressing Europe was that Ireland was showing adaptability. 'The view in Europe is that Ireland is taking steps to put her house in order.'

The steps taken to stabilize the public finances had ensured that the government spending deficit had not drifted to as much as 15, 16 or 17 per cent of GDP, he said. 'This economy will renew and recover and advance. We are going back a few years – we are not going back to the bad years of the seventies or eighties. We had the highest unit labour costs of any country in the eurozone. That is no longer the case.'

Lenihan had been getting some cautious slaps on the back from outside of Fianna Fáil. In February, Jean-Claude Trichet, president of the ECB, had declared that 'Ireland is certainly not the weakest link of the euro area.' He continued: 'there is no weak link. The euro area is a very intertwined, single-market economy with a single currency. Speaking of any particular country in the euro area as a weak link is an error of judgement.'

But in April 2010 the commission warned that we were not doing nearly well enough in trying to address the issue of our public finances. Olli Rehn, the EU's recently appointed monetary affairs commissioner, shocked many people when he said he was 'examining whether Dublin should adopt new austerity measures'. This was not something that we needed when problems were emerging in our ability to borrow on international bond markets.

Ireland had to borrow to fund the near-€20 billion gap between what it took in taxes and what it spent – and that was even before the cost of refinancing the banks was taken into account. The country had gone through a lengthy period of annual budget surpluses, when the income the government received exceeded its annual spending comfortably.

Fianna Fáil-led governments spent some of this money, and used some to reduce taxes and pay down a portion of the existing debt. They did not stop borrowing, however, going into the bond markets with new issues to raise funds to repay loans as they expired, usually on better or cheaper terms (bonds are a form of IOU that involves paying back the amount borrowed at a future date, after a series of interest payments have been made). By the end of April 2010 the difference between the cost of Irish ten-year state borrowing and the cost of benchmark German borrowing had widened to 2.55 percentage points, although this was small compared to what was about to happen. A few years earlier Irish bonds had traded at a discount to their German peers. The new rate was higher than at any time since the immediate aftermath of the introduction of the bank guarantee. Our vulnerability was visible for all to see.

Things had actually gone well in the first few months of 2010. As recently as March, the NTMA had sold €1.5 billion in bonds at a yield of 4.426 per cent. This was the smallest premium compared with the equivalent in German government bonds since December 2008 and 1.58 per cent below the peak spread of March 2009. Although the year was not yet a third old, close to the end of April the NTMA was not far off raising nearly two thirds of its 2010 funding requirement.

The NTMA was busy issuing bonds during the period of the Greek crisis, doing what are effectively door-to-door sales, or roadshows, as they are known in the trade, around Europe's main financial centres. The task was tough and about to get tougher, as sentiment towards Europe's peripheral countries began to change. Investors started to fear that other countries might be masking problems in the way that Greece had. While the Irish effort in reducing the exchequer deficit was appreciated, the size of the gap to be closed became a subject of discussion again, especially when the additional cost of recapitalizing the banks remained unsettled. Questions as to whether Ireland could repay all of its debts began to re-emerge.

The NTMA and Lenihan took a bad and significant blow in April, when Eurostat, which issued the formal statistical information upon which investors relied, decided that the Irish national debt during 2009 was much higher than had been stated previously. Ireland had not been cooking the books Greek style, but there was a dispute as to how the state's investment in new capital for Anglo Irish Bank should be treated for statistical purposes. That may have seemed like a 'so what?' issue, but it wasn't. Eurostat decided that the government's 'investments' of capital in Anglo had to be accounted for immediately, rather than spread over the period for which the money was given. Even though the cash would transfer in lumps, year after year, the entire amount was to be added straight away to the calculation of the government's debts.

This meant that the €4 billion given to Anglo during 2009 brought the government's budget deficit for that year to 14.3 per cent of gross domestic product (GDP), or €23.35 billion more spent than raised in taxes. This was more than four times the EU's 3 per cent deficit limit, and as a proportion it was larger than Greece's.

'This is a once-off impact, and will not affect the government's stated budgetary aim of reducing the deficit to below 3 per cent of GDP by 2014,' Lenihan said. But others could see immediately that it raised serious questions about the accounting treatment of the rest of the money earmarked for Anglo or indeed the other banks. The result was that it changed what the government would have to do to bring the budget deficit down to 3 per cent of GDP by 2014 – meaning further austerity.

Meanwhile the NTMA's John Corrigan wrapped the 'green jersey' around himself and spoke positively. He said there was a 'reasonable prospect' that international ratings agencies would move their outlook on Ireland from 'negative' to 'stable', and that the country was entering 'calmer waters'. Ireland was rated AA1 at Moody's Investors Service and AA at Standard & Poor's, and both had 'negative' outlooks on the nation's debt. Fitch had an AA minus rating on Ireland, with a 'stable' outlook. 'Sentiment towards Ireland as reflected by bond yields has improved,' Corrigan said. The NTMA pressed ahead with the €1.5 billion bond issue and it was sold, albeit at a much higher rate of interest than heretofore.

The Greek rescue failed to impress financial markets because of doubts about that country's ability to implement associated austerity measures – and this had potentially damaging consequences for Ireland. More had to be done, as shown by the crisis in Greece, which had provided a number of uncomfortable truths. One was that the EU didn't have the financial resources or the will to deal with the problem without the help of the IMF, which pitched in €30 billion of the required €110 billion, as happened subsequently with Ireland and Portugal. Nor was the EU as united as the title 'Economic and Monetary Union' suggested: Greece's rescue package was coming from bilateral individual loans from fifteen member EU states, rather than from a united Europe. Few believed Angela Merkel when she said it was a one-off that wouldn't be repeated.

There was a need to do more. Negotiations between EU member states continued throughout May and early June before a fighting fund was unveiled: this would be used to help EMU member countries in extremis to fend off speculative attacks based on the belief that they would not be able to repay their debts. The newly and specially created European Financial Stability Facility (EFSF) would get up to €250 billion from the IMF on top of loan guarantees for €440 billion from the sixteen other euro countries and €60 billion from the European Commission.

But what was also becoming clear was that the European Union was intensifying its campaign to take greater control over the fiscal behaviour of individual governments. At the end of the process EU Council President Van Rompuy confirmed that national budgetary plans would henceforth be presented to the commission and other EU member states. It was said that this was not for checking in detail or for formal approval, because that would be decided by national parliaments. But the main assumptions underlying the budgetary plans, like the levels of growth or inflation, would be examined by a government's peers, and any country that presented a budgetary plan with a high deficit would have to justify itself. There were to be multi-annual budgets too.

Fine Gael was worried by the potential for this even before it was confirmed and raised the subject in the Dáil in May. Enda Kenny called on Cowen to give assurances 'that in no circumstances would the government hand over sovereignty for the running of our economy to anybody else'. Kenny claimed that EU Commission proposals to compel euro states to seek preapproval from Brussels for the amount of borrowing in their annual budgets were effectively 'handing over sovereignty for the running of the economy' to the EU.

Lenihan described as 'mischievous' opposition suggestions that proposals to 'reinforce economic coordination' represented a dilution of Ireland's 'sovereignty over taxation matters'. Enhanced coordination aimed 'to assist member states to be better prepared for any future crises'. Lenihan and Cowen took particular aim at Richard Bruton, who was described as 'anti-European, irresponsible, reprehensible and jingoistic'.

Lenihan reiterated that he was under no pressure from the EU to accelerate his austerity plan. He also said he did not envisage Ireland having to seek help from the IMF should market funding rates remain high. He boasted that 'my prediction in December's budget that the economy would bottom out by mid year and that positive growth would resume in the second half of this year is being borne out.'

Lenihan was buoyed by some international support. 'He made no attempt to gloss over the scale of the sacrifice needed from everyone, politicians included,' the *Daily Telegraph* said approvingly of Lenihan. One of the strongest pieces of support came from the *Wall Street Journal* on 1 June 2010 in an editorial under the headline: 'The Irish Example'. It began 'What a difference credibility makes . . .' and extolled the austerity programme the government had introduced. It detailed how government spending had increased by 138 per cent in the decade before the crash, against economic growth of 72 per cent. 'By September 2008, the national debt was €46.96 billion in the hole . . . By April 2009, Ireland had cut public spending by €1.8 billion. It also managed to squeeze additional tax revenue out of its strapped citizens, though it achieved this largely by broadening the tax base, for instance by including minimum-wage earners, rather than targeting hikes only at the wealthy. Crucially, Ireland maintained its 12.5 per cent corporation tax rate. By the end of last year, Dublin had implemented spending cuts and tax hikes worth about 5 per cent of GDP.

'The government used the report [from economist Colm McCarthy into public finances] to cut its 2010 budget by €4 billion and is going through its recommendations to find a further €3 billion in cuts for 2011. So far, public workers have seen their pay slashed by up to 20 per cent, the state's child benefits have been cut by roughly 10 per cent, and unemployment and other welfare benefits have been similarly gutted.

'The last year and a half of Irish asceticism is now seen as Europe's Ghost of Frugality Future, and politicians around Europe could do worse than to look at Ireland's cuts as a model . . . Meanwhile, the Irish people deserve credit for greeting their government's attempted return to fiscal sanity with, well, sanity.'

The editorial admitted, however, that 'the rewards for Ireland's early frugality have been slow to come. Unemployment remains in the double digits, and citizens know there is more pain to come, even if growth does pick up next year.' It then quoted an OECD report in which the Irish government was commended for allowing 'pocket-books to shrink along with demand'. This had meant that 'the notable improvement in Ireland's price and cost competitiveness could allow growth to pick up more quickly than expected.'

Lenihan seized on the editorial as 'just the latest in a series of favourable opinion pieces in respected international financial media outlets. They reflect real international confidence in the ability of this country to resolve its current difficulties and return to growth. Forecasters are marking up their projections for economic growth in the country, amid mounting evidence that the economy has turned.

'There is understandable anger about the crisis, but the overwhelming majority of our citizens have shown remarkable foresight and maturity in accepting the need for the difficult decisions the government has had to take. Our actions over the last two years have boosted international confidence in our ability to recover. We need now to engender that confidence here at home,' he said.

Joan Burton of the Labour Party observed presciently that while the *Wall Street Journal* praised the Irish people for their tolerant response to government austerity measures, 'it would be wrong, in my view, to confuse this with an endorsement of government policies. The people are waiting in the long grass for general election day to pass their verdict on the policies that created the crisis and the astronomical cost of the bank bailouts.'

With equal prescience, Brian Lucey, an associate professor in finance at Trinity College, noted that the *Wall Street Journal* 'glossed over the monstrous cost, both real and potential, of the government's banking policy'.

And he was not the only one who thought that. In mid April a column by the Nobel Prize-winning economist Paul Krugman in the Sunday edition of the *New York Times* (1.4 million circulation, 6.1 million readers) was headlined provocatively 'Erin Go Broke'.

While using Ireland as a template to warn the US authorities of what not to do, Krugman made some very interesting points about the Irish economy. He said that in trying to satisfy nervous lenders, 'Ireland is being forced to raise taxes and slash government spending in the face of an economic slump – policies that will further deepen the slump.

'As far as responding to the recession goes, Ireland appears to be really, truly without options, other than to hope for an export-led recovery if and when the rest of the world bounces back . . . And the lesson of Ireland is that you really, really don't want to put yourself in a position where you have to punish your economy in order to save your banks.'

Krugman was rewarded with a lash from the tongue of Tánaiste Mary Coughlan, who was at the White House to meet with senior members of the Obama administration: 'There has been comment which has been neither helpful nor, in my view, appropriate, and I would like to move on from that and give the view that we have collectively as a government . . . yes, difficult times, but we have the capacity to deal with these issues and we would like to revert back to the international reputation we had and continue to have.'

The most damaging punch, however, may have been delivered by Professor Morgan Kelly of University College Dublin. He occasionally wrote articles for *The Irish Times*, usually no more than two or three each year, and these pieces had achieved the status of early-warning sirens, now that his predictions from 2006 about the bursting of the property bubble had come true, and his warnings that the bank guarantee and the National Asset Management Agency (NAMA) would fail to stem the crisis had also proved to be justified. His new articles were often greeted with anger by the establishment and understandable anxiety by the rest of his readers.

On 22 May he let loose, with characteristic bluntness, in an *Irish Times* missive. 'It is no longer a question of whether Ireland will go bust, but when,' he declared, to the horror of the establishment. He said that we were different from Greece, in that 'our woes do not stem from government debt, but instead from the government's open-ended guarantee to cover the losses of the banking system out of its citizens' wallets', and warned that the huge costs of the September 2008 bank guarantee would 'sink us, unfortunately, but inevitably'.

'Even under the most optimistic assumptions about government-spending cuts and bank losses, by 2012 Ireland will have a worse ratio of debt to national income than the one that is sinking Greece,' he explained.

Kelly argued that for the previous two years the Irish economy had not been 'shrinking, so much as vaporising'. He pointed out how real GNP and private-sector employment 'have already fallen by one sixth – the deepest and swiftest falls in a western economy since the Great Depression'.

In his typically colourful way, Kelly argued that 'the Irish economy is like a patient bleeding from two gunshot wounds. The government has moved competently to staunch the smaller, budgetary hole, while continuing to insist that the litres of blood pouring unchecked from the banking hole are "manageable".'

He predicted that capital markets were unlikely to agree with the government's optimistic views for much longer and that this would trigger a borrowing crisis for Ireland. 'The first torpedo, most probably, will be a run on Irish banks in inter-bank markets, of the sort that sank Anglo in 2008. Already, Irish banks are struggling to find lenders to leave money on deposit for more than a week,' he observed correctly.

Taoiseach Brian Cowen was drawn into a direct response. 'Really implicit in some of the argumentation is the idea that it would be better for Ireland to default. But we simply don't accept that at all and I think all of the implications from other countries where that happens greatly undermines, not just in terms of financial credibility but also the ability to retain confidence at home.' Cowen said there was 'objective evidence' available that 'confirmed' the government was taking the right approach to dealing with the economic crisis.

A spokesman for the Department of Finance also got in on the act, describing Kelly's analysis as 'extremely pessimistic' and based on a number of 'very serious inaccuracies'. Reference was made to a speech made just weeks earlier by Central Bank Governor Patrick Honohan in which he said the cost of getting the banks out of trouble was 'manageable', as most of them had started the boom with a cushion of shareholders' funds – that is, they would be able to pay their debts from their own resources. The blindfolds were being put on for the march to the abyss.

2.   The Man in Charge

The two Brians had had enough of bad news and didn't want to hear more. They were sufficiently clued in to know that the Greek crisis had consequences for Ireland, but they preferred the comfort offered by friends to the siren sounds – emanating from behind closed doors among their own ranks – that all was far from well and that a sovereign debt crisis was more than likely. It was bad enough having to face adversity from the opposition, the media and many voters without having to listen to Honohan and his ilk warn that further cuts to public spending were required and that even then the harsher economic medicine might not work.

Fianna Fáil was being hammered in the opinion polls and Cowen's popularity was falling as fast as a stone, meaning that they would get no credit for what they were doing – which was, as far as they were concerned, saving the country. Cowen's credibility in handling the economic crisis was always an issue throughout 2009 and 2010, and this just got worse as time went on.

His record as minister for finance was now widely regarded as diabolical: all sorts of examples could be given of his failures of policy and execution prior to becoming Taoiseach in May 2008. The important decisions he had made – introducing the bank guarantee and not nationalizing or closing Anglo Irish Bank at the first opportunity, when it might have been early enough to mitigate the damage – meant that the buck stopped with him. And now his public performances, either in the Dáil or in rare broadcast interviews, were not inspiring confidence either; as he was to tell me subsequently in a radio interview just before he was forced to resign as Fianna Fáil leader in early 2011, he didn't care how people perceived him – he was more interested in substance than style. Unfortunately, the modern era, not to mention the circumstances of the crisis, demanded public displays of leadership that would lift public confidence. Cowen wasn't bothered to deliver, not believing others who told him it was important.

There were other problems too. He was badly conflicted by a desire to serve his party's needs as well as his country's, and by a heart-felt need to believe things were not as bad as his head was telling him they were. He seemed to be racked by guilt for what he knew to be his own failures and the resulting consequences for Ireland, but he also seemed to be in denial about his own responsibilities and the enormous scale of the problems.

Government ministers said, privately as well as publicly, that Cowen was a much better chairman of cabinet meetings than Bertie Ahern, who, like his good friend Tony Blair in Britain, tended to use the cabinet as a rubber-stamp for decisions that had been made outside of the room. But detailed discussion sometimes led to inaction or, at best, deferral. For all the talk of putting the country first, party political considerations were always near the top of Cowen's agenda. He never forgot he was leader of Fianna Fáil as well as leader of the country.

There were also issues about his shrinking circle of advisers. Having made a big play at the start of his leadership about the primacy of elected politicians – even if they didn't necessarily have the required skill sets – he was reluctant to draw on too wide a circle of unelected advisers. But Cowen's mood swings – even more noticeable in private than in public – made it difficult for those working close to him. He didn't always react well to the bearers of bad news. Timing was important, as he wasn't always in good form in the mornings. He suffered from a sleep disorder, apnoea, which his alcohol consumption made worse. While the regularity of his drinking as a means of escape was nothing like the legend that had developed, none the less he did not cope well with hangovers and tended to snap at those who displeased him when he was suffering from them. More importantly, many began to fear that his use of alcohol was a symptom of deeper, underlying problems. Cowen was shell-shocked by what he'd had to go through, as well as by having to deal with feelings of guilt. It was as if he were suffering from post-traumatic stress disorder; some very senior people were worried that he might be clinically depressed. But it was unclear how that could be put to him, even if they genuinely believed it. And there was another problem in that he failed to take any exercise; it would be unimaginable for any other major political leader to show such disregard for his or her own health or to be so unaware that physical well-being is essential to mental well-being, even if attaining it is time-consuming.

Cowen got battered throughout the year during Dáil debates by the opposition, which provoked him whenever possible, partly in the hope of reaping political benefits from another ill-tempered eruption. He was easily goaded, and the public reacted against these outbursts. He got particularly exercised in March 2010 when the Labour leader, Eamon Gilmore, accused him of 'economic treason', alleging that the bank guarantee scheme amounted to a 'blank cheque' and calling for all documentation relating to the expert advice received about the guarantee to be published: 'I believe that the Taoiseach and the government made that decision in September 2008, not in the best economic interest of the nation but in the best personal interests of those vested interests who, I believe, the government was trying to protect on that occasion.'

It was a harsh accusation to make in the absence of firm evidence, but Gilmore's charge that the government had decided to introduce a bank guarantee for Anglo – 'a rotten bank that acted as a piggy bank for property speculators' – simply to 'save the skins' of a number of individuals, some of whom were connected to Fianna Fáil, struck a chord with many. Had Cowen's 2008 round of golf with Sean Fitzpatrick, the Anglo chairman – as disclosed in January 2011 in *The Fitzpatrick Tapes* by *Sunday Times* journalists Tom Lyons and Brian Carey – been known about at this time, it is not hard to imagine that all hell would have broken loose. Gilmore thought he had enough to go with, anyway: 'If my belief is correct, and I have not been convinced to the contrary, then that decision is an act of economic treason for which this country is now paying very dearly.'

'I'm twenty-five years in politics. I am beholden to nobody,' a furious Cowen responded. 'Any decision I ever made in the privileged position I hold in this or any other office has been in the best interests of my country as I saw it. I will not be accused of seeking to cause treason to my country. I find that beyond the Pale.'

Few cared about his huff but many were surprised when Cowen issued a statement later that evening in which he sought to spread responsibility for the introduction of the guarantee. He emphasized that the decision 'was based on extensive analysis and monitoring from the governor of the Central Bank, the Office of the Financial Regulator, and senior officials from the Department of Finance and the NTMA.

'The decision was taken because of the need to take effective action to restore financial stability on the opening of the markets at 7 a.m. the following morning . . . The need to restore confidence required that the guarantee be robust in scope and duration. Protecting the interests of the taxpayer was reflected in the decision to provide the guarantee on commercial terms, and this was also the basis for deciding that Anglo Irish Bank – a bank of systemic importance – should be covered by the guarantee. The option of nationalization of that bank at that time would have triggered direct exposure of taxpayers to all its liabilities, whereas the guarantee gave the prospect of a resolution at a lower cost.'

But much of that was wrong, particularly in relation to the cost of guaranteeing the bondholder, and it didn't let the public know of the alternatives that had been rejected – all documents from that night remained under privilege. Cowen required that the public take him and his government on trust, which most were not prepared to do. The officials whose advice he cited did not inspire much trust either; they were poor policy-makers and inadequate regulators, and they'd had the failed bankers in their ears telling them what to do.

But attention was focused not just on the bank guarantee but also on Cowen's earlier budgets, during which he had spent heavily, assuming that the tax revenues would continue to flow even if the economy slowed. His policy was central to the continued pump-priming of the economy when – because of our membership of the euro and loss of control over interest rates – budgetary strategies were the main weapon left in the state's armoury and there was a requirement to put a more sustainable tax base in place. In his four budgets, from 2005 to 2008, Cowen had increased government spending by 51 per cent, more than twice the rate of growth in the economy. He'd had to keep the bubble inflated to get the tax revenues to pay for it all.

As significant, however, was Cowen's failure to act upon important suggestions from his department officials and the Revenue Commissioners; following up on these could have choked off much of the speculative excess that characterized the bubble years. In 2005 Cowen extended tax reliefs for property developers past the 2007 election, against expert advice. He showed the same lack of courage when it came to imposing stamp duty on commercial-property transactions, ignoring pleas to close off a loophole that allowed property developers to transfer land by way of trading companies, incurring stamp duty charges of 1 per cent on the transfer of shares rather than 9 per cent on the transfer of land. Such taxes, had they been applied properly, would have helped to put the lid on inflation in land values. He'd had the legislative power to act but didn't sign the necessary orders, again, after lobbying by vested interests.

In particular, Cowen had been warned about the dangers of an investment product known as a 'Contract for Difference' (CFD), a device that facilitated large-scale gambling on the stock-markets. CFDs were central to Sean Quinn's disastrous punt on Anglo Irish Bank shares, allowing him secretly to take a 28 per cent control of the bank, which he then had to offload as the share price slid. This cost him nearly €3 billion in losses and control of his own business empire, and contributed massively to the destruction of the stability of the bank (as shown in later chapters). But others were at it too, and there were many ill-fated share purchases by businessmen that wiped out much of their wealth and created major problems for Irish lenders. Following lobbying by a range of vested interests, Cowen abandoned plans to rein in this crazy practice.

More pertinently, the failure of the Financial Regulator and of the Central Bank to stop reckless lending practices during the crucial period of 2004 to 2007 can be explained by an absence of suitably empowering legislation from the Department of Finance. Cowen watched seemingly unconcerned, or perhaps without understanding the dangers, as banks doled out 100 per cent loans, offered loans seven and eight times the true income of applicants and committed people to mortgages lasting up to forty years, all designed to give property speculators and builders a better chance to recoup their speculative investments. Instead of being a wise overseer of what went on, Cowen seems to have been seduced by the game himself: how else do you explain his involvement with a bunch of pals from Offaly in buying apartments in Leeds in England?

Cowen was inert as events unfolded; he was reactive when decisions were forced upon him; but rarely was he proactive in his role as finance minister. His entire career prior to becoming Taoiseach seemed to be based on a strategy of doing as little as possible. Now that it was essential that Cowen act resolutely and decisively, those around him found the decisions that he took to be too conservative, and Cowen himself pig-headed in sticking to them regardless.

It left him vulnerable to regular attack. 'You have levied their sons and daughters for the next generation with a burden that they did not cause and for which they were not responsible,' Enda Kenny told him during one Dáil debate. 'Because of lack of regulation, lack of oversight by you, as minister for finance and now as Taoiseach, you've caused this cataclysmic financial consequence for every person in this country.' Cowen said he would not have his 'integrity challenged by Deputy Kenny'.

A fall in gross national product of over 11 per cent in 2009 meant the country was in the grip of a fully fledged depression, not a recession, and few believed Cowen when he repeated the mantra the 'worst is over'. It could be seen as an act of political deception, a hope that constant repetition would somehow convince the people and make them look to the future instead of the present and the past. The worry was that as well as trying to fool the public he was fooling himself.

Cowen's strategy, in as much as there was one, seemed to be that, in time, the public would forget how we got into the mess and instead appreciate his government's efforts to get us out of it by way of taking what he deemed necessary, if unpopular, measures. The government and its advocates spun the line that people wanted to 'move on' and were no longer interested in attributing blame to those responsible for our recent past – with the exception of greedy bankers and property speculators of course. In any case some of the others who were guilty – be they the top bank bosses, regulators or developers – had been cleared off the pitch, though not necessarily enough of them. Cowen said people did not want a history lesson; they wanted to know 'where are we going to go from here'. Cowen was prepared to hang on, almost, it seemed, for dear life. 'We have to be prepared and we are. I won't walk away from my responsibility. I am accountable for what I do and I will face that accountability at the end of that term,' he said in June 2010.

Cowen was reacting to the publication of two damning reports into what had gone wrong for Ireland. Late in 2009 the government was shamed into authorizing two investigations into how and why the exchequer and the banking system had fallen into such trouble; these constituted the first stage of an inquiry into the banking crisis. Cowen's political antennae convinced him that this would cause trouble but Lenihan agreed to inquiries with terms of reference that he hoped would circumscribe the findings and limit any political damage. The reports finally arrived in early June 2010 and added further to the public distrust in the government.

One of the reports, into overall economic policy, was written by Central Bank Governor Patrick Honohan. The other, focusing on banking performance, was written by a German, Klaus Regling, and an Englishman, Max Watson. Regling, a former IMF official, would later become central to Ireland's fate when he was put in charge of the EU's €440 billion rescue fund.

Honohan did not explicitly criticize individuals when he issued his report but it was clear to everyone whom he held to be responsible. He said that government policy had left the 'public finances highly vulnerable to a downturn'. Cowen was the one who was implicated.

In typical economist speak Honohan laid this charge: 'Macroeconomic and budgetary policies contributed significantly to the economic overheating, relying to a clearly unsustainable extent on the construction sector and other transient sources for government revenue (and encouraging the property boom via various incentives geared at the construction sector).

'This helped create a climate of public opinion which was led to believe that the party could last forever.'

Translated, this meant that the government had constructed a spending pattern that relied on taxes that would be there only for as long as the economy boomed. Personal income tax, VAT and excises tend to be consistent contributors to the national exchequer, even when unemployment rises and spending falls. Instead, the economy had become too reliant on stamp duties and capital-gains tax, and on income tax and VAT that were tied to construction.

Things were made worse by tax incentives that encouraged even more construction when less was needed and that drove wage rates even higher. Honohan referred to studies into the range of tax incentives, including mortgage-interest relief, saying that such measures 'became associated with over-building and high vacancy rates – phenomena which are very evident today'.

At the height of the boom, in 2004 to 2006, schemes existed for urban and rural renewal, multi-storey car parks, student accommodation, buildings used for third-level educational purposes, hotels and holiday camps, holiday cottages, park-and-ride facilities, 'living over the shop', nursing homes, private hospitals and convalescent facilities, sports-injury clinics and childcare facilities. Some clearly were needed and desirable, but it was doubtful if anything like all of them were.

Honohan said Ireland's property and construction bubble was driven by a 'myth . . . an expectation that the Irish economy would grow beyond an unsustainable level'.

And when the tax revenues collapsed, the government's spending commitments subsequently became unaffordable. Honohan said that public-sector borrowing surged quickly with the onset of the crisis because of the rise in government spending after 2004. 'But the main cause of the borrowing surge was the collapse in tax revenues in 2008–9 which appears to have been the most pronounced of virtually any country's during the current downturn.'

Honohan put the figures into historical context. 'Government spending doubled in real terms between 1995 and 2007, rising at an annual average rate of 6 per cent. With the economy growing at an even faster rate, this implied a generally falling or stable expenditure ratio of expenditure to GNP until 2003.'

But thereafter the ratio rose, especially after output growth began to slow in 2007. 'And, in a final twist, real expenditure rose by over 11 per cent in both 2007 and 2008, an unfortunate late burst of spending which boosted the underlying deficit at almost the worst possible time,' Honohan's report said.

Honohan implicitly accused Cowen and Ahern of using the budget of December 2006 to buy the following summer's general election, at just the wrong time in the economic cycle.

The Central Bank governor did recognize, however, that our authorities were not alone in misreading the situation. Foreign borrowing financed the bubble, he said, with net indebtedness of Irish banks to the rest of the world jumping from 10 per cent of GDP to over 60 per cent by 2008. It was a mistake by our banks but also by those who lent to us.

Honohan delivered an ear-catching phrase that not surprisingly got the headlines – and infuriated Cowen. The economist did not explain how he reached the figure, but he said that our crisis was 'three quarters' home-grown.

The second report, by former International Monetary Fund officials Klaus Regling and Max Watson, also castigated the government's handling of budget finances, but it concentrated mainly on the failings of the banks themselves when it came to property lending and the associated failures of the state's regulators to properly monitor and control them.

The duo joined up the dots when they claimed that the banks had acted in response to economic conditions that were heavily influenced by political decisions. Crucially, they found that, while our banking crisis bore 'the clear imprint of global influences', in many important ways it was 'home-made'. Regling blamed 'exceptional financial exuberance' in Ireland, 'governance weaknesses of an easily recognisable kind' and 'a tidal wave of uncritical enthusiasm' for property lending.

The banks had operated within the overall policies set down by the government, but when their lending became excessive the government and regulators failed to rein them in. Alarm bells should have been ringing at the Office of the Financial Regulator, as property prices soared and lending exploded to support this, from as far back as 2003. Instead Regling and Watson found that the culture of supervising banks was 'insufficiently intrusive', and that the number and quality of staff available to perform the hands-on role required were 'seriously inadequate'. Errors of judgement in bank management and governance had allowed financial institutions to go out of control, and the Irish economic crisis was the result.

Watson said he was surprised by the intense concentration of bank lending in property, particularly in commercial property, and by how business had been centred upon 'a couple of dozen' borrowers who were 'very dominant'. And credit-risk control had failed to prevent such concentrations. There had been internal-bank lending decisions of a 'very bad' quality, as well as poor documentation and poor collateral offered. 'The major responsibility lies with the directors and senior managements of the banks,' he said.

The report concluded that property had become a 'national blind-spot' and that even without any tax breaks there would have been a crisis, although it could have been a smaller one. A few crumbs of comfort for the government were included, however. 'There was a socio-political context in which it would have taken some courage to seem to prick the Irish property bubble.' Also helpful to the administrators was Watson's comment that he did not believe that Irish residential mortgages contained the same 'time-bomb' that had been present in commercial- and development-property lending, which was the 'really dangerous element'.

'The crisis management after the crisis broke and after all the criticism that we have in our report, and factors that contributed to the crisis, I'm quite impressed, and I think Max also, about the response to the crisis,' Regling said. 'It's better than in most other EU member states.'

Watson said the authorities had 'got out in front' of the problem in time. 'That was politically difficult, I'm sure. I'm not a political expert . . . it really paid off.'

Despite these endorsements, Cowen was damaged both by the findings of the reports from Regling–Watson and from Honohan, and by his reaction to them. (The reports' findings on the banks and the bank guarantee are discussed in more detail in Part II.) Following the example of his mentor Albert Reynolds from nearly twenty years earlier – when, using just one favourable page from the Beef Tribunal report before anyone else had had the chance to read the rest of it, the then Taoiseach claimed to have been 'vindicated' – Cowen took the line that Honohan had 'strongly vindicated' the government's handling of the introduction of the bank guarantee and subsequent crisis. This rang very hollow in the circumstances, suggesting that there's a fine line between saying something to maintain a political position and appearing delusional.

In an opening statement at a press conference after the publication of the two major reports, he said: 'The Governor's report demolishes the contention that a widespread guarantee was not necessary and highlights the enormous damage which would have resulted if a bank was let fail.' He added that the Honohan report 'finds that Anglo Irish Bank was systemically important as this government has contended. Opposition parties have strongly argued that it was not a systemic institution. Governor Honohan confirms that a disorderly failure of that bank would have brought down the whole banking system.'

Cowen went on: 'I want to emphasize that prior to the crisis, the government took action to reduce the vulnerabilities of the banking sector to the property market, although I fully accept that, in hindsight, it was not sufficient.'

He conceded the reports made clear that, along with mistakes by banks and regulators, 'mistakes were also made by successive governments, some of which reflected fundamental errors in projections by the Central Bank, the IMF, the OECD and others.' In other words he was spreading the blame, which may have been strictly accurate but didn't sound too good from the guy in charge.

Asked if the Regling and Watson report was 'a damning indictment' of his performance as minister for finance, Cowen said the government decisions taken then were based on the advice available at the time, but he added: 'The outcome that we now face is a very challenging one for all our people and I deeply regret that.

'Hindsight is always clear and obviously we would not have taken such a course if we had known of the scale of the property collapse which was facing the country.'

Many of his claims as to his own usefulness did not stand up to detailed scrutiny. Even the stuff that Cowen drew our attention to – Honohan's supposed support for the introduction of the bank guarantee on the infamous morning of 30 September 2008 – got him a pass mark at best rather than honours. Honohan said it was not executed correctly, because it included the cost of subordinated debt – and, more importantly, things should never have had to come to such a pass in the first place.

There were legitimate questions as to why Cowen had not displayed more foresight in his job as finance minister, or at least why he hadn't asked the right questions. Cowen was either too lazy to interrogate those giving him formal advice, or intellectually incapable of it. Blindsided by the seeming riches he had to spend, he acted like a classic politician instead of applying any kind of economic or financial scepticism to the questions of where all the money was coming from and how long it would continue to be there.

Cowen insisted that the first action he took when appointed minister for finance was to bring in 'the most radical abolition of property tax incentives since the foundation of the state', but this was untrue. 'There were property-tax incentives in place over the period from the mid 1990s which, with the benefit of hindsight now, should have been abolished many years prior to my decision in December 2005 to abolish them,' Cowen said. But he had not acted as promptly as he claimed. In 2006 he had prolonged the incentives through a gradual phasing-out process of between six months and two years.

Cowen had responded to vested interests, which had argued that the measures to remove tax breaks for buy-to-let investors, for example, would lead to a 'flight of capital' to Britain and elsewhere. The construction sector fought for deadlines to be put back because of reasons such as 'unavoidable hold-ups in the planning process' and even 'health-and-safety concerns arising from a late rush to complete construction' to make the required dates. And the banks continued to lend furiously to those who wanted to 'invest'.

This had a number of unwanted long-term effects. Those availing themselves of the tax benefits used the extra cash from their incentives as equity to support even more borrowing for further investments, which in turn created an even bigger property bubble. Many of those who received tax breaks to make ill-fated investments have effectively now left their debts with the banks, which just happen to be owned by the government of the state that let them have their tax breaks in the first place.

Lenihan was in a stronger position than Cowen to offer regrets when faced with criticism of poor government decisions, as he had not joined the cabinet until 2007, becoming finance minister only in May 2008. 'Yes we did spend too much money and yes we did neglect our tax base – and they were mistakes. But let's be clear about it, they weren't mistakes that were highlighted by very many at the time and indeed many of those who predicted the collapse of the property bubble did so at a very late stage.'

However, when it was put to him that government fiscal policies should be included in the remit of the subsequent commission of inquiry, he replied that this was 'not an area which was highlighted for investigation' by either Honohan or Regling–Watson.

The two reports, effectively the first stage of the banking inquiry, informed the terms of reference for what would be the second stage: the establishment of a statutory commission of inquiry to be held in private. Cowen was determined that this should take place in secret – and with good reason. Otherwise, he would have to give an explanation in public, and in response to meticulous examination, about what he did, or didn't do, in relation to the calamity that he'd had such a large part in causing.

Lenihan did not totally distance himself from Cowen. 'It is worth noting that Prof. Honohan pointed out that while three quarters of the crisis was home-grown, the primary culprit in the generation of that crisis was the banking sector,' Lenihan argued. 'The secondary culprit was the supervisory system, and the government is in the bronze position in that particular race.'

But the long-attempted – but always wholly unconvincing – defence that our economic woes were caused by international events beyond the government's control was now undermining him.

On 10 June 2010 I met the Taoiseach for a lengthy *Last Word* radio interview in response to the publication of the reports, and asked him, twice, not why he hadn't resigned – because he was never going to concede that he should – but how much time and thought, upon reading the reports, he had given to the idea of resigning. The short answer he gave was that he hadn't considered it and he seemed very surprised that I'd even asked.

Politicians have thick skins but it was hard to believe that, given the catastrophe over which he had presided, Cowen did not doubt his own ability or was not shamed by his performance. The thought that he wasn't up to it and that somebody else might be better off having a go never seemed to have occurred to him.

His tactic of scapegoating the collapse of Lehman Brothers in September 2008 – 'without that, we'd have managed' – had been doubtful at best but was clearly exploded now that these official reports from Honohan and Regling–Watson confirmed that our crisis was self-made. He got quite angry when I asked him if he would promise, in the light of these reports, never to use Lehman as an excuse again.

The Fine Gael leader, Enda Kenny, attempted to take advantage of Cowen's latest troubles during a motion of no-confidence in the government that was heard five days after the reports were published. He claimed that Cowen was guilty of creating an economic disaster that would for ever carry the logo 'Made by Fianna Fáil' and accused Cowen 'of being one of the chief architects of our economy's destruction and of condemning our people to a lost decade of unemployment, misery and emigration'.

He added: 'I accuse him of hijacking our Republic and handing it over to a toxic circle of bankers, developers and speculators who, like a cancer, have sought to destroy our Republic from the inside out. When his policies as minister for finance helped destroy our economy, he also denied all responsibility.' Kenny said Cowen was 'never there when there was a problem, never responsible when there was a failure and never to blame when things go wrong'.

Kenny's problem, however, was that an opinion poll appeared in *The Irish Times* on the very day that the government published the reports by the independent experts into its behaviour. With the media and public becoming bored by the financial crisis, they focused on poll numbers suggesting a slump in support for Fine Gael, and for Kenny in particular. Many in the party panicked, thinking their chances of returning to power were being compromised by their leader. Richard Bruton led an unsuccessful coup, but the main immediate beneficiary was Cowen, from whom attention was diverted while Fine Gael fought in public.

3. The Hangover

In mid September 2010 the Fianna Fáil parliamentary party met in Galway to prepare for the new Dáil session. The most noteworthy conventional news element to come from the meeting was delivered by Lenihan to reporters waiting outside the Ardilaun Hotel. He dropped very strong hints that he would be looking for a deeper reduction of the exchequer deficit in the December budget than the €3 billion that had been indicated previously. This was a reaction to an unravelling financial situation. But, rather than debating that, the nation ended up debating An Taoiseach's sobriety.

Cowen had agreed to mark the second day of the meeting with a radio interview on RTÉ's *Morning Ireland* programme, which was being broadcast live from the hotel. He arrived near the end of the programme, which meant that the interview would be relatively short. It wasn't what he said that scandalized the nation, it was how he said it. Cowen sounded terrible, his voice hoarse and husky. Those who'd had experience of how people can sound after a late night's drinking immediately suspected that Cowen had been on the lash. Traffic on the internet surged and listeners to radio stations began ringing in furiously, demanding to know what was going on. Radio presenters on following RTÉ programmes and on other stations began to speculate openly about whether Cowen had been drunk. TV3's political editor Ursula Halligan confronted Cowen on his way to another meeting and asked him directly about his condition during the interview. Cowen was shocked and angered even to be asked and denied immediately that he'd been either drunk or hungover.

But the genie was out of the bottle as much as the alcohol. Cowen had cut loose the night before in a way that political insiders knew was typical. The shackles were thrown off and he drank, sang and told stories until 3.30 a.m. before going to bed, even going so far as to mimic the high-pitched voice of a prominent golfer. There had been a party, and embarrassed journalists had to admit that they'd been part of it too. Many in the public were furious. This did not tally with the austerity that was being demanded of the country at this time.

Suddenly there was widespread talk among the general public, and within Fianna Fáil, that the time had come for Cowen to step down. Now his personal behaviour was added to the list of failings of which he was accused. But if he refused to go voluntarily who would get rid of him?

To many there was an issue regarding the validity of his mandate, especially when the government was introducing so many unpopular measures. The Dáil arithmetic remained on the side of the government, but only because it refused to hold by-elections to find new TDs for three vacant seats, and because it continued to maintain deals on local constituency issues with independent TDs like Michael Lowry and Jackie Healy-Rae. The Green Party was still honouring the deal it had reached with the former Fianna Fáil leader and Taoiseach, Bertie Ahern, in mid 2007, and had renegotiated with Cowen two years later. In response to criticisms that the electorate had not endorsed him as Taoiseach, Cowen pointed out regularly that it was not a direct vote and that he had been correctly elected Taoiseach according to the constitution.

Yet some within Fianna Fáil wondered if his behaviour in Galway was a subconscious expression of a deep-seated desire to give up the job he'd taken somewhat reluctantly in the first place, even before it became near-impossible. Others pointed out that late nights were nothing new to Cowen and that the media had kept him company in such circumstances before; his misjudgement was to have attended a live radio interview with so little sleep and with his voice so obviously impaired.

There were few outstanding candidates to replace him either. Lenihan would have been required to give detailed evidence about his health, and questions would have arisen as to who would replace him in the Department of Finance, should he be considered especially essential there. Every other candidate was tarnished by involvement with the Ahern governments.

A change of leader probably would have required the almost immediate calling of an election – handily enough, just before budget day – on the basis that the public would not accept a second Fianna Fáil Taoiseach who had not been endorsed, even if indirectly, by the electorate. However, most in the party wanted to postpone this for as long as possible, in the hope that something would turn up to improve the party's standing. In any event Cowen resolutely refused to countenance the calling of an election. Since the time of the bank guarantee, the same excuses had been trotted out regularly: the government had a majority and was entitled to rule on that basis; the instability in the financial markets would somehow be intensified should the people remove the incumbents, as if leaving an unpopular government in place would provide a greater degree of certainty.

Not that the government was admitting that the economic condition of the state was worsening. It seemed to regard coming close to meeting its own budget targets as some sort of major achievement that somehow reflected that the overall economy was doing okay too.

Lenihan greeted the exchequer figures to the end of August with a statement that 'stability' had returned to the economy: the government's deficit of €12.1 billion between income and spending in the first eight months of the year was only slightly worse than he had predicted the previous December. That was scant consolation to most people, because it was only part of the overall picture; the rest of the economy was suffering dreadfully. The rate of joblessness was the highest in sixteen years. The number of claimants of social benefits was 455,000, the highest number in the history of the state. Emigration, especially among young people, was masking the full extent of the crisis, as was the range of educational courses keeping people off the live register. Company failures were soaring, consumer spending had slowed each month since May, and nearly one in twenty mortgages was in arrears. The banks were rarely lending, because, as would soon become apparent, they didn't have the means to do so or any confidence that they would be repaid. When they did lend, it was at higher interest rates and with onerous conditions.

The government's strategy had been to concentrate on getting a grip on public spending to mitigate somewhat the long-term drag on public finances – for which the public would eventually have to pay. However, it was becoming clear that the creation of NAMA and the associated recapitalization of the banks was a tactic that wasn't working quickly enough or as planned. It meant that the government had very limited options when it came to funding efforts at job creation. What it wanted above all was to prevent the loss of any more jobs. Even leaving aside the social consequences of 455,000 social-welfare claimants and their families having to manage without jobs and on small incomes, the government didn't want to be faced with the cost of additions to their numbers. But the government had no idea how or when the jobs haemorrhage could be stemmed, in spite of the confidence with which Brian Lenihan proclaimed, just as he had on the public finances and the banks, that the worst was over.

The tax receipts for the first eight months of the year, at €18.9 billion, were 9 per cent lower than in the same disastrous period of 2009. Income taxes were €270 million behind target, which emphasized not just increased unemployment but shorter working hours and lower incomes. The spending on social welfare was €350 million higher than had been expected. To get the overall budget back on track the government slashed investment in infrastructure projects, which had been conceived with the idea of creating construction jobs as well as benefits for the future. The amount spent was down by €1.3 billion, or 34 per cent, on 2009 and was €803 million behind target for the year. If, as was claimed, better value for money was being achieved, these savings could have been reinvested elsewhere. But they weren't.

The government clearly felt that it had a job to do in trying to persuade people not to be too despondent. Those who had money were saving instead of spending, exacerbating job losses and tax shortfalls, and it was felt that something had to be done to encourage everyday normal economic activity. Lenihan was aware of the growing sense of doom and anger in the public, hostile and adverse comment in the media, and he was finding it very hard to dispel this. Fear was everywhere, and many of those who weren't fearful were ignorant, some wilfully. The figures, not the political spin, were telling all. International investors, upon whom we depended to borrow money, were

neither fearful nor ignorant. They were taking hard-headed commercial decisions about lending to Ireland and the price at which
they would do it because financial instability was now rife.

Near the end of August 2010 the government had to admit that the
cost to the state of funding the losses at Anglo Irish Bank and Irish
Nationwide would be a lot more than had been anticipated. The new
net cost to the government of recapitalizing Anglo Irish Bank was
put at 'about €22 to €25 billion' and of sorting out Irish Nationwide
at €3.2 billion. There was uproar – just imagine all the other potential
uses for that money.

However, that was not the end of it. The ratings agency Standard
& Poor's led the charge in insisting that the cost to the state of covering the losses at Anglo Irish Bank would be even higher than that
enormous sum. There was little or no confidence in the strategy the
bank's management had presented to the European Commission and
the government for controlling and capping the losses. S&P predicted that it would cost €50 billion to finance the bailout of all the
distressed banks. The government furiously denied this, knowing
that the costs for the NTMA in borrowing on international money
markets would rise as a consequence of the bad publicity. It happened anyway, because S&P downgraded Ireland's debt rating from
AA to AA minus.

Anglo's board – with the former Fine Gael leader and one-time
minister for finance, Alan Dukes, as chairman and headhunted Australian Mike Aynsley as managing director – had come up with the
idea of a good bank/bad bank split that would allow for the creation
of a small business lender, of the kind needed in Ireland in the absence
of much corporate lending. To many, giving a complete failure such
as Anglo a key role as one of the few remaining lenders to the business sector in bombed-out Ireland seemed like a bizarre idea. As one
commentator put it, even if the bank managed to generate annual
profits of €100 million, it would have taken more than 200 years to
repay the state's invested capital. Nor did Anglo have the business
skills to deal with loans other than those relating to property.

EU Commissioner for Competition Joaquín Almunia was especially dubious, as state aid was being given to a bank that would

compete with other non-state-owned and foreign institutions. His office didn't dismiss the idea immediately and gave Anglo time to make another pitch. But, in the light of Anglo's 'high level of distress', the 'extreme fragility' of the entire Irish banking sector and the need to pump money into Anglo 'to preserve the stability of the banking sector in Ireland', it was never likely to be on. Nor was the idea that Irish Nationwide would return to its old role as a traditional savings and home-loans provider – in other words, a building society – after its disastrous foray into commercial lending.

In early September the government announced that Anglo would be divided into a savings bank and an 'asset-recovery vehicle', in other words an institution that would act to recover as much of the money owed to it as possible. The reality was that it was closing, but over a long period of time to ensure that there wouldn't be an immediate run on deposits that could bring the bank down. Aynsley said the total cost of the bank to the state would not exceed the now latest estimate of €25 billion. 'We're not going to get to the €35 billion Standard & Poor's suggested. I'm not sure where that came from,' he said.

The latest Anglo announcement failed to instil any confidence. It had all the appearances of a hastily conceived response to the EU Commission's rejection of Plan A. There remained too many uncertainties as to its likely cost and how long it would take to close the bank down. Success could not be predicted with any sense of realism. And the commission's rejection of the plan only served to focus attention on everything that the Irish government had been doing. NAMA, the recapitalization of the banks and their partial nationalization were all supposed to have restored confidence – which in turn would have allowed the banks to lend to help the economy and, what was often missed, reduce the cost of the NTMA's borrowings on the international sovereign debt market. But it wasn't happening as planned.

It was becoming clear that the inability of the government to get to grips with the Anglo mess was only part of the problem. September was turning into a dreadful month as just about everything went wrong on the financial markets for both the Irish State and its banks. Both found it impossible to raise the money that they needed.

The bank guarantee had bought time, but now it was close to running out. It would be extended for another three months by way of a variation, but suddenly the issues relating to the state's ability to meet the contingent liabilities it had guaranteed became very real.

The first problems were at the banks – and these problems weren't restricted to the much commented upon need for capital to cover losses. As with two years earlier, there was a liquidity issue (the availability of money to the banks from other sources) to rival the solvency one (that debts would be repaid by those who had borrowed from them). The Irish authorities had allowed a situation to develop whereby the banks would have to repay huge amounts of bond debts within a very short time-frame. The money to meet the repayments would have to be borrowed, or refinanced. But very few were willing to lend to the Irish banks for this purpose. As the banks were being cut from the inter-bank lending markets, they called upon the European Central Bank, the lender of last resort, for the money they needed. To get money from the ECB, security had to be offered, and so loans that the banks had on their books and regarded as assets were pledged to get cash in return. But what were they really worth?

The Central Bank calculated that, in the two years up to the end of September 2010, the Irish domestic banks, including the Irish retail banking subsidiaries of foreign banks such as Ulster Bank and Bank of Scotland (Ireland), lost overseas deposits of €64 billion and debt securities held by overseas bondholders of €45 billion. The three biggest Irish banks lost a combined €35 billion in deposits in 2010 up to the end of September, most of which left from July onwards, very similar to the amount lost during the crisis of September 2008 that triggered the guarantee. Bank of Ireland alone lost €10 billion in a six-week period over the end of August and the start of September. Downgrades in credit ratings – both for the bank and the state – were largely to blame.

That this had been allowed to happen was bizarre and verging on negligent. The Irish authorities, working closely with the ECB, had allowed the guaranteed banks to cluster an enormous amount of money that needed to be refinanced in a very short period. Knowledge of the situation was not widespread outside of financial markets but that didn't really matter: the key people in the markets were wondering about Ireland's ability to repay sovereign debts as much as banking ones. Political arguments that the two were separate were disregarded. This was where the extent of the initial guarantee, and its concomitant insanity, became apparent.

The ECB had to act in two ways. First, the Irish banks were getting up to a quarter of all the funding the ECB provided across the entire eurozone. (About €130 billion was borrowed from the ECB and a further €34 billion from our Central Bank, much of the latter secured on assets and loans that the ECB would not accept as sufficiently creditworthy.) Second, the ECB was also believed to be active in the sovereign-debt markets, acting as the main price support for Irish government bonds, albeit doing its buying at one remove. Irish rates shot up to a 4 per cent premium over German bonds.

The media, not knowing on a day-to-day basis of the extent of the liquidity crisis at the banks, focused on what was visible: rising yields on government debt and rocketing prices for credit-default swaps. A credit-default swap (CDS) is an insurance policy that allows bond buyers to take cover against the likelihood of the borrower failing to make repayments. The price of this insurance policy increases if there is doubt about the ability of the borrower to repay – and the price increased daily for Ireland.

Cowen took the green jersey approach again. His contention that the rise in the price of Irish ten-year bonds was part of the market's 'ebb and flow' was derided as the type of wishful thinking that fools nobody. Not wanting to spook people (or the markets) is one thing but deliberately evading the truth is quite another. Lenihan admitted that the funding situation for the banks was 'stressed'. With many believing that it was immoral and inequitable for Irish citizens to be paying for the gambling losses of bank bondholders, there was growing speculation that Ireland would also be unable to repay all of its sovereign debts. But anyone who suggested that this was a desirable or inevitable option – and a growing number of economists did – was met with stern rebukes from those in the Irish establishment who were wedded to the idea of living up to Europe's expectations of Ireland.

4.   Brave Little Ireland

When I wrote in the *Sunday Times* in September 2010 that default was beginning to look likely, I received a furious letter from former Taoiseach John Bruton, berating me for daring to raise such a possibility in print because of the damage this speculation might cause. The former EU ambassador to Washington, who now worked as a promoter of the International Finance Services Centre in Dublin and who drew a large pension from the state, was angry that I did not draw a distinction at the very least between sovereign debt and bank debt (at that point I didn't think the difference meant much because of the implications of the state guarantee). He suggested that were we to default, the damage to Ireland's reputation as a country with which to do business would be enormous and could not be contemplated; he was of the belief that Ireland must repay every cent that it owed and that the opinions offered by me in a widely read newspaper were 'dangerous'.

Behind the scenes there were influential figures with strong views who had ready access to government ministers – and whose reputations meant they were heard. Some had the confidence to make their views known publicly too, knowing that they were likely to receive a great deal of attention but relatively little critical examination.

Peter Sutherland was one of those. A Fine Gael man like Bruton, the former attorney general to a Fine Gael and Labour coalition, surprisingly had the ear of Brian Lenihan, who was no doubt impressed by Sutherland's list of international contacts. His CV runs to many pages but among his influential positions is a membership of the board of the World Economic Forum at Davos, the Switzerland invitation-only annual shindig for some of the world's wealthiest and most powerful. He is also the European chairman of a high-powered talking shop called the Trilateral Commission, which promotes closer connections between Europe, Japan and North America. He is part of the secretive Bilderberg Group, an elite group of fewer than 140 invited-only members that meets privately to discuss the state of the world and that conspiracy theorists have accused of attempting to operate a proxy world government, by wielding considerable influence over elected governments. And in 2006 Pope Benedict XVI appointed him Consultor of the Extraordinary Section of the Administration of the Patrimony of the Holy See, which means that he is, in effect, a financial adviser to the Pope.

In addition, Sutherland was a board director at three major global conglomerates and had been chairman of controversial oil giant British Petroleum for years. His most important, and lucrative, source of income was from one of the world's biggest merchant banks, Goldman Sachs, where he had become a partner and chairman of its international division in 1995, sharing in payments worth hundreds of millions annually. However, Sutherland told Simon Carswell of *The Irish Times* in January 2010 that 'I don't consider myself a businessman – I am a man who is passionately interested in public affairs, particularly [those] of Ireland. I am energized by debate and dispute, and I am quite happy to fight my corner. I have a very clear idea as to what I actually believe in.'

Sutherland said the December 2009 budget had 'restored pride in the Irish situation'. It was 'courageous and correct and absolutely necessary', and had created an international perception of 'brave little Ireland'. 'But brave little Ireland has to continue to deliver,' he said. Ireland's competitiveness was 'way down' below that of other countries, and the public sector needed further radical changes. He regretted a failure to 'take on some of the sacred cows', such as the unions, but defended the banks, who he said were 'getting it in the teeth'. Governments, in terms of macroeconomic policy and regulatory oversight, 'carry at least as big and probably a far greater responsibility' than the banks. 'The reaction now has to be one which doesn't simply seek to flagellate but to have a system that actually works. The whole issue of pay and so on, which personalizes everything, is much less important than the systems of regulatory management and oversight which are needed,' said the partner at one of the highest-paying financial institutions in the world. 'It is for the boards of companies to discover and to decide how much of the profits of a company should be distributed,' Sutherland said in defence of the enormous bonuses at Goldman Sachs, controversially still paid after the receipt of major loans from the US government in 2008 to avert a collapse at that institution.

Sutherland also showed limited belief in the abilities of Irish politicians. 'In many ways, our political class have been far too parochial. Only those who have been exposed through council membership [of EU ministers' meetings], and what have you, have enough of a handle on this to make a real contribution to the debate. The result is that the old adage that all politics is local is so much the case in Ireland that it has damaged our capacity to take on bigger issues such as this.'

He did not apply such criticisms to Lenihan. He told Lenihan at one meeting in 2009 that he had the potential to be one of the great Irish Taoisigh of the twenty-first century. When Lenihan learnt of his cancer diagnosis, Sutherland, who had suffered from cancer during 2009, was one of the first people he phoned.

As a multimillionaire, Sutherland tended to provoke a sense of awe among people who should have known better and, as a result, and perhaps fittingly, given his role with the Vatican, his pronouncements on economic matters were treated as if somehow equivalent to a papal bull. The genuflections in Ireland to Sutherland that marked his economic musings – the majority of the audible sounds being those of purring approval rather than probing questions about the standing of his authority – bore an uncanny resemblance to the devoted bowing that used to be accorded to Catholic bishops in Ireland and that was regarded by both parties as rightly due. Mammon had become the new religion so it was no surprise that there was scrapping towards the barrister-turned-bureaucrat-turned-banker who was almost regarded by some in Ireland as a proxy for God.

In September 2010 Sutherland made a rather unremarkable speech that somehow got elevated to the lead item of RTÉ's *Six One News*, as if it was of some great significance rather than merely the opinion of a man who might have been judged by many as the voice of vested interests had the full facts been declared.

Among Sutherland's messages were these: Irish people were paid too much and wages had to be forced down if we were to regain competitiveness; the government must close the deficit between income and spending in 2011 by more than the planned €3 billion; and it would be calamitous to renege on repayment of all of the country's debts.

Sutherland presented larger cuts as the lesser of two evils, predicting 'much greater pain' through higher borrowing costs if the government didn't act to close the deficit further. 'We are told that this [€3 billion] is all that the political system can bear, but if all the mainstream political parties accept that more is required – although disagreeing perhaps about where to find the €3 billion – and are prepared to say it, we can find a way.' Sutherland said the national debt was rising 'at an alarming rate' due to government spending and claimed this was being overlooked in the public debate by the 'constant and intense focus' on the banking crisis. The two issues needed to be separated, he said, and attention refocused on the country's running costs, which were 'still far too high' and way above the European average in the public sector. It was a line very similar to the one Lenihan was pushing at the time. 'We have to recognize that as currency devaluation is not an option, downward flexibility in wages and prices is essential to avoid unemployment,' Sutherland said.

Sutherland might well have been correct in his analysis – and many people agreed with him – but his authority to deliver such sermons might not have been quite as automatic as some of his supporters appeared to assume. The very things for which he was celebrated made him the ultimate in vested interests. As a result of his role in Goldman Sachs, the most powerful financial institution in the world, he was rich beyond the wildest dreams of many, but he was also wedded firmly to the principle of defending the rights of the owners of mobile capital, that they should be able to protect what they regarded as their legitimate interests.

Context was not provided in the RTÉ interview or in others that he gave to newspapers during that year. Most pertinently, viewers were not reminded that Sutherland was still part-time chairman of Goldman Sachs International, the European wing of the investment bank, which traded extensively in government bonds throughout the world and which, since February 2010, had our government's imprimatur as a primary dealer in Irish bonds. They weren't told of Goldman Sachs's extraordinary role in the financial crisis in Greece or of how the US Senate had not long before accused the company of egregious behaviour in its treatment of customers, particularly in playing both sides of the market without telling them. Many independent observers regarded the behaviour of Goldman Sachs as a major contributory factor in the Wall Street crisis of September 2008, which brought down rival investment bank Lehman Brothers and required the state-funded rescue of the insurance giant AIG. The presence of Goldman's former managing partner, Henry 'Hank' Paulson, as President George Bush's treasury secretary during the crisis was regarded as highly significant when it came to the decisions to save Wall Street interests made by the Bush administration.

Sutherland had been on the board of Royal Bank of Scotland (RBS) when it embarked on the optimistic lending that ended in its rescue by the British taxpayer at a cost of over £45 billion. The foolhardy £71 billion purchase of ABN Amro was completed at the peak of the market in 2007, while Sutherland was providing non-executive oversight. He sat on the remuneration committee that lavished huge bonuses on its chief executive, Sir Fred Goodwin.

Nor was there much discussion of Sutherland's former chairmanship of AIB between 1989 and 1993. He may have left the bank long before it embarked on the policy of reckless lending that required state salvation to prevent its collapse, but he had been chair of the board during some of the bank's more notorious crises, including its deliberate facilitation of tax evasion by customers who didn't want to pay deposit interest retention tax (DIRT). Sutherland had washed his hands of this fraud against the state when challenged by the Oireachtas Public Accounts Committee about failures of oversight. 'The issue of non-resident accounts and DIRT was an issue which was essentially one for management. Management, as I understand it, believed that the issue was under control,' he claimed. He said that he 'did not intervene in any way' and had handed the matter over to a subcommittee. 'Everyone, I think, was basically happy with the process . . . If I were to do it all over again, I wouldn't change one iota of the steps that we took in terms of having an objective analysis of the situation and coming to a fair and proper conclusion.'

Nor were we reminded that in an *Irish Times* interview in early 2010 he had argued against the establishment of a banking inquiry. 'It would have been better not to have an inquiry at this time because we have limited resources and a diversion of those limited human resources into an ex post facto analysis of the past is far less important than remedying the immediate problem that we have now,' he said. 'It is a very difficult subject and to have all of these civil servants sitting in listening to bloody evidence on the past when they all know broadly what happened. We know what happened – we know it all. A political football is not what we need. We need to look to the future to get it right.' This was hardly surprising from a former chairman of AIB who had appeared at the 1999 public inquiry into the DIRT tax-evasion scandal.

Sutherland was devoted to the power of the markets and the need to impress the institutions and billionaire individuals who populated its higher reaches. He warned against a slower rate of budget cuts, saying that 'this simply will not fly as an option. Any weakness in one budget will be punished by the market in a manner which we will be unable to take.' In common with others Sutherland warned that a default on state debts would leave the government without the capacity to manage its affairs or raise finance. 'It simply is not an option to choose,' he said.

He said there was 'no way' the country could walk away from the cost of Anglo Irish Bank by letting the losses fall on the institution's bondholders. There had been arguments to that effect made by the influential *Financial Times* newspaper – hardly a bastion of socialism – but Sutherland dismissed its position as 'flawed in theory and extremely damaging in practice'. No OECD country other than Iceland, he said, had allowed a major retail bank to default on what is called senior bank debt, a form of loan to a bank that allows the lender to rank higher among the list of creditors, giving it greater security than so-called junior, or subordinated, bondholders. The amount saved would be small but the collateral damage immense: the maximum saving the government could make by sharing Anglo's rising losses with the holders of senior and subordinated debt would be €5.1 billion and that such a move for a small country would 'surely precipitate a funding crisis both for the sovereign and the banking system as a whole'. Sutherland told us that instead 'we' would have to 'gird our loins to take tough decisions and see it through . . . This is where we show our mettle.'

Outsiders disagreed, however, and concurred with the domestic economist dissidents. In early September 2010 a former chief economist of the IMF, Simon Johnson, warned that Ireland was effectively insolvent. 'The ultimate result of Ireland's bank bailout exercise is obvious. One way or another, the government will have converted the liabilities of private banks into debts of the sovereign yet the nation probably cannot afford these debts,' he said. 'Ireland, simply put, appears insolvent under plausible scenarios with current policies. The idea that Ireland, Greece or Portugal can cut spending and grow out of overvalued exchange rates with still larger budget deficits, while servicing all their debts and building more debt, is proving – not surprisingly – wrong.' He warned that if the current policies continued, 'the calamity of the Irish banking system will lead to a much deeper recession and the consequences will be felt for decades.'

The majority on the markets agreed with people such as Johnson. But politically Lenihan, Cowen and the rest of the government had to be seen to fight. It came as little surprise after the publication of these interventions by Sutherland that Lenihan also rejected as 'unthinkable' the suggestion that Ireland should default on some of its bank debts. 'I do not propose that the country becomes an experiment for default strategy,' he said. Journalists were told that they needed to be aware of the self-fulfilling nature of any 'doomsday scenarios' they put forward and that they were in a position either to undermine or to promote confidence in the economy. He said a crucial element in dispelling fear was the provision of accurate, reliable and balanced information. 'There is a tendency to paint black-and-white pictures, to overstate difficulties, to use sometimes emotive language. And God knows, our problems are bad enough without exaggerating the reportage to present doomsday scenarios.'

We were also supposed to be encouraged by an opinion in a research note by Goldman Sachs, which said that Ireland was 'very unlikely' to experience a financial crisis as severe as the one that had forced Greece to seek an international bailout earlier this year. Yet, by September, Irish borrowing costs hit a new high of 6.55 per cent, while the difference between ten-year Irish bonds and German bonds went to a euro-record high of 451 basis points. Lenihan's response was to claim there was a 'concerted attack' on eurozone nations. The markets, however, noted the revelation that the Irish economy had contracted at a rate of 1.2 per cent in the second quarter, for all the many claims by Lenihan and Cowen that we had turned the corner. In such circumstances, how could Ireland hope to grow its way out of debt? Was austerity, of which more was planned, actually putting the economy into a self-reinforcing spiral?

In the same week that Lenihan urged the media to balance its reporting, NTMA boss John Corrigan asserted that concerns about the refinancing of the country's banks were 'overdone', even though the banks were having to refinance €30 billion of debt that month. 'We've characterized concerns around this like the millennium bug,' said Corrigan. 'We all thought the plans were going to fall out of the sky, the trains were going to stop, the clocks weren't going to work.' Corrigan had managed to sell bonds worth €1.5 billion days earlier, but giving yields to investors at 1 per cent more than in the previous auction was a limited success. Within days Ireland was to withdraw from trying to raise more money in the markets. The naysayers were about to be proved correct.

5. Déjà Vu All Over Again

It was Wednesday, 29 September 2010, and, as the joke goes, it was almost déjà vu all over again.

Some details and personnel had changed. Events similar to those of two years earlier – which had led to the introduction of the bank guarantee – were taking place at Government Buildings, at the Department of Finance, but this time it was Lenihan, instead of the absent Cowen, who was calling the shots. Many of the faces from two years before were to be seen again.

Some, such as the former governor of the Central Bank, John Hurley, the old financial regulator, Pat Neary, and the retired secretary of the Department of Finance, David Doyle, had gone, but Doyle's replacement, Kevin Cardiff, was again involved in a crucial decision. He and Lenihan were joined by Ann Nolan, head of the department's financial services division. Others at the meeting were Frank Daly and Brendan McDonagh from NAMA and John Corrigan and Michael Torpey from the NTMA. Patrick Honohan from the Central Bank and Matthew Elderfield, the regulator, were there too. The topic for discussion was again what to do with the banks and how to limit the state's exposure to their losses.

Honohan made it clear that the ECB would not wear the idea of 'burning' the bondholders. Lenihan, advised by his close friend, Attorney General Paul Gallagher, said that was probably a moot point anyway, as there would be severe legal difficulties in doing so. Just to emphasize the point, a €750 million repayment to Anglo Irish Bank senior bondholders was due to be made the following day and the European Central Bank was providing the money for this, although that was to be kept quiet and revealed only weeks later.

A decision was taken to try to pre-empt activity on the markets the following morning. The latest report on the capital needs for the banks was due to be published by Elderfield on Thursday evening after the markets had closed. As it was ready – and as government ten-year bond yields had reached 6.78 per cent that day, compared to only 4.5 per cent six months earlier – it was decided to publish Elderfield's report first thing Thursday morning.

The news it contained, when unveiled on what came to be known as Black Thursday, was disastrous, fittingly marking the second anniversary of the decision to guarantee all the deposits and bonds at Irish-owned banks, the plan that Lenihan had claimed was the 'cheapest bailout in the world, so far'. Well, now here was 'confirmation' that it was going to cost close to €50 billion in new capital to fix the banks, although some immediately doubted, correctly, whether that was going to be enough.

It had turned out that the latest estimate as to the costs of saving the banks, given at the end of March 2010, had not been sufficiently accurate, or, rather, sufficiently pessimistic. That was the fourth attempt at a figure – and the second by the new team at the Central Bank led by Honohan and Elderfield – and now another number was being offered as the final estimated cost to the taxpayer of the bailouts. The costs were to amount to almost a third of the state's economic output, not including the additional cost of funding the €40 billion National Asset Management Agency or its potential losses.

The following day Lenihan announced that NAMA was to pay less for the remaining loans it would purchase – or, to use the now increasingly common jargon, impose a bigger haircut (discount) on the original value of the loans. The effect was that NAMA was to pay an estimated €30.5 billion for total loans of €73.4 billion, down from the previous estimate of about €40 billion on a total of €81 billion. It also decided that NAMA would change the threshold below which it would not acquire loans. Now anything under €20 million would not transfer, compared to the original plan for a floor of €5 million. This may have seemed like good news, in that NAMA was not overpaying for the loans and was taking fewer on board, but it was a mixed blessing. It meant that the banks were to incur bigger losses, which would have to be filled with new capital, which in all probability would have to come from the state in the absence of other sources. But where would the state get that money?

All of the banks were causing problems but the worst situations were at Anglo Irish and AIB, not surprisingly. The remaining Anglo loans were to be transferred at an expected discount of 67 per cent, up from 58 per cent for the first two tranches, which meant that the bank would require an extra €6.4 billion in capital on top of what had already been provided and perhaps €11.4 billion more in a worst-case scenario. In other words, the cost of meeting Anglo's losses would be at least €29.3 billion, or possibly €34 billion if the property market did not recover as expected. But it would definitely be no more than that, Lenihan promised, even though only a month earlier the public had been reassured that the cost to the state of recapitalizing Anglo would be €22 billion to €25 billion at most.

Honohan said of the Anglo bailout that 'it's costly but it's manageable'; he was quickly reminded of the government's denials of a month ago, when S&P had said that the estimated cost of the Anglo shutdown was still being underestimated.

Not surprisingly there was public uproar and questions as to why bondholders were not being made to 'share the pain' by taking their part of the losses. Anglo's subordinated debt, which did not have to be repaid by the state under the terms of its 2008 guarantee, was only about €2.5 billion, but the remaining senior debt, covered by the state guarantee, amounted to €16.5 billion. Lenihan continued to remain emphatic that senior bondholders would suffer no losses: he described such an idea as 'completely unreal'. He said that to do so would create 'a significant risk of jeopardizing the banking system and indeed the state's access to international debt markets and cannot be countenanced on that basis . . . We are not going to tell the bank manager we are going to default prior to asking for more money.'

Lenihan fell back on the legal position: under Irish law, senior debt obligations ranked equally with those to depositors and other creditors. To impose 'haircuts' on senior bondholders would require that equivalent haircuts be imposed on depositors. Lenihan did begin to talk, however, about asking holders of subordinated debt to share in the 'burden' of bailing out the bank. 'I expect the subordinated debt holders to make a significant contribution towards meeting the costs of Anglo,' Lenihan said, belatedly beginning a process that would save the state some money, if nowhere near as much as if it had been started much earlier.

It didn't mollify Lenihan's critics, who wanted more, but it was as far as the European Commission and the ECB would go. The competition commissioner, Joaquín Almunia, said: 'This is in line with the commission's principles on burden-sharing since it both addresses moral hazard and limits the amount of aid, with benefits to the taxpayers.'

Anglo wasn't the only disaster revealed that day. The other banks would cost a small fortune too. There was a need for €15.7 billion in additional capital to cover losses at AIB, Bank of Ireland, Irish Nationwide Building Society and the EBS (the smallest at €350 million). Irish Nationwide's requirement of €5.4 billion, billions higher than the previous estimate, was incredible because, at its biggest, its loans had amounted to €12 billion. Even the much larger Bank of Ireland didn't seem to need that much from the state, although if it couldn't raise money for itself it would need more than the €3.5 billion it was already getting from the state.

Most of the banks meekly accepted what they had been told, but there were massive rows with AIB. These culminated in Chairman Dan O'Connor and Chief Executive Colm Doherty quitting. Only the previous week the two had been on an international 'roadshow', seeking new investors as they told a tale of restoring AIB to good health. The bank had announced the sale of its Polish interests to Santander, to raise about €2.5 billion; it looked to sell its 22.5 per cent share of US bank M&T; and it hoped to raise about €2 billion by selling its UK assets, including First Trust Bank in Northern Ireland.

Now, however, the Central Bank said AIB needed capital of €10.4 billion to cover the losses, €3 billion above the €7.4 billion target it had set for it in March in 2010. The burden would fall on the state and, in doing so, AIB would be nationalized and the senior management, most of which had hung on so successfully up to this point, were to go. The National Pension Reserve Fund (NPRF) was left to put up the money as 'an investment' on which it was to 'expect' a return. 'It will, I believe, result in a substantial gain to the taxpayer over time as the bank is restored to its proper position,' Lenihan said. Again, many doubted him, especially when he also added that the level of state support to the banking system 'remains manageable' and that the figures represented the 'rock bottom' of the financial crisis.

Honohan, at least, said he was sorry that the regulator's stress tests last March had not been pessimistic enough. Although Lenihan admitted that the costs were a 'nightmare' that the government and the Irish people would have to live with, he was not for taking the blame. 'The Irish people are entitled to be angry with the bankers who lent recklessly over a considerable period of time in the earlier part of this decade. It's clear that these losses were installed in our banking system and in some of the banks by the middle of the decade and it is clear that some of the banks have spent a considerable period of time trying to conceal the existence of these losses,' he alleged.

'With the establishment of NAMA, the state went in, established exactly what the losses were, and we're now dealing with them.' He claimed that the two-year bank guarantee had been justified because it had 'bought the government time'.

'Could we have gone any faster? I don't think we could have if we wished to produce a credible solution to our problems,' he said. 'We haven't taken the toxic assets of our banking system and hidden them in a box and said the assets are worth 80 per cent of what they said they were worth. We have actually gone in there, opened the latch, looked at the loan books and made an independent valuation of them, and, given the natural tendency of bankers to deny problems, that was the right way to go about it and that process necessarily is protracted.'

However, what all of this still didn't solve was the crisis of the outflow of deposits from the banks, and the subsequent need for the ECB to supply more and more replacement cash – a practice to which it wished to put an end. 'This is rock-bottom day as far as the banks are concerned,' Lenihan claimed, wrongly again, as it turned out.

The extra cost involved in saving the banks intensified another associated problem: the growing national debt and the state's ability to borrow to cover it.

The previously announced target of €3 billion in savings for the December budget suddenly became 'an absolute minimum', confirming the hints that had been dropped in Galway in the middle of the month (though these had been somewhat overshadowed by Cowen's infamous drinking session and radio interview, and their aftermath).

Lenihan had to admit that there would be what he called a 'very substantial spike' in the general government deficit for the year, with the ratio coming in at an unheard of 32 per cent of GDP. If it hadn't been for the banks the figure would still have been a hefty 12 per cent. The state's debt was due to rise to 100 per cent of GDP by the end of the year and 115 per cent by 2014, according to the estimates at this date. This compared to a 25 per cent debt-to-GDP ratio in 2007, emphasizing the surge in borrowing. Honohan calculated that just 6 percentage points of the increase could be attributed to rescuing the banks, though, the rest being down to the costs of running the state on a dramatically reduced income.

With further banking costs to come, just how would the government meet its revised commitment of bringing down annual borrowing to just 3 per cent of GDP by 2014, as required by EU budgetary rules? Lenihan said it was important for the state to have 'a credible path to show how we propose to meet this commitment' and that he had emphasized this to our European partners. Significantly, Lenihan announced that he would unveil a four-year plan in early November that would effectively tie in his successor. This move to detailed multi-annual budgetary planning, over four years, was entirely new for the Irish government, but conceded now after prompting from the EU that had gone on over many months.

The press conference at which Lenihan made these announcements ended in some farce. When the bells for a vote in the Dáil began to ring, summoning all TDs, Lenihan dramatically declared that he had to go. 'I'm needed in the Dáil. I don't have a pair,' he explained, much to the confusion of the foreign media, who did not know of the voting arrangements in the Dáil whereby TDs could be excused from a vote if they were matched with a TD from an opposition party who would also be missing, thereby equalizing the numbers. Seizing on the vernacular, one Irish journalist was heard to mutter: 'He better grow a pair quick, so.'

He had to display them when he got to the Dáil because Fine Gael's increasingly prominent finance spokesman Michael Noonan told him: 'You've a great nerve, with a couple of months to go in the life of this administration, to commit a subsequent government to budgetary profiles for the next four years.'

It was part of the normal cut and thrust of politics for the opposition to hit the government hard, but it had extra resonance this time: every decision the incumbent took made it harder for its successor. Noonan bemoaned that 'Anglo Irish Bank was supposed to be too big to fail', but 'it was too big to save. That is the real position.' He said the 'bottom line on the banking strategy' was that Ireland could no longer borrow because its 'sovereign creditworthiness is gone'. He said the government had done what no government should do, which was to 'put the creditworthiness of the sovereign state at risk to rescue a failed bank. The national interest always requires that you protect the creditworthiness of the sovereign. When faced with the choice of the sovereign and a financial institution, you opt for the sovereign.'

Noonan also took a tough personal line with Lenihan when the minister complained that 'reckless lending did not happen on my watch'. Noonan conceded that Lenihan had been badly served by the then Central Bank, by the Office of the Financial Regulator and by expensive advisers, but reminded him that 'You're responsible for the architecture of the banking rescue strategy which is now in broken pieces on the floor.' Lenihan responded that 'I share that anger, but anger is not a policy on its own, and we must now turn to the resolution of our problems.'

That involved bringing Europe centre-stage, but maintaining the illusion that we were solving our problems in conjunction with Europe, rather than having Europe solve them for us. Lenihan told the Dáil that there was 'no question of the authorities in Brussels dictating or suggesting there is a four-year plan', but he confirmed 'intensive discussions' and said 'they are very happy to endorse' it.

His most important early-morning phone call on Black Thursday morning had been to the euro finance ministers, whom he had been unable to join for their meeting in Brussels because of the urgency of matters at home. His key task was to persuade them of the viability of the four-year plan. They were fearful of the costs of having to bail out Ireland.

Most important in that regard was reassuring Rehn at the European Commission, Trichet at the ECB, and Regling, author of one of the key reports into the banking collapse and now head of the European Financial Stability Facility. The German's main interest was in making sure that the EFSF's money was not needed and he expressed confidence, wrongly as it later turned out, that it wouldn't be.

Rehn said the cost of the banking rescue was very large but manageable on condition that the government came up with a convincing austerity plan for the years to 2014. 'We support these plans and we stand by the Irish Government and people in these very difficult times,' he said. 'The Irish Government has now done very thorough work and presented a comprehensive and I trust final cost of the problem of the Anglo Irish Bank and other banks. It's a one-off cost, a one-off measure, which will be reflected in this year's deficit figures.'

Rehn did not specify either the nature or the scale of the fiscal measures he would want next year or in any of the following years. This was characteristic of Europe's approach: it wanted to be told everything, and to approve everything, but it didn't want to be accused of giving the initial instructions as to how everything was to take place. 'What is absolutely key for us is the credibility and the delivery of this unequivocal commitment to correct the excessive deficit by 2014,' Trichet said. The reality was that no matter what was being said publicly, the overall instructions had been given privately.

Lenihan's other major announcement was that the state would stop borrowing on the bond markets until 2011, abandoning plans for bond auctions in October and November. This was forced upon him largely by the price being demanded of Ireland when it sold ten-year debt. Yields on Irish sovereign debt had soared to a record high of 6.78 per cent prior to 30 September, similar to the yield on Greece's debt in early April, a month before it sought international support and three times more than selling such debt was costing Germany. 'It is important to note that the exchequer is fully funded through to the middle of next year. However, in order to fully underline the strength of our resolve and to ensure the necessary fiscal adjustment we will make an additional significant consolidation effort in 2011 over and above the already announced target,' he said.

Lenihan's embarrassment was completed by what happened on a conference phone call the day after and how it was then reported in the *Daily Telegraph*.

The giant US bank Citigroup organized an opportunity for Lenihan to brief over 200 investors in government bonds by way of a conference call. The telephone system malfunctioned as Lenihan delivered his pitch as to why Ireland remained a safe place to invest; instead of everyone in the call merely hearing what Lenihan had to say, everyone else participating in the call could also be heard. According to the newspaper report a few of them started to heckle Lenihan. Bizarrely, there were what were described as 'chimp sounds', recalling nineteenth-century cartoons in which the Irish were stereotyped as being not very far above the apes on the evolutionary scale. One individual apparently called 'Dive, dive' and another shouted 'Short Ireland' before adding 'Why not short Citi too?' As someone, in language well understood by any teenager, said, 'This is the worst conference call ever,' Citigroup officials shut down the line and restarted the call with proper procedures in place twenty minutes later.

A spokesman for Lenihan denied the *Daily Telegraph* report after it appeared. 'The story is pathetic and inaccurate, the *Telegraph* clearly did not listen to the call. A number of media organizations were on the call. None offered a similar analysis to the *Telegraph*'s, which was not on the call.'

6.   A Taxing Issue

Suddenly the pressure was coming from all sides and, ominously, new issues were being added to the existing list of problems. The previous year's second Lisbon Treaty referendum – after the initial rejection – had been passed partly because of the inclusion of a specific codicil, a legally binding undertaking added to the original treaty. It held that decisions on tax rates were for governments to make for themselves. However, that didn't stop the strong-arming of weaker countries – of which Ireland was now one – by the censorious appointed bureaucrats in Brussels and Frankfurt and their political allies.

Our corporation-tax rate of 12.5 per cent had been regarded for many years as a major attraction for foreign multinational investors. The benefits cut both ways. For example, US companies had invested over €165 billion in Ireland and, in 2008, paid 40 per cent of the total corporation-tax take. The feeling was that they won, we won. Lionel Alexander, then president of the American Chamber of Commerce, which represented over 600 large firms in Ireland, emphasized this in a speech in October: 'At a time when the economy is in deep recession, nothing which would impact on the continued investment in Ireland by our existing base of multinationals, or would deter new investment in Ireland, can be countenanced ... The government must clearly and firmly remind the EU Commission that Ireland retains sovereignty in taxation matters and advise Commissioners to refrain from making unhelpful comments of this nature.'

But EU Commissioner Olli Rehn had done so already and would do so again (and would be joined by others in stirring things). The Finn opined that the government should exclude no tax-policy changes in its pursuit of extra revenues. 'I do not want to take any precise stand on an issue which is for the Irish Government and the Irish parliament to decide, but I would not rule out any option at this stage,' he said. 'It's a fact of life that after what has happened, Ireland will not continue as a low-tax country, but it will rather become a normal-tax country in the European context.'

Lenihan responded immediately to this provocation: 'This commitment is protected, in an EU context, by the principle of unanimity in taxation matters. That was further enhanced by the insertion of a legal guarantee in the Lisbon Treaty. The 12.5 per cent corporation-tax rate is a cornerstone of the Irish industrial policy.' It was, but the mood in Europe towards Ireland had turned very sour: we were threatening the stability of the euro, getting plenty of help, as they saw it, and yet we were not prepared to give up something that they perceived to be giving us an unfair advantage over other countries in attracting investment. Ireland's economic model, once in vogue, had made us a pariah; nor had the fuss we'd made about the implementation of the Lisbon Treaty endeared us to the other member states. We were now expected to tax more, according to Continental European norms.

Ireland had been a low-tax country by international standards up until late 2008, when previous cuts in income tax for higher- and middle-income earners, and exclusions for the lower paid – almost half of the workforce – began to be reversed quickly. Our government's tax take was around 30 per cent of GDP, compared to an OECD average of 35–6 per cent and an EU average of 39–40 per cent. Clearly this did not look good to the eurocrats. However, a comparison on the basis of GNP (which excludes multinational profit repatriations) might have been a better measure, as this brought our tax level up to around 35 per cent, not far off the EU average. Indeed, the fact that Ireland did not operate an expensive military apparatus, like so many other countries, was something else that should have been borne in mind. We did have issues to address, though: there were still some very generous tax breaks for high earners – on things such as pensions – even if many of the disastrous property-based reliefs had been brought to an end. We had what was called a narrow tax base, dependent on income and spending, with no property or water taxes, unlike other countries. Social-welfare benefits were very generous by comparison with the EU, particularly on things such as child benefit for all regardless of income.

The government sought to protect as much of this as possible, for political as well as social reasons, but to do so required enormous annual borrowings, irrespective of what money had to be used to refinance the banks. As was pointed out, the expenditure on the banks would end, but the annual deficits would keep mounting and make up well over two thirds of the overall debt. Lenders will only provide, however, if they can be sure they will get their money back. The next priority for the government was to demonstrate that it would at least be able to pay the interest on its loans.

Unfortunately, lenders on international markets were becoming highly doubtful about that and, as a result, were demanding higher interest rates, as insurance against the risk involved in lending to Ireland (even if this made it more unlikely that Ireland would be able to meet its repayments). Essentially, the interest rates were set so high as to deter borrowing. Investors now saw the state and the banks as one – both having large debts and both needing new loans for which the state was responsible. While we had reason to be thankful that we had started to accumulate further debt from a low base, the reality was that we remained a small country with a rapidly increasing and close to unsustainable debt burden. This made us highly vulnerable.

Brian Lenihan claimed that his late-September banking announcements would restore international confidence and credibility. But on the same day that he made this claim the average of the annual interest rates Ireland had to pay to borrow for three and four years remained unchanged at 5 per cent. The sceptics noted that this was the same rate at which Greece was getting its money under its rescue deal. It seemed that we'd just had our Greek moment. Lenihan's admission that S&P – and not him – had been correct about the likely cost to the state of bailing out Anglo wasn't entirely unlike the Greek government's acknowledgement that it had cooked the books and that its exchequer deficit was way bigger than previously stated. Both Lenihan and the government were badly undermined by this.

So, as near politically impossible as it would be for the government to cut back and still survive in office, cuts to the national budget – to reduce borrowing in order to obtain loans – had to be implemented. To impress lenders the government decided upon a four-year budgetary plan to demonstrate how the deficit would be reduced, with the aim of bringing annual borrowing back to 3 per cent of GDP by 2014, as the European Commission had demanded. How could Ireland get from a borrowing requirement of 32 per cent in 2010 to just 3 per cent in 2014 without making the most savage of budget cuts? It was arguably too late already to do this, especially as the catch-22 of Ireland's position was being debated widely. Yes, Ireland had to reduce its deficit, but by making savage cuts how would it be able to stimulate enough economic activity to produce the taxes to pay down the debts? Less cash in circulation means less domestic demand. The economy could continue on a deflationary spiral for years.

Commission officials believed that a prolonged and severe austerity regime would be difficult for the Irish economy but would not cripple it. That was easy for them to say. What would happen if international demand was not sufficiently strong – notwithstanding our enhanced cost competitiveness – and export markets fell back into recession or showed limited growth? It was easy to say that cutting spending would be a more effective policy that would somehow do less damage than tax increases – but it was already clear that the impact of a lack of demand in the domestic economy would be impossible to ignore. Not everyone was an exporter. The issue of the damage that could be done came into sharper focus when the government announced the full extent of its plans.

As politicians were only too well aware, it can be difficult to implement a reduction of services without receiving a massive political backlash. Fianna Fáil feared for its own future should it cut too severely. It had done so much to make itself unpopular that it couldn't risk making itself more so. Yet it was impossible to do otherwise. There was another political issue to be considered too: what authority did the government have effectively to put its successor into a budgetary strait-jacket, especially when it was only clinging to power by avoiding by-elections that might cost it its majority?

Cowen and Lenihan cited the national interest repeatedly, and the Green Party supported that, but many felt the object of the exercise was primarily to stay in government for as long as possible, and hope that something would turn up to limit the losses of seats in Dáil Éire-ann whenever election time came.

The pressure from the European Central Bank in particular was enormous because of the money it was providing to give the Irish banks liquidity – and because of its fears about the value of the secur-ity it was getting in return. Even more important to its thinking and actions was its dread of so-called 'contagion'. It wasn't for our sake that Europe didn't want Ireland to fail. Should Ireland welch on its debts – be they sovereign or banking – other countries and banks might also do so, causing such chaos that it could mean the end of the euro.

On a more prosaic level the ECB's other major priority was infla-tion in the entire eurozone, and it was determined to enforce austerity measures that would dampen fears of higher prices. ECB President Jean-Claude Trichet said it was crucial that Dublin honoured its renewed commitment to shrink the budget deficit by 2014 with 'precise action and precise decisions' to give a 'very credible, highly credible path towards sustainability of public finances'. The governing council of the ECB said a credible multi-year budget plan would 'strengthen public confidence in the capacity of governments to return to sus-tainable public finances, reduce risk premia in interest rates and thus support sustainable growth over the medium term'. That was the the-ory, at least. In reality its only concern was the stability of the euro. If a continued deep depression in Ireland was the price for that, it was one they were more than willing to make us pay.

The European Commission played an even greater role in forcing the Irish government down this path, while simultaneously denying that it was in control of the process. In mid October a team of officials visited the Department of Finance for talks on the four-year budget plan, and one, István Székely, dubbed 'the Hungarian', stayed per-manently. It was presented as routine, but it was not. 'We are in close contact but close contact doesn't in any way mean we are participat-ing in the drafting of the multi-annual plan,' an EU spokesman said.

If the deficit was to be reduced it could be by tax increases, or by spending cuts, or by both, and the method chosen would be up to the government. However, it was clear that if the European Commission didn't like what Ireland was doing, or had no confidence in the measures, then it would act. 'We have no reason to doubt the commitment of the Irish, but it is important that we can assess exactly,' said Olli Rehn's spokesman. 'It's important for us to see how the 2014 commitment can be achieved – year by year, sector by sector.'

Lenihan attended the annual meeting of the International Monetary Fund in Washington on 8 October but tried to make little of it. His spokesman said it was routine, but no Irish finance minister had attended in years. A man from the IMF called Ajai Chopra was in attendance too, but as yet his name did not register in the Irish public's consciousness. Talk of the IMF as an unwanted bogeyman stalked the country: the IMF would close schools and hospitals, eject tens of thousands of public servants and slash the pay of the rest. Its presence had to be avoided, almost at any cost.

The reality, however, was that we were doing to ourselves what the IMF would have done had it been in control, and we were about to do more of it. Our economic sovereignty was being eroded anyway, to all intents and purposes. It may not have been by explicit instruction, but we were still doing what we thought others – our lenders – wanted of us, even if there were those within the state – such as the likes of the independent Economic and Social Research Institute (ESRI), a gaggle of independent economists, a number of newspaper opinion writers and indeed the general public – who believed this was the wrong approach, morally and tactically. Worse, we were not just bowing to what was expected of us, we were doing something that many in government were doubtful would work, most definitely not for Ireland and possibly not even for Europe. If our government did not know what it was doing, as had become the popular belief, it was also possible that it was following the instructions of others who didn't know what they were doing either.

Some argued that our sovereignty went at the time we joined the euro anyway. But our political elite slapped down such doubters back in the 1990s with claims that they were narrow nationalists, insisting that interest rates could be set safely from the middle to the benefit of all the economies within the EMU and reassuring voters that our power to decide our own budgets, including the setting of tax rates, would not be impacted upon. That was an optimistic reading of the situation at best.

Membership of the euro required governments to endure the usually useful discipline of keeping annual deficits down to 3 per cent of GDP. Not all managed to do it, but if they missed a year they normally managed to get back on track in the following one. Ironically, given what was to come, France and Germany were themselves guilty of missing targets in the early part of the century.

The discipline of running balanced, or near to balanced, budgets in the run-up to joining the euro and in the years afterwards had been good for us. In the late 1980s and early 1990s our debt exceeded GDP, and servicing it took more than £1 out of every £5 collected in tax revenue. A series of tough budgets, strong international growth and a devaluation of our currency helped to sort us out. By the time the bubble burst in 2008 we were at a usefully low ratio of borrowing to GDP of under 30 per cent. Debt servicing had taken only €3 to €4 out of every €100 collected in tax revenue between 2004 and 2008, but by 2011 the figure had risen to more than €14 out of every €100. For 2013 and 2014 it was projected to rise to €20 in every €100 – or 20 per cent of all total tax revenue.

The figures emphasized the speed of the decline in the economy. According to Department of Finance figures, the national debt would rise from €100 billion in 2009 to over €150 billion by 2012. Once you added in the cost of the bank rescues – spread over a number of years – the national debt would rise to around €185 billion by 2012 and be close to €200 billion in subsequent years. The key here was that our national debt already exceeded the amount the economy produces each year.

Even though the government had suspended borrowing, the price of Irish bonds on the markets was increasing. By mid October the spread between Irish and German ten-year bond yields had widened to more than 4.5 per cent. This difference was far higher than it had been in the weeks before the 1993 currency crisis and the devaluation of the Irish pound; then the spread stood at just 3 per cent. Fortunately, the NTMA had raised enough long-term funding to cover all of 2010's borrowing needs, and also had €20 billion in short-term cash in the bank. But it was still hard to see how and when Ireland could return in its own right to the debt markets on reasonable terms.

The announcement of an intended €15 billion exchequer reduction in the deficit over the following four years' budgets did not help restore confidence, especially given the government's lack of popularity and the certainty that it would not be in power to implement them. Ireland had received one concession from the European Commission, however. We now had until 2014 instead of 2013 to meet the target of reducing the debt-to-GDP ratio to 3 per cent. Others wanted a longer extension. The ESRI agreed with the Irish Congress of Trade Unions boss David Begg that the government should extend the period over which the deficit was reduced to 2016, warning of 'overkill'. Again Rehn responded that only the European Council – where the heads of government met – could sanction a change to the target and reminded us that the government had confirmed at the end of September its commitment to achieving the 3 per cent target in 2014. Lenihan said the government could get an extension of the 2014 deadline 'after a few years', but only if it showed a credible four-year plan now. Seeking an extension of the deadline beyond 2014 at the moment would render us 'devoid of any credibility'. But it was Lenihan's credibility that was now an issue.

Our government had sent a plan to Brussels that was predicated on a growth average of 4 per cent per year between 2011 and 2014 – but this was based on a degree of optimism that few shared. The plan envisaged growth in nominal GDP from €160 billion in 2010 to €205 billion in 2014. Yet, since mid 2008, the government had taken nearly €15 billion out of the economy in tax hikes and spending cuts, the equivalent of almost 10 per cent of GDP. Core borrowing, excluding the cost of the banks, remained at 11.9 per cent of GDP for 2010. So how would growth return after a further 10 per cent of GDP was removed over another four years? Lower growth means an increase in taxes, which in turn depresses economic growth and social-welfare spending.

The commission was behaving as if we were only just starting on our cuts, and had not already embarked on an austerity programme. It might have been the textbook approach but it verged on self-flagellation. It was all to the benefit of the bondholders; the Irish had become the easiest mark in the world. The privately owned banks had effectively turned their debts over to the state, which insisted that its citizens pay them all on behalf of the borrowers.

In theory the state had to pay these debts to be in a position to borrow other money. The government was borrowing almost €400 million per week for day-to-day purposes and had to reduce this to below €100 million per week by 2014, and ultimately to zero, for Ireland to comply with the rules of continued EMU membership. Even if there had been no EMU membership rules, it was clear that the borrowing had to reduce or more funds would not be made available. Some acerbic Irish commentators noted that our austerity programme was actually a programme of substantial extra borrowing for many years, which had nothing to do with the bank rescue but quite a lot to do with keeping well-paid people in their jobs.

One of the ironies of the situation was that those who despised the capitalism of the bond markets wanted to continue to run high exchequer deficits, which would have to be funded by those same hated bondholders. However, we could only have told bondholders where to go if we were confident that they would lend to us in the future; or if we knew that others would ignore our previous failure to repay on the basis that we'd now be better placed to honour future debts. Ireland was in a complete bind when it came to dealing with bondholders. To many the logical thing to do was to refuse to repay them, especially the senior bondholders who ranked equally with depositors in the hierarchy of creditors at the banks. While the priority given to repaying them may have seemed ridiculous – after all, the bondholders had made professional investment decisions and were getting a higher rate of return than depositors – it was based apparently on their legal standing in Irish law. And on the fact that many of the bondholders were European banks which themselves would have had awful financial problems if they were not repaid.

The bondholders were not all foreign either. The Irish banks were themselves bondholders: they held bonds in rivals, and overseas, in banks and nation states. And they needed these to be repaid. The speculators who were being decried for betting that many eurozone-member countries would default on their debts were only acting logically. It wasn't the speculators who had caused the crisis but the governments that had run up excessive debts – or, as in Ireland's case, that had picked up the bad bets of the banks.

On 22 October 2010 the Department of Finance announced that it had formulated three budget scenarios for 2011: one involved an 'adjustment' of €3 billion, another of around €4.5 billion and a third of €7 billion, the last of which was 'firmly ruled out'. Meanwhile the Green Party leader, John Gormley, much to Cowen's frustration, asked that all the party leaders come together to discuss working out an agreed programme between them. Fine Gael and Labour indulged Gormley but were not particularly interested in getting tied into supporting the government, not with an election almost certainly pending.

Cowen pressed ahead by ignoring domestic advice and doing what the foreigners wanted. He didn't put it that way: he said instead that extending the deadline would only increase the national debt and the debt repayments. Again, this was correct, but it was only part of the story. The budget was set for 7 December and Lenihan confirmed that it would be the basis for Ireland's return to borrowing on the bond markets.

However, according to Lenihan, it wasn't the Irish government's performance in dealing with the crisis that was responsible for the surge in Irish interest rates. During a live radio interview I conducted with him on 4 November, Lenihan became angry with my line of questioning. Instead, he expressed publicly for the first time – but not for the last – his belief that Ireland had been undone by Germany, something that he had kept quiet about for some weeks. And, in fairness, he had a point.

Deauville, in the north-west of France, is a second home to a number of prominent Irishmen. Tony O'Reilly, retired boss of Independent News & Media, and once Ireland's richest and arguably most influential businessman, owns a chateau there that was built on the ruins of William the Conqueror's castle, and was home to the Gestapo officers who led the French occupation of the region during the Second World War. Broadcaster Eamon Dunphy was a regular visitor to O'Reilly's, whenever he stayed at his own holiday home in the area, purchased at the turn of the century. It is the centre of French horse-racing and gambling, an alternative Monte Carlo.

It was also the venue in mid October 2010 for a meeting that turned out to be one of the most important in this country's history. France's president, Nicolas Sarkozy, hosted a summit with his German counterpart, Chancellor Angela Merkel, the first of a number of meetings between the pair at which decisions were made that the rest of the EU was expected to endorse. The outcome of their deliberations stunned the rest of Europe and set off a chain reaction, one that led to the early arrival in Ireland of the IMF as part of a consortium that took financial control of the state.

Sarkozy and Merkel presented a document called 'Le gouvernement économique européen', which set down principles and conditions for the formulation of national tax and spending plans across Europe. EU finance ministers were flummoxed by this: they had been meeting in Luxembourg under the direction of European Council President Herman Van Rompuy and had been planning something else entirely. It would be putting it mildly to say they were shocked and angry when they emerged from a lengthy and difficult meeting to see television pictures of the two most powerful leaders in Europe completely pre-empting and undermining them.

The council had been working on new ways of levelling financial sanctions at those countries that broke EMU rules. Suddenly Merkel and Sarkozy were announcing something completely different: the creation of a temporary rescue net for any euro country, along with stringent new rules imposing greater financial discipline on member states. The French–German joint declaration went so far as to suggest that miscreant countries could have their voting rights suspended temporarily, making it almost certain that changes to the Lisbon Treaty would be required to allow for a 'permanent and robust mechanism'. This would mean a new European referendum in Ireland, of course, with no guarantee at all that it would be passed.

Merkel decided to support the creation of a permanent bailout fund, but only if she could introduce insolvency procedures under which governments could renegotiate the terms of their debt with bondholders in what she described as an 'orderly' fashion. Merkel wanted bondholders to take pain in the form of a 'bail in' and for investors in eurozone sovereign debt to accept that they might have to incur capital losses in some scenarios, after the European Financial Stability Facility completed its work in 2013. Investors wanted to know what would happen after a country got into difficulty and to which bonds the new rules would apply – would it be current bonds maturing after 2013 or only new debt issues after that date?

The proposed establishment of a permanent rescue mechanism also raised a different treaty issue: it would sweep away the no-bailout clause that had been in place since the introduction of the Maastricht Treaty in 1992.

Some of Merkel's critics in Germany were angry that she had dropped her original demand for automatic sanctions for debt breaches, made after Germany agreed to the Greek rescue. But she felt that was an acceptable compromise as long as a new permanent rescue mechanism was in place by the time the EFSF wound up in 2013, one that included private creditors on the list of parties involved in future bailouts of eurozone members.

What was often missed in Ireland was the domestic political pressure under which Merkel laboured. Her country was the biggest individual contributor to the Greek rescue and any further European bailouts, yet simultaneously she was proposing a four-year savings plan that would see her national budget slashed by €80 billion and the loss of 15,000 public-sector jobs.

'Let me put it simply,' she said. 'In this regard there may be a contradiction between the interests of the financial world and the interests of the political world. We cannot keep constantly explaining to our voters and our citizens why the taxpayer should bear the cost of certain risks and not those people who have earned a lot of money from taking those risks.'

Few people were more terrified of the consequences of this new approach than Lenihan and he was quickly in touch with his French and German counterparts to tell them so. Having been forced into the position of paying back every bank bondholder, Lenihan railed against an 'unhelpful' and 'poorly timed' intervention that had spooked the markets. As far as he was concerned, this changed everything. Who now would buy Irish bank bonds or government bonds, when the prospect that these borrowers might not be repaid became a reality? Irish bond yields rose ominously again. There was no relief when, on 29 October, Merkel clarified her proposal for a permanent rescue mechanism: debt restructuring with losses for private holders of sovereign bonds would apply only to bonds issued after 2013. The damage had been done and Irish interest rates continued to rise.

Lenihan tried to deal with this by announcing the outline of his four-year plan, more than a month ahead of the 7 December budget, during an unexpected briefing of political journalists in advance of a visit to Ireland by EU Commissioner Olli Rehn. When the figures came that week they were astonishing. The €6 billion cut for 2011 was confirmed – and it would have been the €7 billion figure that the government had 'firmly ruled out' previously, had it not been for an 'accountancy solution' to the problem of how to handle the annual cost of the bank bailouts. Already €14.5 billion had been cut from the government budget since July 2008 but now another €15 billion would have to go between 2011 and 2014.

Cowen continued to try to be positive. On 6 November he exhorted the Irish 'to look to our strengths rather than magnifying our weaknesses'. He said Ireland attracted 80 times the US investment in Greece and 23 times that in Portugal. 'We are moving into a balance of payments surplus next year, which is unique among those that have high deficits in the euro area.' The economic situation was 'something we will have to manage over the next ten to fifteen years'.

The EU commissioner for internal markets, Michel Barnier, visited on the day Cowen made these comments as a 'sign of solidarity'. 'My conviction is that Ireland has a lot of trump cards. I personally am a very strong believer in your country. First of all the population of Ireland – courageous, hard-working people – have good training and good education.' He said Ireland had an excellent record of attracting high-tech companies, 'which is not the case for every other country', although his hosts could have highlighted the importance of our corporation-tax rates. They were too polite and too scared. Instead they inhaled the bullshit and gagged.

7.   Dinner with Olli

Olli Rehn, the European commissioner for economic and monetary affairs, wanted to go for dinner, but not with somebody who'd be lobbying him on behalf of Ireland. It was the Monday evening, 8 November, of the EU commissioner's highly publicized visit to Dublin to meet not just with Department of Finance officials but with opposition politicians, trade unionists and other interested parties, and to hold press conferences too. He would have enough of listening to them say much the same thing the next day and of having to say much the same thing himself, over and over. They'd get the idea anyway, if they hadn't already, when they listened to the news reports of the briefing he'd just given the Irish media, or read them online, or in the morning newspapers. He'd arranged to meet the Finnish ambassador to Ireland, who'd have the local knowledge about where to go for dinner. His compatriot chose L'Ecrivain on Baggot Street in Dublin 2, directly across the road from the Bank of Ireland's landmark headquarters.

The restaurant is one of Ireland's finest, boasting a Michelin star because of the culinary expertise of the chef Derry Clarke, as well as opulent interiors adorned with tapestries by Graham Knuttel, one of the Celtic Tiger's most celebrated artists. The restaurant was packed. Rehn was somewhat surprised. One of Ireland's most expensive eateries was full on a Monday evening, during a deep recession?

Quickly, the maître d' told his exalted guest that many of those present were from the South African embassy, entertaining guests who were in the country for a rugby international with Ireland. He also emphasized that most restaurants were closed on a Monday evening and that they were providing a service that was not readily available elsewhere. Business was tough, he insisted.

But what if Rehn came away with the impression that the Irish people weren't really undergoing much hardship? Rehn had been having his fill of Ireland and the problems it was causing for Europe. He was visiting an economy (as well as a country) of about 4.5 million people that had been heading towards a value of €190 billion per year, but now had settled back to €160 billion. That could not be described as poor, notwithstanding the costs of dealing with its various crises, especially when Irish wage rates were way ahead of what pertained throughout Europe. That it was an expensive country to live in was something for Ireland to address for itself. Ireland remained a First World nation, and the proof was in these figures: since 1995 Irish people's purchasing power had moved well ahead of the eurozone average, from 10 per cent below it in 1995 to 19 per cent above it in 2009. That's why there were so many Michelin-star restaurants in Dublin.

Rehn knew about economic hardship, because twenty years earlier Finland had suffered dramatically in the fallout from the political and economic collapse of its nearest neighbour, the Soviet Union. Unemployment had soared to 18 per cent of the workforce, from 3 per cent previously; three banks were nationalized; property prices fell more than 50 per cent in five years; and the stock-market fell by more than 60 per cent. GDP fell by 13 per cent in three years. (Most of these statistics were to be surpassed considerably by Ireland.) There was more to it than just the USSR's implosion, though. The Soviet collapse pricked a number of bubbles that were remarkably similar to Ireland's nearly two decades later. Cheap credit was too freely available, which led to the private sector doubling its debt from banks in just four years. There were associated property and investment bubbles as the banks went mad. Soaring exports and full employment masked the reality of what was happening.

Finland reacted much as Ireland did later. It slashed welfare and the public sector, and spent what was to it a massive amount on rescuing the banks – about €6 billion. Recession became depression as the national borrowings continued to rise. There was long-term unemployment – and it took nearly twenty years for employment to return to pre-crash levels, even though the Finns enjoyed one advantage not available to Ireland: they devalued their currency. They did things for which outsiders gave them praise: an investment in making broadband available to everyone, despite the vast population gaps in the spacious country, considerable emphasis on improving educational standards and support for technological innovation by private-sector companies, such as future, if short-lived, world leader Nokia, the mobile-phone manufacturer.

Yet Rehn's political mantra in such circumstances had been always that the public finances had to be balanced, because excessive borrowing creates problems for future generations to bear. He spoke regularly about studies and rules of thumb that showed spending cuts were more effective than tax increases in restoring order to countries' public finances, but he also insisted that Ireland could no longer be a low-tax country and commented that the public sector in Ireland was smaller than the European average.

Rehn's arrival in Dublin earlier that evening had been treated almost as if it were a formal state visit. From Dublin Airport, he was swept through bumper-to-bumper rush-hour traffic in a Garda-escorted cavalcade. He went to meet Lenihan – ostensibly to get more details on exactly how the government would achieve the 3 per cent deficit target by 2014, although it would soon become clear that the EU's input was more than merely supervisory and he had been extensively briefed before his arrival – and then proceeded to patronize the press, who were representing a public still in shock at the €6 billion in cutbacks for 2011 that had been announced the previous week, with another €9 billion to follow over the next three years.

At just after 8 p.m. Lenihan introduced Rehn to the waiting media in the briefing room in the Department of Finance. 'The European commissioner is here not as a director, but as a good friend,' Lenihan said.

'I believe that the Irish and the Finns share a rather similar proverb that was used back home during the 1990s recession which hit Finland particularly hard,' Rehn said. ' "Even the longest night will be followed by a new dawn," the Finnish prime minister Esko Aho used to say at the time. I'm told by an Irish friend of mine that the Irish version says, "The darkest hour is just before the dawn."

'It might feel a small consolation at times like these, but I have no doubt that Ireland, too, will overcome this crisis. You are smart and stubborn people. Time and again you have proved you can overcome adversity. And this time you do not face the challenges alone. Europe stands by you.'

Rehn was asked if that extended to the EU supplying loans if the market stopped doing so. 'It's better not to speculate on a negative outcome,' he said, before turning to another of his Finnish proverbs. '"Better not paint the devil to the wall unless you can wash it off from there,"' he added. Puzzled journalists were informed later that this proverb warned against hyping problems in case it made the situation worse than it actually was.

Rehn said the government's commitment to achieving a budget deficit below 3 per cent by 2014 was an 'important anchor' for financial markets. 'A 2011 budget involving a consolidation effort of €6 billion would be appropriate, as it would strike a balance between allowing the recovery to strengthen and addressing budgetary challenges in a timely and frontloaded fashion,' Rehn said. He also warned that Ireland had no choice but to accept what was happening.

Rehn said the private sector and the EU shared in the responsibility for the financial crisis. 'In the case of Ireland in particular, we need to recall that sovereign debt has not been at the origin of the crisis. Rather, private debt has become public debt. The financial sector has misallocated resources in the economy and then stopped working. It needs reform,' said Rehn.

'So in that sense, yes, we are following very closely the preparations but it is the responsibility of the government of Ireland to decide on the draft budget for next year as well as on the four-year fiscal plan, and once we see the result of that work we will then hopefully be able to endorse this plan,' he said. And then he went off to dinner, in preparation for a round of meetings the following day with opposition politicians, trade union leaders and the Institute of European Affairs. However, he wouldn't be meeting the likes of Father Sean Healy, director of the lobby group Conference of Religious in Ireland, later renamed Social Justice Ireland to downplay its role in the Catholic Church.

Healy, who had enjoyed some influence during the Bertie Ahern era, said Rehn had 'insulted Ireland's poor and vulnerable people' by refusing to meet him as their self-appointed representative.

There was a demand from the public for information about who Rehn was and what his attitude was likely to be. The 48-year-old former policy adviser to two Finnish prime ministers had been given the position of commissioner at the Directorate General for Economic and Financial Affairs, one of the twenty-seven offices within the European Commission, in January 2010. In the previous five years he had been in charge of enlargement and had a brief initial period in enterprise and the information society.

His new job gave him a key role in maintaining a relationship with Ireland. Various newspaper profiles about Rehn described him as 'calm and consensual', said that he did not seek 'the limelight', was 'an archetypal safe pair of hands' and 'a very low-key, upright individual. Purposeful. Serious. Not at all a typical glad-handling politician.' It was claimed that he believed in working with countries rather than dictating to them or trying to punish them for not complying with the rules – the latter being the approach favoured by Germany and France. He was fluent in Swedish, English and French as well as his native Finnish, although his English was somewhat halting in delivery.

What wasn't reported was that he had one particularly close Irish friend: the former president of the EU Parliament, Pat Cox, who had now retired from elected politics but remained highly influential as a behind-the-scenes lobbyist for hire. Cox had been a Progressive Democrat TD but turned to European politics in disappointment when he failed to win a full cabinet position and then lost out to Mary Harney in the battle to succeed Des O'Malley as the party's leader. Cox had been elected as an independent member of the European Parliament but when he secured the presidency he achieved an elevated status among the Irish political and media classes. He was one of those committed Europeans who sometimes despaired of Ireland's attitude towards the EU and lack of what he would have seen as constructive engagement. He was also committed to what might be called right-wing economics. (He was to join Fine Gael in June 2011 and seek, unsuccessfully, its nomination to be its candidate for the presidential election that October.)

Much was made of the rapport Rehn had apparently built with Lenihan. They had things in common such as a passion for soccer and an Oxbridge post-graduate education: Lenihan had studied law at Cambridge University while Rehn had read political economy at Oxford University. At first things went well. Ireland was in favour at the time of Rehn's first meeting with Lenihan and indeed was held up to Greece as an example of how to take tough decisions quickly. In June, Rehn publicly declared that he would not ask our government to accelerate budget cuts, and within a few weeks he said publicly that he agreed with Lenihan's assertion that 'the worst was over' for the Irish economy. Around the time he arrived for his Dublin visit Rehn mentioned that he was personally talking to Lenihan and others every day.

Rehn was clearly preparing for dealings with a new government after Lenihan's certain departure, although ostensibly he was trying to encourage consensus on an agreed strategy before an election took place. The politicians who met with Rehn all emerged to say positive things about him while emphasizing their points of difference – and they all disclosed that they had been put under a degree of pressure by him. Labour's finance spokeswoman Joan Burton said Rehn had asked her to confirm that her party agreed with the target deficit of 3 per cent of GDP by 2014. 'But our view is very much that while Ireland has responsibilities to Europe and to the eurozone, the European Union has responsibilities towards Ireland,' she said. Burton said she had told the commissioner her party's view: that the €6 billion adjustment was too much.

Fine Gael's finance spokesman Michael Noonan told Rehn that a new government with a clear electoral mandate and a stable majority would offer far greater certainty to the financial markets. 'He's a very affable man,' Noonan said. He described Rehn's presence in Ireland as 'important, because he's the commissioner who's in charge of these matters in Europe, and it's very important that whatever government is in power has the support of the EU commission and the European Central Bank.'

Irish Congress of Trade Unions General Secretary David Begg, who went into the meeting wanting a 2016 or 2017 deadline for reducing the annual budget deficit to 3 per cent of GDP, claimed that Rehn had accepted that the approach to be used for dealing with the

public finances was not 'an exact science' but a 'question of judgement'. Begg said Rehn had asked about the ICTU proposal to use
money in the National Pension Reserve Fund to stimulate growth in
the economy without breaching Eurostat rules. He also claimed that
Rehn had 'displayed considerably less arrogance' than many others
who maintained that the government's solution was the only way of
dealing with the difficulties in the public finances. That approach,
however, was praised by the Irish Business and Employers Confederation after its boss, Danny McCoy, met with Rehn.

On the first full day of Rehn's visit, Irish ten-year bond yields
moved beyond 8 per cent. The difference with German bonds widened to a record 562 basis points, or 5.62 percentage points. At the
Institute of European Affairs (IEA), Rehn continued with the soft-
soap. 'In the current political situation in Ireland, irrespective of party
political differences . . . it would be of great benefit for Ireland if
broad political support for the necessary corrective measures of structural reform could emerge.'

Asked about negative perceptions of the Irish economy abroad, he
said that 'it's always essential that the product is right and then you
can do good marketing.' He pointed out again that 'Ireland has formidable strengths which too easily tend to be forgotten in the public
debate in Ireland or outside the country,' but ducked questions on
possible enforced changes to corporation tax. 'Let's not get into the
details,' he said.

While Rehn was meeting the opposition before returning to Brussels, Lenihan was busy on yet another 'charm offensive'. On Tuesday
afternoon he recorded an interview with Jeremy Paxman for broadcast that evening on BBC2's highly influential *Newsnight* programme.
It was a tough interview for Lenihan, given that he was batting on
the stickiest of wickets, and Paxman was in his usual sneering form,
ignoring the elephant in the British room, its own national debt.

Lenihan said Ireland 'absolutely' wouldn't need a bailout and reiterated that the country would honour its debts. 'Absolutely. We intend
to return to the markets next year, and we intend to fund ourselves.
That's our plan. We have put our public finances on a sustainable basis

in the next two years. We have done massive corrections in our public debt and our deficit and we will continue to do so,' he said.

However, when asked to give a cast-iron, hundred per cent guarantee that the government wouldn't have to resort to a bailout, Lenihan couldn't, although his response was logical: 'Of course, nobody can give a hundred per cent guarantee, no state can give a hundred per cent guarantee on anything in the modern world.

'No, I don't accept it's the end and I don't accept it's decimation. We've a workforce of 1.9 million – that's twice what we had twenty years ago. We've a huge workforce, it's shown huge adaptability in the present crisis.

'But the government is not asking people to bring their living standards back ten years. With respect, our tax receipts went back to 2003 levels, we have to increase and augment them to 2005, 2006 levels.'

It was green-jersey stuff, based on fact but not quite accurate, but this was now clearly government policy. In the Dáil that week Cowen accused those in the opposition who exaggerated 'the weaknesses of the economy' of 'driving down national morale'.

Reacting to a jibe from Labour's Pat Rabbitte that the Dáil now resembled the 'last days of the Roman empire' and that Cowen was doing awful damage to the morale of people, the Taoiseach fell back on the line that the government was doing its national duty by bringing forward a four-year economic plan and a budget that would be essential to the country. Nobody else would be able to do that, he said. To emphasize his point, Cowen told Rabbitte that 'if the deputy believes, in the context of the scale of the challenges that face us at present, that a further election based on the divergence of policy that is emerging on the other side of the house would give us an outcome that would provide certainty, he is a better man than me.'

It is doubtful, though, if the opposition understood the full scale of the pressure being put on the government, especially as the government was playing traditional-style politics and not levelling with them. ECB boss Jean-Claude Trichet waded in by telling reporters that the cabinet's decision to frontload the €15 billion four-year austerity plan with a €6 billion package next year was of 'extreme importance' and that the scale of the overall plan was 'not insufficient'.

'We have situations that are very different by many means. The Irish situation is more of a commercial banks nature in comparison with the Greek situation,' said Trichet; this was not entirely true, but it showed where the ECB's focus would be when it came to getting its money back. It turned out that Trichet's senior official, Jürgen Stark, a member of the bank's executive board, had joined Lenihan and Rehn for a meeting in Brussels the previous week. The ECB's interest in Ireland went well beyond the money it was supplying to the banks to make up for the outflow in deposits. On 7 November, the day before Rehn arrived in Dublin, the *Sunday Tribune* had reported that the ECB now owned about €18 billion of our sovereign bonds, a fifth of our current €90 billion of national debt, because no one else in the world wanted to buy and hold our devaluing sovereign bond paper.

Markets were demanding the sovereign equivalent of subprime annual loan interest payments on dodgy residential property mortgages. Irish sovereign bonds were the fifth riskiest and costliest in the world to hold and insure against default on the so-called CDS insurance markets – behind only Bolivia, Greece, Argentina and Pakistan of the major countries involved in such fund-raising.

On the Tuesday evening that Rehn left Dublin, the yield on the benchmark ten-year bonds closed at 7.938 per cent, as Commerzbank, Germany's second largest lender, warned its investors that 'at 600 basis points, Ireland finds itself in the meantime almost in Greek territory' and that 'the likelihood of failure of bonds, as set by the market, lies in Ireland already at 40 per cent'. It blamed Ireland and 'other periphery countries' for the euro's decline against the dollar.

It was against this background that Central Bank Governor Patrick Honohan appeared twice in public on Thursday, 11 November. His first outing was at the International Financial Services Summit 2010, where he said that the type of policy package the IMF would want to see Ireland putting in place was 'very much' the package of fiscal adjustments that the government was implementing anyway. The work was already being done.

He said it was unlikely that Ireland's low corporation-tax rate of 12.5 per cent would be a matter of interest to the IMF, as its aim was to get economies growing again so they could repay their loans

quickly; they would see a low corporation-tax rate as being important to achieving that goal. But he also warned against those who saw
the arrival of the IMF as some sort of 'panacea'. The overall structure
of the fiscal policies laid out by the government seemed 'exactly
right', in his view, and Ireland's borrowing costs would fall from
'crisis' levels to more sustainable rates if the government's fiscal policies were implemented.

Later that day Honohan told members of the Oireachtas Committee on Economic Regulatory Affairs that there was 'no reason to
believe' the spread between Irish bonds and benchmark German
bonds would not return to the more sustainable levels seen in April
2010 when the spread was about 150 basis points, compared to the
spread of more than 600 basis points in November 2010.

He elaborated on his support for the government's four-year austerity package. 'Though we may not like it, we have to jump to what
the lenders expect and convince lenders we can get to the situation
where debt is not spiralling out of control,' he said. The 'wrenching
adjustments' would no doubt be painful, but he believed it could all
be done while also keeping the economy in growth. 'The alternative
is a more damaging inability to fund,' he said.

The next day Honohan's remaining confidence evaporated quickly
when he was the first senior Irish official to be presented with hard
evidence of how the rest of the world's attitude to us was dramatically changing. When Honohan started his Oireachtas presentation
at 2.30 p.m., Irish ten-year bonds were trading at around 8 per cent.
By the time he stopped speaking at about 5 p.m. the rate had risen to
close to 9 per cent. That wasn't his fault. Events in South Korea were
about to take control of our fate. The meeting of the G20 group of
leading industrial nations was fixated on how an Irish default might
destabilize the euro and cause a global economic meltdown. Decisions were being made about our future in our absence. We were
about to be sacrificed, apparently for the global good.

8. Surrender

The off-the-record briefings of journalists started shortly after a European Central Bank telephone meeting of its council – including Patrick Honohan, the governor of our Central Bank – had ended on the morning of Friday, 12 November.

The meeting had been a very tough one for Honohan, more so than he had expected. His colleagues were angry and scared by what happened on international financial markets the previous day, as the euro came under selling pressure and the spreads on Irish government bonds, and others in the EU, soared. The world's main political leaders wanted them to do something to stem the rising panic. Irish borrowing rates had climbed above 9 per cent for ten-year money (this was the yield implied by the price at which existing bonds were being traded), even though the Irish government had withdrawn from the borrowing market. It was an extortionate rate that was more than three times the comparable price for Germany. It meant that Irish plans to re-enter the debt markets in 2011 would now be relegated to the fantasy category: such rates were unaffordable and indicated that nobody really wanted to lend to us.

But suddenly it wasn't just Ireland that had the problem. Contagion was afoot and fear spread like a virus. What was happening to Ireland could happen to other euro currencies with similar exchequer and banking problems. It was enough to drive rates for Italy and Spain to levels unseen since the euro had been established.

Action was taken at Seoul in South Korea, where the G20 meeting of the prime ministers of the world's leading industrial nations was dominated by talk of the euro and the threat Ireland posed to it. At the behest of the forceful US treasury secretary, Tim Geithner, Germany, France, Spain, Britain and Italy issued a statement designed to clarify Angela Merkel's previous comments on forcing bondholders to share the burden of bank losses and sovereign defaults. It said the holders of existing eurozone debt would not be compelled to take a write-down in a sovereign crisis. 'Any new mechanism would only come into effect after mid 2013 with no impact whatsoever on the current arrangements,' said the belated statement from Seoul. This would prove highly significant for Ireland in all sorts of ways.

It did mean, though, that Honohan caught the ire of his colleagues full-frontal. His Spanish counterpart, Miguel Ángel Fernández Ordóñez, was particularly strident in his comments, demanding that Ireland stabilize the euro by applying to use funds from the EFSF and the IMF immediately. Honohan was not authorized to do that, as it was a matter for the government, but there were things that the ECB could do. In fact, two major decisions were made by members of the ECB Council that morning, if not formally. One was to be kept secret for the time being; the other, which followed from that, was to be communicated unofficially for the rest of the evening, with the European Commission also playing its part in ratcheting up the pressure on Ireland.

The first was that the ECB had decided that it could no longer continue to fund the Irish banking system on the same basis that had applied in recent years. The deposits leaving the banks were just too large, and nobody other than the ECB (or the Irish Central Bank) was providing the cash to keep banks liquid. The amount owed to the ECB had touched €100 billion, and our Central Bank was owed €30 billion. This was about a quarter of all the money available to the ECB for all of Europe. Things were likely to get worse. Bank of Ireland, by far the strongest of the Irish banks, had just reported that it had lost €10 billion in corporate deposits in recent months, money that the ECB would have to replace, and similar bad news about AIB was about to be made public. The ECB reckoned its exposure to Ireland had to be reduced before it ran into trouble itself, and to do so the Irish banks had to be reduced dramatically in scale so that they would need less funds.

To bring this about, the Irish banks would have to sell assets and accept more losses on loans than they had done previously, a process that would necessitate the need for even more capital by the banks; and, as this money could not be secured on the private markets, it would have to come from the state. This was where the second of the ECB's decisions came into play, albeit covertly. The markets had to be persuaded that Ireland would soon be the beneficiary of a major financial rescue, courtesy of the EFSF and the IMF, even if that wasn't the truth of the situation, as far as our government was concerned, but more of the ECB's wishful thinking. Like a dud cheque, Ireland was about to be bounced.

It was the economic equivalent of waterboarding, the torture technique where the victim is made to feel as if drowning. The Reuters news agency quoted 'sources' as saying that 'Ireland is in talks to receive emergency aid from the EU and it is likely that the former "Celtic Tiger" will become the second eurozone country after Greece to require a rescue.' It said 'aid discussions' were under way and that it was 'very likely' that a deal would be done. A later, updated version of the report added a denial from our Department of Finance that any application for aid had been made and that there were no plans to do so. The words were chosen carefully. It did not deny that talks were ongoing.

Little more than an hour after the initial report Lenihan went on RTÉ Radio 1's *News at One* programme. 'The state is well funded into June of next year to fund the budget,' he said. 'I think that's important, we have substantial reserves, so this country is not in a situation or a position where it is required in any way to apply for the facility . . . So why apply in those circumstances? It doesn't seem to me to make any sense. It would send a signal to the markets that we are not in a position to manage our affairs ourselves.' But that wasn't necessarily true: our reserves were not particularly substantial and they were dwindling. Knowing you have enough money to last for six to nine months was not a strong position, and it was one that was weakening by the week.

Lenihan also knew that his own Department of Finance officials were firefighting. A group of his senior officials had gone to Brussels that Friday morning for what they thought were the normal preparations for the scheduled meeting of Economic and Financial Affairs Council (ECOFIN) ministers on the following Tuesday and Wednesday. Instead they were blindsided.

Officials from Olli Rehn's office raised the issue of Ireland applying for assistance to the IMF and the EFSF, and began to discuss
what measures for introducing change would be implemented once
the application was made.

The civil servants were shocked by that (they would have been
more shocked, had they known what was going on at the ECB). The
first moves against Ireland were being made not by politicians but by
bureaucrats who had tired of their engagement with Irish politicians
and who believed they had a higher and more immediate calling to
serve: that of Europe as a whole.

All manner of conversations began that day. Dublin was bom-
barded with phone calls from the offices of European Commission
chief José Manuel Barroso and European Central Bank chief Jean-
Claude Trichet. Even German foreign minister Guido Westerwelle
got in on the act. More media briefings followed: it was 'disclosed' by
unattributed 'sources' that Irish officials had been involved in 'technical' discussions about the procedures to be followed in the event of
any aid application being made to the EFSF.

Cowen was briefly drawn on the issue by reporters in Donegal,
where he was canvassing votes for the Fianna Fáil candidate, Brian Ó
Domhnaill, in the 25 November by-election in the Donegal constituency. 'We have made no application whatever for funding,' he said
carefully. 'As the minister for finance has outlined, we have funding
up to mid year because of the pre-funding arrangements done by the
National Treasury Management Agency. So the sovereign, if you like,
has that funding arrangement in place. We don't have to borrow any
money in respect of the sovereign issues that affect the government.'

This was true but he knew this was no longer the real issue, which
was the funding of the banks. And the European Commission response
did not inspire confidence: Ireland had not asked for financial assistance so therefore no further comment would be made.

That night the Bloomberg news agency went further: 'Ireland is
being urged by European policy makers to take emergency aid to
contain a debt crisis rattling their markets.' The source was a person
who had been 'briefed on the discussions'. It referred to the pressure
that had been brought to bear by the ECB on Honohan and the Irish

Central Bank to make the application to the EFSF immediately. The fact that details were emerging was immediately understood to be at the behest of people who were close to the very top or who worked on their behalf; such things do not leak from ECB meetings unless decided so deliberately. Reference was made to the EU finance ministers' meetings to be held the following Tuesday and Wednesday and what would be expected there. Ireland was being bullied for the sake of the euro: the ECB officials were fearful that a real run on an Irish bank could trigger runs elsewhere in Europe.

The pressure mounted. By Saturday a number of 'well-placed sources' briefed Irish journalists that Irish officials had been involved in 'technical' discussions about the procedures to be followed in the event of any aid application being made to the EFSF. Irish government sources dismissed reports of the 'technical' discussions and instead claimed that there had merely been routine talks between Dublin and EU officials ahead of the ECOFIN meeting of EU finance ministers. Although the Irish journalists knew who they believed, they didn't want to be right.

Also on Saturday, the BBC reported that 'preliminary talks' on financial support were taking place; recourse to the EU bailout fund was 'no longer a matter of whether but when'. On Sunday morning the lead headline in the *Sunday Independent* read: 'Cowen Fury at BBC "When not Whether" Bailout Claim'. Cowen and Lenihan had met privately for hours that Saturday but did not inform their colleagues of what was really going on. Instead, they were told to hold the line. The minister for enterprise, trade and innovation, Batt O'Keeffe, told RTÉ radio on Sunday afternoon that Ireland was unlike Greece, and not in bailout talks. 'No. It hasn't arisen,' he said. 'We have every confidence that we will be able to manage this economy. It's been very hard-won sovereignty for this country and this government is not going to give over that sovereignty to anyone.' His cabinet colleague, the minister for tourism, culture and sport, Mary Hanafin, said, 'There is no question of it,' when asked if Ireland was in negotiations.

The minister for justice, Dermot Ahern, went further during a *Week in Politics* interview recorded on the Sunday afternoon with

Sean O'Rourke and broadcast later that night. 'So where is all this speculation from reputable international news organizations coming from? Is it just total fiction?' asked O'Rourke. Ahern seized on a word in O'Rourke's question. 'It is fiction because what we want to do is get on with the business of bringing forward the four-year plan and deal with the budget . . . We have to be calm in all of this, we have to be decisive, and we will be decisive in the next few weeks. We obviously have to ignore a lot of this speculation because it is only speculation. We have not applied; there are no negotiations going on. If there were, obviously the government would be aware of it and we are not aware of it.' To top it off Ahern said, 'I spoke to the Taoiseach this morning, I spoke with the minister for finance, and absolutely nothing is taking place in respect of this.'

The definite language of Ahern's comments surprised many. Just what was going on so? It got worse for him the following day as he and the minister for transport, Noel Dempsey, launched the 'Go Safe' speed cameras for the road network. With Dempsey alongside him nodding in agreement, Ahern said, 'We have to be very careful in relation to this. People need to be calm. Ultimately, there are people who may have their own particular interests in making comments. It's vital that the less said about these issues, the less speculation there is. Speculation does lead, as we have seen, to some fairly significant spikes in the cost of funding not just Ireland but a number of other countries across Europe.' Junior minister Dick Roche, who held responsibility for European affairs, said there was 'no reason whatsoever why Ireland should seek external support'.

Around 6.30 p.m. that Monday evening, Taoiseach Brian Cowen did an interview on the RTÉ *Six One News* and he continued to insist that Ireland was not in bailout talks. 'In a context where there is a lot of turbulence and worry and concern, I am just making the point that we will calmly and in a considered way deal with these issues in the days and weeks and months ahead,' he said in an effort to reassure. He called the word 'bailout' a 'pejorative' term.

But behind the scenes all sorts of mayhem abounded. Cowen and Lenihan were desperately trying to work out the best thing to do and what kind of deal might be struck. They hit the phones, ringing whoever they could among other European leaders and finance ministers, whom they hoped would show support and understanding. They wanted to present a deal that was clearly a bank rescue, as opposed to a rescue of Ireland – one in which they would now borrow to recapitalize the banks while still being able to return to the debt markets in the new year to resume borrowing on behalf of the state. They knew that Lenihan would come under enormous pressure at Tuesday's meeting of ECOFIN ministers; Cowen had to face the Dáil and the Fianna Fáil parliamentary party, both of which were showing increasing signs of panic.

There was a cabinet meeting to be had first, on the Tuesday morning. Lenihan told fellow ministers for the first time of what the ECB was doing and of the Friday meeting his officials had conducted with Rehn's staff. His colleagues were stunned, especially those who had been giving interviews that could now be said to be misleading at best. The Fianna Fáil members of the government waited until Green Party ministers John Gormley and Eamon Ryan, and independent Mary Harney, left; and then Ahern, Dempsey and O'Keeffe let rip at Lenihan.

It wasn't just that they had deceived the public, and would have to face the consequences of that; it was that they had been deceived themselves and, as far as they were concerned, deliberately, if not maliciously, by Lenihan. Collective cabinet responsibility requires trust. They hadn't been told the truth. Ahern's and Dempsey's subsequent decisions not to stand for re-election at the 2011 general election were strongly influenced by their disillusionment at what had happened, although they would not confirm that publicly.

On Tuesday afternoon the Dáil and the media were informed that Cowen would make a major statement on the economy at 5 p.m. that afternoon. Speculation heightened that Cowen would announce the surrender. But, even though the country was on tenterhooks and the world's media was watching and reporting, he waffled in his usual administrative and clichéd language about things such as an 'impending sense of crisis' and 'front-loading of consolidation', leaving his audience wondering what all that had been about and angry at yet another missed opportunity to find out what was going on. It undermined his position further.

Cowen then went to a meeting of Fianna Fáil TDs and senators, where he continued to maintain the line that the 'sovereign' was well funded and that Ireland had plenty of cash available to it and would not need to borrow again until the middle of the following year, by which stage interest rates should have fallen to manageable levels. He insisted that there was no question of a bailout. Quite deliberately he did not mention the funding position of the banks, and, even though the outflow of deposits from the Irish banks was known to his audience, they assumed that the ECB would continue to cover this, without fully understanding that this was pure folly.

Meanwhile, Lenihan was having serious trouble at the meeting of the ECOFIN, the finance ministers of the seventeen EMU states, in Brussels. Unfortunately, Lenihan was over an hour late in getting there. It wasn't his fault – fog had temporarily closed Brussels Airport and his plane couldn't land – but it didn't improve the mood of Germany's finance minister, Wolfgang Schäuble, who had arrived more than thirty minutes early. He spoke in German to waiting reporters: the translation was that Ireland had not asked for a bailout, so there was no deal to announce. But his grim demeanour left few doubts as to what he wanted; what wasn't clear was what his tactics would be.

Lenihan was to be shocked at the approach taken by Schäuble. The ECB clearly was no longer Ireland's only adversary. Germany was gunning for Ireland. Schäuble demanded that Lenihan leave the meeting and address the media, in order to announce that Ireland was accepting a bailout. Lenihan was appalled and angry. Drawing on all of his legal eloquence, he declared that he would not be 'dragooned' into agreeing any course of action without the authority of his government to do so. He had been asked to do the impossible, and many other ministers sympathized with him and cavilled at this latest example of German arrogance. A compromise was reached: four hours after the meeting started EU Commissioner Olli Rehn and the Luxembourg premier, Jean-Claude Juncker (who represented his country at these meetings), issued a statement saying that a delegation would travel to Dublin to tackle its stricken banks. Crucially, they mentioned the IMF would participate and soon that body had issued its own statement: 'At the request of the Irish authorities, an IMF team will participate in a short and focused consultation, together with the European Commission and the ECB, in order to determine the best way to provide any necessary support to address market risks.'

The following morning Lenihan went on RTÉ's *Morning Ireland* programme and promised that 'the Irish government will fully engage with this process and will work with the mission to ensure that everything possible is done to secure the Irish banking system.' Again, he carefully chose his words. Cowen hadn't mastered that ability. In the Dáil he insisted 'what we're involved in here is working with colleagues in respect of currency problems and euro-issue problems that are affecting Ireland, they're affecting other countries. They're particularly affecting Ireland at the moment ... there has been no question, as has been stated all over the weekend, of a negotiation for a bailout.' He was hooted at when he stated 'we were not involved in negotiations and we are not involved in negotiations.'

Predictably and understandably, the opposition tore into him. Cowen responded to Labour's Eamon Gilmore in his usual belligerent yet convoluted fashion: 'If the deputy thinks it is in the essential national interest of this country for me, as head of government, to indicate what our negotiating position is before negotiations have even begun or before we have agreed to enter into them – pending these discussions that have to take place on a whole range of technical issues including regulation, structure and others – then he is not very clever.'

Cowen turned on the domestic media now, moving on from the previous weekend's attacks on the international media, claiming organizations were trying 'to suggest there is something problematic here'. He insisted he was levelling with the people and protecting the country's interests as discussions continued. 'We haven't started any negotiations. I want to get away from this word game,' he said.

But his own party started to round on him too. His former junior minister, the Fianna Fáil TD for Kildare South, Sean Power, declared, with unusual eloquence and force, that: 'We failed the people and treated them as if they could not understand the complexities of the financial situation. We engaged in a game of semantics. We started trying to play a cute game about words and what they meant or might mean instead of using the opportunity presented to us following a number of statements on television and radio about the state of the nation and the difficulties we are experiencing.'

Later that evening Lenihan confirmed that the team from the IMF would arrive the following morning (they actually arrived that same evening), but he still didn't spell out what was going to happen.

Patrick Honohan did that for him instead. On Thursday morning, 18 November, the Central Bank governor instructed his press officer to contact *Morning Ireland* and ask that it make time for him to appear, via telephone from Frankfurt, on the programme before 8 a.m.

Honohan confirmed what everybody believed – that the country was set to get a rescue package from the IMF and the EU worth at least 'tens of billions' of euro. 'It will be a large loan because the purpose of the amount to be advanced, or to be made available to be borrowed, is to show Ireland has sufficient firepower to deal with any concerns in the market,' he said.

'The ECB would not send large teams if they didn't believe first of all that they could agree to a package, that there is a programme that is fully acceptable to them that could be designed, and that it is likely to be acceptable to the Irish Government and the Irish people. I think this is the way forward. Market conditions have not allowed us to go ahead without seeking the support of our international collaborators.'

He said the huge sums of money put in by the government to support the banks had not generated sufficient confidence, partly because of the concern of investors about the government's finances and the prospects for growth and employment.

Cowen was furious, and offered some veiled blows at his own determinedly independent official. 'The governor gave his view. He is entitled to give his view. I am entitled to give the view about the decision the government will take when the necessary discussions are over. The governor is part of the governing council of the ECB, and it is a matter of public knowledge what the ECB general view has been,' he said in a comment that was more understandable later than it may have been at the time it was made. 'At the end of the day, we have to determine what is the best option for our country, and for our people at the time. As I have said, it will require further consideration.'

But he had little time left in which to think. An Indian man called Ajai Chopra was about to become one of the most famous faces in Ireland as he set about his work.

9.   Welcoming Mr Chopra

On 18 November 2010, Ajai Chopra stepped out of Dublin's five-star Merrion Hotel with three colleagues and crossed the street like a man on a mission. One of the group of journalists and photographers waiting on the far side of Merrion Street, at the entrance to the Department of Finance, recognized the acting head of the International Monetary Fund in Europe, and the media posse quickly surrounded the delegation, firing questions and taking pictures as they walked. Chopra was about to become an unlikely celebrity.

Instead of going straight into the Department of Finance, Chopra went left up to Merrion Row and then veered right towards St Stephen's Green, using a map on his mobile phone to find his way. He walked past the deserted former Anglo Irish Bank headquarters, providing great opportunities for the photographers, but at the top of Grafton Street came the image that was seen in newspapers and television newscasts throughout the world: he and his colleagues passed a beggar (a foreign national, as it turned out, when the media tried to find out his story) sitting on the ground, holding out a coffee cup for alms. Chopra ignored him, headed off down Grafton Street, where he must have noticed the many vacant shop units on what was once one of the most expensive shopping streets in Europe, and moved towards Dame Street and the headquarters of the Central Bank and the Office of the Financial Regulator.

That an IMF representative, apparently in town to take measures that would outrage the public, could walk the streets so confidently – and would continue to do so even after his photo was widely publicized – illustrated the compliance of the Irish in what was happening, despite their anger. Chopra had started preparatory work for this day some months ago and had met with Lenihan in New York the previous month. As deputy director of the IMF's European Department, he was not paying his first visit to Dublin. Four years earlier he had been the lead author on a report about the Irish economy and banking system. The report was filled with superlatives and plenty of praise for the government of the time, which had Ahern as Taoiseach and Cowen as minister for finance. He said, 'economic performance remains strong, assisted by good policies . . . fiscal policy has been prudent.'

'Reflecting the strength of the economy,' wrote Chopra, 'the banking system is well capitalized and profitable, and non-performing loans are low . . . even in an extreme scenario involving a sharp rise in unemployment and a sharp decline in house prices, capital remains adequate in every bank.' He claimed that 'recent stress tests indicate that the major lenders have adequate buffers to cover a range of shocks.' Related to this, he said that 'a contraction of the construction sector to a more sustainable size over the medium term is likely to be smooth.'

There was more: 'even a substantial withdrawal of private-sector deposits would not exhaust the stock of liquid assets at any major lender.' He claimed that the 'general approach of the Central Bank and Financial Regulator is appropriate for the mature and sophisticated financial market'. Nobody at those offices, where he now arrived, chose to remind him of this. It was too late for that and probably would only have been counterproductive. Chopra had the power and that had to be respected.

But his knowledge of his own mistakes may explain why it was the Irish officials found Chopra somewhat more accommodating than the European Commission and the ECB, especially over issues such as corporation tax, not forcing a faster and more aggressive reduction in the exchequer deficit and the restructuring of the banks. The IMF had been painted as the bogeyman, but it regarded the Irish government as having done what should have been done; it was our partners in Europe who were less appreciative, understanding and forgiving.

It was because of the pressure from Europe that the government continued with its work on the four-year budget plan, to the fury of opposition politicians, who did not want to be bound by it when they came to power. An eight-hour cabinet meeting that Thursday signed off on nearly all of the four-year plan's major points: there was an agreement to introduce a property tax to raise €530 million annually by 2014; to bring low-paid workers into the tax net; and to reduce the social-welfare budget by €2.8 billion by 2014. Interestingly, a €1 cut in the hourly minimum wage was agreed, even though this would have no direct budgetary impact; it was seen as a way to help in reducing social-welfare rates.

The government had two priorities: one was to come up with a plan that would be passed by the EU; the other was to be able to say that the plan was its own and not forced upon it, because it feared that to admit such a loss of sovereignty would play dreadfully with the section of the electorate it still hoped to seduce come election time.

But if the government was acting in conjunction with the EU, and acting in accordance with what it perceived to be the wishes of the IMF, it may as well have been an IMF document. To try to counter this impression, Cowen ordered his government colleagues to have the four-year budget plan ready for presentation to the Dáil ahead of any move against Ireland by the IMF and the EU, so it could be claimed as Irish. The cynics said he was months too late; it all should have happened before the end of September, to stop the bond markets closing to his government. And, as Fine Gael's Michael Noonan told the Dáil: 'If [the IMF/EU/ECB] are going to lend us €90–€100 billion over the next four years for government spending, I don't see how any minister can say that won't have an influence [in policy] on the fiscal side.' 'It is very hard to see the economy growing with that burden of debt,' he continued. 'I don't know what scope will be left.'

As it happened, things could have been even worse. Many of those who offered approval to the government, mainly foreigners but some domestically such as the Irish Business and Employers Confederation, doubted the growth forecasts on which the four-year plan was based. Incredibly, however, some wanted even further cuts to compensate for this, the European Commission and the ECB looking for an adjustment of up to €8 billion in the first year, with the IMF having to step in to say that was too much on top of what had been done already and that it would be counterproductive. The government did not want to go even as far as the €15 billion in cuts over four years, but it was forced upon them.

The Irish negotiating team was not an elected political one. It included Honohan; the financial regulator, Matthew Elderfield; the secretary general of the Department of Finance, Kevin Cardiff (who had replaced David Doyle but who had been a key figure on the night of the bank guarantee); and senior officials Ann Nolan, Michael McGrath and Jim O'Brien. The head of the NTMA, John Corrigan, was involved, as were the NTMA's head of banking, Michael Torpey, and the Central Bank's Tony Grimes. Attorney General Paul Gallagher and his senior advisers also took part. The team reported back to Lenihan, who in turn spoke to Cowen.

On the day that Chopra arrived, Lenihan told the Dáil that he was in charge of the negotiations but that he was 'not participating in the conduct of the discussions because they are of a technical nature'. He said 'the job of government is to protect the taxpayer' and 'that is what we have been doing.' (Some of his critics cavilled at the use of the word 'taxpayer', saying he should have said 'citizen'.) Lenihan also said: 'If the government has been reticent in making public comment, it has been in the interest of protecting the taxpayer. Jumping to conclusions ahead of the facts is not to the benefit of the taxpayer, nor is it in our interest to do this in advance of the discussions that are now taking place.' He said the 'facts can best be established after a short and focused discussion.'

The overall interest rate to be charged for the entire package of loans was something that exercised Lenihan in particular. Before that, however, he had to endure many political arrows: Gilmore said Fianna Fáil had 'effectively put the country into receivership', while Kenny delivered the less memorable, but popular and accurate, line 'The government has long since lost any shred of credibility.'

Rehn was not present on behalf of the EU, instead putting a ten-man team into the country, with no stated leader of the delegation. Many suspected it was effectively István Székely, the Hungarian who was director of economic and financial affairs at the European Commission, and who had been such a regular visitor to Ireland in the previous months that he had been dubbed the 'tall Hungarian' by Labour's finance spokeswoman, Joan Burton.

Other nations spoke of becoming involved supportively. The British chancellor, George Osborne – whose family were from Tipperary originally and who maintained strong links with the country – made it clear that Britain stood willing to help, raising the prospect of bilateral loans across the Irish Sea: 'Ireland is our closest neighbour and it's in Britain's national interest that the Irish economy is success-ful.' This irked *The Irish Times* no end. The newspaper, committed to the European Union at all times and positive in its attitude to Britain, surprised many when it published an editorial that asked whether Ireland's republican fighters in 1916 had died for 'a bailout from the German chancellor with a few shillings of sympathy from the British chancellor on the side'. The paper lamented 'the shame of it all. Hav-ing obtained our political independence from Britain to be the masters of our own affairs, we have now surrendered our sovereignty.'

Meanwhile, to add fuel to the fire, AIB released a trading update that disclosed that customers had withdrawn €13 billion in deposits so far in 2010. This was 17 per cent of its overall deposits and served to reinforce fears that a run on the banks was effectively under way. The ECB had lent €130 billion to Irish banks by the end of October, at a bargain interest rate of just 1.5 per cent, which was a 60 per cent increase in the position since the end of March. Indeed, six months after the September 2008 guarantee had gone into place the ECB exposure to our banks, by way of provision of emergency liquidity, was just €35 billion, and it was supposed to come down from there.

The government continued to behave in public as if in denial. Lenihan said on Friday, 19 November, that 'we have not, contrary to much speculation, applied to join any facility, or avail of any facility.' However, the crafty lawyer, as ever, gave himself a get-out-of-jail card. 'But, of course, we're an inter-dependent part of the eurozone, and we're in constant liaison with the [ECB] and with the [Euro-pean] commission,' he said. 'If banking problems are too big for this small country to manage, Europe has made it clear, they'll help.' The increasingly detached minister for health, Mary Harney, made a rare public comment and began her effort to play the béal bocht over what had gone wrong. 'There may be areas we would have done differently in hindsight,' she said ruefully. 'Should we have had a benchmarking exercise, benchmarking public-sector pay against private-sector pay?'

she asked, as if this, rather than banking, had been the main cause of our problems. 'Perhaps we should have benchmarked public-sector pay against public-sector pay in other countries, for example . . . There is no point in going forward in a blame game. The last thing we need now is to take our eye off the ball.' She insisted that the decisions taken by the government in the past two years had been 'saluted' internationally.

Minister for agriculture, Brendan Smith, appeared on RTÉ's *Saturday View* radio programme and insisted that the government had not applied for a bailout but rather was in 'technical discussions' with the EU, the ECB and the IMF. Smith had been promoted to cabinet by Cowen; he was not going to let down his mentor.

Cowen did not find a shortage of people willing to kick him when he was down, however. A day earlier he had rejected calls for his resignation. 'You would expect me as leader of the government to conduct these discussions in a way for which the best outcome for Ireland can be achieved,' he said. The media had joined his political opponents regularly in doing so, as had many of his own party, both publicly and privately. But he had reason to seethe when the flamboyant Ryanair boss Michael O'Leary decided to pull a stunt that got international attention.

It was Cowen's misfortune that the official opening of the new, massively expensive Terminal 2 at Dublin Airport had been scheduled for Friday, 19 November, which meant that the event happened while the world's media were in Dublin to report what was going on with the IMF. The incongruity of opening a gleaming new state-of-the-art facility, at an estimated cost of €823 million (when all other associated work at the airport was added), was not lost on many, especially O'Leary.

O'Leary was never one to miss an opportunity to embarrass a politician with whom he was in conflict – and O'Leary's rows with Fianna Fáil-led governments had continued long after the exit of Bertie Ahern, whom he had often castigated bitterly. Arguably Ireland's most successful businessman, and certainly its best known in Britain and beyond because of his Richard Branson-esque publicity stunts, O'Leary had insisted even long before construction had started that the terminal was an expensive and overblown folly.

Just before Cowen arrived in the cavalcade of state cars, a hearse pulled up at the entrance to the new terminal. Out stepped O'Leary, dressed in an undertaker's garb of black tails, white shirt and black tie, and sporting a small moustache, in support of that month's Movember campaign for the Irish Cancer Society in which men were sponsored to grow facial hair.

'It's a statement of modern Ireland. A big, bankrupt property development. It's a nice place to welcome IMF executives,' gloated O'Leary, as a coffin, draped in the Irish tricolour, was ushered inside. Even many of his fans thought he might have gone too far this time, but his comments attracted attention and support because O'Leary was a proven success. While many decried Ryanair's customer service and staff relations, the reality was that it was the biggest Irish business success story in living memory, the creation of a major European brand from an Irish base. When fans of Finland cited Nokia as an inspiration, others noted that these people should have been celebrating Ryanair for what it brought to its customers: airline tickets at prices most could afford. Many would now use Ryanair to emigrate.

Later that day the IMF fund spokeswoman in Washington, Caroline Atkinson, said the focus of the discussions was 'to look at whatever measures might be needed to support financial stability'. She said talks would include the IMF's views 'on the government's budget plans . . . on tax and spending measures'. Meanwhile, news of the IMF's arrival had done little to soothe the markets: the ten-year bond interest rates were still running at over 8 per cent. This suggested that big international investors didn't believe our debt levels were sustainable and that there was a sizeable risk they wouldn't get all of their money back, no matter what EU leaders said.

There was near-panic outside of Ireland on Saturday, 20 November, as world leaders pondered the possibility of a run on global markets when they reopened on Monday morning. The publicity about the run on deposits at AIB and Bank of Ireland was a major worry: what if more deposits fled Ireland, leaving the ECB to step in, and what if money then started to drain from other banks and countries in Continental Europe? The eurozone big boys decided that Ireland's 'insolvency' was now jeopardizing the ability of other bigger countries, Portugal, Spain and even Italy, to keep borrowing. The eurocrats engaged in a cynical and, many claimed, misguided attempt to calm down the markets in the hope that yields would stay relatively low for Spain and Portugal, allowing them to continue with their borrowing.

The US treasury secretary, Tim Geithner, was deeply involved again in many conversations over the weekend – and he repeated his insistence that Ireland be dealt with quickly – but it went even higher than that. US President Barack Obama was phoned that evening to be briefed and consulted. The call was made by European Council President Herman Van Rompuy and by European Commission President José Manuel Barroso. Word emerged that the US was pledging 'moral support', whatever benefit that had, to Ireland. Essentially, however, Cowen and his government were told that their attempt to stave off the inevitable had to end because the delay in agreeing a deal was becoming a danger in itself. Just a week earlier they had believed that they had at least a couple of weeks in which to negotiate, but that idea was now blown away.

Cowen was almost in despair. He had continued to hope that some way could be found to spare the country, and indeed him, from this fate. He knew that it was catastrophic for Ireland and that years of penury beckoned. But he also knew that his own reputation had been destroyed and that things would get worse for him come general election time. The party that he loved would suffer the consequences of his failures and he would go down in history for that ignominy. But he had no other options open to him, as he saw it. The talks with the foreigners progressed quickly on Saturday, and Lenihan became involved personally on Saturday evening, which was taken as a signal by his colleagues that the end was nigh.

Surrender was formally declared on Sunday, 21 November, days after Cowen had denied Honohan's confirmation of the IMF arrival. That it had been expected did not make it any the less shocking.

Just before lunchtime the Department of Finance alerted favoured journalists and warned them to listen to an interview that Lenihan would be giving on the RTÉ *This Week* programme at 1 p.m. In it, he said he would be formally applying later that day to his fellow finance ministers of the eurozone countries for use of the EFSF and other funds by Ireland. And that he would be 'recommending' that his government colleagues should approve this – as if they had a choice.

Lenihan attempted to downplay the humiliation by emphasizing that the rate of corporation tax had been saved and that the Croke Park deal for public servants would be implemented without change. He said the amount sought would be less than €100 billion. Lenihan admitted finally that his banking strategy had failed – although he did not say that directly – and that it was too big a problem to be solved by the government alone. He said that yet another review, or stress test, of the banks would take place, less than seven weeks after he said that the issue had been sorted. The banks would then be 'restructured'. 'You have to stabilize your banks,' he said. 'This type of process cannot continue indefinitely.'

The devil, however, was in the details, and those – the interest rates on the loans, the amount of time we'd get to repay them, the distribution of the money borrowed and the continued approach towards fully compensating bondholders for their losses – were not yet forthcoming.

Lenihan left RTÉ and headed to a cabinet meeting, where the application was discussed and yet more work was done on the content of the next four budgets. The mood was grim. Having to approve a formal application for aid from the IMF and the EU was something that no predecessor of this government had ever had to do. It was a mark of failure for all concerned, no matter how hard they had worked to try to avert what was happening.

Lenihan left the others to their work because he had to attend the telephone conference of the eurozone ministers, one that had been organized over the previous twenty-four hours and that had only Ireland on its agenda. The meeting was conducted more in sorrow than in anger. Nobody kicked Lenihan when he was down, but afterwards a few blows were aimed by other ministers during briefings, with some wanting to discuss our corporation-tax rate at a later date. Their post-meeting statement made it clear why they had acted. 'Ministers concur with the European Commission and the European Central Bank that providing assistance to Ireland is warranted to safeguard financial stability in the EU and in the euro area.' This wasn't about Ireland; it was about them.

The press conference that night was a humiliating affair. It began about ninety minutes later than expected, at 8.30, although some suspected that this was to coincide with the RTÉ TV schedule. Cowen and Lenihan took to the podium and announced that a formal cabinet decision had been taken that afternoon to apply for external funding and that they'd agreed to external oversight of the government's economic performance on an ongoing basis. Lenihan told of the meeting of the finance ministers from EU eurozone states, where the package had been ratified, and of how the G7, comprising the seven most powerful economies in the world, had also met to approve the deal.

In another indication that the announcement had been rushed to suit the international markets prior to Monday opening, Cowen and Lenihan could not disclose the sum that would be borrowed, and said it would be decided over the coming two weeks of negotiations. Lenihan confirmed it would be less than €100 billion, however.

Significantly, Cowen began with the latest attempt to restructure the banks. 'Irish banks will become significantly smaller than they were in the past,' he said. This would involve the sale of what were called non-core businesses, essentially anything outside of the island, forced mergers between institutions and, ultimately, the sale of the institutions themselves to foreign banks. It was a doubtful strategy, as a fire-sale almost guaranteed assets would be sold too cheaply. Having international diversification at the banks was actually a good thing, because it provided a flow of profits and reduced dependency on the small island economy of Ireland.

The EU, however, was having none of forcing losses on the bondholders. It would not risk contagion spreading to other European banks by burning the lenders. 'In the course of these negotiations I did raise the issue of senior debt, and the unanimous view of the

European Central Bank and the commission was no programme would be possible if it were intended by us to dishonour senior debt because such a dishonouring of senior debt would have huge ripple effects throughout the euro system,' Lenihan said. What he didn't say publicly at the time was that the IMF was wholly in favour of burning the bondholders, which is why he left it out of his comments. The IMF would have been in favour of burning up to €30 billion of these bonds to reduce the size of the package, but the ECB and the European Commission had the support of Geithner again, who believed that lenders should not suffer the consequences of their reckless behaviour.

Lenihan insisted that so-called junior bondholders – who had been paid higher rates of interest but had less security – would not be repaid in full, a process that was already under way. 'They will be expected to bear steep losses and make a contribution towards this,' he said. 'As far as senior bondholders are concerned, I've always made it clear that as long as we were in the markets, that senior debt was fundamental for Ireland.' In other words, Lenihan hadn't just been influenced by the EU; in time, he wanted to return to the markets to borrow, but was afraid that anyone burned by us would steer clear of Ireland for a long time. This was a matter of judgement. Some market experts believed that such investors would write off their losses and come back again if certain they would get their money on the next loans – something that would be more likely if the Irish economy had been restructured by way of debt write-off. Others, particularly in government who would suffer the consequences if the gamble did not pay off, were not prepared to take the chance.

Returning to the markets eventually was central to the announcement of the four-year plan for the budgets and the €15 billion reduction in the amount that would be borrowed over the period. Cowen said the forthcoming budget and four-year plan were an Irish initiative that would not be changed by the external bodies, but also that 'a small, open economy like Ireland did not have the luxury of taking decisions without reference to the wider world.'

While the latter part of Cowen's statement was true, the first part was not. The rules of the EFSF made it clear that the conditions attached to any loan to Ireland would be political, and not purely economic. So, just as an Irish government would look for changes over time, so would EU ministers demand changes as well, especially to things such as corporation tax. The head of the EFSF bailout fund, Klaus Regling, said that with the rescue would come 'drastic conditions' and 'dissuasive costs', while the head of the eurozone finance ministers, Jean-Claude Juncker of Luxembourg, dismissed Lenihan's claim that Ireland's 12.5 per cent corporation-tax rate was safeguarded in the agreement and therefore 'off the table'.

'It is essential that we maintain economic continuity, that everyone understands that ATM machines function, that salaries are paid, that the big workforce that has built up here continues to be employed, that a large number of overseas investors continue to invest in enterprise,' Lenihan said.

Lenihan came through the ordeal of the press conference somewhat better than Cowen did. Cowen denied that his party or the people had lost faith in him, and also confirmed it was his intention to lead Fianna Fáil into the next election. One of his former ministers, Willie O'Dea, said that day that the government's handling of the crisis had 'been disastrously mismanaged by a total lack of a coherent communications strategy. A general election can't be far away.'

Cowen denied that the rescue plan would lead to a loss of Irish sovereignty. 'I don't believe there's any reason for Irish people to be ashamed and humiliated,' he said. 'We're not ceding any policy-making decisions,' he claimed. 'The IMF or people like that don't micro-manage the Irish economy. We're not ceding any policy decision in relation to how we're going to continue with the direction in our own public finances.'

'The size of the crisis means that no one can be sheltered,' Cowen said. 'We find ourselves in a situation where we need to take some steps back before we go forward again. We can and we will pull through this as we have in the past.' Cowen refused to shoulder any personal responsibility for the crisis, saying 'circumstances' were to blame. It was questioning from TV3's veteran current affairs presenter Vincent Browne that prompted the 'circumstances' comment and various other excuses. 'Why can't you see you're a liability, not just to your party, but to the country?' Browne charged. 'Why don't you get out now?'

'I don't accept the premise of your question,' the Taoiseach replied. 'Circumstances change . . . we were hit by a financial crisis . . . I would defend my decisions throughout my political career, any decisions I took, the context in which I took them and the rationale for taking them.'

Browne kept at Cowen in a manner that reflected public anger, but Cowen did not flinch from defending himself. 'I don't accept your contention, the premise to your question that I am the bogeyman that you're looking for . . . All these decisions were taken in the national interest.'

Even that exchange gave Cowen fresh problems, because RTÉ decided to leave coverage of its press conference to return to a short studio discussion with staff reporters before an ad break brought the time up to the start of the *Nine O'Clock News*. Those who wanted to see the exchange continue had to do so on Sky News if they had access to the channel. Conspiracy theorists thought either that RTÉ was doing the government a favour or that it had not wished to highlight the fact that a rival station's broadcaster was asking the questions RTÉ should have asked. The station insisted afterwards that it had not engaged in censorship but privately admitted that it had made a mistake. But it had plenty of opportunities over the coming weeks to continue with wall-to-wall coverage. The twists were to come fast and plenty, starting the very next day.

10.　Playing Politics

The opposition was not slow to castigate the government, which was hardly a surprise: not only had ministers surrendered ignominiously, they would be leaving the opposition to pick up the pieces when it came into government, with both hands tied behind its back.

Fine Gael's finance spokesman, Michael Noonan, claimed that sovereignty had been relinquished. 'The IMF can intervene on a quarterly basis. That shows who is in charge,' he said, in words that he would have reason to recall many times when he replaced Lenihan later and found that he could not make much difference himself. His soon-to-be-cabinet-colleague Joan Burton claimed the application was the 'final epitaph for a Fianna Fáil government that has plunged the country into the financial abyss and that has consistently and deliberately lied to the Irish people'.

To everybody's shock, however, there was support for these views from within the government itself. On the Monday morning, 22 November, not long before noon, the Green Party effectively usurped Brian Cowen's authority by setting the date for its withdrawal from government and demanding that a general election be held before the end of January 2011.

It was an extraordinary demand. Secretly, the Greens had been looking for an opportunity to leave government for months, but a number of things had delayed the making and implementation of such a decision. Ministers John Gormley and Eamon Ryan genuinely believed that they had been serving the national interest by participating in the decisions that were being made about the economy, but the always present tensions meant that they and their government partner had grown further and further apart. The Greens were briefed regularly by Lenihan, and in particular by his adviser Alan Ahearne, with Party Chairman Senator Dan Boyle very involved in that process, but they became increasingly unsettled by what they regarded as

Ahearne's continued insistence that everything was being brought under control when they saw that it clearly wasn't.

The Greens knew also that they had become every bit as unpopular as Fianna Fáil because of the economic collapse, but would face an even bigger electoral punishment. More experienced politicians than they were often given credit for, they were relatively sanguine about the unfairness of that: even though they had not contributed to the policies that inflated the bubble, they understood that there would be punishment for their endorsement of the bank guarantee and all that followed. They also knew that the public blamed them for keeping Fianna Fáil in power. If the Greens had walked at any stage after September 2008, the remaining Fianna Fáil/independent coalition would not have survived. Their grasp of the situation went only so far, though. They clung to the hope that the electorate would not penalize them unduly, that they could save at least a couple of seats in the next Dáil, that enough people would recognize their efforts to act in the national interest. Just like Fianna Fáil, they hoped that the passage of time would be their ally and allow the public to see that they had done the correct things.

The Greens wanted to do a number of things in the time that was left to them, to justify their presence in the cabinet not just to voters but to their own members, who had become increasingly sceptical throughout the lifetime of the government. They had voted in 2009 on a revised programme for government that had been negotiated with Fianna Fáil: it contained items such as a climate-change bill, and a procedure whereby there would be directly elected mayors for Dublin and, in time, the other major cities. These were not popular suggestions. The proposed climate-change bill was opposed by the Irish Business and Employers Confederation and the Irish Farmers Association for allegedly adding to the costs of their members at just the wrong time in the economic cycle (although they would probably have argued against this even if the economy had remained in growth). Few saw the benefits of the proposed increased powers for local government in a country with a population of little more than four million people. Measures of which the Greens were proud – such as a new carbon-emission-based motor-tax system and the introduction of a carbon tax on fuel – were reviled by large sections of the public.

Green TD Paul Gogarty was something of an embarrassment for his party, and his public venting caused other members to be more careful about what they said. But John Gormley cracked in the Dáil late in 2010. Particularly dismissive of Enda Kenny, whom he liked personally but did not rate politically, Gormley complained about how hard it was to be in government and how what Fine Gael and Labour were saying now wouldn't necessarily come to pass once they were in power. He was in fact correct but commentators thought he had shown weakness in saying it. It didn't undermine the Greens, though – that job had been done long before.

So for the Greens it was all about picking a moment to leave government with their heads held high. It had become clear that the climate-change bill would not get through. Fianna Fáil TDs in rural constituencies planned to oppose it in an attempt to save votes in their local areas. A rump of senators with their own ambitions was particularly vocal about making sure it would not pass. Cowen was not going to force it through and bring even more trouble upon himself within his own party. He was relying on the Greens' sense of honour to keep them in government and also on his belief that they too would want to delay an election until the last possible moment. Yet he didn't give his relationship with the Greens a great deal of thought; he had too many other things on his mind.

Fianna Fáil was caught completely unawares, then, when the Greens dropped their bombshell. The timing was extraordinary and the disclosure handled badly. Gormley did not tell Cowen what he was doing. Instead, the deputy government press secretary, John Downing, rang his boss, Eoghan Ó Neachtain, just ten minutes before the Greens told the media about their sudden press conference and explained to him what would be happening.

The press conference started sixteen minutes late, at 11.46 a.m. The Greens set out their demands, apparently more in sorrow than in anger. They would stay in government and support the budget on the condition that a general election would be held by the end of January. 'People feel misled and betrayed,' Gormley said about the

IMF application, which the Greens had endorsed at a cabinet meeting the day before. He added that the events of the past week had been 'traumatic' for the electorate. His colleague Eamon Ryan complained also about the way the public had been treated. 'It was terribly uncertain, it wasn't well managed, communications were poor. If you were to say "We are in discussions but not in negotiations, this is a formal process where it will be considered" – in hindsight, that would've been okay. But not saying – that aggravated the public.'

There was immediate turmoil in financial as well as political circles. Would there be an immediate general election, and, if so, how would this affect the IMF/EU/ECB deal? Independent TDs Jackie Healy-Rae and Michael Lowry, whose votes were needed by the government to stay in power, even should the Greens stay, immediately went on radio to say that their support could no longer be relied on. When, therefore, would the budget be introduced? Irish bond prices began to rise, bank shares plummeted, and EU officials were immediately on the phone to Cowen and Lenihan wanting to know what was going on and what the government was going to do. The 1 per cent improvement in the value of the euro that had occurred within hours of the Sunday-evening announcement was reversed almost immediately. Bond yields in the other European peripheral countries, as well as Ireland, soared.

Fianna Fáil was furious at what had happened. Lenihan was at a public event in his constituency in Blanchardstown when he was told. He couldn't hide his amazement or anger, or his fear of the possible consequences. He felt that he had tried to accommodate the Greens at all times but that this was a betrayal.

Cowen was calmer than many would have expected. The man who had sprung to prominence at a Fianna Fáil ard fheis nearly twenty years earlier by taking an anti-coalition line with the PDs – 'if in doubt, leave them out' – had to be mature. Cowen had many Fianna Fáil voices to hear, most of whom wanted immediate retribution taken against the Greens. Some regarded their actions as an arrogant betrayal; only the Taoiseach had the constitutional authority to decide if there would be an election and when. Others were angry that they'd been outdone by the type of 'stroke' upon which

Fianna Fáil prided itself and depressed by having their impotence highlighted. Traditionalists such as Éamon Ó Cuív and Cowen's closest political friend, Batt O'Keeffe, wanted the Greens sacked from cabinet immediately. They said that the Greens could still be shamed into voting for the budget, even from the opposition benches. Others told Cowen to call an election immediately.

He had two main concerns: one was that the EU would go ballistic should the deal it was forcing upon Ireland be derailed, even if temporarily, and that international markets would punish not just Ireland but the euro as well. In addition, Fianna Fáil wasn't ready for an election, not having all of its candidates in place. Besides that, who would vote for Fianna Fáil in these circumstances? As he saw it, he needed more time for the public to understand what he'd had to do.

Cowen had to address the issues publicly. As it was a Monday, he could not do it in the Dáil, which did not sit until Tuesday. Instead, he held a press conference on the steps of Government Buildings. Surrounded only by his Fianna Fáil ministers, he declared that there was a 'clear duty on all members of Dáil Éireann' to pass the budget. He invoked the 'national interest' to defy calls for him to resign immediately, which were coming now from inside his own party as well as from almost everywhere else. 'There will be a time for political accountability to the electorate. The interests of the electorate, of all our people, would not be served by delay or, worse, casting into doubt the steps that are necessary to secure our economy and financial stability.'

'The greatest statement of confidence in this country should be passing the budget on December 7,' Cowen said. 'We have entered into discussions with European partners on the basis that we are going to implement a budget with a €6 billion adjustment to it and that we will provide a four-year plan this week. The interests of the electorate . . . will not be served by delaying, or, worse still, casting into doubt, the steps which are necessary to secure our economy and financial stability.'

Later that evening Cowen rang Gilmore and Kenny to ask them to support the budget and the four-year plan. Reportedly he was met with a polite but frosty reception; it was not in their interests to let Cowen off the hook no matter how understanding they were of the national situation. Fine Gael's deputy leader, James Reilly, came forward to make the argument for an early election. 'What's the point in people preparing a four-year plan that they're not going to preside over? And they won't be there to implement and they haven't consulted the people on. If we have an election tomorrow, it can be all done and dusted within eighteen days. We would all have an opportunity to put forward our plans – our respective plans for the country – and people can vote on that,' he said.

Behind the scenes Fine Gael had concerns that it was not prepared for an election either, notwithstanding the fact that one might happen suddenly had been obvious for some time. More pertinently, some of its leading strategists calculated that things had gone so far that it had become impossible not to ratify the IMF/EU deal, no matter how bad it was, and that the budget had to be passed. Tactically, it would be better to allow the government to introduce the budget and for Fine Gael to decry it while allowing it to go through, before dealing with the consequences once in power.

The following day the two Green ministers walked into a cabinet meeting. Noel Dempsey took it upon himself to convey Fianna Fáil's anger. Once that was done, work continued in the way that then passed for normal. There was a four-year plan to announce, the budget had to be finalized, Fianna Fáil had to fight a by-election in Donegal South, and there was the little matter of finalizing negotiations with the IMF and the EU.

Fianna Fáil had a parliamentary-party meeting to get through first that Tuesday evening. Volatile backbench TD Noel O'Flynn from Cork North Central announced that there would be a 'bare-knuckle fight' with the Taoiseach. Former chief whip Tom Kitt denied rumours that he had been collecting the eighteen signatures that would be needed to formally put down a motion of no-confidence in Cowen. In the end the meeting was something of a damp squib. The fight had gone out of Fianna Fáil. Many of the TDs, including ministers, had decided not to contest the next election; those who would do so believed that their survival depended entirely on their own local efforts and that the identity of the leader of the party was almost irrelevant. What was the point of having a major fight when the outcome would make so little difference? Cowen was free to continue to canvass for the by-election and take updates on the progress of negotiations with the IMF and the EU.

One of the biggest points of debate during the negotiations was whether Ireland could force senior bondholders at the banks to accept only partial repayments of the money that was due to them – 'haircuts' as they had become known. Cutting these debts would be the fastest and most effective way to shrink the banks' balance sheets as demanded and could save the state at least some of the likely extra bill for recapitalizing the banks.

There was another good reason for doing this. Lenihan had maintained that it was impossible to burn the bondholders if Ireland was to return to the sovereign debt markets. The reliance on the IMF and the EU for government money for the next three years meant that was no longer an immediate concern. The hope of some was that we could burn the bondholders and that they would forgive if not forget by the time Ireland was back in the bond markets.

There were a variety of complications, however. One was that bonds issued since 30 September 2008 – worth about €24 billion – carried an explicit state-sponsored guarantee of full repayment. These bonds may have been issued by private banks but it was sovereign debt to all intents and purposes. Legally it would have been very difficult to avoid repayment.

Many of the bonds issued prior to that date had benefited from a state guarantee that had now expired. There was about €35 billion in such bank bonds still outstanding. The bondholders could have been given shares in the banks instead, forcing them to take ownership. They could then run or sell the banks themselves, albeit under the auspices of the European Central Bank, which would still have to provide liquidity.

The ECB had reasons of its own to avoid such an outcome. First many, though far from all, of the bondholders had already been repaid in full and the money had come from the ECB, which now had to be repaid instead; subsequently there were fewer bondholders to burn, and one big creditor in the form of the ECB itself. The ECB was not inclined to write off any part of the money owed to it.

More fundamentally, the ECB did not want to set a precedent. The UK bank Barclays Capital had estimated that Irish senior bank debt was 38 per cent of its GDP; what was highly significant about this was that the percentage was actually smaller than in Belgium, Spain, the UK and Holland. If the Irish banks were allowed to default, the contagion effect could result in banks in those countries refusing to repay their lenders in full. The French and German banks were among the biggest lenders to banks in those other countries, as well as in Ireland. The impact of an Irish default on them would be bad enough but add in banks from those other countries and it could have been catastrophic, especially when you consider that European banks had raised more than €560 billion in bondholder debt between them in the first eleven months of 2010. The bank bond markets had to be kept open, as far as the ECB was concerned. The government was being killed by public sentiment in Ireland – where popular opinion demanded the burning of the bondholders – for their failure to do something that the ECB and the European Commission had made impossible.

The issue had been complicated somewhat by alterations to the original guarantee scheme that had taken place in late 2009; these had gone unnoticed by a weary public, media and political opposition – by almost everyone except Labour's Joan Burton, who was one of the few to try to highlight what would be significant changes. The original guarantee was due to expire in September 2010, and the government was worried about the ability of the banks to raise finance after that date. With full approval from the ECB and the European Commission, it introduced the so-called 'Eligible Liabilities Guarantee' (ELG) scheme in December 2009, to help the six covered Irish financial institutions raise longer-term funding. This provided an unconditional and irrevocable state guarantee for what were described as 'certain eligible liabilities', which included all deposits (other than retail deposits of up to €100,000, which were guaranteed by a specific deposit-guarantee scheme that does not have an end date); senior unsecured certificates of deposit; senior unsecured commercial paper; and other senior unsecured bonds and notes. The ELG scheme came into existence on 9 December 2009 and is due to expire at midnight on 29 September 2015, subject to the EU Commission confirming, on a six-monthly basis, that the financial support provided by the guarantee scheme continues to be necessary and is compliant with state-aid rules.

Had the ECB been inclined to help, the extension of the guarantee could have provided opportunities for the reduction of our debt. Certain subordinated debt and asset covered securities, which had been guaranteed under the scheme that expired on 29 September 2010, were not covered by the new one. In order to qualify as an 'eligible liability', a bond had to have a maturity date of less than five years and had to have been incurred during an 'issuance window' in the period that commenced on 9 December 2009 and that had been extended to 30 June 2011. This meant that some senior bonds – previously regarded as untouchable – could have been burnt. There was about €16.4 billion in senior debt not covered by the ELG and not secured by collateral, about two thirds of it with AIB and Bank of Ireland.

The IMF was sympathetic to the idea, put forward by Department of Finance officials, that such bonds at the very least were vulnerable to burning. It believed there was only so far that Ireland could go in cutting its public budgets; it did not automatically advocate the burning of sovereign debt but saw merit in taking that approach with certain types of bank bonds. Unfortunately for Ireland the presence of the ECB did for that hope. Again, apparently encouraged by Geithner, who wanted to protect the banks, seemingly at all costs (although this is unlikely ever to be confirmed officially), the ECB dug in its heels.

Chopra expressed sympathy to Lenihan and his team over the issue. However, the IMF's own appraisal of the situation – not to mention the vehemence with which the idea of haircuts was dismissed by the ECB, the European Commission and various euro-member governments – left the finance minister in no doubt that this was an argument Ireland could not win, even with IMF support. In particular the ECB let it be known that its appetite for supplying cheap money to the Irish banks to replace fleeing deposits – an amount that now came to over €130 billion, or a quarter of the ECB's entire liquidity assistance to banks under its watch – would be at risk if Ireland did not do as it was told. Some thought this was an empty threat – no lender of last resort could walk away from its job and retain credibility – but nobody wanted to test that proposition.

Central Bank Governor Patrick Honohan subsequently confirmed that there had been 'no enthusiasm – I shall put it no more strongly than that' for the idea of making bondholders share the losses at the Irish banks. 'I think there is a certain amount of quid pro quo involved,' he said. 'There is a liberal attitude being demonstrated by the European Central Bank in regard to the funding of Irish banks, and it continues and will continue while confidence is being restored to underpin the Irish banking system . . . So there is a balance. We are working in a collaborative setting.'

The argument against burning the bondholders wasn't just made by the ECB or the governments of euro-member countries. The British got in on the act as well, and with good reason: British-owned banks had more than €120 billion tied up in Irish assets. Having somehow escaped meltdown from its own banking crisis, Britain did not want its banks taken down by an Irish collapse.

The British chancellor, George Osborne, said senior debt holders in Ireland's banks could not be forced to take losses if 'financial and economic stability' was to be safeguarded. 'That is exactly what did happen in late 2008 in some of the US bank rescues, with pretty disastrous effects. That is why the decision was taken. Subordinated bondholders will suffer losses and that is appropriate,' Osborne said, repeating the line that had been decided at the G20 meeting in Seoul earlier that month.

As a result Britain had to offer a loan to help its 'friend in need' out of 'its incredibly difficult situation'. 'It is in our national interest that we should be prepared to help them at this difficult time,' Osborne said. Because of the deep ties between Irish and British banks, the British government was 'in the room', Osborne said, discussing the terms and conditions, adding that he was 'certainly conscious' of Ireland's 'considerable assets' in the UK. Britain was struggling to stave off its own financial crisis – and was imposing severe cuts upon its population – but it was also Ireland's biggest creditor. And the British banking system wasn't the only thing heavily exposed to Ireland's crisis. Ireland is a bigger market for British export goods than the four BRIC nations (the major emerging economies of Brazil, Russia, India and China) put together. UK businesses had invested enormously in Ireland, retailers as well as exporters and banks.

Four years earlier Osborne, then just a Conservative MP, had written an opinion piece for *The Times* entitled 'Look and learn from across the Irish Sea'. 'The Irish Republic was seen as Britain's poor and troubled country cousin, a rural backwater on the edge of Europe,' he had written. But that had all changed – Ireland was 'a shining example' of long-term economic policy-making, and Osborne had gone to Dublin 'to listen and to learn'.

In spite of Osborne's glowing words, one of the criticisms that had been levelled at successive Irish governments was their failure to conceive long-term strategies. After months of preparation the 140-page four-year budgetary plan was finally presented to the media by Cowen at 2 p.m. on Wednesday, 24 November, a day before the Donegal South West by-election and the day after Standard & Poor's downgraded Ireland's credit status again, notwithstanding its knowledge of the deal being negotiated with the IMF and the EU.

The government's credibility, in tatters anyway, was in no way improved by its undue optimism as to the scale of economic growth required to deliver the plan. Taking €15 billion out of the economy over four years was going to depress consumption dramatically and therefore retard economic growth and the ability to raise taxes as required. The four-year plan said that the debt-to-GDP ratio – the key measure on how sustainable our debt position is – would peak at about 102 per cent in 2013 before declining gradually. This would require 20 cents in every euro of taxes collected in 2014 being used by the government to meet the annual interest on debts, compared to 11 per cent in 2011.

With those figures in mind, investors doubted that GDP would rise by 1.75 per cent in 2011 and by over 3 per cent in 2012 and 2013. Standard & Poor's said it expected no growth in our economy in 2011 or 2012. Slow or zero growth would result in lower than expected tax revenues, which would lead to higher borrowing or further reduced spending. The budget could therefore not be reduced by the planned €15 billion without inflicting enormous pain on the Irish people.

While the IMF and the EU were apparently ready to endorse the plan, the consensus among independent commentators was that it couldn't work. Although Ireland was no longer borrowing on sovereign markets, the rates on its existing ten-year loans continued to rise. Cowen's talk about certainty and hope and confidence in the future was ignored internationally, as was the support from Rehn in Brussels. The extra debt that Ireland was taking on was not regarded as sustainable and there was little to suggest that this time the banks would actually be sorted out properly.

There was also the issue of how much the loans would cost. Clever management by the NTMA over the years meant that the average cost of servicing our national debt repayments worked out at about 4.5 per cent. Some of the cheaper, old debt would have to be refinanced in the future, meaning that as it was paid down, newer, more expensive loans became a larger proportion of the total.

This made the issue of the rate to be charged for our new loans an essential one.

There was consternation when, near the end of the week of negotiations, RTÉ reported that the interest rate would be around 6.7 per cent, at the high end of expectations, and above the rate of 5.2 per cent secured by Greece for its €110 billion package.

Fine Gael's finance spokesman, Michael Noonan, described the suggestion as 'very disturbing' and Labour's Eamon Gilmore said, 'If true, it would be an appalling capitulation by the Irish government. And it would be a betrayal of the founding principles of the European Union.' Noonan also said: 'The government must take a hard line in its negotiations. Even though the government is in its last days in office, it must not abandon the national interest and settle on unaffordable terms in its negotiations,' adding that anything over 6 per cent would be 'unacceptable'.

Some people began to smell a rat when Lenihan gave an interview to the *Sunday Independent* in which he said he could not accept an interest rate that high and would get a lower one. Suspicions increased when Green minister Eamon Ryan said the 6.7 per cent estimate was incorrect and that it was unfortunate this figure had entered the public domain. Could it have been that Fianna Fáil was looking to pull one last stroke, by raising expectations of an utterly disastrous deal so as to benefit in some small way when things did not turn out to be quite as bad?

The pressure to do the deal at almost any price was mounting, however. Things were made even worse when Irish banks were curtailed in their ability to use the Irish sovereign debt that they owned as collateral to raise cash. This was blamed on an outfit called LCH Clearnet, which is used by banks and financial institutions in so-called repurchase transactions, where sovereign bonds are exchanged by them for cash.

LCH acts as an insurer: it allows banks to reduce the risk of a counterparty – such as the Irish State – failing to pay them. In other words, it shares the risk of a potential bond default by the Irish State. The price it charges for offering this insurance, and the security it demands, are therefore of paramount importance. LCH increased the charges, or margins, from 30 per cent to 45 per cent above normal requirements to trade Irish bonds in November. Without LCH Clearnet insurance attached, many institutions would simply refuse to accept Irish State bonds offered by the banks as collateral in exchange for cash. Ireland's banks were subsequently made even more dependent on the ECB, which was the opposite of what the previous Sunday's announcement was intended to achieve.

Meanwhile Mohamed El-Erian, chief investment officer of the powerful bond manager Pimco, added to the anxiety by describing Ireland's banks as 'bleeding deposits'. He said: 'What you advise your sister in Ireland now is that you'd say take your money out of an Irish bank and put it in another bank headquartered elsewhere.' The German parliament was told of the gravity of the situation by Schäuble. He said that if Germany did not play its part in bailing out Ireland, 'our common currency is at risk' and the 'economic and social consequences for our country will be incalculable'. Yes, but what about the outcome for Ireland?

11. Terms and Conditions

Terms and conditions for the surrender were announced one week after the 'application' to the IMF and the EU had been made. The public was treated to another live Sunday television event involving Brian Cowen at Government Buildings, this time after the details of the size of the loan and the interest rates had been announced in a prior event in Brussels. The 'package' was worth €85 billion and the average interest rate on the loans was 5.8 per cent – better than the speculation of recent days but still way higher than the average rate Ireland had been paying on its loans. What shocked possibly even more was the list of things that would have to be done by the state to get this money.

With Lenihan detained in Brussels, Cowen was accompanied to his press conference by Fianna Fáil ministers Mary Hanafin and Pat Carey, and by Eamon Ryan of the Green Party. There was a rare public appearance by Kevin Cardiff, the general secretary of the Department of Finance. Cowen tried his now familiar approach of accentuating the so-called positives and of refusing to accept the disaster that had occurred. He claimed that he had secured 'the best available deal for Ireland' and provided 'vital time and space' for the state to address its unprecedented economic problems and be put on the road to recovery. 'This agreement is necessary for our country and our people. It is in the best interests of Ireland and of the European economy on which our future prosperity depends,' he claimed.

What Cowen had to say got far less attention than the financial details in the agreement. While the deal amounted to €85 billion, €17.5 billion was coming from Ireland itself – €5 billion from its remaining cash reserves and €12.5 billion from the savings in the National Pension Reserve Fund. A loan of €22.5 billion was arriving from the International Monetary Fund and the same amount again from the European Commission. The temporary bailout fund of the

EFSF was pitching in €17.7 billion. Another €5 billion was coming from so-called bilateral loans from non-euro members of the EU: the UK (which was to provide €3.8 billion), Sweden and Denmark.

It was hoped that not all of the money would be needed, especially the €35 billion earmarked for the banks. Of that, €10 billion was for extra capital, a 'contingency' that would most likely be used to provide liquidity should the ECB pull back on its provision of loans to replace disappearing deposits. The remaining €50 billion was to fill the gap between the government's revenues and spending over the next three years, money that would have been borrowed anyway had the markets still been open to Ireland.

To get this money from these new sources the government had to make an enormous number of promises about what it would do with it and how it – and its successors – would reform the economy to ensure that this type of crisis would never happen again. The humiliating list implied that we had failed completely to enforce proper regulation across a range of sectors – not just the banks – and that major reform would be imposed upon us by people who knew better. The hubris of the Celtic Tiger years – when our authorities boasted that it was they who knew better – was exposed fully now.

The governments during the period of the deal would also be subjected to very regular and very detailed audits, and if they failed to meet the commitments of the agreement they would run the risk of the loans being withdrawn, with no other source of finance available to the state. The government, the NTMA and the Irish Central Bank had to provide the IMF and the EU with the following: details of all the government's expenditure and income on a weekly basis; its end-of-week cash position; a statement of the assets and liabilities of the Central Bank; and the balance sheets of the big banks. Each month they had to supply details on adherence to budget targets and on the prospect of meeting targets for the rest of the year. They had to come up with a whole range of information relating to the debts of the government and the banks. Each quarter they had to supply data on the public-sector pay bill, the number of employees and the average wage. They had to furnish data on debt falling due at state-guaranteed companies and local authorities over the following thirty-six months.

They also guaranteed to meet exacting deadlines on taking required actions. The banks were to be recapitalized and further transfers of bank loans to NAMA were to be completed by March 2011, although this was to become a major issue during the subsequent February general election campaign and, after it came to power, one of the new government's first major crises.

Legislation to increase the state pension age was to be enacted by May 2011, as was a cut in the minimum wage. To the delight of employers and the anger of trade unions, there was to be a review of registered employment deals covering pay rates and conditions for jobs in agriculture, catering, construction and electrical contracting that paid in excess of the minimum wage.

The introduction of unemployment-benefit reform was intended to 'incentivize early exit from unemployment'. This would involve 'improved job profiling and increased engagement', with more effective monitoring of jobseekers' activities through regular 'evidence-based reports'. There would be sanctions applied to 'beneficiaries not complying with job-search conditionality and recommendations for participation in labour market programmes'. In short, the government was being told to crack down on dole fraud and to show proof that those getting payments were actually seeking work, as happened in most other European countries. If they couldn't, they'd have their payments cut. To which some people asked why this hadn't always been the case and why the targeted savings of €2.8 billion in social-welfare payments over four years hadn't been achieved previously if they were genuinely achievable/attainable.

The cost of pensions was to be reduced as well, with a pay freeze for state pensioners until 2015, and public-sector pension payments to be reduced by an average of 4 per cent. Pensions for new state employees would be based on career-average earnings instead of on final salary and the retirement age for new entrants would be linked to the state-pension retirement age. The age at which people would qualify for the state pension was to be raised to sixty-six years in 2014; to sixty-seven in 2021; and to sixty-eight in 2028.

Measures to limit the cost of local government were to be brought in by August 2011, and reform of the legal, medical and pharmaceutical professions – to reduce prices to consumers – had to be achieved by the same month. The latter was a first for any country that had received IMF help and showed just how out of kilter with the international norm professional fees in Ireland had become.

Most importantly perhaps, if the Croke Park agreement on public-sector reform did not start to deliver savings by this deadline, there would have to be 'appropriate adjustments' to the public-sector wage bill.

In one of the most controversial decisions of its last year in office the government undertook not to cut public-service pay or to introduce compulsory redundancies before 2014, as long as it got cooperation for a lengthy series of reform and efficiency measures. However, this was a major challenge, with the government now having to save up to €400 million a year on public-service pay from 2011. As a result the government warned that it might have to break its promises and go after pay again – following earlier savage cuts on public-sector pay – if there weren't changes to work practices that saved money, as well as voluntary redundancies.

There were longer-term decisions required as well by the end of 2011, such as which state assets would be sold – with the European Commission showing particular interest in state-owned electricity and gas providers – and how water charges would be introduced at a later date. Property taxes had to be decided upon too. There was also to be legislation on dealing with personal debts and a reform of bankruptcy laws by March 2012. For some reason the European Commission insisted on an examination of the cap on the size of retail premises, to allow for the creation of gigantic out-of-town supermarkets, as if lower prices there would somehow compensate for the damage that would be done to smaller towns and property values by the inevitable move in trade.

The documents set out the targets for budget adjustments over the next three years, although the government continued to insist that the targets had been set by it alone. The December 2010 budget for 2011, due less than a fortnight after the deal, would have tax increases and spending cuts of €6 billion in total. There would be another €3.6 billion and €3.1 billion respectively in the following two budgets. Of that €15 billion in the four-year plan, a total of €6 billion in social-welfare and public-sector cuts, including pensions, would be required and another €4 billion in spending reductions. There would be €5 billion in what were called euphemistically 'revenue raising measures', another description for tax increases, through a combination of lowering of income-tax bands and credits, reducing pension reliefs and other tax breaks, increases in excise duties and the carbon tax, the introduction of a property tax called a site-valuation tax, and changes to capital-gains and acquisitions taxes.

Even though the government was sticking to its plan for the €15 billion over four years, the Europeans agreed with domestic critics that it would be impossible to get the budget deficit down to 3 per cent of GDP by 2014: the nature of the cuts would make the government's ambitions for economic growth – 1.7 per cent in 2011 and 3 per cent in 2012 – unachievable.

Rehn's new prediction was for the Irish economy to expand by 0.9 per cent in 2011 and by 1.9 per cent in 2012. (Rehn himself had said previously that the economy would grow by 3 per cent in 2011.) And he now set a new target of 2015 (two years later than the original target) for the reduction of borrowing to 3 per cent of GDP. The government, however, indicated that it was ready to implement further austerity measures beyond the €15 billion in the four-year plan, if it failed to meet the targets set down for it.

Ireland's corporation-tax rate was safeguarded, for the time being at least. 'How Ireland makes its tax decisions is to be respected as I would want German tax decisions to be respected,' said Schäuble. 'We don't want to communitarize everything; tax is not a community concern and will not be communitarized.'

He praised Ireland's austerity ambitions, but warned that he expected all future administrations in Dublin to honour the deal. 'Ireland has to create circumstances in which there isn't senseless waste of these loans, that's the way things are when a country cannot get out of a situation of its own accord,' he said. 'We are not forcing anything on the Irish . . . nor are we wasting money on those who have acted less sensibly. We are doing this because a successful European Union, politically and economically, is in the interest of Germany . . . and Ireland.'

The IMF's Chopra said, 'A very simple answer to the corporate-tax rate is that it is not a part of the programme.' But Chopra later said spending and tax issues would be included in its annual review of Ireland's compliance with its programme. He described the €85 billion bailout package as a 'very good deal for Ireland'.

'We've been involved in countries and devised programmes with countries on the eve of elections and the experience has overwhelmingly been that even after an election given the sense of common purpose, which is particularly striking in Ireland, that one can continue to proceed,' said Chopra in a newspaper interview. 'In terms of the specifics we leave this to the country authorities. We work with them in devising the overall strategy, we work with them in how they can make the strategy operational, there is always going to be a number of nitty gritty details and these will have to be left to the experts on the ground who know Ireland.

'We have discussed a particular route, there may be other routes of getting there, as long as they are efficient, as long as they are not going to be hurting the poor, we will certainly work with any government on those objectives.'

Not surprisingly opposition politicians attacked the government on the day of the plan's announcement and for many days afterwards.

'The government was cleaned out in the negotiations and has not acted in the best interests of Ireland. At the very least we could have expected a low rate of interest on the loans, EU agreement on a jobs-and-growth package, and agreement to share the cost of rescuing the banks with the bondholders. The government came away with none of these,' Michael Noonan said. 'I believe that the negotiators on the Irish side were soft. They have given up €17.5 billion of our own resources in sacrificing all of the National Pension Reserve Fund. The fund has been cleaned out.'

He said the decision to allow Ireland another additional year (until 2015, as against the original 2013 and then revised 2014) to meet the 3 per cent target gave the state no advantage. What the extension would entail, he said, was an extra year of austerity measures if the targets had not been met by 2014.

Sinn Féin Dáil Leader Caoimhghín Ó Caoláin also objected to the deal and said 'no party should feel bound by any deal struck by this government, which has no mandate or political authority' and which was 'seeking to strap the people' into a 'sell-out deal with the IMF and EU' that would 'dictate the shape of the fiscal affairs of the state' in the future.

Labour's Eamon Gilmore went into the Dáil and told Cowen that 'the Fianna Fáil government has shown no backbone, no negotiating ability and no authority . . . You have no shame after what you have done to this country to stand up here on the day that you come back with a lousy deal like that and claim that you have got a bargain.'

Gilmore complained that the government had entered into commitments that the Dáil had not approved. 'It amounts to a surrender of the country's economic freedom,' he said. In one of a number of comments that would later come back to haunt him, Gilmore said 'the Labour Party cannot be bound by what is contained in the document, not only for democratic reasons but because it won't work.'

His colleague Pat Rabbitte said the deal would 'pauperize' the country. 'Now we are going to bend the knee and do as we are told by our European masters,' he warned. The party's deputy leader, Joan Burton, also got stuck in: 'The negotiators on the Irish side had no negotiating power left. If they played poker they lost. The Pension Reserve Fund has been given up. That is an enormous sacrifice. We no longer have any room for manoeuvre. Developers and bankers here were crazy borrowers. But so were German and French banks which backed them with finance.' The deal 'buys time for the rest of Europe to get its banks in order, but it makes Irish taxpayers the sacrificial lambs for European financial stability', Burton said.

Fine Gael's Enda Kenny asked Cowen if he had the 'courage' and 'gumption' to put the package to a Dáil vote. This was important. The government was entering into an extraordinary deal that would bind its successors but without first having got the consent of the elected representatives of Dáil Éireann, let alone the consent of the people through a referendum, as some wanted. Attorney General Paul Gallagher gave a legal opinion that the deal did not represent an international agreement as set out under Article 29 of the constitution – on the basis that the article refers only to treaties lodged with the United Nations – and therefore did not require Dáil approval.

Meanwhile, the ECB's Trichet described the package as the best programme 'to preserve the medium- and long-term stability and prosperity of Ireland'. 'These times are obviously very difficult. They're coming after times that were very, very good and affluent of course, and now adjustment has to operate,' he said. 'I am confident that the Irish people realize that it is extremely important to be for the long run competitive and to prove what they have always proved in the past – namely that they are able to cope with difficult periods.'

One of the more important aspects of the deal, given all that Ireland was surrendering, was that the ECB would continue to provide short-term funding at 1 per cent to the Irish banking system. The implied threat to abandon its role as lender of last resort to the Irish banking system was being explicitly removed. Trichet also said the ECB would continue to buy government bonds to ease the borrowing costs of member states and would postpone its exit from emergency liquidity measures to help ease the ongoing volatility in the bond markets.

Despite all that was becoming known about how Ireland had been bounced into this bind, Trichet insisted that it was the government's decision to request the aid package. 'The government of Ireland in my opinion took the decision that was really necessary, absolutely necessary to redress the situation with the help of the international community and with the help of the Europeans.'

But others were not prepared to be disingenuous, especially one man who had been called exactly that just a fortnight earlier. Minister for Justice Dermot Ahern decided that he would announce his retirement from politics at the forthcoming general election. Mindful of the embarrassment to him caused by his interview with Sean O'Rourke on RTÉ's *Week in Politics* just two weeks before, he went on O'Rourke's RTÉ Radio 1's *News at One*. He let fly at the 'quite incredible pressure' that had been put on Ireland. 'There were people from outside this country who were trying to bounce us, as a sovereign state, into making an application – throwing in the towel – before we had even considered it as a government,' he said.

'I've been going to EU meetings for thirteen and a half years as a minister and you hear a lot of discussion about solidarity. I accept that the European partners were giving us solidarity, but I strongly believe that Ireland should look for this type of solidarity from people and we shouldn't be cast to the wolves.' He said 'time and time again there is considerable pressure on us as a country to give up on the 12.5 per cent corporation tax.'

Most pertinently, he said that if officials were discussing bailout deals ahead of a meeting of European finance ministers, 'they had no authority to talk about bailouts because the government hadn't discussed it and the government hadn't authorized it.' He said the cabinet only formally gave Lenihan authorization to go to Brussels to discuss the issue of an application on the morning of the eurozone finance ministers meeting – after Ahern's two interview disasters. 'It was a difficult thing to be accused of being deceitful. My conscience is clear. I gave the factual position – there had been no discussions and I was not aware of any discussions,' Ahern said.

Lenihan kept quiet at that stage, talking privately afterwards to journalists and slowly unburdening himself of what had happened. But in April 2011, not long before his death and free of the responsibilities of being minister for finance, he decided to talk publicly, for a BBC radio documentary. While those now in government accused him of trying to rewrite history to suit himself, some of what he said seemed to make sense, and highlighted how the public was given only half-truths the previous November.

Lenihan shared Ahern's concern that members of the seventeen-strong governing board of the ECB – whom he did not name – had damaged Ireland by briefing against it. 'On the betrayal issue, I did feel that some bank governors should not be speaking out of turn and that only the president should speak for the bank,' he said. 'While I found Mr Trichet very helpful throughout the crisis, I have to say I could not say that of all of his colleagues. Some of them were inclined to brief newspapers in their own member states, giving them an assessment of the Irish position, which I viewed as damaging.'

Lenihan went on to admit in that interview that in many respects the deal he championed was a bad one. The interest rate on the loans was too high, the scale of the budget cuts required too deep – he had not wanted to go beyond €4.5 billion in his December budget but

was forced to add another €1.5 billion – and the amount of fresh capital that the ECB wanted put into the banks excessive. But we heard
none of that at the time the deal was being done. Held captive by the
need to borrow money, and intimidated by the need to do what Europe wanted to protect the euro, our government told us that our
surrender was anything but.

12.   Saving Face

In the days that followed Sunday, 28 November, Cowen, Lenihan and other members of Fianna Fáil tried to argue that the deal they had signed on Ireland's behalf was not as bad as critics suggested, that it gave Ireland money it would not otherwise have had to pay important bills, and that it did not equate to a surrender of sovereignty.

They seemed to have convinced themselves, even if it was almost impossible for them to convince others. Few had any sympathy for them, but Cowen and Lenihan had been through a great deal, and felt that they had taken brave decisions – which meant that their sense of self-worth was now dependent upon convincing themselves that they had done the right thing by their country and by their party at all times, even if they were ruined politically. If they didn't believe this, how else could they live with themselves? They felt that they had been bounced unfairly into the deal but were not in a position to claim or admit this publicly at the time.

They had legacy issues too to contend with: Cowen had come into office hopeful of emulating his hero, Sean Lemass, and, although he never said so publicly, many felt Lenihan had wanted to take the prize of leader that had been denied his own father by the presence of Charles Haughey. Now political misfortune was going to tarnish whatever legacy Lenihan had hoped to establish and his own ill-health would limit his opportunities to recover it over time.

They had to save face as much for immediate political reasons as for personal ones: a budget had to be introduced on 7 December and then passed. Otherwise, the IMF/EU/ECB deal, which they continued to insist was essential even if they knew it was not a good one, would be lost and their humiliation complete. A defeated budget would have meant a general election either just before or just after Christmas; and Fianna Fáil knew that to fight it in these circumstances would have been impossible. The party felt it needed the passage of time to mitigate the certain heavy political losses.

When Cowen made his first appearance in the Dáil after the confirmation of the deal, he said he had 'taken every step possible in the national interest to try and bring this country forward again'. Cowen's credibility was so badly damaged that few believed him when he claimed that instead of crippling the country the IMF/EU/ECB deal would put it on the road to recovery. He said that at its worst the burden of debt the country would suffer would be 102 per cent of GDP, roughly where it was in 1992/3 when Ireland was on the cusp of the Celtic Tiger period. He also reiterated that the debt burden in 1985 was even higher. But he left out two major crises that did not apply back then: Ireland did not have a banking crisis to be paid for out of state funds; and the level of private indebtedness, particularly mortgage loans for almost an entire generation, was paltry then compared to now. In addition, many estimated that the debt burden would be much higher than he predicted.

Cowen was on somewhat stronger ground in asking the opposition for plausible alternatives. 'If Deputy Kenny's view is that this deal should not be taken up, I ask him where he expects this state to get funding,' Cowen said. Indeed, Kenny clearly irritated Cowen: the Taoiseach was greatly annoyed that the Fine Gael was scoring what he saw as cheap populist shots, especially as he reckoned Kenny would have done little differently had he been in power and would do much the same once in office. Cowen accused Kenny of retreating 'into flights of rhetoric' any time a serious matter was discussed in the house. 'What we do need in this country perhaps is to rise above partisan politics now and again,' the Taoiseach said. 'Far from referring to Ireland as either banjaxed or an economic corpse, we need to recognize there are people going to work ... and we need to be supportive of what they are trying to do.'

Cowen was supported loyally as ever by his Tánaiste, Mary Coughlan, who asked Kenny to explain how he would get access to the €400 million that had to be borrowed each week to 'keep this country going'. She asked how the Labour Party would access funds for key public services, the social-welfare system and the health system if it 'does not agree to the measures being taken by the government'. Cowen's closest political friend, Minister for Enterprise Batt O'Keeffe, claimed that public servants and social-welfare recipients would have had to endure a 38 per cent cut in income had the government not agreed a deal. He also said the government had played hardball by delaying agreement to the deal, refusing at first to do as the ECB had wanted and, as a result, using the time to engage in 'pre-negotiations' that had resulted in the four-year plan. An angry public was not buying any of it.

The most eloquent defence of the package came from Lenihan in a Dáil debate just days after it had been announced. Lenihan went on the offensive, particularly in dismissing claims that the deal should not have been entered into without a vote in Dáil Éireann. 'I am advised by the attorney general that the programme, and these supporting documents, do not represent international agreements and do not require the approval of the Dáil,' he emphasized.

Lenihan blamed 'the sometimes hysterical and contradictory reaction to the external assistance programme' and argued that without it 'our ability to fund the payments to social-welfare recipients, the salaries of our nurses, our doctors, our teachers, our gardaí, would have been extraordinarily limited and highly uncertain.

'There has been the usual barrage of criticism of the outcome accompanied by the personal abuse of those involved that has become common place in our debased public discourse. But none of the critics explains how we could have secured the funds we require at less cost to the state.'

He attempted to minimize the cost of the deal to the state, saying that €50 billion was money that the government would have had to borrow in any event. Trying to turn disaster into triumph, he said the government had accessed these funds 'at a much lower rate than currently available to us in the market'. He said the state was in the 'happy position' of being able to contribute €17.5 billion towards the €85 billion from its own resources, provoking incredulity by his choice of phrase. He said it was right to raid the National Pension Reserve Fund. 'Why would we borrow expensively to invest in our banks when we have money in a cash deposit earning a low rate of interest? And how on earth can we ask taxpayers in other countries to contribute to a financial-support package while we hold a sovereign-wealth fund?' he asked.

He claimed that Ireland was not 'a delinquent state that has lost fiscal control. We enter it as a country that is funded until the middle of next year; as a state whose citizens have shown remarkable resilience and flexibility over the last two years in facing head on an economic and financial crisis the severity of which has few modern parallels.'

He also claimed that his and the government's performance of the previous two years was judged as a success by the very institutions that had now forced Ireland to accept the deal. 'The team with whom we have negotiated has acknowledged our success in stabilizing our public finances and they have endorsed our banking strategy. They have also accepted our four-year Plan for National Recovery and have built their prescribed programme around that plan,' he said.

To cackles from the opposition benches, Lenihan repeated the claim he had made many times now, with less and less credibility. 'Our economy is showing signs of recovery,' he insisted. He cited growth in exports, but ignored the desperate state of the domestic economy. He boasted of improvements in competitiveness and claimed that conditions in the labour market were also beginning to stabilize, although unemployment was at its highest rate in nearly twenty years and emigration had returned. Choosing, again, to disregard the concerns of independent economists, and even the EU and the IMF, he declared: 'The outlook for next year is much improved. As forecast in the plan, growth is expected to be around 1.75 per cent next year again driven by a remarkably robust export performance.'

He did not concede that he had engaged in a failed banking-rescue strategy and made the highly debatable claim that it was 'surely appropriate that our cash reserves should be deployed to help solve that problem'. In explaining that Ireland required external assistance 'because the problems in our banking system simply became too big for this state to handle on its own', he provided no clues as to how and why that had happened or why responsibility for private debts should have been taken on by the public. 'Our public finance problems are serious but we were well on the way to solving them. The combination of the two sets of difficulties in circumstances where the entire eurozone was under pressure was beyond our capacity,' he said.

'We have been through a traumatic two years. Of course, we would have preferred to avoid resort to external assistance. But we can emerge from it a stronger and fitter economy. The attributes that brought us the boom – the quality of our workers, our entrepreneurship, our pro-business environment – all of these remain intact. During the boom we built a top-class transport infrastructure, sport and cultural facilities and educational sector. Over the last two years, we have won back much of the competitiveness we lost during the boom.'

He finished his speech by telling his audience that 'we have every reason to be confident about the future of this economy.'

The opposition doubted this very much. When Labour's Pat Rabbitte wanted to know what freedom the next government would have to change the agreement, given the very specific parameters that had been set, Lenihan said it would have as much freedom as he'd had since his appointment as minister in May 2008. The implication was clear: not very much at all.

'It is important to remember that when you are borrowing, and borrowing at unsustainable levels, you have to take certain decisions in the public interest . . . decisions which might not be popular in the political sense but are essential for the long-term interests of the country . . . I do not believe the practical options open to this country in the next four years would have been any different were funding to be available to us in the markets than were we to adopt the programme,' he replied.

Lenihan had to move on then to the introduction of a budget on 7 December that would satisfy the IMF and the EU but would also secure a majority in Dáil Éireann. He had to be careful not to alienate Fianna Fáil TDs – some of whom might have been tempted to 'make a stand' against controversial decisions in the hope that it would help them with local voters at the general election – and independents such as Jackie Healy-Rae and Michael Lowry, upon whose votes the government depended for a majority.

To cut his borrowing requirement by €6 billion Lenihan decided to attack social-welfare payments, implement departmental spending cuts, reduce public-sector pensions and widen the tax net. 'The scale of this adjustment is demanding, but it demonstrates the seriousness of our intent,' he said.

Lenihan started the effort to reduce social-welfare payments by reducing working-age social-welfare rates by approximately 4 per cent from 1 January 2011, cutting the basic dole payment by €8 a week to €188 to save just under €400 million. Old-age pensioners were spared any reduction at this time, but €8 a week was removed from welfare payments to the blind, the disabled, widows and carers under the age of sixty-five, saving just €96 million from the state's annual budget but causing enormous distress. It was intended that for the 2011 tax year the cuts would provide the government with savings of €873 million and, given that some of the cuts would not be introduced immediately but later in 2011, the full-year savings would be €920 million in future years. However, many of the intended savings were not disclosed. 'Every government of whatever colour will have to ensure that social welfare is kept under strict control because it is now €20 billion of our total expenditure. That is not sustainable for this country,' he said.

People at work were also expected to contribute a lot more. The 1.8 million still in work saw their take-home pay cut further with even more tax increases. In his budget speech, just three years after Cowen's last effort, Lenihan said the income-tax system was 'not fit for purpose' and that he had to 'widen the tax net'. Cowen's emphasis in his last budget had been on taking and keeping people out of the income-tax net, a process that was now being reversed at speed. All had changed utterly and how.

The government sought to take an additional €945 million in income taxes for 2011, rising to €1.25 billion by 2012 (before additional increases were levied). Although the headline income-tax rates remained unchanged, there was a reduction of 10 per cent in the tax credits and bands, meaning that more people would pay at the top rate of 41 per cent. In addition, there was the new tax, the Universal Social Charge (USC), introduced to replace the 'temporary' income levies of previous years, amounting to up to 7 per cent of gross income. The USC was to apply to all but the first €4,000 of pay, and wage earners would now pay tax on all income over €16,500. The ceiling beyond which people stopped paying PRSI was removed. Employees would now also have to pay PRSI and the USC on pension contributions, while their employers would have to pay 50 per cent PRSI on their contributions to employees.

Economists worried about what all of this extra tax would do to consumer spending and economic activity, as those on the standard rate of tax would effectively be paying tax of up to 31 per cent, when changes in PRSI and the USC were added to the standard 20 per cent. By the same calculations, those on the top rate of 41 per cent might actually be liable for tax of up to 52 per cent when the USC and the increase in PRSI were included.

After tax increases and current spending cuts, Lenihan still had to find more to make up the €6 billion demanded by the IMF and the EU. Infrastructure spending was slashed by €1.8 billion, to just €4.7 billion, half of the peak amount reached in 2008. It meant that another of Cowen's promises from his last budget speech had been dismantled: 'In the past governments have reacted to economic slow-down by stalling capital investment. I will not do so.'

Enda Kenny described it as 'a budget of booby traps and landmines that will go off' in the homes of thousands of low- and middle-income families over the following twelve months. His finance spokesman was scathing too. 'This budget is the budget of a puppet government who are doing what they have been told to do by the IMF, the EU Commission and the European Central Bank,' Michael Noonan said.

'No, this is the budget of the Irish government approved by the Irish parliament . . . which is the sovereign parliament of the Republic of Ireland,' said the spokesman for the economics commissioner, Olli Rehn, when asked by *The Irish Times* about Noonan's remarks. 'It is a tough budget, no doubt about that. It is an ambitious and indispensable consolidation budget but it is tough and of course the commission acknowledges the social impact of some of the measures contained in this budget, no doubt.' The IMF also weighed in: 'This is a clear sign of Ireland's strong commitment to tackle its problems and harness the impressive growth potential of this open and dynamic economy.'

Lenihan's efforts to explain and defend his budget in a round of media interviews got very much caught up in continued explanations as to why he had not forced senior bondholders in the banks to accept the repayment of a fraction of their money instead of getting it all in full from the state.

In the Dáil and on radio, Lenihan took issue with those who offered default on those debts as an option. 'The idea which is now commonplace, that somehow there are no costs associated with default, is entirely incorrect,' he said, ignoring the fact that many proponents of default had not said it would be painless, but merely the lesser of two evils. Indeed, he had conceded previously that he'd sought default on senior bank debt himself, except he used the euphemism 'burden-sharing'. However, he had been stopped by the ECB from implementing this, on the basis that no European bank had dishonoured senior bondholders throughout the crisis nor would one be allowed to do so.

He chose to criticize those who had advocated debt write-off by saying that the airing of their opinions had somehow contributed to the economic crisis. 'In recent years there has been much commentary about the need for senior bondholders to accept their share of the burden of this crisis. I have to say that there has been far too much discussion . . . When those who deplore the gradual erosion of the deposit base of the Irish banking system come to reflect on it, they will see the substantial contribution that was made to that by the amount of domestic noise generated in this area.'

'People should not be surprised that there's a huge erosion of trust in the Irish banking system when we've an endless debate on whether we should be defaulting on the payment of our obligations,' Lenihan said on another occasion. 'A small country like Ireland cannot default without the support of a central bank because you have to have the bank loaded with cash while you're engaged in such a default and it's not feasible for us to do this. We really need to face up to this because we've allowed public discussion to become dominated by it and it has done huge damage to the country,' he added.

Now that the budget was out of the way, without the violent reaction that many within the government had feared, some observers felt that Lenihan was angling to replace Cowen as leader. Certainly he went out of his way to dispel suggestions that his ill-health was inhibiting his performance. 'I have had very, very busy times since late August and I have been working all the time. I have been in this department a lot. Certainly I have been working seven-day weeks for some time, working continuously, liaising with officials, international authorities and my colleagues in government,' he said. The chance he wanted would soon arise but not in a manner or at a time that suited him.

13. A Long-awaited Heave

The move against Cowen's leadership of Fianna Fáil finally came in early January 2011, but it was by accident and, bizarrely, was prompted by revelation of a game of golf he'd played in July 2008 with the then-chairman of Anglo Irish Bank, Sean FitzPatrick. Cowen survived the initial challenge to his leadership but fell almost immediately afterwards, as, in the adrenalin flush of victory, he blundered badly and was left with no option but to resign.

Cowen seemed to fight to retain leadership of his party almost harder than he fought about anything else. There had been plenty of speculation about a possible challenge to his leadership immediately after the budget, enough to rouse him to a series of broadcast interviews in which he pleaded his case and to a performance in front of the parliamentary party that, according to some members, was his best since he became party leader.

In that speech to Fianna Fáil members he denied that he was worried about a possible challenge from Lenihan and condemned those who'd put that word about. He might have looked close to home for that: many people believed the speculation about Lenihan's intentions was being floated deliberately by some of Cowen's handlers, without Cowen's knowledge, to flush Lenihan out. Lenihan himself was tempted by the idea of leading a rebellion but was not giving dissidents nearly as much encouragement as they wanted. Indeed, as time passed, he may have been damaged by the actions of some of those perceived as close to him.

His aunt Mary O'Rourke, the former minister and deputy party leader, called for the leadership to be discussed at a parliamentary party meeting in early January, which was interpreted as an effort to clear the way for her nephew. But she went a step too far, in the view of many, when she wondered aloud during a radio interview if Cowen's wife, Mary, might be able to persuade her husband to step down. And Lenihan's brother Conor may have done his sibling few favours either: in a column in the *Evening Herald* he wrote: 'The poll ratings putting [Fianna Fáil] at below 20 per cent and the party leader Brian Cowen on 8 per cent make for sober reading, as will the budget and its impact on public opinion.' That may have been accurate and temperate, but coming from a junior minister, whose brother was regarded as the main contender, it was an incendiary intervention. O'Rourke effectively withdrew her challenge to Cowen when he emphasized that he was staying. 'We have a party that is going to fight this election under my leadership,' said Cowen, who denied Lenihan was one of those plotting behind his back. 'I welcome Brian Cowen's statement,' O'Rourke said. 'It was quite straightforward. [He is saying] "Listen, guys, I'm here, I'm bringing you all into the next election, so buckle down."'

Cowen delivered his commitment to stay during an interview on RTÉ Radio 1's *News at One* programme. He also apologized to the Irish people, but the problem was his expression of regret seemed to be as much for the position in which he found himself as for the failure of his actions.

'I am extremely sorry that we are in this situation. Everyone in this country is, and I take responsibility – as Taoiseach day and night, as leader of the government, I've been seeking to deal with it . . . I have said it from day one that I am sorry we are in this situation, but it is my job, and it is the job of all of us, to move on and get this country moving back to where we have to get it,' Cowen said, before claiming that the government had acted on the 'best possible advice available to it' during the financial crisis.

'I'm proud of the fact that during the good times we were able to make many social gains as well as economic advances . . . and it does nothing for the confidence of this country to suggest that after the economic tsunami which hit us in 2008, everything has gone out with the sea . . . I believe we can manage this to the extent where we can maintain many of those gains and in future regain some of those lost.'

Cowen continued with this approach in the Dáil, where he also justified the state's borrowing to provide social-welfare support. 'The levels of income support provided by the Irish State to those on welfare are still among the highest in Europe and we're all proud of that. And people who live in Border counties know what the social-welfare budgets and payments are across the Border.' He added: 'Many people used to look in the past down to the Republic and suggest patronizingly that we weren't capable of looking after our own people.' The argument, however, was that we had to borrow money on outrageous terms to do so now.

While Cowen's regained initiative impressed his party colleagues – most of whom retained some affection for him on a personal basis – it seemingly did nothing for the electorate, at least as far as opinion polls were concerned. The amount of baggage he was carrying meant that he was always on the defensive during interviews, and that his strategy of going on the offensive by attempting to point out the differences between Fine Gael's and Labour's approaches simply got no traction. Yet some TDs clung to the idea that Cowen would come good during a sustained election campaign, just as he had in the very different days of 2007, and minimize party losses.

Many of the Fianna Fáil parliamentary party were disabused of this hope by the reaction they received in their constituencies over Christmas and the New Year. The previously unimaginable was becoming a distinct possibility. The opinion poll findings were getting worse and worse, culminating in a 14 per cent showing for Fianna Fáil just days before Christmas. This compared to a near 42 per cent share of first-preference votes in the 2007 general election. However, even though they were becoming increasingly nervous about the prospect of Cowen leading them into an election, they still would not act.

The possible obliteration of Fianna Fáil at the forthcoming general election – and not just its end as the dominant force in Irish politics – loomed more and more clearly into view. Many of the TDs, including ministers, simply had given up and had little interest in a change of leadership, believing it would make little or no difference. Others, serving TDs and new candidates alike, were preparing campaigns in which they planned to run effectively as independents, with minimal reference to their Fianna Fáil credentials. They intended to trade almost exclusively on local personal loyalties rather than on national interests. What difference would a change in party leader make to that?

On 9 January, the *Sunday Times* carried details from a new book to be published the following day. *The FitzPatrick Tapes* was a remarkable piece of work by that newspaper's business journalists, Tom Lyons and Brian Carey. It was based on a series of exclusive interviews conducted with the disgraced former chairman of Anglo Irish Bank, Sean FitzPatrick, but was balanced by exhaustive interviews with other key players in the whole Anglo debacle. FitzPatrick may have cooperated and put across his side of the story, but it still did not read well for him.

It read worse for Cowen and his government. Amid the complexities of financial mismanagement, one easily understood fact stood out. In July 2008, a little more than two months before Cowen apparently declared 'I'm not fucking nationalizing Anglo' and opted instead for the ruinous bank guarantee, he had played a round of golf with FitzPatrick at Druids Glen. The two men, and Cowen's close friend, a former director of Anglo, Fintan Drury, had later been joined for dinner by Alan Gray, a director of the Central Bank, and another Anglo director, Gary McGann. (Details of the dinner were disclosed subsequently in the Dáil, almost by accident, because Sinn Féin's Caoimhghín Ó Caoláin happened to be at a wedding in the hotel that day and remembered seeing Cowen at dinner with other men whom he didn't know.)

Cowen insisted that he had never discussed Anglo's financial position, either on the golf course or at dinner afterwards. It was during his holidays. He was damned either way. If he had engaged in such discussions and admitted to them, he was open to the allegation that his subsequent actions were an attempt to look after his pals. If he maintained his insistence that nothing had happened, he appeared negligent, given what he had known about Anglo previously.

What the book confirmed was Cowen's role, from March 2008, in trying to help Anglo deal with the crisis of Sean Quinn's proxy 28 per cent shareholding in Anglo, held by way of those ruinous CFDs, a form of stock-market gambling that allowed him to profit or lose on the movement of shares without actually physically possessing them or having ownership publicly declared. It linked Cowen to the extraordinary sequence of events that followed the share-price collapse on Saint Patrick's Day. There had been an undercover attempt to place a chunk of the Quinn shares, representing 10 per cent of Anglo, with a group of select investors – who were effectively given the money by Anglo to engage in a covert share-support scheme. It had the appearance of being highly dubious legally, even if state agencies appeared to be giving it tacit support. Cowen was in Singapore at the time; he took a phone call from FitzPatrick about the problems Anglo was facing then.

Did Cowen authorize those in positions of regulation or authority to use the green jersey to justify their actions in the so-called 'national interest', or did he deliberately turn a blind eye to allow them to get on with sorting things out? That, and his subsequent attendance at a special Anglo dinner in his honour in April, to mark his promotion to Taoiseach, opened up Cowen's own personal Pandora's Box. He should have been all over those present at the dinner, wanting to know what was happening at Anglo in relation to its shareholding. He said he wasn't. If he wasn't, it was because he was too lazy, or uninterested (which, given his past record, was very possible, unfortunately), or too worried about the consequences of knowing about the sharp practice that was involved.

This meant that it was actually possible that Cowen was telling the truth when he said he did not ask anything of FitzPatrick or other Anglo directors during the July golf outing and subsequent dinner; again, he didn't want to know. Yet he remained so enamoured of these people, despite the already accumulating evidence of their recklessness and their loss of favour in the stock-market, that he was asking them for advice on the general economy (which is what he said was the topic for discussion). It was another massive blow to his credibility.

It also lent credence to conspiracy theories. This closeness to Anglo – which was not replicated at other banks – might explain why nobody from that bank had needed to directly influence Cowen in its favour on the night of the infamous bank guarantee in September 2008. His reported explosion as to the future ownership of Anglo – that he would not nationalize it under any circumstances – could be explained as much by a subliminal desire not to do something that would wipe out the wealth of his Fianna Fáil friends as shareholders or bond-holders as by a reluctance to cause enormous collateral damage to the overall economy.

Cowen was the type of guy who must have gone to his political grave wondering how a round of golf, and dinner afterwards, could have proven almost fatally toxic to his career and reputation. But he didn't seem to have the imagination or the wit to understand context; nor, it appears, did the tribal members of his dwindling band of supporters, who spent the week after the book's publication trying to paint him as a victim of misrepresentation and misunderstanding, angrily trying to make the debate an issue about people wrongfully trying to impugn Cowen's truthfulness.

Micheál Martin started his move against Cowen's leadership the day of the book's publication – the Monday after the *Sunday Times* story – by going for a private meeting with his party leader. Martin broached the issue carefully. After they spoke about the forthcoming election and organizational issues, Martin raised the possibility of Cowen stepping down as party leader but remaining, until the election, as Taoiseach. The idea was that this would allow a new leader time to try to revitalize the party while Cowen continued to perform the normal duties of Taoiseach, including getting the Finance Act passed.

Cowen was against the idea for a number of reasons. The obvious one was that, despite everything, he wanted to lead the party into the next election. Nor did he think it would be possible for him to act as caretaker while Fianna Fáil got itself a new leader: an immediate election would be required. The meeting was cordial, despite the difficult topic being discussed, and the two men reached an agreement: Martin would keep quiet for the remainder of the week and await developments.

There was a significant twist to come that Wednesday. The Dáil returned from the Christmas break much earlier than was usual, but this meant that Cowen had to face questions about the revelations in the book. The Taoiseach's performance was typical of him when on the defensive, as he shouted down legitimate questions. But then, at the death, he was bounced, almost accidentally, into revealing the identity of those other dinner guests at Druids Glen.

It was the tipping point for many Fianna Fáil TDs, and rumours abounded that a motion of no-confidence would be put. Martin used the Sunday newspapers on 14 January to float the idea that he was ready to mount a challenge. Cowen reacted immediately by declaring that he was going to call a vote of confidence in himself and that it was to be held the Tuesday evening, giving his opponents little time to organize themselves, though they should of course have been ready for months. Martin reacted quickly, saying within hours that he would be voting against his leader; but notably, when he held an evening press conference to state this, he stood on his own, with no colleagues. In what appeared at the time to be a tactical blunder, he did not resign his position, something that was brought up regularly in the radio interviews he conducted over the following thirty-six hours as he sought to canvass support.

Cowen was reinvigorated by the challenge, going on his own round of broadcast interviews. Again, it was notable that Cowen became animated when he was confronted by a political challenge to himself, rather than by an economic crisis to the state. One thing that could be said by the media in Cowen's favour, however, was that he wasn't afraid to be interviewed by those who had written or said critical things about him; he did not appear to hold grudges and he did not doubt his ability to be able to confront his critics. I had written about his political performance in trenchant terms in the *Sunday Times* and *Irish Examiner*, but he realized that it was never personal and he was up for defending his record when he came to *The Last Word* studios at Today FM.

It was the fourth major on-air interview I had conducted with him during his time as Taoiseach. He was in good humour, influenced no doubt by the fact that the contest seemed to be going his way. The main point that emerged from the interview, and which was picked up by many others afterwards, was his boast that he had not relied upon advisers to tell him how he should deport himself in public. He scoffed at the very notion, clearly regarding this as a badge of honour. He felt that this helped to mark him out as a politician of some substance, not one obsessed with style, someone who could think and act for himself without asking others what he should be saying, someone who could make what he knew to be the right decisions without worrying what anybody might think of them.

This twentieth-century approach to dealing with twenty-first-century-media demands appears to have been one of his most serious mistakes. Communication had become an essential part of the job, particularly given the wide spectrum of existing media, compared to what was available to politicians of previous generations; and it cannot be done occasionally or only at a time of extreme crisis. The fact that some of his distant predecessors 'got on with the job', as he saw it, without having to bother regularly with explaining themselves or convincing others, didn't excuse his attitude. A leader can't be too busy to explain, especially if he wants people to accept and support actions that have a very negative impact on their lives, at times of great trouble.

Cowen's style of language continually let him down. He failed to offer his message in a jargon-free, empathetic fashion. Indeed, Cowen preferred to rely on the emphatic rather than the empathetic: in efforts to be strong and convincing in his arguments, he simply seemed to be shouting, be it at interviewees or at the opposition in the Dáil. When he was calm, his almost robotic use of technocratic language emphasized the notion, rightly or wrongly, that he didn't care too much what people thought; he was just getting his speaking duties out of the way. Too often Cowen seemed to feel sorry for himself as he trotted out nonsense about the courage of taking tough decisions, trying to dupe people who knew instinctively, as well as intellectually, that many of the government's solutions to the economic crisis were plain wrong and that, to make it worse, it had tried to deny the extent of its own responsibility for the mess.

With all of these weaknesses very much evident, many people wondered how Fianna Fáil's best communicator would respond. Despite being minister for finance at the most difficult time in the history of the republic, Lenihan was still held in affection by much of the public. He had shown great bravery in committing himself so diligently to the job, in spite of his need for debilitating treatment for cancer. Surprisingly, nobody was demanding publication of his medical records to give assurance that he would be able to take on the leadership of Fianna Fáil on a long-term basis, although if they had they would have learnt just how serious his prognosis was.

But now he made a tactical misjudgement and alienated many of his supporters.

On the day of the vote of confidence he gave what was a blundering interview to Sean O'Rourke on the *News at One* on RTÉ Radio. He said Cowen was 'the best person to lead us into the next election', but tried to have it both ways by referring to what he called the Taoiseach's 'lapses of judgment', such as his drinking at Galway and his game of golf with Sean FitzPatrick. More significantly, he also claimed to have rejected approaches from backbench TDs who were interested in his taking over as leader. 'I made it clear at all stages that I was very flattered at their interest in me being leader of the party . . . but made it clear that current financial matters made it impossible for me to disrupt the good working relationship,' he said.

Some of those TDs were shocked and went public to say so. 'He did encourage dissent, he did encourage us to look at the numbers, he did express an interest in the leadership, and that is what is shocking about what he has revealed today, because that is not what he had to say to us,' John McGuinness said. 'In all of our discussions, we were led to believe that Lenihan would have been a candidate, that he was interested, and that he was seeking support from the backbenches.'

Kildare South TD Sean Power said he was 'surprised and shocked' that Lenihan was backing the Taoiseach. 'I along with colleagues have spoken with Brian over a long period of time and the concerns we expressed were very much shared by him,' he said. When I conducted a live radio interview that afternoon with Michael Kennedy, the Dublin North TD, he said: 'Any discussion I've had with Brian Lenihan, he has shared my own view that our poll ratings were very disappointing. I never asked directly "Will you challenge Brian Cowen?" but I would certainly have been of the view that Brian Lenihan would like to be the leader of Fianna Fáil.'

Cowen's victory was assured, although many agreed with Power when he said he did not believe Cowen 'could do in eight weeks what he couldn't do in two years'. While the result of the vote was secret, it was widely speculated that Cowen had a two-to-one winning margin, remarkable in the circumstances. Martin quit his position as minister, saying that he had agreed this course of action with Cowen in advance of launching his challenge. It was to prove the catalyst for the most unexpected and dramatic turn of events.

Testosterone seemed to be coursing through Cowen's veins in the Dáil the morning after his party victory. He was cracking jokes, emphasizing the divisions between Fine Gael and Labour, as Kenny criticized what he called an 'ill-judged and ill-timed' Labour Party motion of no-confidence in the government. The Fianna Fáil press office was emboldened enough by Cowen's performance to post a clip of it on YouTube and to e-mail the attachment to party members and the media.

Cowen had dreamt up what he thought was a cunning plan even before Martin's resignation, and now he thought he had more scope to implement it. He would change his cabinet, moving aside those who were not going to stand for re-election and introducing those whose profile could be raised in time for the campaign. The few people he consulted told him it was a really poor idea, that it would appear to be a 'stroke' and that the public would react against it. He would not be dissuaded. A combination of arrogance and ignorance was at play. Cowen's reasoning – that he was entitled to do anything the constitution allowed the Taoiseach to do – was actually correct but illustrated his failure to see the bigger picture during his time in office.

He hadn't contemplated the reaction of the Green Party to the idea. As far as he was concerned, he could do what he liked when it came to deciding upon the identity of non-Green Party members of the cabinet. But the Greens had put themselves under pressure by demanding a January election. They clearly weren't getting this and could not be seen to agree to something that would be perceived as an attempt to prolong the life of the government.

A massive set of rows with the Greens broke out, both public and private. Things were made worse for Cowen by a negative internal Fianna Fáil reaction to his plan: he couldn't even find people who wanted to be promoted. Frightened that the Greens were going to immediately withdraw support from government, Cowen backtracked, but unfortunately the resignations of Dempsey, Ahern, Harney,

Tony Killeen and O'Keeffe had already been sent to Áras an Uachtaráin and been accepted by President McAleese. The Green Party's Gormley and Ryan also quit. Remaining ministers now had to double up in their jobs. It was a mess.

Immediately talk of a fresh vote of confidence was rampant, just a day after Cowen had won. Many of those who had voted for Cowen had had enough. Martin waited and called upon TDs to 'reflect again' on their vote in favour of Cowen.

On Saturday, 20 January 2011, Cowen called a lunchtime press conference for the Merrion Hotel, base of the IMF mission when it came to Dublin. He would do exactly what he had told Martin he could not do: resign as leader of Fianna Fáil but not as Taoiseach, and remain in Government Buildings until the general election, which he set for 11 March.

'I'm concerned that renewed internal criticism of Fianna Fáil is deflecting attention from this important debate,' he said. 'Therefore, taking everything into account after discussing the matter with my family, I have taken, on my own counsel, the decision to step down.'

His time as seventh leader of Fianna Fáil was over, but even if he wasn't good enough to be leader of his party, he felt sufficiently qualified to remain as Taoiseach; he was prepared to step down for the sake of his party but not for the sake of his country.

Some people felt sorry for Cowen personally, but many had gone past the point of caring. He had been undermined not just by his actions and behaviour as Taoiseach but by his determination to stay in power regardless of how many disasters had been caused by his government.

There had been many points at which Cowen could have called a general election to ensure that a new government was able to deal with the Fianna Fáil-induced crisis on a basis of popular support. However, Fianna Fáil kept confusing its own interests with the national ones. It denied or partly excused its own failures and it boasted of its bravery in implementing solutions, when many of those had been forced upon it, and done little to solve our problems anyway, even if well intentioned. Every time it was suggested that Fianna Fáil should offer itself to the electorate because it had lost the confidence of the people, as measured by opinion polls, it offered two rebuttals: it had a majority in the Dáil and the economic condition of the country was too perilous to risk the 'instability' that would be caused by an election.

Both were spurious arguments. The Dáil majority was manipulated artificially by Fianna Fáil's cynical and deliberate failure to hold by-elections it knew it would lose, and with them the government's majority. Lowry and Healy-Rae were given the power to hold the government to ransom over local issues and to posture as statesmen, particularly in the ludicrous Lowry's case. The idea that only Fianna Fáil could provide financial and economic stability and restoration was utterly arrogant, given its own failings; it is not just hindsight to say that a four-week campaign at any time during 2009 or 2010 would actually have done more to provide certainty because it would have produced a government with a proper mandate of popular support.

The irony is that Fianna Fáil's own medium- and long-term interests as a political force might have been better served had it resigned and called an election much earlier, perhaps even as early as late 2008. Fianna Fáil almost certainly would have lost power, but having fifty or sixty seats, as might have been possible the earlier an election was called, would have placed it in an excellent position to return to government at a subsequent election, which might not have been too long in coming either. It is arguable that the granting of the blanket guarantee in September 2008 was itself such a momentous decision that it should have triggered an election.

The lowest of all points was the surrender of economic sovereignty to the IMF and the EU, both a practical and symbolic humiliation, the likes of which the country had never experienced before. The government decided to offer its successor a strait-jacket instead of a life-jacket, by entering into a formal agreement on the basis of a four-year plan from which the new administration cannot deviate to any significant extent. Not content with having ruined the economy, this government had the arrogance to believe that only it could come up with a rescue strategy. The main responsibility for that lies with its then leader, Cowen.

For all of the claims made on Cowen's behalf over the years about his alleged range of skills, most of which were grossly exaggerated, he also lacked the necessary dimension of emotional intelligence that must be applied to modern-day political dealings. He often failed to understand that his decisions did not appear to others as they appeared to him. He didn't seem to grasp that how people feel about things can be even more important than how they rationalize them. Decisions cannot be made based on perception, he complained prior to his resignation, denying the widespread belief that he had attempted an old-fashioned political stroke in changing his cabinet members. But misunderstanding and misapplication of communication was one of Cowen's many shortcomings.

Cowen did not run from responsibility for his own actions. Nor was he corrupt. His faults were on display but his transparency meant we could see he wasn't personally mendacious or duplicitous, like a couple of his predecessors. He was unlucky too at times. Those who dealt regularly with him sensed some underlying guilt arising from his realization that he had not been attentive enough as minister for finance while the bubble was inflating and saw that he worked hard to try to atone for that. He had his pride but even that became a liability, because, despite his protestations that he had done what he believed was best for country and party, he gave the appearance of wanting to hang on for the sake of proving his love of country and party to himself. He will be remembered also for how he blew his last chance of survival. It is sadly laughable that a leader who survived near-removal then managed to undermine himself so thoroughly that within less than forty-eight hours his opponents were sufficiently emboldened to demand his removal once more and this time get their way.

When he came to the Today FM studios for interview during the leadership challenge, he bumped into his *Gift Grub* impersonator Mario Rosenstock in the lift. After a brief silence Cowen deadpanned: 'I'm giving you a lot of material these days.' Rosenstock paused and responded: 'You're the gift that keeps giving.' Cowen laughed heartily and his entourage then joined in. He didn't laugh last, though.

PART TWO

Bailing Out the Banks

14. Why Did It Happen?

The bank guarantee was supposed to be the solution to our problems. Instead, it only made matters far worse. The Credit Institutions (Financial Support) Scheme 2008, to give it its proper title, decided upon by the government in the early hours of 30 September 2008, was approved by a cabinet meeting that many ministers attended by telephone. They were presented effectively with a fait accompli by Taoiseach Brian Cowen and Finance Minister Brian Lenihan. They rubberstamped the most expensive and calamitous gamble in the history of the state. The ministers who remained in their beds returned to sleep, but everyone would have nightmares for years to come.

The decision to guarantee all those who had deposited money in the six Irish-owned banks and building societies, or who had bought bonds issued by the banks to raise money for their lending, involved taking on an enormous contingent liability, one so large that it would bankrupt the country if ever called upon. The sum of money involved – €440 billion – was a multiple of the annual income of the country. The stakes were so high that, should this bluff by the government be called, the state would be bankrupt and everyone who lives here cast into penury. Therefore everything from that day forth had to be done to ensure that didn't happen.

Even though it would be some time before it was exercised partially – as deposits were withdrawn and bondholders demanded repayment of their money from banks and got it in full – the very existence of the bank guarantee accelerated a sequence of events that would be financially ruinous to the economy. While the guarantee itself may not have been the cause of our problems, it exacerbated them and was one of the most important steps towards the loss of sovereignty involved in the November 2010 arrangement with the IMF and the EU. Without the guarantee, the cost of rescuing the banks and the state might have been, probably would have been, a whole lot less.

The introduction of the guarantee – originally to last for a maximum of two years before things returned to 'normal' – bought time and space to sort out the problems. It succeeded in its initial aim, stopping and indeed reversing the haemorrhage of deposits from the accounts of our banks and allowing the banks back into the money markets to borrow. It allowed for the continuance of the payments and money-transmission systems of the banks, which otherwise might have stopped.

However, the government did not use the time it had to put the banks back on a sound footing and to sort out the non-bank issues relating to its public finances. If it acted reasonably quickly on the public finances – although not as quickly as it might have, had it not been worried about the political fallout – it procrastinated on the banks when it needed to move speedily. Accordingly, the problem grew and the scale of what it had to try to achieve became too vast. The ECB, which was central to the whole process, failed to realize the urgency of the situation too and panicked when it realized that things were not working out as intended.

Indeed, the European Commission may have been guilty of delaying the necessary action. It seemed more interested in dealing with theoretical competition issues than with the important practical ones.

These failures meant that just over two years later the perceived worthlessness of the guarantee – and its role in making it more difficult to deal with the capital issues at the banks – prompted a new flight of deposits and the closing of the bond markets to the banks, forcing the ECB to fulfil grudgingly its legal role as lender of last resort.

The guarantee led directly and indirectly to all sorts of things. It increased the cost of government borrowing just as the government needed to borrow more to cover the gap between its revenues and spending. It led to the creation of NAMA, the National Asset Management Agency, which was to be our rough equivalent of a so-called 'bad bank', dealing with the failed property loans of the banks and providing them with the means, both in terms of cash and time, to get on with servicing the normal economy. NAMA did not solve the bank's capital problems and could be said to have worsened them, although this latter opinion, while held by many, remains debatable.

However, had the guarantee not been introduced in the form that it was, and had something different been done, it is entirely possible that we would not have reached a situation where the arrival of the IMF was inevitable.

The 'Why did it happen?' and 'What if something else had been done?' elements to the guarantee consumed political debate for much of the two years after its introduction and may have deflected attention away from the questions of why it wasn't working and how it could be replaced. Central Bank Governor Patrick Honohan gently tried to warn of this, even though he took on the task of writing a major report on what had happened. The only excuse for this diversion of his time was that if he could understand what had taken place, he would be in a better position to fix it. But he had to be careful not to be seen to play to a political agenda.

The government knew that its place in history – and in the next Dáil – would depend upon its economic performance. The success or otherwise of the guarantee was central to that. But the determination to show that it had been correct in its decision became absolute. A mistake could never be conceded for political reasons. The same applied to NAMA once it was formed. It had to be held out as the best way, the only way. This had the practical effect of committing the government to standing by courses of action even if it suspected that they were the wrong ones.

Since the circumstances surrounding the inflation and bursting of the property bubble were set out in *Who Really Runs Ireland?* (published in 2009), more details have become available about the weeks running up to the introduction of the bank guarantee and the events of the night on which it was decided. A limited amount of information has been released under the Freedom of Information legislation, and there have been three official reports with pertinent revelations and comments: one was by Central Bank Governor Patrick Honohan; another by Klaus Regling, the German who later became head of the EU's bank rescue package, in conjunction with English banker Max Watson; and the third by a Finnish banker called Peter Nyberg. (The implications of the first two, published in June 2010, for Fianna Fáil ministers are discussed in Part I of this book.) While the Omertà-like silence of many of those who were present on the night the guarantee was decided is disappointing – if understandable because nobody wants to admit to their failings – it has meant that speculation remains as to why things occurred as they did.

What has become clear from these reports, newly released documents and my private interviews is that the authorities had more than an inkling that problems were emerging from early 2008. However, officials underestimated and misidentified the problems, and succumbed to the hope that things would work out without extensive intervention. When they did intervene, they did so at times in a way that may have serious legal implications if ever fully investigated and revealed. This is especially true of their dealings with Anglo Irish Bank.

Many factors contributed to the political unwillingness to face up to what was happening. The government was convulsed in the early part of 2008 by Bertie Ahern's troubled evidence at the Mahon Tribunal, his departure from power, long lap of honour and replacement by Minister for Finance Brian Cowen. Then it was distracted by the referendum that failed to endorse the Lisbon Treaty, creating all sorts of difficulties for our relationship with European Union bureaucrats and other EU governments.

Officials in the Department of Finance had started preparing contingency plans back in February 2008 in case there was the sudden onset of a banking crisis, even though the Central Bank, the Financial Regulator and the banks themselves were insistent that there was no need to worry because the banks were so profitable and well capitalized. This wariness was not necessarily as impressive as it might appear, even if it took place well in advance of the eventual debacle: this was more than six months after the Northern Rock crisis in the UK in the autumn of 2007. Worse, documents show that the officials had decided on a policy of maintaining 'constructive ambiguity': in other words the government would demonstrate support to the banking sector without making any commitments as to how it would actually do that, leaving it to the banks themselves to sort out their problems. The officials were also determined not to let banks think that they were 'too big to fail' in case they became complacent about government support or even reckless in their efforts to gamble their way out of trouble. And they examined the prospects for encouraging 'covert takeover', forcing a troubled bank to sell itself to a rival before anyone became aware of its problems, thereby stopping a possible run on deposits or difficulties in securing liquidity. Whatever happened, though, government officials did not want to intervene, and state money was to be used only in the most extreme of circumstances.

Department of Finance documents noted, intriguingly, that 'the Central Bank is liaising with the major domestic banks at CEO level, to explore the options that may be available for mutual support between the Irish banks in a crisis situation, and to respond to any problem in small institutions in a collaborative fashion.' Given the subsequent revelations of how Irish Life & Permanent engaged in providing balance-sheet support to Anglo – making massive loans available that were classified wrongly as deposits, and claiming that it did so with the full knowledge and support of the state, despite denials – this document was sure to have been of interest to investigators at the Office of the Director of Corporate Enforcement.

The collapse of Lehman Brothers has often been claimed by the former government and its supporters as the reason for the economic implosion. This excuse failed to acknowledge properly that the banks had already been ruined by their insane lending to all sections of the property market, and that the liquidity issue, while real, merely brought forward the timing of what was going to happen anyway.

Yet all the government and its officials focused on was the liquidity issue. There was an emergency meeting on 18 September 2008, a note of which revealed: 'John Hurley [the Central Bank governor] gave a report. Liquidity under great strain. Potentially serious crisis.' Crucially at the same time the idea of an 'all-deposits' guarantee was being floated, particularly because of newspaper articles by the likes of solicitor–property developer Noel Smyth and economist David McWilliams. Hurley told Lenihan that an 'all-deposits' guarantee would potentially be counterproductive and warned against its implementation. Instead he suggested that a €10 billion emergency fund should be available as a liquidity provision structure in the event of a 'pressure scenario'.

It wasn't just the regulators but externally hired advisers who failed to see the full extent of the problems at Anglo and Irish Nationwide, even if the advisers certainly seemed more wary of various shortcomings at the Irish lenders. Everyone was convinced they were dealing merely with a liquidity problem – the getting of enough money for a bank to supply its customers with cash on demand and to repay whatever it had borrowed itself. Solvency – the ability of the bank to recover the loans it had made to its customers and therefore have enough money to continue in business – was not considered a problem. Former financial regulator Patrick Neary told Cowen and Lenihan five days before the bank guarantee was introduced that there was no evidence that Anglo was insolvent 'on a going-concern basis' but that the threat to its existence came solely from an inability to access liquidity. Neary said Irish Nationwide was in a similar situation to Anglo's.

The banks themselves were in denial. Anglo had given a presentation to the government on 18 September in which it claimed that its financial situation was sound and that it had 'no requirement for external equity capital'. It was greeted with some scepticism, but not nearly enough. Rather than trust its own officials, the government asked accountants PricewaterhouseCoopers (PwC) to carry out an urgent review. It came up with a worrying assessment as to the quality of some of Anglo's property lending, but it was still far too optimistic.

On 24 September, the giant American investment bank Merrill Lynch was contracted to advise on the options available and told to report quickly within two days. (Ironically, Merrill was itself in the process of being taken over by Bank of America in order to rescue it from the same fate as Lehman Brothers.) It too got some of its assessments badly wrong. 'Liquidity issues aside, all of the Irish banks are profitable and well capitalized,' Merrill said in a memo dated 28 September. 'However, liquidity for some could run out in days rather than weeks.' It warned, moreover, that Anglo had used its available collateral to secure outside funding, that it would run out of money in two days, and that the bank was heading for a deficit of €4.9 billion by 24 October. Amazingly, Merrill said the commercial loan book at Irish Nationwide was 'regarded as being generally good'. It focused instead, legitimately but partially, on the behaviour of its chief executive, Michael Fingleton. Merrill queried whether Anglo and Irish Nationwide could survive because of their difficulty in raising money from the wholesale markets to finance their ongoing business. It said both should be dealt with quickly to avoid a 'systemic issue', their possible failure somehow creating knock-on effects for Irish and international banks.

While the liquidity assessment was correct – if rather obvious – these expensive experts also failed to identify the solvency and associated capital crisis that would arise because the profitability that the banks had been reporting was somewhat unreal.

Merrill drafted a series of crisis-management options from which the government could pick and choose, outlining the pros and cons of each, and presented it to the NTMA on 26 September. In a phrase that would be seized upon later by the government, it said that a blanket guarantee would be 'best, most decisive, most impactful from market perspective'. It said such a move would stop the outflow of deposits and actually bring money into their coffers. Importantly, it said that it would protect senior and subordinated creditors, the later to be famous bondholders. However, it warned presciently that such a guarantee would be detrimental to Ireland's credit rating and deeply unpopular with the European authorities. 'This would almost certainly negatively impact the state's sovereign credit rating and raise issues as to its credibility. The wider market will be aware that Ireland could not afford to cover the full amount if required.' Merrill made it clear that this option would not deal with the difficulties facing Anglo and Irish Nationwide; it also made up just one paragraph of the seven-page document.

Merrill had a different idea, what it called a secured lending scheme (SLS). The six Irish lenders could use their existing commercial loans as collateral to borrow loans from a special government-created €20 billion pool to provide the money they needed. 'The SLS scheme is recommended because it would offer immediate liquidity and stabilize the sector,' said Merrill. 'The option to subsequently own or separate assets out of the banks into state ownership or to stronger banks will be preserved, and can be done with full market support.'

In the end, Merrill hedged its bets by admitting there was 'no right and wrong answer' available. But it was against allowing an Irish bank to fail and go into liquidation without any government intervention. 'The resulting shock to the wider Irish banking system could, in our view, be very damaging.' The fear was that if a solution was implemented in which the weakest bank was saved, the market would simply turn on the next weakest.

Merrill was contacted again on 29 September at 6.37 p.m. Kevin Cardiff from the Department of Finance stated that he was in a meeting with Cowen and needed the Merrill 'pros and cons' document. He got it within six minutes. It did not recommend the guarantee, but that was the option that the government decided upon later that evening and formally approved at its cabinet meeting in the early hours of the following day. When they met again the next day a tired Cowen muttered that 'we came close to the brink last night.'

There was something of an air of unreality in the initial aftermath of the decision. It was due largely to a misreading of the situation. The government believed the risk in providing a €440 billion guarantee scheme was offset by the assets held by the banks, which it believed wrongly were worth €500 billion. Department of Finance officials – in a briefing document presented to Cowen on the day the guarantee was announced – suggested the financial exposure to the taxpayer was mitigated by a 'very substantial buffer' of assets. It did not take into account the possible severity of the looming recession or the collapse in property values that was already under way and that would worsen. Instead, the document claimed that the asset quality in the financial institutions remained good. Rather than focusing on the amounts lent for development and investment mortgages, it focused on residential mortgages and reassured Cowen that these were safe because of a relatively low loan-to-value ratio. 'While Ireland along with all developed economies has experienced a sharp decline in its property market there is very significant capacity within the institutions to absorb any losses,' the document claimed confidently, and incorrectly.

This wrong assessment of the situation was emphasized on 2 October, when John Hurley claimed that the Irish-owned banks, unlike their international counterparts, had 'not had to write off significant losses on loans and investments so that bad debts and loan losses were not the key issues for our financial system last Monday evening'.

Kevin Cardiff, now the secretary general of the Department of Finance, but then in charge of banking before his promotion, lashed out at the banks during a July 2010 meeting of the Dáil's Committee of Public Accounts, for their 'self-delusion' and 'over-optimism' in the weeks leading up to the announcement of the bank-guarantee scheme in September 2008. He said nothing about whether the same characteristics could be attributed to his own officials, not necessarily in that month but in the long period of the bubble that preceded it.

The lack of reality about the extent of the crisis was underlined in the days after the guarantee by a relative failure to take any action against the banks. Once it was decided that none of the institutions would be nationalized, the debate centred on issues such as demanding an annual levy from them to cover the cost of providing the guarantee, the imposition of restrictions on executive bonuses and the introduction of closer scrutiny of lending practices. All were warranted, but they did not deal with the core issue: the looming capital crisis. Professor Morgan Kelly appeared on RTÉ's *Primetime* programme to emphasize that this was more important than the liquidity issue, but he was largely ignored.

The arguments as to how much the levy should be, and how it should be spread between the six covered institutions – AIB, Bank of Ireland, Irish Life & Permanent, Anglo Irish Bank, Irish Nationwide and EBS – raged. A total of €1 billion over two years was the maximum that the six wanted. The government wanted double, but the banks argued this would wipe out too much of their capital. AIB and Bank of Ireland asked for a levy based on the quality of the lending at each institution, hubristically believing they had acted more conservatively than others. Anglo Irish Bank asked for a levy based on the amount of deposits in each institution. Anglo boss Sean Fitz-Patrick stated publicly that 'it would be terrible if the cure killed the banks.' Ominously, while all of this was ongoing, the cost of government borrowing began to increase, slowly but noticeably.

There was a combination of reactions amongst those responsible for the guarantee. Some, who feared that they might have done the

wrong thing and that they and the country would be punished subsequently, remained silent. Some were near to euphoric: pumped by
the adrenalin of the drama they had faced, they were convinced of
their own bravery and brilliance. Some, quietly, didn't quite understand what the repercussions of the guarantee could be, but it didn't
suit to admit this publicly.

Soon the overwhelming response was to justify, as people sought to
protect their own positions, and this was to become the dominant
mode of behaviour in the coming years. Eventually Cowen and his
government would be forced to admit responsibility and apologize
for what had happened to the country, but most of their sorrow and
regret was restricted to what had occurred during the boom years, the
failure to prepare for downturn. Nobody was ever going to admit that
the guarantee had been the wrong course of action, because to do so
would be to admit to an absolutely enormous mistake. But equally
disastrous was the decision to defend and bolster that mistake.

Not surprisingly, many demanded to know what had brought
about the guarantee and why that decision had been taken. Eventually the government succumbed to the political and public pressure
to conduct investigations. Cleverly, though, it managed to keep the
events of the evening of the decision out of the terms of reference,
refusing to lift the veil on what had happened, why it had happened,
and who was responsible.

Peter Nyberg's report was published in April 2011. He discovered
that there was no official record, or 'paper trail', of what took place,
that neither the department nor anyone else had ever bothered to
look at 'alternative options' or to fully understand what they were
doing by granting the guarantee. The option of buying time, rather
than rushing to meet a midnight deadline, was not considered, apparently. The government had based its decision on 'deficient' information
on the extent of the problems, he said. Had accurate information been
available, it is likely that the guarantee would have been more limited
and the state would have 'more seriously contemplated' taking over
at least one bank. Yet he said that he wasn't surprised, because it had
all been agreed at such a frantic time. As a former public servant he'd
had experience of such a scenario. While it may well be true that

events were moving at a phenomenal speed, the more sceptical might conclude that a deliberate decision was taken to commit as little as possible to paper, lest a subsequent release of that paperwork cause problems for the decision-makers.

None of the reports gave us the answer to a question that was later to become fundamental to the country's economic collapse. Whatever about guaranteeing deposits, who recommended the idea of paying bondholders in the banks all that they were owed?

That was to prove another calamitous part of the overall decision, indeed one that exacerbated the damage. In a normal corporate restructuring – and that's what was needed here – owners of shares are the first to bear any losses. If necessary, their entire investments are wiped out. Bondholders, who have lent money to a company or bank, are next in line, with junior bondholders, who receive a preferential rate of interest in return for their loans, the first to lose out. Then senior bondholders, who enjoy more security but are paid less in interest for their loans, come next in the queue. If a business is to continue, the usual situation is that the bondholders are handed ownership of the business in return for agreeing to write off all or part of what's owed to them. They get their return if the business returns to good health.

Banks are different in that they need a licence, which most companies don't, and certain restrictions are placed on who can be shareholders. But there is little to stop a two-step process by which banks are taken into state ownership – or nationalized – and then turned over to bondholders at a later date as part of a recapitalization.

The government set its face firmly against nationalization. It claimed that, somehow, publicly owned banks would be less well operated than privately owned and managed ones, a theory that would be blown apart as details of the mismanagement of the Irish banks became clear. Another excuse was that foreign multinationals and others would not hold large deposits in state-owned banks, because sometimes they were prevented by their own rules from doing so; the reality was that they would hold them in any bank that was not in danger of failing. The common belief was that nationalization would wipe out the investments of its citizens and pensioners, held either directly in bank shares or through pension and investment funds, and the government wished to avoid this – although the sceptical thought that the large blocks of shares owned by the well-connected, especially builders, provided the real motivation.

There was another possible reason, though, that went beyond the legal advice that bondholders ranked the same as deposit holders under Irish law, and therefore had to be repaid everything in the same way. While there was an easily obtained share register – not that it was always simple to identify who owned shares because of the existence of nominee accounts – public disclosure of who owned bonds was nowhere near as straightforward. This raised questions as to whether some of Ireland's wealthiest and most influential had as much interest in protecting the repayment of bonds as they had in saving their shares.

Lenihan fell back on the crutch of one of Honohan's findings many times: his belief that 'given the situation that had developed by September 28, 2008, it was too late to avoid an extensive guarantee.' However, Honohan had questioned whether it should have been extended to all classes of bond investors in the banks.

That wasn't surprising. What was, however, was that he gave even qualified backing to the guarantee, in the light of his past views on the subject. Back in 2002, when working at the World Bank, Honohan had co-authored a major study on forty banking crises throughout the globe. In it he concluded that 'governments that provided open-ended liquidity support and blanket deposit guarantees incurred much higher costs in resolving financial crises . . . open-ended liquidity support, regulatory forbearance, and a blanket guarantee for depositors and creditors all significantly contribute to the fiscal cost of banking crises.

'Countries that used policies such as liquidity support, blanket guarantees, and regulatory forbearance did not recover faster. Rather, liquidity support appears to make recovery from a crisis longer and output losses larger. Thus it appears that the two most important policies during the containment phase are to limit liquidity support and not extend guarantees.'

Lenihan seized upon Honohan's reported belief in Anglo's 'systemic importance' to the economy, emphasizing that Honohan was 'our foremost expert on banking', as if the governor of the Central Bank would have done exactly the same thing had he been in the room on the night the guarantee was introduced. He seized upon quotes from the document produced by Merrill Lynch, which, he reminded us, had described a blanket guarantee as the 'best, most decisive, most impactful from market perspective'. And he seized upon another of its recommendations: 'the only option which Merrill Lynch discounted, after full consideration, was the option of allowing an Irish bank to fail.' But even Lenihan had to admit that it was 'wrong to suggest that Merrill Lynch [had] recommended one option over another'.

One thing that Honohan was very clear about, though, in his June 2010 report was that the weakness of the Irish banks had been caused not by the collapse of US bank Lehman Brothers in September 2008, but by their overexposure to property lending. He said this had been driven by excessive overseas borrowing 'to support a credit-fuelled property market and construction frenzy'. Anglo and Irish Nationwide were 'well on the road towards insolvency' by the time of the Lehman collapse, and AIB and Bank of Ireland could have survived without state-supported bailout only if the international financial markets had calmed. Shortly after the issue of the Honohan report in June 2010, I interviewed Cowen, live on air, in the Today FM studios. I asked him if he would promise now to never again use the collapse of Lehman as the excuse for the failures of that month. He got very angry, to put it mildly.

The report itself was very damaging for Cowen because it pointed directly to a failure of regulation under his watch – and also to a complacent attitude towards assessing the risks to the economy. Cowen had been depending on the experts but he hadn't put enough pressure on the experts to do their jobs.

Cowen should, must, have been aware of the existence of plenty of warnings from outside of establishment circles that things were going wrong, particularly during 2007. Honohan in particular criticized the Central Bank's Financial Stability reports, which predicted 'a soft landing for the economy' as late as 2007. This was not based on any quantitative calculations or analysis. 'This appears to have been a "triumph of hope over reality". More generally, a rather defensive approach was adopted to external critics or contrarians.' Concerns expressed by commentators should have 'raised more warning flags' and prompted a rethink by the bank. He could have said that the same should have applied politically. '"Rocking the boat" and swimming against the tide of public opinion would have required a particularly strong sense of the independent role of a Central Bank in being prepared to "spoil the party" and withstand possible strong adverse public reaction,' Honohan said. But, just as with the Department of Finance, as is detailed in a later chapter, nobody was prepared to confront a government determined to milk the good times.

Given that he had just taken on responsibility for the people working in the Central Bank and the Office of the Financial Regulator, most of whom remained in their positions and whose cooperation he needed, Honohan's criticisms were unusually brave. He effectively accused the organization of cowardice and incompetence, even if that message was delivered between the lines.

There was insufficient awareness or willingness to accept 'how close the system was to the edge' and that it was the responsibility of the Central Bank and the regulator to pull it back from the edge, he said. There was an aversion to taking 'on board sufficiently the real risk of a looming problem and act with sufficient decision and force to head it off in time'. Problems that had been identified long before the crisis were not corrected, and by not adhering to deadlines the regulator 'allowed some important matters to drift'. The people in charge failed to comprehend the scale of the potential exposure of banks to a fall in the property market. When the problems developed, they thought liquidity was the key issue and failed to realize 'the underlying lack of solvency'.

'The potentially very large loan-losses that would threaten insolvency in several institutions were not foreseen in the supervision documentation even as far as late 2008,' Honohan's report said. 'Even the detection of serious deficiencies in loan appraisal and approval procedures of the major banks did not seem to trigger alarm.'

The rate of growth of Anglo – the fastest in the market, with a loan book increasing at an average rate of 36 per cent a year – should have been 'the trigger for much more intense scrutiny of its business than it received' and forced the regulator to consider restraining its growth directly. Stress-testing of Anglo's €72 billion loan book did not raise warning flags until April 2008, when concerns about the books brought the bank up to the regulator's 'high-priority' risk level. 'The weakest bank was given a relatively favourable assessment until close to the edge of the cliff,' said Honohan.

The regulation of the banks was 'excessively deferential and accommodating' and 'insufficiently challenging and not persistent enough . . . Given the model of engagement, decisive corrective action that might have prevented the deterioration of the situation was unlikely ever to have been imposed.' The regulator's appetite for taking on legal actions was 'very limited'.

They did not move 'decisively and effectively enough against banks with governance issues', and corrective intervention for the system was 'delayed and timid'. Regulatory inspection focused on whether banks complied with governance rules and procedures, rather than on whether they had too great a concentration of property loans and whether these loans could be recovered. Inspection records and correspondence at the regulator revealed 'a pattern of inconclusive engagement' with the banks on prudential matters and lack of 'decisive follow-through'.

There seemed to be two major problems. One was political: there was 'undue emphasis' on fears of upsetting the competitive position of the domestic banks and simultaneously on encouraging the financial services industry 'even at the expense of prudential considerations'. In other words, the banking business was oiling the economy and the politicians didn't want that to end.

The second was that the banks were able to bully regulators by going above their heads to their bosses. 'It would have been known within the Financial Regulator that intrusive demands from line staff could be and were set aside after direct representations were made to senior regulators,' Honohan alleged. There was a mismatch between the expertise and seniority of staff at the regulator and those at the institutions that they supervised, which 'hampered effective supervision'.

The Regling–Watson report supported Honohan in this when it said that regulation was not 'hands-on or pre-emptive' and was 'insufficiently intrusive' and 'forceful'. The available resources were 'seriously inadequate for the more hands-on approach' required. The regulators had seriously underestimated the funding risks linked to the banks' overexposure to property. 'The fact is that supervisors, right to the end, clung on to the hope of a soft landing for the economy and the property market,' they said.

Honohan did not shirk from exposing the hubris of bank management either. He accused them of failing to maintain safe and sound banking practices in their greed for market share and the profits – and resultant personal reward – they thought this would bring. They lowered their lending criteria and did not follow their stated policies. He related that the banks had incurred huge external borrowing in the international money markets 'to support a credit-fuelled property market and construction frenzy', money that had come with no intervention either by our own Central Bank or – and it was every bit as relevant – by the European Central Bank.

What none of the reports detailed was the role of the ECB in encouraging the Irish decision on the guarantee. It had been said that the ECB was shocked at the solo run engaged in by the Irish. However, ECB President Jean-Claude Trichet rang Brian Lenihan over that fateful weekend in September 2008 just before the introduction of the guarantee. He had a very clear message. Lenihan was to do whatever it took to prevent an Irish bank from failing. The obvious inference was that the ECB would play its part in support of Ireland. The proof of that was its central role in the establishment and operation of the National Asset Management Agency, a bastard child of the guarantee that came to be greatly unloved by its guardians. The NAMA debacle will be explored in more detail in Part III.

15. The Bad Bank

If one bank could be held responsible for making Ireland go bust, Anglo Irish Bank fitted the bill, at least as far as the public was concerned. If one man came to symbolize hubris, it was the bank's former chairman, Sean FitzPatrick. Truth was that all of the banks were to blame for the economic catastrophe, but Anglo and FitzPatrick managed to hold a special place for many good reasons. Anglo's losses were bigger than any other bank's in the world in both 2009 (at €12 billion) and 2010 (at more than €17 billion), its need for state-supplied capital more voracious, the behaviour of its top executives more egregious. Its infamy provoked the *New York Times* in September 2010 to pose the question as to whether one bank could bring down a whole country, as ratings agencies speculated that Ireland could not bear the cost of covering Anglo's losses on top of all its other commitments.

The horror for the Irish citizen, who had to pay for it all, and who had to watch as international investors used Anglo as an excuse to shy away from lending to the government, was seemingly never ending. There was a symbolic moment of closure in April 2011, when the sign over the bank's old headquarters on Dublin's St Stephen's Green was removed. Crowds gathered to cheer the workmen, and the bank's Australian chief executive, Mike Aynsley, recruited in 2009 to clean up the mess, watched on approvingly. 'It's over, it's gone,' one observer was heard to shout. But it wasn't, unfortunately. This was a never-ending horror movie with many sequels, each less palatable than the last.

The cost of cleaning up Anglo would continue for the Irish citizen for a decade to come, creating a bill of thousands of euro per head, to be paid for by increased taxes and reduced public services. The disaster at Anglo contributed directly to the arrival of the IMF-led 'rescue troika' and to the enforced economic austerity. Some of those

responsible faced the possibility of high-profile prosecutions and
court cases – and relative poverty, at least compared to their old lifestyles but not compared to the lives led by most people – although
many wondered if that would ever happen due to the snail-like progress of the criminal investigations.

There were so many questions that demanded answers. Why had
the regulators allowed Anglo to run up such enormous debts in such
a reckless fashion? What political patronage and protection did it
enjoy? What collusion had there been between bank and authorities
during 2008, and, if there had been none, how seriously were state
representatives misled? Why had it been included in the September
2008 guarantee and not just left to fail, as the normal rules of capitalism dictated? Why had it failed to own up to the extent of its problems
in the crucial months following its rescue? Most importantly, why
was the Irish taxpayer required to pay for it instead of the bank's
investors? And why wasn't this toxic bank just closed down immediately instead of allowing its poisons to continue to seep into Irish
society?

In the end it was the European Commission that took the decision
that Anglo could be no more. It had been presented with a plan by
the bank's new board in the summer of 2010 to put some life into the
zombie. This had been endorsed implicitly by the government, which
decided to test if it would pass EU competition barriers, despite
strong objections from Patrick Honohan and Matthew Elderfield,
who felt that the business plan for the new bank was unduly optimistic and the use of scarce resources for such a gamble too risky.

There had been enough gambling done already, at too high a cost.
The old management had done a hell of a job in bringing Anglo
to the brink, and the guarantee had sorted out Anglo's liquidity
issues, temporarily at least – but none of this seemed to alert people
inside the organization to the reality of its pending insolvency. Just
two months after the guarantee Anglo announced 'record' profits of
€724 million for the financial year that ended on the day the bank
guarantee was announced. Finance Director Willie McAteer told
stockbroking analysts that he expected the scale of loan losses
'through the cycle' would be 125 basis points, or 1.25 per cent of its

total loan book. By then AIB and Bank of Ireland were predicting loan losses of 2 per cent of their respective loan books, but McAteer, incredibly, boasted of Anglo's 'superior collateral'. Chief Executive David Drumm decided that a €500 million provision for loan impairments, on total loans of €72 billion, sufficed.

Donal O'Connor was formerly managing partner of PricewaterhouseCoopers and had served with FitzPatrick on the board of the Dublin Docklands Development Authority. He was already on the board of Anglo as a non-executive director (and was later to be appointed as chairman by the government after FitzPatrick was forced to resign). He took on the task of conducting a review of the loans with the assistance of another director of both bodies, Lar Bradshaw, who would later be revealed as a co-investor with FitzPatrick in an exotic Nigerian oil venture, financed with loans from Anglo.

Having examined 82 per cent of Anglo's Irish loan book, O'Connor concluded the 'extreme case potential loss' was just €797 million on Irish loans of €43 billion, an underestimate of a mere €14 billion or so, as it turned out. Adding a potential €200 million loss on loans advanced to businessman Sean Quinn brought estimated losses to just €1 billion. When the bank accepted an offer of €1.5 billion in capital investment from the government in December 2008, it was presented as a way of attracting deposits and improving liquidity, not as a way of dealing with a looming solvency crisis.

That was the real issue. It was clear that Anglo had been lending huge percentages of the prices of assets purchased by borrowers, sometimes as much as 100 per cent. Falling property prices – and it was obvious that this was happening – meant not only that the limited equity provided by borrowers was gone but that the ability to recover most of the debt through the sale of the asset had also disappeared, should Anglo have chosen to call in its loan.

The rental income on these commercial properties was also falling or had disappeared, not just reducing the capital value of the assets but also depriving the borrowers and the bank of the cash needed to pay the interest on the loans taken out to buy them. Worse, Anglo had diversified out of property to provide loans to some of its so-called HNWIs, high-net-worth individuals, customers who had borrowed to fund their stock-market purchases. But the stock-market had slumped, particularly in bank shares, and there were many Anglo-funded, mini-Sean-Quinn-lookalikes caught by bad investments they couldn't repay.

In mid January 2009 the government did what it had sworn it would not and nationalized Anglo. Just eighteen hours before a scheduled extraordinary general meeting to approve the originally planned €1.5 billion state investment, Lenihan stepped in with the compulsory acquisition of the bank, wiping out the investment of all ordinary shareholders.

Events and a drip-feed of damaging information had forced Lenihan's hand. The previous month a scandal involving Sean FitzPatrick's 'warehousing' of massive personal loans to avoid detection in the annual accounts had forced his departure as chairman. He had borrowed up to €129 million from Anglo, but just before each financial year-end he took out a personal loan from Irish Nationwide for that amount, before then returning to the original position by repaying Irish Nationwide and taking out a new loan from Anglo – which effectively kept his Anglo borrowings off the books. Now it emerged that many other directors had been taking out massive loans as well, at this point up to €179 million in aggregate. The quality of the security on these loans was to become an issue. So too was the secrecy involved and the scale of the borrowing. Very few banks would have allowed their directors to borrow such money for speculative investment. Drumm and McAteer followed FitzPatrick out of the bank.

Lenihan reassured everyone that the state was investing in a bank that remained solvent and that had a cushion of assets over liabilities amounting to €4 billion. Immediately, the value of the assets was queried. What was the security on the loans actually worth? What if the security was valued at today's market prices rather than at historical levels? Already it was clear to external observers that getting repayment on loans would be a problem. Yet Taoiseach Brian Cowen said it was 'business as usual' at the bank.

To carry on, Anglo needed new management. In early 2009, at the recommendation of former Bank of Ireland boss Mike Soden, an Australian called Mike Aynsley pitched up in Dublin. Former Fine

Gael Leader Alan Dukes, already a public-interest director appointed by the state, took on the role of chairman. After over a year spent trying to get a handle on the scale of the losses, they came up with a plan for a new-look Anglo.

Aynsley and Dukes wanted Anglo to pick itself up and go again, albeit under a new name, despite losses that had already required government investment of €24.5 billion in new capital and, on top of that, a further investment of at least another €2.5 billion, this time not to cover losses but to allow lending to resume. The new Anglo – name not yet decided – had a plan, one that was devised for it by international consultants Bain & Company, at a cost to the state of €11 million.

Having already transferred nearly €36 billion of loans to NAMA, they wanted to put another €24 billion of bad loans – which had nothing to do with property development and therefore weren't eligible for NAMA – into a separate bad bank, or asset-management company, which Anglo would own and operate. The new 'good' bank would have just €12 billion of so-called clean loans, split a third each in Ireland, Britain and America. Aynsley wanted to keep the €12 billion retail-deposit bank to assist with funding a bank that would be just one fifth of the size of the old Anglo.

Aynsley apparently saw himself going into competition with AIB and Bank of Ireland, offering a new form of banking to support businesses, as well as earning profits to give the state a return on its new investment. More detailed analysis of the plan suggested that its greater focus would be lending to large corporate customers, entering a business space already occupied by massive international banks HSBC and Barclays, which remained prepared to lend to foreign companies exporting from Ireland. 'There will be a return on the new bank. By the time we flip the assets over from the current entity, Anglo, into the new bank, we will be very clear about the quality of the assets going in, and we will have a profitable business model. We will have €2 billion to €2.5 billion of capital underpinning that in taxpayers' money. That's not lost. There will be a return on that. That's not money down a black hole,' Aynsley claimed in a *Sunday Independent* interview in August 2010, as he tried to build public support for his grand plan.

However, Anglo had little or no experience with non-property lending, which was one of the reasons why it had failed. It would have to buy such expertise now – and it could hardly ignore property lending if it was going to be profitable. Aynsley promised a 'balanced' approach to such lending but didn't rule out that his new bank would get into the business of financing those who would buy property assets from NAMA.

From a business point of view that had a certain logic but it wasn't the type of idea that would endear itself to politicians or the public, let alone the regulators. Although the senior management had changed entirely, it was still Anglo that the politicians and public were dealing with, and a change of name was not going to shift perceptions or erase memories.

Aynsley's main argument was that his idea was cheaper for the state than a long-term wind-down, even one that was to last for over ten years, because more capital would be required for a wind-down. He believed that in 'normal circumstances' Anglo could recover 80 per cent of the value of the loans it would keep, but if it was put under pressure to sell everything, even over a ten-year period, it would be forced to accept lower prices on selling the loans or the assets that backed them. He estimated that with a wind-down Anglo might recover only 68 per cent of the loans' value, thus increasing the capital requirements from the state to plug holes. He also argued that deposits would leak from the bank if it was to go into wind-down and that it might cost the state as much as €22 billion in funding to cover this.

Aynsley and Dukes had a credibility issue. They had to keep revising their estimates of how much money they needed from the state in new capital. Only a year earlier they had been saying that another €9 billion in capital, on top of the €4 billion already invested, would be the maximum the state would be required to invest. That number had since climbed to €22 billion (and would get bigger).

This wasn't necessarily all their fault. Elderfield had increased the capital requirements for all banks significantly. The transfers of loans to NAMA had taken place at prices that shocked Anglo. Instead of transferring €28.4 billion of loans to NAMA at a 30 per cent discount, as it had expected – which would have led to a €8.5 billion loss – Anglo ended up moving €35 billion of loans to NAMA at an aggregate discount of 59 per cent. That implied a loss of €20.6 billion and a requirement for a massive extra amount of capital.

Whatever about people in Ireland, the European Commission was not impressed by Anglo's rationale. 'The European Commission is saying, "This bank has dropped €25 billion, and it doesn't deserve to survive," and they're right. But you have a dysfunctional banking system,' said Aynsley. Competition Commissioner Joaquín Almunia could not see Anglo funding itself and knew it would need fresh exchequer capital. He wasn't prepared to give money to a bank that could potentially be in competition with banks that were owned by private investors who hadn't received state capital support.

Lenihan insisted that our government made the eventual decision for a ten-year wind-down itself, having being informed of the commission's thinking, although not, as usual, under formal direction from it. This was somewhat at odds with his and the government's previous statements and behaviour, when he had stated consistently that it was not possible to close Anglo. As recently as March 2010 he had said: 'I understand why many want us to close this bank [Anglo]. I understand the impulse to obliterate it from the system. But I cannot, as minister for finance, countenance such a course of action . . . Winding up [Anglo] is not and was never a viable option.' And two days later he said, 'We would all like to see the back of this institution [Anglo], but it is not possible.' But by the end of April he was wobbling: 'I do accept that a longer-term workout is an option that has to be examined.' And by mid August he said that 'Second to the good-bank plan is the option to wind down Anglo Irish Bank over a very long period.' By the time the European Commission's opinion tipped the balance he was resigned. 'You can call it a wind-down if you like [of Anglo]. It's over an extended period of years, and it's an orderly workout of the institution in question,' he said on 9 September 2010.

This raised questions as to why it had not been possible to make this decision much earlier, perhaps even a year earlier. Ten months had been wasted in trying to convince the commission to approve something that was never likely to be endorsed. Lenihan excused that on the basis that Anglo had not engaged in new lending during that time, but international confidence in the state's ability to deal with Anglo had deteriorated during the time, with disastrous consequences, as speculation about the size of the capital requirements intensified.

Even if Anglo was to be closed, albeit over ten years, the issue of who would pay for it all was the subject of highly contentious public debate – which related directly to the decision that no bank should be allowed to fail, and the European Commission's role in that decision. Although it was not appreciated fully at the time, it was a concrete example of how Europe had decided that Ireland would bear all the costs of the crisis it was enduring. The commission and the ECB had decided that Anglo's senior bondholders – most of whom resided on Continental Europe – would not share Ireland's pain but be repaid in full.

The EU fear was that imposing losses here would make it more difficult for banks elsewhere in the eurozone to raise debt. It was spelt out in an EU Commission document, published in February 2011: 'For legal reasons, but also to avoid contagion to other parts of the financial system both in Ireland and elsewhere in the euro area, the measures agreed with the Irish authorities do not include steps that would affect senior debt holders.'

Ireland's weakness in this regard went all the way back to the introduction of the guarantee and the inclusion of bondholders as well as depositors as those who would get all of their money back. Nobody was arguing that deposits should not be paid in full, even those of more than €100,000, which were covered by the increased guarantee that the government had introduced less than two weeks before the blanket guarantee. It was felt that any failure to repay depositors in full, most especially large corporates which provided employment in Ireland, would destroy not just Ireland's reputation but also the ability of banks to attract deposits in the future. There was also €26 billion in deposits from the European Central Bank and our own Central Bank.

The big issue with all the banks, but particularly Anglo, given that it was to be wound down, was what to do with bond or debt holders. Anglo had €2.4 billion in subordinated, or junior, debt and three quarters of this was not due to be repaid until after the state guarantee expired, providing an opportunity to save money by not repaying it in full. Anglo sought permission from the government to buy back this debt at a discount, saving some money at least. As it was already trading at a deep discount on the money markets, at about 33 cents in the euro, it implied that investors did not expect to be repaid most of their money.

The problem came with senior debt that Anglo had to repay. These investors lent to Anglo at a cheaper rate of interest but enjoyed a higher level of security in return. At one stage Anglo had such bonds of about €14.5 billion on which it owed repayment. But just to complicate things, those bonds themselves fell into different categories. There were those that had been issued prior to the announcement of the state guarantee and that were covered until September 2010; and there were those that were issued after the introduction of the Eligible Liabilities Guarantee scheme of December 2009. The consensus was that bonds issued after the ELG had been introduced had to be repaid: the government would be sued if it was to renege on explicit agreements to make such repayments and it would lose any court cases and incur additional costs and possibly suffer damages. Not only that, but the damage to Ireland's reputation and ability to borrow further, either as a state or through its state-controlled banks, would be enormous; it would be regarded as the equivalent of a sovereign-debt default.

But what about reneging on Anglo bonds issued prior to the introduction of either guarantee, which were worth nearly €7 billion? The government had had a chance to act before 30 September 2010, when bonds worth just shy of €8 billion fell due for repayment; they were a mix of types but more than half had been issued prior to the introduction of the original guarantee and theoretically were suitable for burning.

There were a couple of problems with this. Unlike in other countries, Irish law seemed to rank bondholders on the same level as depositors. The guarantee had copper-fastened that position. So any non-payment to senior bondholders could open up the possibility of legal action. However, the bigger problem was with the European

Commission and the European Central Bank, because the full repayment of bondholders, who had supplied either the state or the banks, was essential to the strategy they were following to protect the euro.

The Department of Finance explored ways in which it could induce senior bondholders in Anglo to negotiate and accept lower repayments, or at least those who were in place already before the guarantee was announced. Even if they could be persuaded to take just half of what they were owed, it would save the state over €2 billion. Honohan emerged from the Central Bank to warn that it 'simply could not be done', and brought what was described as the 'firmly expressed opposition' of the ECB with him.

The government was in a bind. It was under pressure from some economists, politicians and sections of the media to burn these bondholders, but the pressure from the EU was enormous. It was reminded of how the ECB was funding deposits at Anglo. It worried about the likelihood that more help would be needed from Europe, not just with the recapitalization of the banks but with their ongoing liquidity. The day-to-day funding of the state was also a very live issue, as Ireland was at risk of being priced out of the sovereign-debt market even before it had administered a bloody nose to some of those upon whom it depended. The EU could pull the plug on Anglo. It wasn't just the government that would lose money but all of the pension funds and Irish credit unions that had put money there, confident in the strength of the government guarantee. Private investors would suffer too. Quietly, Lenihan authorized the repayments in full but made no fanfare of it. Instead, the word leaked out on internet discussion forums.

Speculation about the final cost was rife during the summer and early autumn of 2010. When Standard & Poor's joined the fray to estimate that the cost to the taxpayer of bailing out Anglo could be €35 billion – at a time when the government insisted it would not be more than €24 billion – it was joining a long list of pessimists. However, it had the most international clout, and the alarm bells were deafening when investors realized that this sum was more than Ireland's entire tax take for 2010. Efforts by Brian Cowen to calm fears by way of an RTÉ news interview failed, predictably. Yields on traded Irish bonds increased in a way that would make returning to the markets for extra borrowing near to impossible and, given that Ireland raises 85 per cent of its national debt from overseas investors, the crisis was obvious.

Essentially, the government believed that it was faced with four options for Anglo's future. It could close it immediately; close it over a short period of time, such as a couple of years; wind it down over a lengthy period of between ten and twenty years; or just keep it going with new capital invested as required, and as management wanted.

The immediate closure was ruled out on the basis that it could cost as much as €70 billion. Few could quite understand why it would cost so much; but apparently the immediate repayment of all liabilities in a situation where assets would be difficult to sell would have led to that cost. A short wind-down apparently would cost nearly as much. A forced seller of so-called distressed assets always gets a bad price.

The solution decided upon was the ten-year wind-down. The cost of following this option would be €29.3 billion in total capital investment by the state, rising to €34 billion if things went wrong. This was announced on 30 September 2010 as the absolutely final cost to the exchequer of rescuing this delinquent bank. The capital would not be paid out in one huge sum; rather, payments would be spread out over ten years – a small mercy.

The remaining loans that Anglo held as assets would be 'run off' at a rate of about 10 per cent per annum. The loans could be sold to other banks or borrowers would be persuaded to find new bankers who would replace Anglo as part of a refinancing. The option of foreclosing on distressed borrowers – taking their assets in lieu of the repayment of loans – was a very live one and would happen far more often than in the first couple of years of the crisis. Anglo also had to raise money to repay loans worth €56 billion that it had drawn from the Irish and European central banks to provide it with liquidity, much of that money borrowed in the previous six months as deposits drained away.

Some good news for the state came in April 2011. While the bank confirmed further enormous losses, this time of €17.7 billion for

2010, Aynsley said that Anglo had gone further than the Central Bank capital stress tests to quantify the scale of losses on problem loans, and that there was no need for additional capital. Indeed, he emphasized that the requirement for another €5 billion to bring the total bill to €34.3 billion would arise only if values of commercial property dropped by 80 per cent from their peak. 'With a fair wind behind us we don't think the taxpayer is going to have to put in any more money,' said Aynsley. 'We think we are at the bottom of the problems in the books that we have. Now the job for us is to get the best value for the loans.' Meanwhile, Anglo merged with what was left of Irish Nationwide, got rid of its wealth-management division and closed overseas offices in Jersey, Vienna and Düsseldorf.

Anglo was entering a new stage of its corporate life but it would not be an easy one. 'We are a wind-down bank in a sector of the market that is incredibly stressed and we are having to deal with very litigious customers,' Aynsley said, even before relations with the Quinn Group deteriorated to prove his concerns well founded. Anglo, having failed itself to run its own business, was going to be in the rather bizarre position of overseeing the behaviour of businesses it knew little about, such as the Quinn Group and the retail department store Arnotts.

The sign over the old Stephen's Green headquarters was gone, and Anglo had moved to Connaught House on Dublin's Burlington Road, built by one of NAMA's biggest clients, Treasury Holdings, with money provided by Anglo. It used to be the home of its private banking division. There was no need for that service now.

16.   Sean Quinn vs the Financial Wreckulator

Given all that had happened for which he was responsible, business-man Sean Quinn might have considered himself lucky that Taoiseach Brian Cowen took his call in the first week of April 2010. Such a thought is unlikely to have passed through Quinn's mind. Quinn had been used to getting his way for years and was surrounded by people who agreed with him and who sorted things out for him as he wanted. He still had sufficient clout for a phone call to Cowen not to go unanswered, but he was about to have it confirmed that his power was so diminished that he would be heard and then politely ignored.

Quinn was angry and, although he probably would not have admit-ted it, scared about how things were running away from him, now that others were pointedly doing the opposite of what he wished. He was angry that the Financial Regulator had called his bluff after lengthy talks about how the financial stability of arguably the most important part of his empire, Quinn Insurance Ltd (QIL), could be re-established had ended badly and the regulator had taken control of it away from him. Quinn was frightened, justifiably so, that he was on the verge of losing his best chance of pulling off some kind of financial recovery: without the profits from QIL, he would have no way of repaying even part of the debt of over €3 billion he owed to Anglo Irish Bank. This would mean surrendering ownership of his entire group and other personal assets as well.

For many years the Quinn story had been a great one. He had cre-ated something out of nothing in a part of the country that had seen little investment and where emigration was the alternative to pov-erty. Quinn broke the Irish Cement monopoly and branched into glass and radiator manufacturing. He bought pubs, hotels and golf courses both in Ireland and, in time, abroad. He also supplied much needed jobs. The bulk of the estimated 6,000 people employed by the group in Ireland were based in border counties or near by. Other businesses thrived by trading with Quinn. What was not to admire or applaud, other than occasional rows with non-unionized workers and complaints about the way some insurance claims were settled?

He seemed to wear his massive wealth with ease, as if it didn't matter to him. His lifestyle somehow was the opposite of ostentatious, a trait that endeared him to many, even if he did own a corporate jet and helicopter. He was happier at GAA matches or, as folklore had it, playing games of cards with old friends for no more than €5 a night. The *Sunday Times* 2008 Rich List not only placed him in first position in Ireland, with a net worth of €4.7 billion, but, due to his place of birth if not his Irish nationality, he even made it into the list of Britain's twenty richest people.

What Quinn didn't realize was that whatever about the hero worship he enjoyed in the Cavan/Monaghan/Fermanagh region, he was thought of very differently in the rest of the country, at least among those who examined the facts and didn't fall for his maudlin claims about being merely unlucky but determined to make things right. Others put it about that he was some sort of unwarranted victim of the establishment. They all chose to minimize the truth: that his behaviour had undermined the already flimsy foundations of Anglo; that it threatened to bring about an expensive destabilization of the insurance sector; and that it had undermined his own group of companies and the prospects for those who worked for him. These consequences ultimately would have to be borne by the citizens of the state, already paying for the recklessness of the once privately owned banks.

The regulator had put Quinn's prized insurance company into administration days before the phone call to Cowen. Matthew Elderfield had secured High Court approval for a pair of accountants to take provisional responsibility for the management of the business to the exclusion of Quinn's management team, prior to subsequent confirmation of a permanent arrangement in the courts. He did so in circumstances that would have been extraordinary at any time but even more so given what had gone before.

Cowen took Quinn's phone call only because he was aware of the misguided popular support for the businessman in his local area – and the potential impact for Fianna Fáil in the next general election if it was seen to be dismissive of efforts to save jobs. But he did not buckle in the face of Quinn's pleading. The best he could offer was help from Enterprise Ireland in setting up a task force for the region if required.

To have done otherwise would have been to interfere with the entirely justified actions of the recently appointed financial regulator. Had Cowen done so, Elderfield would have had no option but to quit, just three months after taking up the job. The negative impact upon Ireland's already tarnished reputation would have been catastrophic. The donning of the green jersey had taken on a new meaning. This time it meant doing the right thing, no matter what xenophobic taunts would be hurled against Elderfield by some Fianna Fáil TDs in the coming weeks.

The history of Quinn's early business career and his insane gambling in Anglo shares is set out in *Who Really Runs Ireland?*, but it is worth including a summary of the latter here.

Quinn lost nearly €3 billion in buying the rights to nearly 28 per cent of all the shares in Anglo. He did not use his own cash to do so but borrowed much of the money for his gambles from Anglo itself. But this wasn't all. To use a sporting analogy, Quinn received what could be called a 'yellow card' from the Financial Regulator in late 2008 when it was discovered that he had used money from QIL to finance some of his disastrous gambling on shares in Anglo, to the tune of €288 million, without getting approval from the insurance company's investment committee.

In addition, QIL paid €300 million in October 2007 for property assets owned by entities controlled by the Quinn family. The payments were made without independent valuations having first been carried out. When this was done later at the insistence of the auditors, it was decided that a valuation of €211 million would have been more appropriate. The regulator was told nothing of it until the auditors insisted Quinn confess to it. Later, Quinn would claim that the value of the assets had fallen – accounting retrospectively for the write-down – but he couldn't explain who had been responsible for the transfers initially at that price. Fortunately for Quinn the regulator agreed that it would take no action that would affect the group's ability to continue as a going concern, and the auditors signed off its 2007 accounts, staving off crisis for a while.

Quinn did not go unpunished for all of this. He was fined €200,000 personally and ordered to step down as a director of the insurance company that he still owned. It was fined €3.5 million, effectively his money, given that he was 100 per cent owner. Many argued that the punishment was soft, even if of record dimensions, and they wondered why it had taken over a year for the news to be revealed publicly. But few wanted to see QIL put out of business – because of the jobs it provided, because of the possible cost to the state of an immediate wind-up or sale, and because of the impact such an immediate action would have on the state's ability to recover as much as possible of the €3 billion debt Quinn had to repay to Anglo.

But a second, equally serious breach of the regulations – not discovered until early 2010 – was to sunder the difficult relationship between the regulator and Quinn entirely; this ultimately cost Quinn control of the insurer and, eventually, his entire group.

On 24 March 2010 QIL Chairman Jim Quigley phoned the Office of the Financial Regulator. That was not unusual; there had been ongoing regular discussions between QIL and the regulator, often fraught, for more than a year about QIL's deteriorating financial position. Only two days earlier the regulator had rejected the latest attempt by QIL to provide evidence of a plan to rectify the solvency issues that threatened its ability to continue in business. What Quigley was about to reveal put the tin hat on things, as far as the regulator was concerned.

A day earlier a bondholder at Quinn Group (the bondholders comprised a large group owed about €1.2 billion; their composition was changing regularly as bonds were traded) had informed the group that it believed the existence of guarantees provided by QIL to Quinn Group over the repayment of bonds had a material impact on the solvency requirements of the insurance company itself.

Quigley decided that he had better inform the regulator formally of this. It was a bombshell to the recipient. The regulator's office did some quick calculations and decided that the effect of these guarantees was a reduction in the value of QIL's assets by €448 million. Although these assets were owned by QIL, the legal right to their ownership would transfer to bondholders in Quinn Group if the latter failed to make its own repayments to its lenders. QIL was now no longer sufficiently solvent to conduct insurance business, as its liabilities exceeded its assets; there was now a €200 million hole in the balance sheet of the insurance provider that needed to be filled, and fast.

Elderfield didn't care about Quinn's status in his local community or his role as an employer. He saw the bigger picture. He quickly contacted PricewaterhouseCoopers, auditor to Quinn, and asked if the bondholders would release the guarantees to improve the position of QIL. He also asked for an immediate €35 million cash payment from Quinn Group to QIL as an interim provision for improved solvency. Neither request was agreed to, and Elderfield moved on Tuesday, 30 March 2010, to appoint an interim administrator, even though he had been told by his officials of the likely political impact.

Elderfield's action had to be approved by the High Court. He had made an *ex parte* application, meaning Quinn wasn't represented at the initial hearing; Quinn's opportunity to fight the appointment of provisional, or temporary, administrators – two partners from accountancy firm Grant Thornton, Michael McAteer and Paul McCann – would not come for another fortnight. In its affidavit, the regulator said that the 'manner in which the business of the insurer is being and has been conducted has failed to make adequate provision for its debts, including contingent and prospective liabilities'. The business was being managed in such a way 'as to jeopardize and prejudice' the right and interests of the policy holders, and that the company had not complied with solvency requirements. It was concerned that if Quinn Insurance were to 'continue as at present, there might not be sufficient funds to meet claims', and that it had 'failed to make adequate provisions for its debts'.

Quinn and his family remained the sole shareholders of Quinn Insurance, for the moment at least. This gave them time to find some way to get the money to cover the hole in the balance sheet and restore solvency. Quinn Group claimed that it merely required a capital injection of around €150 million to meet the required solvency rules. Quietly, the regulator suggested the real figure was actually €700 million.

Predictably, Quinn's reaction to the regulator's actions was furious. He claimed he was '100 per cent right' and had broken no rules. The regulator, said Quinn, had been aware of the guarantees for five years because details were contained in the accounts, even if not explicitly notified to the regulator. Quinn also claimed that it was not obliged to disclose the existence of the loan guarantees in the solvency returns that it supplied to the regulator.

The regulator denied ever receiving the company filings (raising questions as to why it hadn't sought them) and insisted that details of the loan guarantees should have been included in the solvency returns that QIL submitted, specifically in the section relating to solvency ratios. There was no indication that the guarantees, some of which had been in place for five years, would be called in, but Elderfield could not take that chance. And in any case why was the insurance company taking the risk of providing guarantees to Quinn Group companies? The implications were too obvious.

None of this stopped Quinn from embarking on an offensive that served to muddy the waters politically. To his shock, however, even if Cowen did speak to him once, other personal messages to government ministers went unanswered, so he decided to make his case publicly, by way of press releases and television interviews. Quinn attacked Elderfield's actions as 'highly aggressive and unnecessary' and claimed the move 'endangered' employment across the Quinn Group by making 'the repayment of outstanding debt extremely difficult'. He asked the ministers why the regulator was taking this action when 'the group and Quinn Insurance are in a position to meet all their respective obligations from a cash perspective'. To anyone who didn't know the true story, and many did not, it might have been swaying.

In 2009 the public was informed about Quinn's fine back in October 2008, for earlier irregularities connected with the use of QIL money to buy Anglo shares. But the public wasn't told of how, back in May 2008, QIL had been forced to submit a financial-recovery plan to deal with falling property and share values affecting the investments in its portfolio.

The first serious hint of trouble to emerge publicly, other than stock-market rumours that Quinn had been taking large losses on his undeclared investments in Anglo, came in July 2008, when Quinn Group stopped providing information to credit-ratings agency Moody's, preventing it from offering further opinions on Quinn's ability to repay its debts. Worryingly, it was a response to Moody's decision to revise its outlook on QIL from positive to stable. At the time Quinn said the change was immaterial, as the company had no publicly traded debt in issue, but it remained highly indicative of the deteriorating state of the QIL accounts.

On 18 November 2008 QIL informed the regulator that the Quinn Group, its parent company, was unable to meet its financial obligations as owner, derailing a plan to restore the insurer's solvency margins and solvency ratios to the required levels.

The Office of the Financial Regulator demands that non-life insurers operate a solvency margin of 150 per cent and a solvency ratio of 40 per cent, measures designed to guarantee that an insurer can meet all the claims on its books. The solvency margin is the excess of an insurer's assets over its liabilities, and the regulator required assets to be one and a half times the estimated value of its liabilities. In 2008 the Quinn solvency margin was 133 per cent and it admitted that it would not be able to reach the 150 per cent target for 2009. The solvency ratio is arrived at by measuring a company's after-tax income against its total debts and is meant to reflect how likely a company is to be able to continue to meet its debts. In 2008 Quinn Insurance had a solvency ratio of 25 per cent, as against the required 40 per cent; by the time the administrators were appointed, it had been brought up only to 31 per cent.

In April 2009 QIL forecast that its Gross Written Premiums (GWP) – effectively the total of all its insurance policies – would be limited to €972 million in 2009 in order to improve its solvency. Less than two thirds of its sales would be in Ireland, and more than one third in the UK, where major efforts would be made to improve the position in commercial and motor insurance while withdrawing from the solicitors' personal-injuries market. QIL said it would meet the year-end solvency ratio for 2009 of 40 per cent and claimed 'significant improvement' in its British operations over the previous twelve months. At a further meeting on 10 June 2009 QIL said it would be doing more business in Britain and less in Ireland. Apparently, the regulator did not object.

More meetings were held. At a presentation in December 2009, the insurer said that it was unlikely to meet the 150 per cent solvency margin at year-end. 'The presentation stated that the profits had not materialized in the opportunity in the Great Britain motor business highlighted by the insurer during the June 2009 meeting,' said the court affidavit in April 2010, supporting the application for the permanent appointment of the administrator.

On Christmas Eve 2009, QIL sent an e-mail to the regulator warning that it was breaching its agreements with lenders because its financial performance had fallen below minimum standards, which conceivably could lead to the lenders demanding immediate repayment. This major development was not disclosed to staff in a 'New Year message' displayed on the company's website. Instead, Quinn boasted that his insurance company had enjoyed a 'robust' year, making record profits. He outlined his 'renewed excitement' for the year to come. It was more bluffing by the man who had boasted previously that his only vice was playing poker with friends in Cavan once a week for a fiver.

On 18 January 2010 the regulator asked QIL to draw up 'contingency plans' in case the larger Quinn Group was to fail. The plans received on 29 January did not satisfy the regulator, even after further negotiation. On 11 March, Colm Morgan, Quinn Insurance's chief executive, was told by Elderfield during a phone call that he was 'exceptionally disappointed' with the recovery plan being presented to it, that QIL's forecasts for investment returns were 'very optimistic' and that profit forecasts 'were unrealistic'. A few days later Jim Quigley offered 'a substantial price adjustment' at the British operations to reduce its risks. This was not enough for the regulator, who remained worried 'about the insurer's equity exposures and the insurer's continued over-exposure to property'. Another new business plan was demanded, and received on 22 March, but again rejected by the regulator at a meeting with Quigley and Morgan the next day.

The accounts of the Quinn Group and QIL were both complicated because of the myriad of structures used to hold assets. Overall, the insurance business accounted for €1.1 billion of the group's €2.2 billion of turnover in 2008. The company accounts showed that at the end of 2008 it had managed to pay Quinn personally, as owner, a dividend of €75 million, having paid a larger dividend of €135 million the previous year.

But that was only one part of the QIL story.

Another was how it invested its reserves and the annual insurance premiums it received. QIL was massively exposed to the downturn in property values. Of its €1.8 billion in total assets at the end of 2008, 28 per cent (€514 million) was held as property, land, fixtures and fittings. By contrast, Hibernian Aviva, the largest competitor in Ireland, had invested just 1.3 per cent of its €2.2 billion assets in property, and FBD had 9.4 per cent of its assets in property.

QIL held none of its money in government bonds, instead preferring to keep over 40 per cent of its money as cash on deposit in the banks (which made it far more vulnerable than others prior to the introduction of the bank guarantee). Hibernian Aviva had over 70 per cent of its assets invested in government bonds and FBD not far short of half. Having the money in cash meant that it was far easier for Quinn to use it for other purposes.

The other problem that the regulator identified was putting suitable values on the property assets, particularly in markets where the prices were falling. These assets included pubs in Ireland, property companies in Switzerland and Poland, hotel companies in Bulgaria and Holland, and landfill-waste and wind-farm businesses in Northern Ireland. Many of these insurance-company assets had been bought from the Quinn Group. One example of a wind farm called Mantlin and its sale to QIL raised eyebrows. The cost of building the wind farm was €35 million but, based on its perceived potential, this was revalued at €136 million prior to transfer of ownership. Once on the books of QIL its valuation increased again, to €200 million.

That Quinn had an unorthodox investment pattern did not surprise competitors, who had complained for years about his way of doing business – and who had been rewarded with claims of sour grapes. In particular they argued that QIL made its profits by underwriting insurance at levels that did not provide adequate protection to clients. This is why Quinn had a reputation for putting pressure on clients to settle for lower amounts than many other insurers might have offered. If they didn't accept a swift settlement as offered, to the advantage of the company, they faced the prospect of an expensive court battle, enough to deter many nervous claimants who were also in need of quick cash. QIL's explanation – that it had a more efficient, low-cost business than other insurers, which allowed it to lower prices – was not about to stand up to intense scrutiny.

Little of this was encouraging when QIL needed around €150 million to bolster its solvency reserves. Where would the Quinn Group get this? And where would it get another €500 million to pay bondholders to release QIL from its guarantees of other Quinn company borrowings, in order to satisfy the regulator? When other borrowings in the Quinn Group were taken into account, there was borrowing worth €780 million that needed to be refinanced.

The other businesses in the group were under pressure too. After all, they were highly vulnerable to declining consumer spending. Less profits were likely from businesses such as container glass, building products, plastics, packaging, radiators, a fitness centre, eight pubs, nine hotels and thirteen retail-business centres, along with warehousing properties throughout Eastern Europe and India.

And in any case the profits being declared by Quinn Group were not all that they seemed. It emerged only later, courtesy of a report in the *Sunday Tribune*, and confirmed by Quinn, that more than 40 per cent of Quinn Group's operating profit for 2008 came from fees for property-development services provided to investment and finance companies owned and controlled by Sean Quinn, his wife and close family members – who of course owned and controlled the ultimate parent. Quinn Group booked €150 million in income from these related undertakings, understood to be Quinn Property Investments and Quinn Finance Holdings.

Loyalty meant that Quinn's claims that he was a victim of an overzealous regulator got more than just a hearing: they were reiterated with zeal by local politicians who played to domestic interests.

In Seanad Éireann, Fianna Fáil's chief whip, Diarmuid Wilson, from Cavan, claimed that he knew that the regulator had made a serious mistake. 'I want fairness for him and I want justice. There is no justice in a one-sided argument,' he claimed. He described Quinn as a 'patriot' – a strange description when one considers how his losses ended up being borne by the people of Ireland.

There were huge protests outside the Dáil and rallies of support in Cavan and Enniskillen, two towns that had benefited hugely from the jobs provided by Quinn. Posters decried the 'Financial Wreckulator'. The GAA weighed in alongside the local chambers of commerce. 'Despite the contrary assertions of the regulator and the Minister for Finance, we have no hesitation in accepting Sean Quinn's word that he would pay all his liabilities as they fell due and that there was no risk to policy holders,' the chairman of the Fermanagh County Board, Peter Carty, declared. Quinn's brother Peter had been a previous president of the GAA. RTÉ pundit, former Meath all-Ireland medal winner Colm O'Rourke, signed off his *Sunday Independent* column on Gaelic football with this postscript: 'Here's a message for a great GAA man: don't let the bastards grind you down.'

But Elderfield was not to be deterred, even when Quinn went on to RTÉ to declare that Elderfield had made a 'huge mistake'. He emphasized his family's probity and, in an odd use of the third person, made reference to 'Sean Quinn's' desire to clear his debts. Quinn denied there was any risk to policy holders at QIL and said, in now typical hyperbole, that the decision to appoint administrators was the biggest mistake in Irish corporate history. He said that the Quinn Group had 'plenty of money' and did not need a big injection of cash.

Elderfield set the personal insults aside. His decision to put QIL into administration was based on clearly set-out principles, as listed in the affidavit to the High Court. He was worried that the business was being run without adequate provision being made for debts; that it was being managed in such a way as to jeopardize the material interests of policy holders; and that it was not complying with financial regulations.

Within a week of the confirmation of the appointment of the administrators, Quinn eased his position, admitting later that the regulator had been 'technically right'. He tried to move the guarantees away from QIL and over to other companies within the group. 'We will not need new borrowing to cover the guarantees,' said his chief executive, Liam McCaffrey. 'We hope to move those guarantees to other assets, probably manufacturing assets.' McCaffrey maintained that the other divisions were performing well enough to be able to bear the burden of being mortgaged. 'All of the businesses are profitable and cash generative,' he said. He also claimed that the debts in the rest of the group could be serviced from its cash flow, even without QIL. However, that didn't sort out the Quinn family's position on repaying Anglo its debts or help Elderfield achieve his aim of shaking up the way QIL operated.

Quinn was influenced greatly by the appointment, on 13 April 2010, of Talbot Hughes McKillop – an expert in financial restructuring services that had a stellar international reputation – to sort the business out. Murdoch McKillop went in to run the group as interim executive director and quickly started to demand change. With as much as half of the group's daily cash flow being lost each day because of the closure of its UK insurance business, McKillop was determined to bring order to proceedings as fast as possible and to prevent the contagion effect of a disorderly contested wind-down.

McKillop also insisted that Sean Quinn cease to have any executive responsibility within the group. Liam McCaffrey claimed this was to 'ensure that executive management are not excessively diverted from the vitally important job of running our manufacturing business'. Quinn would supposedly concentrate on salvaging the other family assets held outside the country, although, as subsequent events proved, this was not necessarily the case.

Properties such as the Slieve Russell Hotel in Cavan and the Belfry golf resort in Britain had been placed outside the group and were owned by his children through a variety of foreign-registered companies in the British Virgin Islands, Cyprus and Sweden, even though they were listed in various brochures as Quinn Group assets. The family-owned Swedish company held shares in retail outlets in Ufa, the capital of the Russian Republic of Bashkortostan; in an unfinished hotel in Hyderabad, India; in a warehouse in Kazan, Russia; in other warehouse parks in Russia and business centres in Moscow and the Ukraine; and in a few pubs and properties in Ireland.

Sean Quinn returned to RTÉ in early June 2010 making another vain appeal to public sympathy, claiming on *Primetime* that he would be able to repay all of the money owed to Anglo within seven years if Quinn Insurance might be allowed to stay under the control of Quinn Group. 'In seven years' time, we have a projection to 2017, we would have enough profit made in the meantime, plus the value of the company in seven years' time would clear 100 per cent of the debt,' he said. He also implied that family-owned property could be sold to add to the proceeds.

His sums didn't stack up, however. He made no reference to making any interest payments on the debt, which could have amounted to close to €1 billion over the following seven years. He didn't say how he would raise the €150 million needed to meet solvency regulations (according to his estimate – the regulator had put it at €700 million), or how the group would be able to meet its repayments on debts connected with the proposed movement of QIL's guarantees to other companies within the group.

Quinn claimed the insurance company had earned €3 million per week in the first quarter of 2010, but had been losing €3 million per week since it went into administration. But this was because the administrators had been taking a more realistic view about the performance of the business. How would Quinn be able to return it to profitability, now that the previously declared figures were shown to have been based on hopeless optimism? Even if one believed Quinn's figures, that would imply profits of about €1 billion over seven years, nowhere near enough to clear the debt to Anglo.

Given his misbehaviour in running the business, why would the regulator trust Quinn to behave better in the future? Quinn proposed the appointment of a new independent board to run the business as it was being run before administration. But if really independent, would it do things as Quinn had done? And who would it answer to? The Quinn family as the owners, the very people who needed to have maximum profits to help clear their debts?

Quinn accepted that there could be a gap of €2 billion between Quinn assets and the Anglo debt. 'Could be, could be – which is very easily paid back,' he claimed.

The sum was enormous clearly but not to a man who had previously taken so much cash directly from QIL. In the interview he disclosed that he had taken €800 million in dividends personally from the company over five years: 'it drained Quinn Direct, and then we wasted it by buying shares . . . We wasted it, and that is a tragedy.'

He said that although these dividends had been approved by the regulator, a further €288 million had not. Maybe he was confused and misspoke, because a withdrawal of €288 million – which led to his fine by the regulator in October 2008 and his departure as chairman – had been described as a loan, not as a dividend.

This was just one of a number of comments that he made in the interview that cast doubt on previous claims he and his group had made, intentionally or not. He admitted for example that he had not resigned voluntarily as chairman of QIL back in 2008, as had been stated at the time. 'The regulator got rid of me,' he said. This was grist to the mill of reporters, who are always put in legal strait-jackets by officially agreed statements that someone has 'resigned' when in truth they have been fired.

Extraordinarily, the story changed on the issue of the guarantees that the regulator had been told about officially only in March, but which Quinn had claimed had been known about for years because of the freely available public filings. In an incredible twist Quinn said neither he nor anyone in his company even knew about these guarantees until earlier this year. 'It turned out we gave guarantees on subsidiaries of a regulated entity. We didn't know that,' he said. 'Nobody knew they were given – it just happened.'

Suddenly, it seemed, the regulator was correct about the issue and Quinn was supporting him. 'There is going to be a big legal case, and the regulator is inquiring about this and has asked for statements,' he said. 'I'll be supporting him all the way, because this has taken our company down. We have paid so many people so much money, and we are left in this sort of mess. This should never have happened.'

More, however, was to happen at Quinn.

A year after he lost control of his insurance business, Sean Quinn lost ownership of his entire empire.

The denouement occurred in two related events that took place in the space of less than three weeks in April 2011. First Anglo Irish Bank, in conjunction with the US insurance giant Liberty Mutual, seized control of Quinn Insurance from its administrators, with the approval of the Financial Regulator. Then Anglo, acting with the full authority of the state – in the form of a cabinet meeting of the new coalition government – and using guarantees it had been given by Quinn personally, had a 'share receiver' appointed to the Quinn Group. (The guarantees had been over shares in the Quinn Group, which had stood as security for Quinn's loans from Anglo.) This effectively ended not just Quinn's ownership but his involvement with the companies he had created. He was removed unceremoniously from the offices in the company's Ballyconnell, County Cavan, headquarters, barred from returning unless invited, and had his company-supplied mobile phone confiscated.

The state took his empire from him because of his repeated failure to provide a credible plan for repaying his debts. The new coalition government acted decisively against him, whereas its predecessor had appeared to dither somewhat, allowing Quinn the misplaced hope that he would be allowed to retain control of his business and be given time to attempt to repay €4.1 billion, mainly to Anglo Irish Bank but also to a group of about forty international bondholders.

The new government ended Quinn's fantasies, ruthlessly and effectively, ignoring protests from Quinn employees, who, no matter what evidence was presented to them, failed to realize that their hero had gambled recklessly and should suffer the consequences of his losses accordingly.

There was understandable nostalgia for what Quinn had done in the previous thirty-eight years, when he created about 6,000 jobs in the Cavan/Monaghan area that otherwise probably would not have existed. There was loyalty too even if much of it was misplaced: notwithstanding all of the evidence that had come into the public domain over the previous two years, his supporters failed to acknowledge how Quinn's personal excesses – most manifest in the misuse of insurance-company money to fund his private gambling in Anglo Irish Bank shares – had damaged not just his own business interests but also the economic capability of Anglo and the state itself. Most of all, though, there was self-interest: many employees apparently believed that only Quinn would be committed to retaining their jobs, so that was why they backed him. They confused Quinn's retention as their boss with their campaign to 'save our jobs, save our communities'.

Various lobby groups championed Quinn following the announcement of the new arrangements for QIL and before the April 2011 announcement that the state, via Anglo, was exercising its legal right to take control of the group's businesses. They continued to do so afterwards. On the same day that the cabinet privately gave approval for the move against Quinn, which came less than two days later, a meeting of the Quinn stakeholder groups, held in the Slieve Russell Hotel in Ballyconnell, heard of plans to present a petition of 90,000 names in support of Quinn to the regulator, Matthew Elderfield. They organized a convoy from factories and offices to the Central Bank in Dublin to hand a letter and petition to Elderfield. They did so two mornings later and most probably passed the Anglo bankers and receivers travelling in the opposite direction, on their way to apply the coup de grâce to Quinn at a curt meeting at his company headquarters.

As had been decided at the cabinet meeting, the new government stood firm. There were no easy or good options but this course of action looked like the one with the most chance of relative success, even if the optics of engaging Anglo – itself to be wound up – in the process looked debatable. In late April 2011 Taoiseach Enda Kenny made a visit to Leitrim, where he was heckled by a hundred protestors and presented with a letter claiming that removing Sean Quinn from a 'successful' business was 'deplorable'. 'The workers were looking for an assurance that Sean Quinn would be put back in charge of the [Quinn] group,' Kenny said calmly afterwards. 'I can give no such assurance, obviously.'

The campaign continued none the less, but gained little traction outside of its local area. A spokesman for some workers, Padraig Dono-hoe, asked: 'What was the sense, economic or common, to remove Sean Quinn and his senior board of directors in the Quinn Group? . . . They have built the group up over the last thirty-eight years . . . They know all the customers – it makes no sense to remove them.' On its website the group Concerned Irish Businesses declared: 'Quinn pays his bills and helped us at times of need.' Maybe he had, but with whose money had he done so in recent years and how would he pay his debts to Anglo and, by extension, to the rest of the country?

What the government knew, although it would not be made public for another six weeks, was the actual size of the losses at the Quinn Group and the near-impossibility of recovering that money under the existing management. It already knew of the losses at Quinn Insurance – and had endorsed the transfer of that business from the Quinn Group to full state ownership and control – but that wasn't the end of things. In 2009, the last year in which the group was under the full control of Sean Quinn, it had made a pre-tax loss of €852 million, with the losses at QIL largely, but not entirely, to blame.

Not surprisingly, central to the Quinn strategy to regain control of his group's business had been his effort to recover QIL from the administrators, the presence of whom he had accepted reluctantly a year earlier. He tried to achieve this through a populist promise of jobs, saying he'd be able to create 1,800 jobs in three years, most of them local. Yet, in something of a contradiction, Kevin Lunney said a new 'independent' board would be appointed and the family would take a 'back seat' if QIL was returned from the administrators.

But what the regulator was more interested in was money. The Quinn family offered to help recapitalize the insurance business with €200 million from the sale of so-called unencumbered personal assets that were held outside of the group structure (instead of using their sale proceeds to cover the father's gambling debts). They also requested

€500 million to €600 million in new capital from the state, through
Allied Irish Banks or Bank of Ireland rather than through Anglo,
with whom relations had broken down, although this would have led
to state-aid issues with the EU. The idea that the state would become
a co-investor with Quinn, and trust him to keep his oar out while
running the business along the same principles that he had established, was an optimistic one to say the least.

Yet Quinn argued that he could repay all his debts within eight
years if he was left in control of the insurance firm. Anglo – with the
approval of the regulator and Department of Finance – was having
none of that. It had engaged with Quinn throughout 2010 in its
attempts to take control of the insurance company but got tired of
doing so. Instead it sought out other partners and eventually picked
Liberty Mutual of the US, with its experience, capital and ability
to enter the Irish market without creating competition issues, as its
partner. Together they would put about €150 million into the recapitalization of the company, with Anglo having a marginally bigger
share at 50.1 per cent. The idea was that, in time, Anglo would sell
the balance to Liberty.

This deal happened because Quinn's creditors had become impa-
tient at the seeming lack of progress in sorting it all out. The group's
other banks and bondholders, led by Barclays, Bank of Ireland and
AIB, were owed €1.3 billion by now, a large chunk of which had
fallen due in September 2010; they were prepared to be patient for
only so long.

By March 2011 the bondholders had written to both Anglo and
Quinn berating Quinn's apparent unwillingness to address issues
about corporate governance and management. They also believed
that Quinn's financial proposals were unrealistic. Repaying all of
what Quinn owed at a time when the non-insurance businesses were
making profits of not much more than €100 million per annum, and
when the insurance business was in state-enforced administration
because of doubts about its insolvency, looked near impossible. They
wanted him out.

The argument was strengthened when it was confirmed that the
insurance company had run up losses of €706 million for 2009 – with

€559 million of that incurred in the UK – and probably another €160 million for 2010. There was an 'investment loss' of €147 million, mainly because of a reduction in the value of assets, chiefly those held by Quinn Property Holdings, a Quinn Insurance subsidiary, which owned the Slieve Rushen wind farm in County Fermanagh, and hotels in Cambridge, England, Krakow, Poland and Sofia, Bulgaria. Those assets were valued now at €464 million and were to be sold: €200 million of the proceeds were to be used to pay creditors of QIL and the remaining €264 million were to be used to reduce the amount the company would need from the state's fallback, the Insurance Compensation Fund. All of this more than wiped out QIL's shareholders' funds, which showed a deficit of nearly half a billion euro by the year-end 2010.

Buying the shares in Anglo had not been the only massive and wrong gamble that Quinn had made. By offering cheap insurance Quinn had managed to command a 19 per cent share of the market in Ireland. He tried to do the same in Britain, with disastrous consequences. (Interestingly, one of Anglo's English former directors, Noel Howarth, who had worked in the industry in the UK, warned years previously against Anglo giving loans to Quinn to finance this strategy.) Premiums were priced too low, and the administrators, Michael McAteer and Paul McCann of Grant Thornton, were forced to push prices in the UK up by an average of 44 per cent to bring them to realistic levels. They did so after taking independent advice from actuarial consultants, who believed that QIL was under-provided for future claims losses, just as Irish rivals had long been saying. Most pertinently, as far as the administrators and Elderfield were concerned, QIL was still failing to meet regulatory requirements: there wasn't enough cash being held to meet a sudden influx of claims, based on the number of policies the company held.

Sean Quinn reacted angrily to these announcements. He blamed the administrators for wrecking the business. He said that Milliman, Quinn's own actuarial consultants, and PwC, its auditors, had projected underwriting losses for the UK operations of only €40 million for 2009, just before the administrators had been appointed. He went on the offensive, claiming that QIL had €1.1 billion in assets and

€464 million in property when the administrators had been appointed just thirteen months earlier and that the actions of the administrators in 'over-providing' for future claims were causing unnecessary and potentially fatal losses. He reminded anyone who'd listen that in October 2010 lawyers for the administrators had told the High Court they had kept 'a tight eye' on the company and Quinn Insurance would not have to avail itself of the Insurance Compensation Fund.

His family said if documents relating to the involvement of the insurer's new owners were not published, 'then the cover-up of the erosion of value at the expense of the Irish taxpayer at Quinn Insurance will never be revealed'. Quinn claimed that if QIL had not been placed in administration, there would never have been a demand on the ICF for money. He claimed that the insurer had seen its turnover fall by two thirds in administration and allowed its costs to soar. 'It is a truly appalling admission by the administrators of enormous damage they have caused to one of Ireland's most successful companies in just thirteen months,' he said in a statement designed to cause doubts among the public as to the performance of the administrators. McAteer replied by saying that all of his actions since becoming administrator had been designed to stop the losses on existing insurance contracts and that any new contracts were undertaken only on the basis that the prices charged gave them a good chance of being profitable.

Liberty Mutual, one of the largest car insurers in the world, was chosen as the new controlling force at QIL because its presence would ensure competition in the Irish market – not having been there previously – and jobs. It needed the 1,570 staff Quinn had in Ireland and, as it was newly arrived, had no intention of 'rationalizing' by cutting staff. Liberty also offered the potential for further job creation, as its ambitions went beyond Ireland: this deal offered it a foothold in the European market.

Liberty Mutual got into the deal for just €102 million, with Anglo investing €98 million, which was due to be repaid first out of any future profits. It looked a reasonable deal for Anglo financially. A quarter of the future profits made by Liberty–Anglo would go towards reimbursing the state's Insurance Compensation Fund, which was being used to bolster the assets in the company. Another quarter of future profits were to be used to repay part of the €2.88 billion owed by the Quinn family to Anglo. The remaining 50 per cent of profits were to go to Liberty. The deal was constructed so as to give Liberty the option of buying out Anglo in future years, providing a return to the state on its unwanted investment in QIL. Importantly, the guarantees over debts in Quinn Group that QIL had undertaken were no longer a factor for the reconstituted insurance company (having been moved by Quinn to other companies in the group), giving it a stronger balance sheet and allowing Anglo the opportunity to get on with fixing the Quinn Group, just as Liberty was getting on with fixing QIL.

There was bad news for Irish citizens, however. Anybody who purchased any form of non-life assurance in the state would end up paying towards this deal. The administrators said the losses would lead to amounts of up to €600 million being extracted from the state's Insurance Compensation Fund. As the fund had only €30 million available in its reserves, and as €180 million would be needed in the first year, a levy of up to 2 per cent on all motor and household insurance policies in Ireland would be applied. The public was told that this was the lesser of two evils. The administrators estimated that the cost to the ICF would have been 'well in excess of €1 billion' if this deal was not done.

But it wasn't just the insurance firm that Quinn lost. Quinn Healthcare, which had been bought from Bupa, was not part of the Liberty–Anglo deal. Instead, it was put up for sale separately, the proceeds, again, to be used to pay down Anglo's debt. All of the companies in the group outside of the insurance company were about to be placed in the hands of receivers, at the direction of Anglo Irish Bank and with the support of bondholders. When Anglo lent Quinn €2.88 billion, it had taken the right to ownership of the group as its security; and it was now exercising that right. It therefore became the majority owner of the Quinn Group, with 75 per cent of the shares, the balance to be held by bondholders.

Beyond that, Anglo sought to take control of various properties owned by Quinn family members outside of the Quinn Group, but pledged by Sean as security against loans in the event, as was happening now, of his being unable to repay the loans. Anglo reckoned it could recover up to €600 million from sales of properties that had once been valued at €1.1 billion. These included the Kutuzoff Tower in Moscow, once said to be worth €192 million, and the Hilton Hotel in Prague, once valued at €246 million, where US President Barack Obama had stayed and been welcomed personally by Quinn in 2009. There were other properties in India, Russia and Turkey. These included, among other things, a chain of DIY stores and office blocks. The family's corporate jet and helicopter would also be sold.

But it was the fate of the Quinn Group's manufacturing businesses that interested people the most, because more than 6,000 jobs depended on it. The bondholders had to be persuaded of a partial default on the debts Quinn owed (in a way the state or the banks it had taken over were being denied). In return for its quarter share in the remaining business the bondholders agreed to write off €500 million of the debt owed to them. Instead they received €80 million in cash and €125 million from the sale of assets, including hotels in Sofia, Krakow and Cambridge. The state was to get 75 per cent of any dividends paid out of future profits and 75 per cent of the proceeds of the sale of the group, once the remaining €800 million of debt still owed to the bondholders, and secured on the assets of the group, had been paid off in such a sale.

There was a certain irony involved in Anglo becoming the major shareholder in the Quinn Group: here was a bust bank taking over the profitable remnants of a business brought low by its owner gambling on that bank before it went bust.

In addition to their quarter of the shares in the new Quinn Manufacturing Group, the bondholders would get 74.9 per cent of the voting rights; Anglo would own 75 per cent of the shares but only 25.1 per cent of the voting rights.

Anglo nevertheless had to do something to try to get at least some of its money back. It had made a provision of €2.2 billion against the €2.8 billion owed to it by Quinn, but that didn't mean, as popularly believed, that it had written off that money as unrecoverable. It would try to get as much as possible, although not necessarily the full amount. Anglo Chairman Alan Dukes admitted in late April 2011 that Anglo might recover less than half of the €2.8 billion owed by Quinn and his family. With this end in view, Anglo decided on a five-year business plan for the Quinn Group and changed the management to implement it. 'We're reducing the risk on the money that we're owed because we have access to a stream of income that we wouldn't have access to without this arrangement,' Dukes claimed.

So how much was the new Quinn Manufacturing Group – with its four divisions of building products (including cement), glass, plastics and radiators – worth? Much of the public debate was framed around what were then the most recently available accounts, from as far back as 2008, when the full effects of the recession had not yet hit. These showed a turnover of almost €800 million. The earnings before interest, tax depreciation and amortization – a measure of profit that tends to produce bigger numbers – was around €185 million at that stage.

Late in 2010 Quinn Group Chief Executive Liam McCaffrey had sent an e-mail to staff arguing that, no matter what, Sean Quinn would not lose control of the group he founded under the refinancing plans, despite widespread speculation. 'I think it is important to clarify that, contrary to these reports, the board has made no proposal to the banks and bondholders which offers equity in the group's assets,' he said. He said the various Quinn businesses 'have all performed well in 2010, despite a very difficult economic climate' and the group was enjoying 'continued profitability and cash generation'. The reality, however, was that manufacturing turnover fell 28 per cent in 2009, reflecting the collapse in the construction sector. Heavy cost-cutting kept gross profit margins at 27 per cent. Earnings before interest, tax and write-offs of depreciation costs and amortization (EBITDA) – a measure of cash generated – totalled €104 million in the manufacturing business for 2009, which was nowhere near enough to effect a successful rebuilding.

There was a certain degree of bravado to this, which ended when Anglo's Dukes, its chief executive, Mike Aynsley, and executive Richard Woodhouse arrived in Cavan on 14 April 2011 and demanded immediate repayment of the money owned to it. Quinn, accompanied by his close lieutenants Dara O'Reilly and Kevin Lunney, went to seek advice from his lawyers, Eversheds O'Donnell Sweeney, but by 10.30 a.m. the banks had appointed Kieran Wallace of KPMG as share receiver. By 11 a.m. the trio, David Mackey and Patricia Quinn had been voted off as directors and by 4 p.m. Paul O'Brien had been installed as the new Quinn Group chief executive.

He faced many difficulties in the early weeks, including sit-ins and a sustained campaign of sabotage. An effort was made to damage the weighbridge at the group's Derrylin plant, fibreoptic cables were smashed, the power supply was cut off, and a vehicle was parked to block access to the gates of the plant. The protests continued even when it was emphasized that the 2,600 Irish jobs in the division were safe; there were further damaging incidents in July as tensions simmered locally, and in August an arson attempt was made on O'Brien's home.

Bitterly, Sean Quinn left the business he had built. He conceded some mistakes and expressed remorse for the impact on those who had worked for him, but he was eager to blame others too and did not seem to fully understand the effect of his actions on the wider Irish economy. He was in denial, not uncommon among those who are in shock.

'Our mistake was to place an overreliance on the Irish banking system and the many predictions for continued sustained growth in the Irish economy from some of the country's leading financial services experts,' he said in one of his RTÉ interviews.

He believed that he should be given a second chance, no matter how extensive the damage he had caused. 'My colleagues and I have spent the past year developing a proposal that is economically sustainable and which would allow us to discharge fully all of our family's obligations to the Irish taxpayer,' he claimed about his plans to regain control of QIL. 'During this process, we consulted with and secured the support of some of the most respected and experienced individuals in Irish and UK business. I am utterly convinced our proposal could achieve the retention and increase of skilled employment in the group.' But what about repaying the debts? 'Ireland needs enterprise and entrepreneurs more than ever at this time but mistakes in business should not result in a life sentence.' But what about punishment for someone who had been caught twice secretly using the money of QIL to fund his personal gambling on shares in Anglo Irish Bank?

Quinn faced the possibility of losing everything. It had become clear that he and his family – his wife, Patricia, and his children, Sean junior, Brenda, Aoife, Collette and Ciara – had attempted to reduce their risk, not holding all they owned within the Quinn Group, even though four of the children drew an income from working in businesses in the group. The children were equal shareholders, however, in Quinn Group (RoI), the ultimate parent company for the various manufacturing, financial services and leisure businesses that were owned by the family.

This created some confusion as to who would be responsible for the repayment of the debts Sean Quinn had incurred. If he wasn't the owner, how could the right to ownership of the company be offered to Anglo as security in return for its loans? There were conflicting stories as to the giving of personal guarantees. Did they or did they not exist, had they been properly executed, and if so could they be used to seize the homes of the children or other assets that were held in ownership outside of the group and over which no direct charge may have been laid? Rightly or wrongly, the family felt that it was being treated with undue harshness, that it was being denied the right to work itself out of its situation. The state took the view that enough chances had been given.

This led to another extraordinary development in mid May 2011. Patricia Quinn and her five children lodged a High Court action seeking damages from Anglo and the removal of the receiver that had been appointed to Quinn Group, with ownership and control returning to the Quinn family. The lawsuit alleged negligence, breach of duty and intentional and/or negligent infliction of economic damage and sought the removal of the receiver from his position. They sought damages: although their father's actions had cost the state billions, they now wanted hundreds of millions of euro of state money paid to them as compensation.

The six claimed that charges made in favour of Anglo from late 2003 up to 2009 over shares held in Quinn Group (RoI) Ltd, Quinn Quarries Ltd, Slieve Russell Hotel Ltd, Quinn Finance Holding, Quinn

Group Hotels Ltd and Quinn Group Properties Ltd were invalid, unenforceable and of no legal effect and that, as a consequence, Wallace's appointment as receiver was invalid and unenforceable. They also sought declarations that undated guarantees provided by them to Anglo over the liabilities of several Cyprus-registered companies were invalid and unenforceable.

The Quinns made a very serious allegation. They claimed that the loans were made for the purpose of 'an illegal objective of market manipulation' – support of the Anglo share price. Even if this had been true – and it was not immediately clear that it was in fact the case – it would have been to their benefit, given that they still held about 15 per cent of the bank's shares by way of CFDs (following the sale of the rest of Quinn's CFDs to the Maple Ten). Aoife Quinn claimed in an affidavit that she and her family signed personal guarantees in late 2008 over certain loans by Anglo to Cypriot-registered companies owned by the family without being told of the 'precarious' financial position of Anglo. They'd had no independent legal or financial advice and the nature of the loan documents had never been discussed with them, she said. She said the plaintiffs, when they were asked to sign the execution blocks to the personal guarantees, had not known, and were not made aware, that the guarantees were 'a purported condition' of the advance of the loans.

How could they not have known? The share price was crumbling. The state's bank guarantee had been put in place, even if Anglo would not fall into state ownership for a few months yet. Were they not under a duty to independently check for themselves what they were signing? Had they not objected to what their father had been doing? Had they not known about his gambling on Anglo shares? Had they not authorized his use of their shares as security?

The intent of the action seemed clear: it was designed to repudiate responsibility for the repayment of loans to Anglo, make the guarantees unenforceable and regain control of the business. But the implication of it was that Sean Quinn had acted beyond his powers in offering shares in their business as collateral for his gambling, and that Anglo had not investigated properly the title to the security it had received. That raised the prospect of a lengthy and expensive court battle, at further cost to the state.

But there was a risk to the Quinn family in their actions beyond the financial. There was a danger that the court could come to the conclusion that Quinn had acted fraudulently in offering security over which he had no entitlement or that the Quinn Group had constructed an ownership structure that was of the 'have your cake and eat it variety', where control and/or ownership rested with Quinn or his wife and children depending on when it suited them.

A long and bitter game of legal poker loomed. What would be unveiled during the 'discovery process' for the legal action, for example, on both sides? In the preliminary hearings it was noted by Judge Peter Kelly that none of the guarantees provided for the Anglo loans were dated, while copy documents of two personal guarantees in the names of Aoife Quinn and Sean Quinn junior over certain loans by Anglo to companies registered in Cyprus were unsigned. Would there be other problems with documents? What information would the discovery process turn up in the way of internal Anglo memoranda or files, or contacts with the regulator, the Central Bank and the Department of Finance? But by the same token what would it reveal about Sean Quinn's behaviour?

Paul Gallagher, the former attorney general, was now acting for Anglo. He warned that his side would consider whether to join Sean Quinn himself and others as third parties to the action, in other words whether to make him a co-defendant with Anglo against the action by his own family. The family was alleging illegal behaviour by Anglo but might that not apply to Sean Quinn, depending on what emerged? The case, unless settled out of court, would constitute the largest ever claim in the Commercial Court's history and was due to be heard early in 2012. But how could the state be seen to settle with Quinn? The legal arguments moved to Sweden, Cyprus and Russia, where the Quinn family had established structures to control its global collection of assets, and where Anglo now sought injunctions to freeze the movement of money by members of the Quinn family and to take control of their assets. The allegations being made became more and more remarkable, and promised to be sensational should they ever receive a full hearing in court. In the meantime the issues were made more complicated when four of Quinn's adult children, Ciara, Sean junior, Brenda and Collette, claimed that they had been 'either sacked, made redundant or constructively dismissed' from their positions in the Quinn Group.

Some things were clear through all of the confusion, though. The ultimate cost would be borne by the Irish taxpayer, and the actions of Sean Quinn, his self-pity notwithstanding, had done much to undermine the economy of Ireland. No matter how the court case finished, everyone else would end up paying for it.

18.   It's So Hard to be Humble

AIB didn't cost the state quite as much in capital as Anglo – at €20.5 billion it came in at €9 billion less than the cost of Anglo – but on top of that enormous sum the unquantifiable damage it did to the wider Irish economy must have been sizeable. Whatever about the dubious merits of the argument that Anglo was 'systemic' and therefore had to be saved, there was no doubt that AIB was essential to the proper working of the Irish economy and that there would have been chaos had it failed suddenly. The bank had more than 270 branches across the Republic, more than a third of all bank branches in the country, employing almost 13,000 people at its peak. It was entwined in the fabric of every town and city. Almost half of the country's adults had their current and savings accounts with AIB, and one in five mortgage holders had got their loan from AIB. But this meant that the damage it caused went deeper than what Anglo had done: although AIB had lent heavily to developers and deliberately gone after Anglo's customers, it had also provided loans for the end customers who would buy these units. It was AIB, more so than anyone else – and not Anglo with its dependency on those with high incomes – that had sucked ordinary people into the casino, with its aggressive marketing of loans, mainly when the property market was at its peak. It was AIB to which small businesses had often turned; and it was small businesses that were now finding that its capacity to provide simple services such as overdrafts, much less bigger loans for investment, was constrained enormously by its own financial recklessness.

AIB and the government had thought initially, back in December 2008, that just €2 billion in new capital would be enough to put the bank back on a sound footing. This turned out to be less than one tenth of the final figure.

AIB had gone on a lending splurge from 2004 onwards, aimed at both developers and the end buyers, having made a policy decision to regain market share from Anglo. The warning signs appeared in relatively small things such as chartering a plane in 2004 to fly sixty developers to golf's Ryder Cup match between Europe and the United States in Michigan. They were clearly visible in the decision to bankroll Ray Grehan in his ill-fated €171 million purchase of the two-acre former veterinary college site in Ballsbridge, less than a mile from its own headquarters, a deal that left most observers of the property game agog and that, even then, drew comparisons with the madness in the Japanese property market of two decades earlier. Senior executives were involved in property development themselves as a 'sideline', and there were reports of property-lending managers earning commissions so large on loans that they ended up with seven-figure annual incomes.

At the 2008 annual general meeting of AIB, the bank's chairman, Dermot Gleeson, another barrister-turned-businessman who had been attorney general to the Rainbow government of 1994 to 1997, told shareholders that the bank had no need to ask them for extra capital. Some analysts had been suggesting that this would be a prudent course of action in what many could see was a sharply slowing economy. He said the capital, asset quality and funding at AIB were all robust. The provision against loans not being repaid was a mere 0.2 per cent. He spoke of the bank's 'diversity and resilience' and boasted of a 'carefully chosen spread of businesses', not just in Ireland but internationally. They had just spent €216 million on buying a half-share in a Bulgarian bank (which would be sold just three years later for €100,000). Further proof of this arrogance came in August 2008, when Gleeson and his board decided to increase AIB's interim dividend by 10 per cent, costing AIB €270 million in cash. But the balance sheet was primed to collapse. AIB's total Irish loan portfolio in 2008 was €92.6 billion, with €33.2 billion related to construction and property. Lending to that sector had grown by 124 per cent over four years, and the bank's lending to property developers and construction was ten times the size of its loans to the manufacturing sector.

Yet Gleeson and his Bank of Ireland counterpart Richard Burrows were not humble when they went to the government on the evening of 29 September 2008, as the crisis for funding of the Irish banking system reached epic proportions; it wasn't in their nature to demonstrate anything other than total confidence in their position. They conceded that they had big problems with raising cash to meet their liabilities, but this, apparently, was because of the international crisis caused by Lehman Brothers and the perilous condition of the disdained Anglo, not their own shortcomings. Their own situation remained relatively good, or so they said, even if privately they might not have believed it.

The government had good reason to be distrustful of whatever AIB said. The bank had a long history of corporate irresponsibility and of leaving the state in a position of having to pick up the tab. Many in the Department of Finance still had bitter memories of the circumstances of the state's bailout of AIB in 1986, when losses at its disastrous acquisition Insurance Corporation of Ireland nearly bankrupted it. Within months of that rescue, AIB dished out big dividends to shareholders. It was the single biggest banking facilitator of tax evasion by Irish residents over a lengthy period and ended up making a massive settlement with the Revenue Commissioners as a result. Many of its own senior executives from a previous board had availed themselves of a special offshore entity into which tax-avoiding investments had been made. AIB had a colourful history of being caught ripping off its own customers and of having to make subsequent compensatory payments. It was also careless in management of its employees' behaviour: in 2002 a rogue trader in the United States called John Rusnak lost $691 million of AIB's money through wild speculation that nobody noticed until it was too late.

Just weeks after benefiting from the state guarantee AIB tried to emphasize that it had no need for further rescue. Its defiant chief executive, Eugene Sheehy, declared that he would rather die than sell equity to the state, but his bravado failed to inspire any confidence in AIB's ability to assess and deal with its situation. During the following year a pattern emerged in which AIB consistently issued statements admitting that things were actually worse than they'd said previously.

The government went into 2009 still not realizing how bad the situation was at the country's main banks. At a January 2009 Oireachtas committee meeting Central Bank Governor John Hurley claimed that the share prices of the main Irish banks quoted on the stock-market were 'not really indicative' of their actual situations. It was presumed that he meant that the shares were undervalued rather than overvalued, because he said they were 'strong institutions' and 'solvent institutions'. Hurley commented that AIB and Bank of Ireland had 'a very good opportunity' to raise €1 billion each from private investors as part of the new €2 billion capital fund-raising each was attempting. He said this effort 'should be allowed to run its course'. By 12 February it had to be announced that the amount of new capital required at each bank would be €3.5 billion and that it would have to come from the state.

Yet the government continued to set its face against nationalizing the banks. It had become an article of faith that this would be off-putting to international investors in the country. It decided that its investment would be made in preference shares rather than in ordinary shares. This meant that the state would not get voting rights but it would get a 'guaranteed' annual return on its investment; and if the bank failed to make the dividend payment, an equivalent amount of ordinary shares would be given to the state in lieu.

Things continued to deteriorate, and at speed. In March 2009 AIB said that it could write off up to €8.4 billion in bad loans between 2008 and 2010 and still have enough capital, once the government's €3.5 billion injection was taken into account. Unfortunately, the government's advisers, as they prepared to announce NAMA, then estimated that the likely losses would reach €12 billion. The rising figures were causing panic within AIB, and its provision of finance to customers began to dry up. This was the main reason why the state began its rescue of AIB and the calls for immediate nationalization mounted. The one thing the government and AIB agreed upon was that neither wanted that.

Sheehy said in March 2009 that 'it is very important that the staff know the bank has done nothing to be ashamed of, that it is going to support its customers through this downturn.' But his position, and that of Gleeson and Finance Director John O'Donnell, now became the subject of much public speculation. The government tried to stay aloof, encouraging the AIB board privately to consider the situation rather than dictate anything in public.

Eventually, Lenihan had to force the resignations of the trio when AIB announced all were standing for re-election to the board at the 2009 annual general meeting that May. Lenihan warned that he would vote publicly against their re-election at an annual general meeting if they did not step down. A deal was done whereby the state actually voted for them to continue in office on the understanding that they would subsequently resign at a time of their own choosing. Gleeson might have wished that he had quit earlier. One angry shareholder pelted him with eggs to protest against the destruction of shareholder value. On that day, shares that had traded at a high of €23.95 in 2007 changed hands at just 87 cents. AIB's value had fallen by over €20 billion to not much more than just €1 billion.

Sheehy was not to leave for months, however. A massive row broke out as to who should be his successor. AIB wanted an internal appointment, believing that Colm Doherty, a main board director for many years and head of its capital markets division, should be promoted to the top job. It said that he was the best man and that, in any event, it had been unable to find a suitable external candidate who wanted such a big and difficult job at a newly imposed government maximum salary of €500,000, hard as that might have been to believe.

The idea of promoting from within appalled many. Doherty had been a main board director since 2003, although he claimed to have opposed the property-lending strategy vocally at board meetings during that time. Lenihan at first refused to endorse the promotion, still smarting from the criticism he had attracted for allowing Richie Boucher to step up to become new boss at Bank of Ireland. Twice he tried, unsuccessfully, to persuade Chairman Dan O'Connor to take the job of acting chief executive. After a lengthy stand-off, Lenihan compromised by allowing Doherty to become managing director instead of chief executive, although few understood what the difference actually meant. He asked O'Connor – a former General Electric executive who had been on the main board since 2007 – to assume his role on a permanent, full-time basis.

The idea apparently was that Doherty would run the business and raise private capital, while O'Connor would deal with the government and with the EC in Brussels. As some critics chose to make pay, rather than suitability, the main issue for debate, Lenihan boasted that he had forced AIB to accept that Doherty must be paid no more than €500,000, a fall of €133,000 on his previous package. The idea of a clean slate, of getting rid of those who'd overseen the mess at the bank, to be replaced by people who were not responsible, seemed to disappear.

Few doubted that Doherty was highly able and qualified, someone who could argue his case, and the bank's, forcibly and stylishly, depending on the circumstances. But his presence on the board since 2003 compromised his status, and his promotion sent out signals that not all was changing at AIB.

Doherty's main responsibility became the search for new capital from private sources, in order to keep AIB out of state hands. He held off on retrenchment of staff numbers, although he drew up plans for over 2,000 job losses, largely because he didn't have the money available for redundancy payments. His idea was that the new capital would pay for that. The bank also cut back savagely on its new lending, much to the frustration of consumers and businesses who argued that the only reason the state was rescuing AIB was so that it could fulfil its role as a lender. Doherty had to start considering the sale of the bank's prized overseas assets in Poland, the UK and US, to raise money and to reduce the overall capital needs.

Doherty had two unexpected problems, courtesy of the European Commission. AIB was due to transfer loans of over €24 billion to NAMA. The EC's changed position on the price NAMA could pay – demanding that this be at existing market value rather than at long-term economic value – was of great significance to the losses AIB would have to report. In August 2009 AIB had announced that €4.9 billion of the loans it had given would not be repaid. However, by November it was admitting that its bad debts could be €1 billion higher, at least, and that another €10.5 billion of loans were 'impaired', a near €4 billion increase on its previous estimate. Having already received €3.5 billion in state investment, by early 2010 AIB required another €4 billion at the very least.

The European Commission had also refused to allow the payment of guaranteed dividends on preference shares. AIB had been due to make annual repayments of €280 million in cash under the terms agreed with the government for its investment. The state now had to take ordinary shares instead of cash, representing 18 per cent of the overall equity. This provided little scope for fund-raising, because any new investment by the state would make it the majority owner, thus bringing about nationalization. By March 2010 Lenihan began explicitly preparing investors and taxpayers for that likelihood, and Doherty's job became far tougher.

The target set for Doherty in March 2010 was near impossible: he had to raise €7.4 billion through a combination of new capital and asset sales if he was going to keep AIB out of state hands and he had to do it by year-end.

He pulled off one coup. He sold AIB's 70 per cent share in the Polish subsidiary, Bank Zachodni WBK, for €3.2 billion, a price about €500 million higher than anyone had expected. But that, in itself, told a tale. Santander paid this price because it regarded it as a very lucrative asset, one that in normal circumstances AIB should have held. BZ WBK was the fifth largest bank in Poland and one of its most profitable, earning a return on capital of 17 per cent. Would it not have been better for the state to take ownership of AIB, hold this stake and use it as an attraction for the subsequent planned reprivatization of AIB?

The government had decided, however, that it wanted as much as possible of the money for the restructuring of AIB to come from the private sector, and that was what Doherty wanted too. He didn't want to become a civil servant. The €2.5 billion profit he turned on the deal meant that he had 'just' another €4.9 billion to raise to meet the capital target set by the Central Bank. He managed to negotiate the sale of AIB's 22.5 per cent stake in US bank M&T for about €1.5 billion. He felt he was getting places.

But selling the British side of the business, which included First Trust in Northern Ireland, was essential . . . and it was nightmarishly difficult. A sale would have removed €20 billion of loans from the group balance sheet; this would have effectively knocked the equivalent of €1 billion off the €7.4 billion capital target. But there was a short-age of buyers in the UK.

It didn't stop Doherty from pressing ahead bullishly. He went to various investor conferences in Dublin and London in September 2010 and spoke very confidently about AIB's improved position, not-withstanding the ongoing economic crisis in Ireland and how that would impact on day-to-day profits. He promised that he would put the bank 'on the path of profitability through 2011 and 2012'. He said that there would be a big initial hit to the bottom line because of the cost of job cuts and other restructuring, but he claimed the payback to the profit line would be fast. He implied that AIB would ruth-lessly take advantage of its return to its old monopoly position. 'Much higher margins will be achieved on new and re-priced loans,' he was reported as telling analysts. 'The new competitive landscape will mean that AIB will be a price-maker rather than [the] price-taker that we have been, given the level of competition in this market over the past number of years.' Doherty was confident he could con-vince a sufficient number of investors to give him all the money he needed.

His fear was that he did not have enough time and that Elderfield would not be flexible or 'reasonable' if things failed to go to schedule. His fears were to be realized spectacularly at the end of September 2010.

It was NAMA that did for Doherty's efforts. Having been sup-portive initially of the concept, Doherty became disillusioned about the practicalities of how it operated. He had already been angered by the prices paid to AIB for its loans, believing that the 'mark to mar-ket' approach, where the accounts reflected the assumed value of the security in the property market at that time, even if perhaps unnatur-ally low, had been self-defeating, driving property values downwards. Now he was to get the news that dealt the final blow to his hopes of raising capital from the private sector.

On the last Saturday of September the bosses of all the banks were summoned to the Central Bank on Dame Street to a meeting with Matthew Elderfield. He had asked NAMA for estimates of the dis-counts that would be applied to the next three tranches of loans that it was purchasing. AIB had been forced to accept a 45 per cent haircut on the first batch of loans – about €6 billion – that NAMA had taken in April. But now NAMA proposed a 60 per cent discount on the next €13.5 billion of loans it would take, bringing the losses that AIB would suffer on all of the loans combined to more than €9 billion.

Doherty was furious, because he had told potential investors and analysts in previous weeks that the next set of discounts would not be much higher than the previous 45 per cent figure and that there would be no need for any more capital than previously announced. Now he was being told that his losses would be much bigger than he had expected and that he would have to raise more capital again after all. He couldn't go to private investors and ask them for more equity, so he demanded an extension of time, in the hope that he could sell the UK business to make up the shortfall. Elderfield – mindful of the government's need to clarify the position about the banks in an effort to stave off the mounting sovereign crisis – refused.

The tensions between AIB and the state now turned to open conflict. The following Wednesday evening the regulator contacted AIB to say that it wanted the new capital requirement to be €3 billion higher at €10.4 billion. AIB's board met at the Ballsbridge headquarters, only to be hit with another shock demand. At about 8 p.m. a message arrived for Michael Somers, the former NTMA boss who was now deputy chairman at AIB. It came from John Corrigan, his successor at the NTMA. Somers was instructed to tell both Doherty and O'Connor that they were to resign and that if they didn't AIB would not get its money from the state.

It may have seemed an idle threat; there was no way that the state would allow AIB to go under, given the chaos that would ensue. The board was furious and rowed through the night as to what to do. But by 6 a.m. they had bowed to the inevitable. Without the state, AIB would go bust; with the state in control the government had the right to decide who it wanted in key positions. O'Connor resigned and Doherty's contract was terminated; there was to be enormous controversy the following April, when it was disclosed that he had been paid nearly €3 million in compensation.

Lenihan said AIB was a bank that was 'viable but unattractive to private investment'. He also described it as one that needed 'a new beginning'. The official end of its life as an independent entity – even if it had effectively been a dependant for over two years – came two days before Christmas. The government secured a High Court order allowing the state to invest an immediate €3.7 billion in capital into AIB without requiring the approval of other shareholders, a move that nationalized it.

The urgency of the pre-Christmas move and the decision not to consult shareholders was not explained – but it was implied. The government used emergency bank restructuring legislation that had been signed into law by President Mary McAleese two days previously. Two *Irish Times* journalists had been excluded from the court on the basis that the application was a matter of 'extreme commercial sensitivity' and of 'urgency' and related to issues that had not yet been aired in the media – even though it had been reported the previous day that a move on AIB was imminent. A heavily edited version of the legal affidavit explaining the minister's application was released later by the courts, but the sections explaining why the minister felt the use of his new powers was necessary were blacked out.

It quickly became clear, however, that AIB's very banking licence may have been at risk, because it was close to breaking the rules set by the Financial Regulator about how much cash and other assets it must hold in reserve to meet potential losses. 'We wouldn't have had Allied Irish Banks on January 1st if this investment wasn't made,' Lenihan said later. AIB issued a statement that the money was 'critical for the continued activities of the company'. But one of the biggest economic transactions ever undertaken by this state on behalf of taxpayers had been conducted in secret. 'This level of secrecy is entirely unsatisfactory in the case of AIB, which has consistently underestimated its liabilities. And to find that the minister is now prepared to go into a private hearing to cover up its latest position is utterly unacceptable to taxpayers,' an *Irish Times* editorial thundered. 'Why was AIB nationalized? What is it they don't want us to know? What is being hidden from taxpayers under the now familiar guise of commercial sensitivity?'

AIB had found a new executive chairman by this stage, an English career banker called David Hodgkinson, whose softly spoken manner belied an international career based on taking tough decisions. He wasn't long in the job before he admitted, 'I have never worked with quite as many problems as AIB had, particularly in the property sense.'

He had to announce in early 2011 that AIB had made a loss before tax of €12 billion in 2010, compared with €2.7 billion the previous year, by far its worst performance in its 45-year history. But he insisted 'the worst was over for AIB' and that the recovery was 'under way and clearly signposted'. The bank hoped to return to profitability by 2012, he said.

The worst wasn't over. The all-important March 2011 stress tests of the banks, as demanded by the IMF, decided that the government's previous investment of €7.2 billion in capital did not go nearly far enough in addressing AIB's problems. Another €13.3 billion had to be added.

But AIB was to have a future, albeit a limited one. It was to be the 'second pillar' in the government's proposed reconstructed banking sector, tied to EBS Building Society. Hodgkinson insisted that the 'vast bulk' of the new cash to be invested in capital would be returned to the state as AIB became smaller. The intention was that an already smaller bank would become even smaller still. AIB would be left with between €80 billion and €90 billion in loans after the shrinking of the bank, compared with a balance sheet of €180 billion at its peak. The bank was told to focus on Irish customers at home and Irish expat customers abroad through the UK business it wasn't able to sell. One of Ireland's few multinational success stories, once valued at more than €21 billion, had just about survived, but only as a shadow of its former self. Thousands of staff prepared to lose their jobs.

Michael Fingleton's greed and recklessness cost the Irish people €5.4 billion. Nobody who had the power to touch him did so as he went about destroying the Irish Nationwide Building Society, and nobody with the responsibility to enforce some kind of retribution went after him later, even though this meant that the money he'd cost us would never be recovered. The former chief executive of Irish Nationwide may not have enjoyed as comfortable a retirement as he had planned, but it was a damn sight more relaxed than he deserved.

Fingleton suffered brief moments of unpleasantness, such as being questioned against his will as he walked through Dublin Airport by RTÉ business reporter David Murphy and having the results broadcast on the television news that evening. There was occasional publicity too about his brazenness in holding on to a €1 million bonus that he took from Irish Nationwide just before his exit and that he refused to return to the state; the *Sunday Independent*, with which he had enjoyed a long, cordial relationship, said that he was giving the money to charity, but there has never been any proof subsequently that he did so. Fingleton continued to live in some style behind the high-gated walls of his Shankill, Dublin, home, commuting to his Spanish holiday retreat, apparently without fear of state-sponsored investigation or censure, even after his close friends in Fianna Fáil left power.

What Fingleton did at Irish Nationwide was incredible; that he was allowed to get away with it was disgraceful. He headed the building society – which was in the business of providing home loans – for thirty-seven years until leaving in April 2009, and somehow managed to run it like a personal fiefdom. From 2004 onwards he engaged in a madcap expansion into commercial-property lending, particularly to large-scale developers, not just lending to them but getting involved in partnerships to try to grab a bigger bit of the profits that might arise. From having development and commercial loans of €3.6 billion outstanding at the end of 2004, he more than doubled this amount to €8.5 billion by the end of 2008. This meant that for every €1 the building society lent to mortgage customers – its reason for being in business – it lent €4 to property developers. The society was hopelessly overexposed to the property bubble, and the regulators had allowed this to happen.

Confirmation of just how bad this lending was came with the eventual transfer of loans to NAMA before Irish Nationwide was closed in April 2011. NAMA took on loans with an original recorded value of €8.5 billion. It paid just €3 billion for these, a discount of two thirds.

Of the €2.6 billion in non-development loans – mostly home loans, but also a large number of 'buy-to-let' investment loans – a full third were overdue or unlikely to be repaid.

Between 2005 and 2008, while most of this bad lending was going on, Fingleton received total remuneration of over €8.5 million. He was doing so well personally out of it that he couldn't decide whether he wanted to sell the society; he had persuaded the government to change building society legislation to allow him to do so and he had suitors. While at the time it was thought that he feared not getting enough money personally out of the sale, in retrospect it seems that what he feared may have been a 'due diligence' investigation by a potential buyer. Anyone looking into the company would surely have found out what accountants Ernst & Young and solicitors McCann FitzGerald did in late 2009 and early 2010, when they conducted a full review of the business and presented it to the new Irish Nationwide board. The board, in turn, gave it to the Financial Regulator and the Department of Finance, but up to a year later it had still not been published. Details have emerged, however, and they have revealed an extraordinary level of deliberate mismanagement and an extraordinary amount of power concentrated in Fingleton.

For example, he persuaded a compliant board to give him powers to personally set, vary or alter interest rates charged on loans; to decide the fees for these loans; and to make arrangements on loans with individual clients of the society. This allowed Fingleton to circumvent the credit committee when it suited him – and he broke no Irish Nationwide rules by doing so. The investigators found evidence of loans paid out before approval and of the amounts lent being different to those that had been approved. Sometimes the loans went to associated companies rather than to the named borrowing entity. Millions of euro were paid to UK offshore companies linked to borrowers for consultancy services. Fingleton, together with another former executive, was found to be in control of an Irish Nationwide account that was used for immediate disbursement of money on behalf of the society; payments without limit could be made from it, and it was used for settlement of disputes and to make loans. The paper trail for many loans was not just incomplete but without basic information. There were cases of the same solicitors and valuers being used in transactions both by the society and by the borrower.

There were well-founded serious rumours in early September 2008 about Irish Nationwide's ability to stay in business, strenuously denied by Fingleton at the time with threats of legal action against those who published them. The Department of Finance was worried but seemed to take the society at its word when Fingleton wrote to its secretary, David Doyle, to emphasize that the society did not have a 'seriously impaired' loan book. Fingleton estimated bad debts for 2008 would amount to just €100 million. Had the regulators been doing their job properly, they would have known that this was a hopelessly optimistic and self-serving projection.

They might also have insisted that Irish Nationwide not be covered by the infamous bank guarantee of September 2008. Much has been made of the decision to cover Anglo Irish Bank but far more unforgivable was the decision to include Irish Nationwide. It had no 'systemic' value whatsoever. Most of its depositors had small amounts invested, usually of about €20,000 in size, in an attempt to qualify for free shares should the society be sold. They would have been covered comfortably by the existing state guarantee, had the society been allowed to fail, and this would have been far cheaper for the state than the bill it eventually received.

But Fingleton benefited from the friendship of sections of the political establishment and the media. His closeness to Fianna Fáil was legendary, but details began to emerge only during this period. There was a loan of €1.6 million to former Fianna Fáil Minister for Finance and European Commissioner Charlie McCreevy in 2006 to buy a property at the K Club golf resort in County Kildare. The property had been valued at €100,000 less at the time (and would be worth less than half that now) but approval and payment was fast-tracked. In 2008 Fingleton quickly arranged an emergency loan of €40,000 for Celia Larkin at a crucial time in the Mahon Tribunal's investigation into the finances of her ex-partner Bertie Ahern. Michael Lowry, the disgraced former Fine Gael minister – who became the subject of the most damning judgment possible at the Moriarty Tribunal in early 2011 for his handling of the government's issue of a valuable mobile-phone licence in 1996 – was another who benefited from his relationship with Fingleton.

Sections of the media, particularly a generation of journalists in their fifties and sixties, did not cover themselves in glory either. Many years earlier Fingleton had started an annual golf tournament for Oireachtas members, journalists, gardaí and the army. He got business out of it, selling mortgages to people who might otherwise have struggled to get them, mortgages being far harder to obtain in pre-Celtic Tiger days. He provided these without looking for extensive documentation or large deposits, and charged heavily for the privilege.

He received extraordinary loyalty in return. The most surprising intervention came from former *Magill* magazine editor Colm Tóibín, who had moved on to become one of the country's most outstanding novelists. 'I was in the Conrad Hotel [in Dublin] earlier this year and Michael Fingleton came in, alone,' Tóibín told an *Irish Times* interviewer. 'I was proud to stand up and shake his hand. He gave me my first mortgage. When he mightn't have. When I wasn't the most solvent person in Ireland. And I think if you're going to do witch-hunts, you should do your own personal ones. Pick your own people. But joining an Irish witch-hunt, whether against priests or against bankers . . . I'm afraid not.'

When somebody who is regarded as one of the country's leading intellectuals, and formerly a formidable journalist who had been willing to subject the establishment to forensic investigation, excuses Fingleton on the basis that he once gave him a loan, it becomes clear just how unwilling this country can be to confront serious issues. Perhaps the most bizarre defence of Fingleton came in the Jesuits' quarterly magazine *Studies*. 'Are we being unfair to Michael Fingleton?' it asked. 'Has he been singled out amongst Irish bank bosses because of his uncommon family name and his distinctive appearance?'

Fingleton was lucky to find people who were willing to cut him a break, because he had a reputation for ruthlessly hunting down homeowners who had missed payments on their mortgages, sometimes going so far as to call round personally at a borrower's front door to demand money. But in recent years he has himself not been without financial problems, and would discover that he was no longer beyond pursuit. He had dissipated the extraordinary €27 million pension pot that Irish Nationwide gave him at his retirement. It was estimated that this pension pot had shrunk to €4 million in value by 2009, unless Fingleton had had the foresight to divest himself of the major shareholdings in other banks that he had accumulated.

Fingleton still had assets, mainly in property, though he had assigned his interest in his family home and lands at Liskeen, Shankill, County Dublin, to his wife, Eileen, in October 2009. He retained an investment in a development site at Kotor, which is located on a bay in Montenegro, where a hotel was planned; he valued this at €4 million. He owned four apartments in the Mespil complex next to the Burlington Hotel in Dublin 4, acquired in controversial circumstances in the early 1990s; a retail property in Phibsborough, Dublin; and a house in Leopardstown, Dublin. These were valued at just over €3 million combined, which may have been a tad optimistic. There were more properties in Donegal, Mayo and Wicklow. He had €1 million in the bank in cash, possibly his Irish Nationwide bonus money. His income for 2009 'was in excess of €400,000'. He had also 'initiated legal proceedings to recover €10 million plus held in trust by a third party from actual earned and received profits in relation to a major Northside development'.

This was an extraordinary claim, which he launched two days before Christmas 2009, against his close friend the property developer Gerry

Gannon. Fingleton held that he owned a quarter-share of a Clongriffin project in North Dublin because of a £75,000 (€95,000) investment he had made with Gannon in the late 1990s. Given the indebtedness of the Clongriffin development – and of Gannon himself – it was hard to understand why Fingleton wanted to establish his rights in that regard. It raised all sorts of questions as to what other deals Fingleton had been involved in over the years with Irish Nationwide borrowers.

All of this became known because of a High Court case undertaken by Ulster Bank seeking repayment of €13.6 million owed by Fingleton, former Fianna Fáil Senator Francie O'Brien and two other Cavan businessmen. The four had purchased fifty acres of land at Swellan in Cavan with the intention of building 433 houses. As they failed to get planning permission, it was reckoned that the land was now worth no more than 10 per cent of what they owed. Ulster Bank explained that it had lent the money for this speculative development on the basis of Fingleton's 'perceived wealth' and because he was a 'man of substantial means', even though it had never dealt with him directly.

Fingleton made a couple of small repayments against the arrears, and in March 2010 sent a letter with a handwritten net-worth statement showing his assets and liabilities. Ulster Bank discovered that it was 'significantly less than was previously understood' – a common outcome for banks dealing with many of the titans of the Celtic Tiger era.

20.　The View from Abroad

If the Irish banks had been guilty of insane optimism and imprudent lending as a result, the same could be said of the Irish subsidiaries of foreign-owned banks. Indeed, there were instances when their behaviour was just as bad as that of the local banks (and sometimes even worse), which in turn put pressure on Irish banks to take even more risks to prevent the erosion of their market positions. The foreign banks were lucky, though, in that they could be rescued either by the British government or by the profits from Continental European operations – a luxury the Irish banks did not have.

The arrival and departure of Bank of Scotland (Ireland) from the Irish market was a typical story. Owned by Halifax Bank of Scotland (HBOS), it had entered in a small way back in 1989, taking over Equity Bank and developing a modest niche as a business lender. But the Irish chief executive, Mark Duffy, had big ambitions and was given full support by the British owner to expand the business. In 2000 it bought the reliable state-owned bank ICC – which had played its part in providing capital and loans for businesses when others wouldn't – for €340 million, and began to aggressively offer loans to Irish businesses, in competition with the established banks. It also began to lend to property developers.

It didn't stop there. BoSI decided to target the residential-property market: both those buying their own home, especially first-time buyers, and those investing in so-called 'buy-to-let'. The bank made a virtue of undercutting the interest rates offered by other lenders, thus making too much money available too cheaply and inflating the price bubble. What had at one time seemed good for consumers was ultimately very bad for them.

In 2005 BoSI made what appeared to be a major move at the time. It decided to establish a major branch network, paying €120 million for the chain of ESB electrical shops. The idea was that these stores had a highly visible presence, being well located and of a suitable size (which was not always the case) to draw in customers. They would enable the bank to attract deposits and to sell a larger range of profitable products.

BoSI was the first bank to roll out a new branch network in Ireland since the 1890s, but the plan didn't work anywhere near as well as it claimed publicly. Irish people showed a reluctance to switch from their existing banks; and, when they did move, they sometimes transferred only some of their accounts or loans. Many of BoSI's new mortgage holders did not open current accounts or take out credit cards with it. By the time it closed its operations it had just 50,000 customers with each of those key products, a little more than 1,000 per branch, a disastrously low number given the money spent on pulling them in. And if these customers weren't availing themselves of so-called 'vanilla', or plain, financial services, they were even less likely to be buying personal loans, life assurance, pensions or investment products, where the real profit for the bank was to be made.

Meanwhile BoSI was increasing its risk in the Irish market by becoming an investor as much as a banker. It started taking stakes in developments such as Bernard McNamara's ambitious plans for a site surrounding the Burlington Hotel. This would provide more 'upside' if things went well but potentially greater losses if things didn't go well – and they didn't. It also started to attract some of the big names in the property business, taking lower profit margins to seduce the likes of Liam Carroll, Jim Mansfield, Sean Quinn, Pat Doherty and Michael O'Flynn away from their usual bankers. A substantial relationship developed with Derek Quinlan, who ended up owing the bank €330 million. Soon its top-ten borrowers accounted for 58 per cent of the bank's own funds, and there was talk of BoSI possibly buying Irish Nationwide Building Society. This reliance on developers was a very dangerous concentration of interests, but the bank's British owner, HBOS, was happy when its 2007 profits were reported at €272 million.

This crashed to a pre-tax loss of €250 million in 2008, however, and Duffy left early in 2009, receiving a generous severance package. He departed claiming that the bank continued to have 'a strong underlying business' and that he was 'leaving the bank in good shape'. Denying that the Lloyds takeover of HBOS would lead to his bank's closure, he asserted that an immediate €750 million capital injection by the parent company had provided a 'solid foundation' to grow the bank in the future.

But if that loss was a setback, it was only a tiny foretaste of what was to come. The bank reported a further pre-tax loss of €2.9 billion in 2009 and provided for further losses on loans of €1.5 billion for the first half of 2010. It had suffered deposit outflows too, as investors were not covered by the Irish State guarantee, the bank having rejected the offer to be included.

BoSI had a total loan book in Ireland of €33 billion, but by June 2010 nearly 44 per cent of this was impaired. In other words, almost half of the borrowers were not making any repayments of principal or interest. BoSI admitted that it had lent €13.3 billion for development and investment property. Some 46 per cent of this loan book, or €6 billion, was for property development and 90 per cent of these loans were impaired; the remainder of the loans were for property investment and 45 per cent of these were impaired.

BoSI had taken enormous risks in its lending to individuals for investments in rental property, many of their loans equating to the full 100 per cent 'value' of the asset, requiring only interest repayments during the life of the mortgage, with the principal to be repaid at the end of the term. Everything was dependent on a continued healthy letting market. It was discovered subsequently that BoSI had been lending to investors on the basis of the property generating rental income of just 1.2 to 1.4 times the annual interest bill. This meant that it would take only relatively small increases in interest rates to make these investments unprofitable, even without a fall in property prices creating a situation where the properties would be worth less than the loans attached. Often the loans were secured on nothing more than the 'value' of the property being purchased. Losses at the branches before they closed were running at €400 million per annum.

Not surprisingly all of this meant that BoSI incurred massive losses that had to be covered by extra capital. Lloyds Banking Group, the newly established owner of HBOS, had to keep topping this up, spending €4.5 billion in two years (with more after that, bringing the final bill to €8 billion).

It wanted an end to that. HBOS had itself fallen victim to the September 2008 credit crunch and been rescued by a British-government-enforced takeover by Lloyds TSB; the new combined entity was now owned 43 per cent by the British government. However, it declined the opportunity to move its Irish loans into a new toxic unit established by the British government – a less ambitious version of NAMA – because to have done so would have increased its own capital needs and triggered full British-government control. That was not good news for the Irish operations, because once it decided to manage the loans itself it indicated that it was in wind-down, rather than recovery, mode for Ireland. The first people to be affected were the 750 employees who lost their jobs in the forty-four Halifax branches that were shut.

Efforts were made to sell the bank. The US venture-capital investor Blackstone looked closely and said no. To the surprise of few, BoSI took two big steps in 2010: first, it shut its branch network; and then, having denied initially that it would, it shut the rest of its business, establishing a separate special company of Irish managers to recover as much money from its existing loans as possible while making no further ones. It gave up its banking licence entirely. The only consolation was that most of the 840 people employed on the business-banking side were re-employed by this new venture, called Certus, which was given the contract to manage BoSI's commercial-loan portfolio over the next seven years.

However, BoSI's exit was to leave significant problems for the economy in general. BoSI had secured about 8 per cent of the overall business-banking market in Ireland but much more of particular sectors, particularly hotels, pubs, pharmacies and other relatively small businesses, often stand-alone and with little or no other banking relationships. BoSI had advanced about €10 billion there.

Repaying existing loans was one thing, but how were such clients to obtain new working capital and overdraft facilities, given that their bank was withdrawing these? What other banks would take on the risk of dealing with them? Not only might there be difficulties for small companies in finding new capital loans but also in financing their day-to-day needs, particularly if they had made bad property investments. The exit of BoSI exacerbated the consequences of the banking crisis, which saw good companies with good strategies struggling to realize them because of an absence of cash.

Other banks decided to stay, but to scale back operations dramatically. Danish bank Danske cut its National Irish Bank branch network from 54 to 32 and abolished cash transactions, focusing only on wealthy and corporate clients, a far cry from its ambitions when it bought the bank from its previous Australian owners in 2004. It said there was 'nothing attractive' about operating banks in Ireland but that it would not sell or seek to expand by buying others. It had gone into a holding pattern.

The Dutch-owned Rabobank required its Irish subsidiary, ACC Bank, to close 16 of its 28 outlets after the bank lost €394 million in 2009, but maintained a similar wait-and-see approach to the one Danske adopted. 'We want to wait it out and try to recover as much as we can,' the bank's chairman, Piet Moerland, said, adding that it could take four to five years before the Irish economy recovered and that Rabobank had supplied 'quite a bit' in the way of additional capital during 2010. He wouldn't say how much, other than that it was less than the €275 million that had been transferred during 2009.

What was most noticeable about ACC, though, was the way it went about recovering as much as possible of its €4.6 billion loans – of which, it reckoned, nearly a quarter would not be repaid. It was the first to move aggressively against borrowers, often via the courts through the appointment of receivers and the seeking of judgments for immediate repayment, prompting Cork developer John Fleming, for example, to opt for bankruptcy in the UK.

All of this made the position of the Royal Bank of Scotland-owned Ulster Bank – long the third biggest bank in the Irish market but well behind AIB and Bank of Ireland in its market share and influence – even more important. Would it stay or would it go?

This was a big decision for the British government, now an 87 per cent shareholder in Royal Bank of Scotland, to make. At face value it seemed obvious: do what Lloyds had done at BoSI and pull the plug. After all, since the start of the crisis RBS had conceded that

€8.6 billion of its loans in Ireland could not be recovered: this meant that €7 billion had been contributed in new capital to keep Ulster Bank afloat, with the prospect of much more being required as the losses mounted. It also meant that these two Irish subsidiaries of British banks had received over a third of all the capital made available by the British government to save RBS, HBOS and Lloyds at the peak of its crisis in the autumn of 2008.

Ulster Bank's losses (stated in sterling) were worse than seemed at first glance. For example, in the first three months of 2011 alone the bank reported an operating loss of £377 million (€441 million), with bad debts more than double what they had been during the first quarter of the previous year. A surge in losses on mortgages had pushed the figure for bad debts up to £461 million, wiping out any profits Ulster had made on its usual activities.

But this did not include additional losses on loans that had been transferred out of the bank into a so-called 'non-core division'. RBS had treated its Irish subsidiary differently from the way Lloyds had treated BoSI, having moved nearly £20 billion of property-related loans into a quasi-NAMA, the British Asset Protection Scheme, internally run but kept off the new RBS balance sheet. Those loans accounted for losses of another whopping €839 million in that period alone.

Yet political reasons dictated that the British government continue to support Ulster and take responsibility for its £52.5 billion (€62 billion) of loans. Although an all-Ireland bank, its main business was in the six counties of Northern Ireland, which were under British rule. RBS watched the losses increase at its Irish operations, but, while it was forced to sell most of its overseas assets – many of which were profitable – Ireland had to be kept.

Sympathy for Ulster was limited. After all, it had been the bank that had introduced the 100 per cent mortgage for consumers to the Irish market, providing no margin for error should property prices slip, let alone collapse. Ulster had taken this risk because of the 'success' of its acquisition of the former building society First Active (once known as First National) in an €883 million purchase in the early years of the century. Ulster used the First Active name to become a bigger residential mortgage provider in the Republic than it could have become by establishing its own brand name locally. So impressed was RBS by its achievements that First Active boss Cormac McCarthy was promoted to run the entire Irish business.

McCarthy sought to become more active in lending to the Irish development sector, determined to get business that was going to other banks. Disastrously, the bank backed Sean Dunne's folly of a major Knightsbridge-style development for the Ballsbridge area of Dublin, but it was not the only mistake made. Ulster concentrated heavily on lending to property developers who believed that retail spending would continue to rise and that leisure spending would continue to soar, becoming a major lender to the ubiquitous hotel developments. As with other banks it seemed to work, and enormous profits were made. McCarthy was rewarded handsomely, getting €1.4 million for his efforts in Ulster's 'best' year. But it merely built up a crisis for the future. For in 2008 Ulster lost £689 million and in 2009 another £368 million. But this didn't tell the whole story, because the transfer of loans into the bad-bank scheme masked the full effect of the losses. In August 2010 Ulster said it had lost £314 million in the first six months of that year, which, compared with other Irish lenders, did not look too bad. However, another £1.2 billion was written off against the loans that had been transferred to the bad bank.

Remedial action had to be taken. Although McCarthy remained in favour – indeed he was given additional responsibility in Britain – he decided to offer his notice to quit late in 2010 and was replaced in mid 2011 by a New Zealander called Jim Brown. But before going McCarthy was required to dismantle much of what he had done, and more than 1,000 jobs were lost as a result. His First Active brand was abandoned, and 45 of its 60 branches were shut, the rest to be converted into Ulster-branded units.

Ulster made a big play of its commitment to the Irish market. 'Are we a foreign-owned bank?' Mike Bamber, its head of retail operations, asked rhetorically during one interview with the *Sunday Business Post*. 'We are a foreign-owned bank, but we are hardly foreign, as we've been here for 174 years.' It emphasized a new customer charter, which included things like a promise not to close any of its 236 branches, a commitment to Saturday opening, queues of less than five minutes in branches and free text messages to help customers take action to reduce avoidable current-account charges.

But caution was the watchword at Ulster. Far from seeking out opportunities to capitalize on the weakness of its main rivals, AIB and Bank of Ireland – which continued to hold more than 70 per cent of the current-account market, compared with Ulster's 12 per cent – Ulster pulled back. It allowed its mortgage rates to become among the most expensive available, effectively pricing itself out of new business as it concentrated on improving its profit margins on existing loans. It became very unpopular with some mortgage customers, as it refused to pass on ECB rate cuts and then began increasing rates for non-tracker mortgage customers even when the ECB didn't. Just as importantly, small business owners began to complain that Ulster had become very difficult to deal with when securing overdrafts or business loans.

If the foreign banks already in the country were reluctant to lend – or were scaling back their operations – what hope was there that other foreign banks could be persuaded to buy the Irish-owned banks from the state, as Central Bank boss Patrick Honohan clearly hoped would happen?

There would be a number of advantages to such an outcome, not least the improvement in liquidity as well as capital provision that such purchases would entail. Foreign-owned Irish banks had a number of advantages over state-supported institutions. They could get much cheaper inter-bank funding on the international money markets; they could issue bonds, when the reputations of Irish banks prevented them from doing so; and they had the ability to supply capital, something with which the Irish government was clearly struggling. But, although Irish banks might find it useful for foreign banks to fill the holes in their balance sheets, why should the foreign banks bother? The prospects for profitable business in the Irish market were constrained by the overall economic situation, and a higher return on their capital might be available elsewhere. If Ireland didn't seem an attractive proposition for many of the Irish, why should it be for foreigners?

The political and media debate during a lengthy portion of Ireland's crisis focused on the exploding exchequer deficit – and how the public would be forced to pay for it – the cost of bailing out the banks, and the return of high unemployment. But one largely ignored element of this economic crisis – which differentiated it from the 1980s and made it worse – was the enormous element of personal debt that had been lumped upon a generation. Then, at least, a much smaller number of people carried personal debts and the size of those debts was much smaller, not just nominally but in relation to income. During the so-called boom, private debt soared from 46 per cent to 170 per cent of national income, itself a statistic that emphasized how unreal and unsustainable the whole thing had been. This meant that when the crash came it hit a far greater number of people hard. People didn't just lose their means of income because of unemployment or see it reduced because of pay cuts, less overtime and higher taxes; now they had debts to worry about paying on top of the normal everyday bills.

By the end of 2009 principal private-residence mortgage debt amounted to €118 billion. This was purely for the homes that people lived in: it did not include mortgages for buy-to-let investments, holiday homes or foreign-property investment. Such mortgages, as well as loans for cars, credit cards, investments and more, amounted to another €60 billion. This total overshadowed the national or public debt considerably. Irish householders carried the largest mortgage debt per head in the world.

But not every citizen laboured under this burden. Only 40 per cent of homeowners had mortgages at that time (790,000 in total), and some of them had paid down a lot of their debt. This meant the rest of the country's homeowners, mainly older ones, had little or no debt to worry about, only the performance of their pensions or investments. But younger people, usually but not always aged from forty-five downwards, often with children to care for, were the ones who faced a greater crisis. They had been persuaded by greedy banks, with the encouragement of the state's tax policies, to borrow for a period of thirty-five or forty years, and to buy their accommodation at wildly inflated prices.

They had wanted homes, be it houses or apartments, in which to live, maybe even with gardens where kids could play, near to schools and to family. They bought because they didn't want to be reliant on the state to provide housing for them. The vast majority had not borrowed for stock-market investments, or for 'buy-to-let' properties in Dubai or holiday homes in Bulgaria, or for spending on cars or holidays, or for credit-card-fuelled shopping sprees, as is sometimes alleged. Many of those purchases were made by members of older generations: they had paid off their mortgages or had small amounts outstanding, and were seduced by the notion of 'equity release'. If the younger generation had additional borrowings it was for things like cars, which they needed to commute from their expensive new homes to their places of work, often many kilometres distant and not serviced adequately or at all by public transport. They didn't pay inflated prices for their homes because they were greedy but because those were the prices they were required to pay for what was often very ordinary and sometimes very badly constructed and finished accommodation. Renting wasn't much cheaper and the money paid out was considered 'dead money', because it could never be recouped. To own your own home was a perfectly reasonable aspiration. Buyers made choices in the situation in which they found themselves and for many years that situation – fuelled by government tax breaks to developers and landlords, and a lack of regulation of the lenders – was frenzied.

Worse, the crash in property values meant that the loans these borrowers had to repay, even before interest was added on, were now often larger than the value of the properties they occupied. The curse of negative equity was to stalk hundreds of thousands, as residential property prices fell by about 50 per cent on average and further falls loomed.

Negative equity is not a problem, some experts have said, as long as you don't have to sell your property and take a real-cash loss; it is supposedly merely an irritation if you continue to live where you are. But negative equity seemed far from benign to many people: for example, those who faced financial crisis because of seriously reduced incomes and lost jobs, or who feared they would lose their homes if they could not keep up repayments. Increased interest rates and lower household incomes – because of pay cuts or job losses, reduced overtime and higher taxes – created intense pressure for borrowers. And the knowledge that one is repaying far more than the house or apartment is worth and that any necessary sale will bring about a major loss is highly stressful, to say the very least. Large numbers of people had bought 'starter homes', small but seemingly affordable, in the hope that they could sell at a later date and, assuming their income increased, buy something bigger. But now homeowners faced the prospect of being stuck in the same property – which had perhaps become unsuitable for their needs – for decades, paying back way more money to the bank than their 'asset' was ever going to be worth.

Such situations are likely to encourage a borrower to pay off debt as quickly as possible, which, at a time of falling net incomes and higher taxes, means less consumer spending. This dampens demand in the economy and impacts on the tax revenues the government can collect. There would be no recovery in consumer spending while people tried to get a more sustainable and realistic grasp on their finances.

The banks and government played down the problem, presenting the figures in such a way as to reinforce their approach. The number of those in arrears was deceptive, for example, being relatively small, at 40,000 mortgages, or 5.1 per cent. This figure was a reflection of those who had been in arrears for over ninety days at the end of September 2010, up from 26,000 a year earlier. Twenty-eight thousand of the mortgages were in arrears of more than 180 days. But it was estimated that the number of 'rescheduled' mortgages – where the life of the loan is extended to reduce the monthly repayments – was at 45,000; and, as there was an overlap between the two, the number of 'troubled' mortgages was actually about 70,000. This sort of 'creative accounting' helped to make the situation appear not quite as bad as it really was.

The Irish Banking Federation boasted that it had a policy to help mortgage holders who were struggling and issued details of a voluntary code of practice to which ten member institutions subscribed. It urged people to admit potential repayment problems quickly and promised at least a six-month window before any legal action was initiated that could result in repossession.

That seemed reasonable but self-interest was at work. The banks didn't want to engage in widespread repossession of homes either, as there was no market for resale and they didn't have the money to provide loans to new buyers. There was also the potential for a double-whammy: if a sale took place at a very low price, the bank would have to recognize a loss immediately; but if the bank provided a loan at what was still an excessive value, it would suffer the loss at some stage in the future.

But none of this dealt with the key problem: many borrowers would never be able to repay the full amount they owed. It suited the banks to switch them to interest-only loans or to extend the life of the mortgages because then they didn't have to suffer an impairment charge. It was only a postponement of the evil day for both sides.

The banks were under government instruction not to act against borrowers, and to wait at least a year before beginning court-enforced repossessions. As recipients first of the guarantee and then of capital, they had no choice but to obey. The banks were also lucky that people went to whatever extremes they could to make their monthly repayments and protect their homes. But they'd stopped spending on almost everything else, doing enormous damage to consumption in the domestic economy, leading to further job losses in the retail sector and, ironically, a further property-price decline.

Not everyone was sympathetic to those in trouble over their mortgages. There was an issue of personal responsibility involved. As many people who rented, or who did not 'trade up' for bigger accommodation, have pointed out, nobody was forced to take out a mortgage. It was a decision into which people entered freely and supposedly with maturity. However, it was not as simple as that. People were suckered in by the financially powerful (with the assistance of the government, which offered them tax incentives) through intensive advertising and measures such as the ubiquitous 'tracker mortgages' and repayment holidays. It was the 'generosity' of the banks in issuing large loans – sometimes for seven or eight times income and for terms way longer than the traditional twenty years – that got many people into trouble.

The banks seduced the ordinary borrowers of this country into what was little better than a Ponzi scheme. First, the banks lent insanely excessive amounts of money to land speculators and developers, who built intensively – with the size of many overall units seemingly smaller, even if the price per square metre occupied soared. They then had to find someone to buy the units they had created. The banks, who wanted repayment from those speculators and developers, helped out. They lent further insanely excessive amounts of money to people to buy the properties. This worked fine, for the banks and the developers at least, until the scheme blew up because everything was overpriced.

The banks ended up transferring any remaining development loans to NAMA, which is seeking full repayment – an unlikely outcome. Developers knew how to fight, had cash squirrelled away, and used lawyers and financial advisers who made things difficult for the banks. Many of these developers hadn't even been paying interest, let alone principal, on their loans for years, and had not lost their homes. The ordinary borrower of the end unit was an easier mark for full repayment, however. The more you owe, the more likely it is that a bank will do a deal for partial repayment. Owe what is a relatively small amount – relatively small, that is, to the bank if not to you – and you may find that you are pursued ruthlessly.

Identifying the scale of the problem – and holding people responsible for what had happened – was easy enough. What was more difficult was coming up with a solution, for a variety of reasons.

In May 2010 I addressed the issue as part of a four-section documentary programme for RTÉ called *Aftershock: Where to Now?* I suggested a form of debt-for-equity swap for hard-pressed homeowners that would involve lenders taking part ownership of the homes of people in negative equity in return for writing off part of the outstanding debt, giving people a lower debt, more realistically related to the present value of the home, to be repaid.

I suggested this because, without doing something, a generation of people would be left to labour with an unfair millstone round their necks and our economy's chances of recovery would be greatly hampered. It was also common in the business sector for debts to be written off or debt-for-equity swaps to take place. Banks were doing deals to get whatever money it was practicable to recover, the only way to ensure that businesses would survive. The banks lose some money as a result but it is often the best way to get more money in the future.

None the less homeowners seemingly were expected to pay every cent back to the banks, even when they didn't have the income. Then Minister for Justice Dermot Ahern, when asked subsequently about debt-forgiveness, said: 'I don't accept people will never be able to pay their debts.' The former solicitor's opinion seemed very harsh, but his comments played to a sizeable audience that would likely agree.

The objections to my idea were twofold. First, as mentioned previously, people had to take responsibility for their own mistakes and did not deserve to be bailed out by those who had not made such mistakes. Why bail out those who took reckless chances? Who borrowed money that they could not repay? Who wanted more than they could afford? Who lost the run of themselves?

Well, the answer to that is, who hasn't made mistakes in their lives? Who hasn't followed the crowd and done what everybody else said they had to? Should the punishment be as severe as what was being imposed on our young people and those with families approaching middle age? Pragmatism means that people get cut breaks all the time, particularly the richer they are. Nor would a swap of debt for equity be pain free for the borrowers, as they would lose part ownership of their homes.

Second, the banks and government were bust and simply couldn't afford to get involved in financing an idea like this. Any deal would certainly have required an injection of extra capital into the banks by the state – but if the state was prepared to borrow from the IMF so the banks could repay bondholders, why wouldn't it do the same for its citizens?

The Fianna Fáil-led government kept telling us that we needed fully functioning banks, but what about fully functioning citizens? In the United States, where they decry socialism, a government guarantee has been provided for 'troubled' mortgages, with the aim of bringing about lower monthly repayments through refinancing. Other ideas are being examined, as they know the problem has to be fixed.

The government engaged in a minimalist approach. It outsourced assessment of the problem to a specially established Mortgage Arrears and Personal Debt Review Group, which included government civil servants, regulators and members of the banking fraternity as its members. Consumers were represented in the group, but it decided, none the less, that there will be no measures to write off debts, save for some nice little gestures to give the appearance of a government both caring and doing something.

Matthew Elderfield pre-empted much of the debate when he gave a speech in which he said that 'there is a need for a sense of realism as to what can be achieved given the financial constraints affecting both government and the banks.' He warned that there were 'no silver-bullet solutions' for mortgage arrears. Specifically, he mentioned the costs involved in providing support for struggling borrowers – which was a political policy issue rather than a regulatory one.

'We must be careful that any approach doesn't provide financial incentives for the arrears problem to get worse,' he cautioned. 'And, in seeking to assist households in difficulty, we need to recognize that the cost of any support will be borne by those neighbours who avoided excessive borrowing themselves or are gritting their teeth and meeting their obligations,' he said, stepping even further away from regulatory matters and into the realm of the political.

But it was clear that the public finances and the banks dominated the thinking of government. They did not want to see beyond those things for which they had immediate financial responsibility because they did not want to make things more complicated for themselves. They had enough on their hands. But the economic situation was so catastrophic that the government and its officials were not really in a position to pick and choose which fires they wanted to fight; they had to look at the bigger picture, whether they wanted to or not.

The dismissal of debt restructuring on the basis of fairness and morality did not stand up, particularly when set against the background of how the economy had been, and still was, run. It could hardly be said that Ireland took a fair, ethical and moral approach to all economic issues. The introduction of debt forgiveness wouldn't exactly have thrown a rotten apple into an otherwise perfect barrel.

The entire system by which our taxes are collected and allocated at present could be said to be unfair, unduly rewarding some at the expense of others. Where, for example, was the morality in a system that, at one stage, allowed nearly half the workforce to pay no tax at all? Or that allowed the better-off to receive tax write-offs against their pension contributions, or that allowed high-income earners to shelter part of their income from tax by way of state-sanctioned incentives? The unfairness and inequality of tax exiles, for example – citizens who demanded a say in how we ran our society and who often got it, despite sheltering their non-Irish income from tax here – was 'justified' on the basis of the investments they had in Ireland, as if they might withdraw should they be subjected to the same taxes as the rest of us. Go back further, to 1988 and 1993, and you find tax amnesties that allowed cheats and frauds to get away with paying only a fraction of what they owed. But did they serve a useful function in cleaning up the black economy?

When the Mortgage Arrears and Personal Debt Review Group finally reported, the best it could offer was the creation of a deferred interest scheme, which might save borrowers only €1,000 over five years and buy a bit of time. Elderfield said the state couldn't afford a debt-forgiveness scheme and claimed it might give mortgage holders a 'perverse incentive' to stop making their monthly repayments.

Instead, the group's report suggested that the Department of the Environment should allow borrowers at risk of losing their homes to become eligible for social-housing assessment before a repossession order was made. It proposed changes to the bankruptcy laws and measures to allow repossessed borrowers to remain in their homes until such time as a local authority could find them an alternative.

And it called on lenders to facilitate trading down by borrowers who were in negative equity, if that would result in more affordable monthly payments.

The report was made public on 17 November 2010 and press briefings were held on the top floor of the Central Bank. The next day the same offices would be used for meetings with Ajai Chopra and his IMF team, who had come to seal a new loan agreement that would rescue bank bondholders but not bank customers.

PART THREE

Welcome to Namaland

22.   Solution or Problem?

Once the original bank guarantee was in place, the government seemingly had two years in which to come up with a plan to rescue the banks. Something had to be done to provide protection against the flight of money, so the ATMs could work, but also to allow for lending. Still believing that the priority was providing liquidity to the banks, with solvency lower on the list of things for repair, the government came up with the idea of the National Asset Management Agency. NAMA, the name of the property-management company that would take property-backed loans, both good and bad, from the banks and deal with them, was to become one of the most famous and hated words in Ireland.

The primary goal, at least initially, was to provide a mechanism to give the banks sufficient cash. This was a process with which the European Central Bank was involved intimately and approvingly. The idea was that the government would not give the banks cash in exchange for the transfer of loans from their balance sheets, because, quite simply, it didn't have enough cash to do so. Instead, it would present the banks with bonds, with an interest rate, or coupon, of just 1 per cent attached. The banks would then be able to present these government bonds to the ECB or other lenders as collateral for whatever money they wanted to borrow from them. This gave the banks affordable access to cash and also allowed the government to account for its potential liability on the bonds 'off-balance sheet'. It was complicated but it was regarded as 'creative' accounting. Few cared to remember that such an approach had created many of the problems now faced by the banks and the country.

One key drawback was that this mechanism failed to deal with the other major problem that the banks faced: their imminent insolvency. The full extent of the crash in property values and the losses that it would cause to the banks – and how it would wipe out their capital – would not be appreciated for some time, although many were screaming warnings. Wishful thinking again prevailed with officialdom. At every stage along the way the hope for a 'soft landing' remained, or at least a somewhat softer one than the pessimists had suggested.

Lenihan turned to economist Peter Bacon in February 2009, asking him to flesh out ideas he was kicking about with officials in his department. Bacon was asked to examine whether a 'bad bank' asset management firm or risk-insurance programme should be established to deal with development and property loans in Irish banks, but he was encouraged to concentrate on the former. Bacon had history with both property and banking. He had written two major reports into rising house prices at the turn of the decade, which led to the introduction of government policy to try to control this (after lobbying by the construction sector, this policy was reversed). Bacon, who had been managing director of AIB's stockbroking subsidiary, Goodbody, for some years, then joined Sean Mulryan's Ballymore Properties group as a consultant on foreign expansion.

Bacon did not act alone in drawing up his proposals. He said that he spoke daily with top officials in the NTMA, such as Chief Executive Michael Somers, his later successor John Corrigan and Brendan McDonagh, the man who would become NAMA's boss. Simultaneously Lenihan was having his own conversations with the NTMA, asking it to assess the insurance proposal from the banks nine days after he had hired Bacon. Lenihan's instruction to Somers was that he was to make proposals that would limit the potential financial exposure to the exchequer, improve the timing of any call for state financing and minimize the burden on the national debt.

Bacon lent towards the idea of an asset management agency quickly and made presentations on his plans to Lenihan, the Department of Finance, and Central Bank officials before bringing forward his final ideas. By April he had persuaded Lenihan and Cowen to back him, and his formal proposal was put into a government memorandum and presented to officials from the NTMA, the Central Bank and the Financial Regulator at a meeting in Government Buildings on 3 April. Bacon would later say that support for the plan was 'unanimous', and nobody contradicted him. The government decided it would announce the details of NAMA to coincide with the emergency budget it was launching to try to deal with the growing budget deficit. Unfortunately, it decided not to publish the reports upon which it based its decision – another example of a lack of transparency and the belief that the public should just 'trust' the government to act in the country's best interests.

Lenihan announced his NAMA decision in his budget statement of 7 April 2009 'with a view to addressing in a comprehensive way the problem of impaired or potential impaired assets in the banking system'. Lenihan said 'the continued denial or postponement' of bank liabilities carried 'a significant economic cost' to the country. 'Postponing these losses, delaying these losses and rolling up interest on these losses – the extent of that cannot be sustained by our economic system.' This was true, but unfortunately NAMA itself was to delay Lenihan's attempts to deal with the inevitable even further.

Bacon promised that NAMA would clean up the balance sheets of Irish banks and allow them to resume lending to the wider economy. He said the loan values would be 'set by reference to the market' and that it was possible to 'offset the risks of potential errors' associated with paying too much, or too little, for the assets. He said that his proposal assigned responsibility for the losses to where they should go: 'namely the borrowers in the first instance, bank shareholders in the second instance. And it cleans banks' balance sheets and allows them to move forward and provide the kind of services that the economy needs if it is to recover from the deep recession.'

Bacon had given an estimate in his report of the possible write-off on the property loans to be purchased by the state – the discount, or 'haircut', that would be applied – but it was never revealed. The initial figure that became popular in the public domain – floated by the stockbroking firms that wrote research reports on the banks afterwards – was 15 per cent: NAMA would pay the banks €76.5 billion for property loans of €90 billion. It was to be far from the eventual outcome.

When asked why he hadn't opted for a risk-insurance scheme, similar to what was being implemented in Britain, Bacon said it was because his chosen method would ensure that the banks would have to take their losses upfront. A risk-insurance scheme would have left big contingent liabilities on bank balance sheets, he believed, limiting their ability to lend. Bacon also claimed that NAMA would break the 'link' between the banks and their developer customers, something that played to popular opinion.

But few other things about NAMA did. Its creation raised numerous questions, as well as numerous potential problems. How many loans would be transferred from the banks to NAMA? On what basis would they be chosen? At what price would they be transferred? If NAMA paid too much for the loans, how much of a loss would that mean for the taxpayer? If the banks incurred heavy losses on the transfer of the assets, how much new capital would they need to repair their balance sheets and where would it come from? Would it be only so-called bad loans – on which repayments were not being made – that would be transferred or would good loans go in too, to give NAMA an income? How long would it take for NAMA to take control of the loans and, once it did, what would it do with the underlying property assets? How would the banks behave as NAMA came into being? If NAMA tried to sell the assets, what would happen to the market? But if it held on to them, would NAMA itself have to become a bank in order to fund any work that was required on land or properties?

Not surprisingly there was speculation as to who NAMA was really supposed to help, other than the banks. The most regularly stated claim was that NAMA was designed by Fianna Fáil politicians to somehow provide breathing space for the developer classes – friends of Fianna Fáil – to allow them time to get their affairs in order and to protect them from aggressive moves by the banks to recover debts. While that was disputed, there was little doubt that NAMA would act as a form of professional dole, giving massive sums to financial advisers, lawyers and property valuers for 'services', at a time when they were struggling for income because of the collapse of the property market.

Immediately, supporters of nationalization as an alternative, or at least as the necessary missing step in the NAMA process – came forward.

The idea of nationalizing the banks had some merits. First, a change of control would bring about swift board and management changes and, with those, a new attitude in the banks. Leaving those responsible for the mess in situ meant that there was a danger of them acting to justify their previous behaviour, should moves be made to hold them accountable; and of them trying to protect their ongoing relationships with borrowers, should they be held responsible for the circumstances in which deterioration had occurred. Nationalization also meant that the problem of the price to be affixed to each loan transfer would disappear: as the state would own both sides of the transaction in their entirety the price wouldn't matter and there could be no allegations of providing a subsidy to the private sector by overpaying banks for their loans. Time wouldn't have to be spent on determining a fair price for the transfers; and the legal establishment of NAMA itself would also take less time, thus avoiding delays in an effective remedy of the situation. Indeed, this gave rise to questions as to whether or not NAMA would be necessary at all, because surely the nationalized banks would then be able to get on with sorting out their loans and drawing down new capital from the state as required.

Clearly, nationalization would not change the extent of the initial losses at the banks, although arguably the stability it would have provided might have obviated the need for the massive further write-offs that occurred as the economy went into tailspin. But what nationalization could have done was leave the banks with the good loans, moving only the bad ones to NAMA, leaving them with stronger balance sheets and less need for capital. A group of economists writing for *The Irish Times* on 17 April 2009 presciently argued that 'a circumstance where a drip-feed of recapitalizations is required would be the worst of all possible outcomes.' They pointed out that if the state was going to have to fund the rescue of the banks, it might as well own them and have the benefit of the upside once they were restored to reasonably good health and subsequently sold.

The government set its face against nationalization and rolled out the advisers in support. Bacon argued there was little real difference between the NAMA proposal and nationalizing the banks, saying nationalization would not solve the bad debt problem but merely 'change the name over the door'. Lenihan's adviser Alan Ahearne said the difficulties with valuing the loans would remain, irrespective of whether the banks were temporarily nationalized in full. He claimed nationalization created 'a significant risk of undermining the capacity of the banks to raise funds internationally for domestic lending', that it was 'difficult to see a credible exit strategy from wholesale bank nationalization' and that the returns for the taxpayer reprivatizing later 'would probably be disappointing'. 'The simple inescapable truth is that nationalization creates a significant risk of a political rather than a commercial allocation of credit,' Ahearne said. 'This would be bad for the banks but even worse for the country.' They seemed to think that nationalization, as much as insolvency, threatened to cause a run on bank deposits, and they wanted to avoid any recourse to the guarantee at all costs.

The government did not want to take the liabilities of the banks on to the national balance sheet, although in effect that's what it had done already with the guarantee – and that's how the markets would later come to see things. Yet the NAMA announcement brought a favourable response from the dreaded ratings agencies. Moody's described it as an 'ingenious mechanism' that was good for the government and for the banks, and Standard & Poor's said the 'clarity' achieved on the amount of recapitalization that would be needed by the banks was 'a major step forward' in the process of repairing them.

There continued to be opposition from domestic economists, however. Another sizeable group returned to the fray in late April 2009, twenty signing their names to another attack on how NAMA would operate. In their letter they claimed that there was a 'fundamental internal contradiction' in the government's plan: how, they wondered, could the government simultaneously purchase the bad loans at a discount that reflected their true market value while at the same time keeping the banks well or adequately capitalized and out of state ownership. They forecast, correctly, that the three outcomes were 'simply mutually incompatible, and we are greatly concerned that the NAMA process may operate to maintain the appearance that all three objectives have been achieved by failing to meet the first requirement. This would arise if NAMA purchases the bad loans at a discount, but still well above market value . . .

'To conclude, we consider that the government's approach of limited recapitalization supplemented by NAMA represents only a partial solution to our banking problems, and one that is unlikely to protect the taxpayer. A nationalized banking system with a mandate to restructure and reprivatize would be a preferable approach at this time.'

Their worries were not assuaged over the summer and they returned to print in late August, their number now swelled to forty-six. They mocked Bacon's promise that NAMA would 'mark to hope', assigning a value to the properties that reflected what those properties might be worth in the future, not what they were at present.

The government's strategy was motivated by the knowledge that, should the loans be transferred at pertaining market prices, the banks would suffer enormous losses, so enormous that their capital would be wiped out and the institutions bankrupted unless the state moved to take control.

Whatever else, the government was set against nationalization. But this had one interesting consequence. Back in 2009 there was little or no talk of burning the bondholders, because at that stage the shareholders hadn't yet been asked to bear any losses, and they had to lose their money before the bondholders did. The group of economists spotted that many of the bonds were not due to be repaid until after the guarantee had expired in September 2010 and suggested that 'the government is in a strong position, if it chooses, to negotiate with bondholders to engage in some debt for equity swaps.' Even then, they agreed, this was unlikely to provide enough capital to the banks.

'We therefore urge the government to reconsider its approach to payment for loans to be taken into NAMA, to pay no more than current market value – which can be ascertained even in these times – and to require the investors in the banks to bear some of the cost of restructuring the system. Moreover, we also argue that the government should not burden the state with more debt than is absolutely required. To do otherwise would be economic folly,' they argued. The government went with folly.

There were critics from outside of the country too. Gabriel Smith, a director of Lombard Street Capital, an independent economic consultancy in London, had been involved in the bad banks set up to take over property loans from Swedish banks during its banking crisis in the early 1990s, often cited by Lenihan as having provided the model for NAMA. He argued that the Irish model was 'fundamentally flawed'. 'If the objective is to repair the banking system, then why would you take perfectly good, fully performing, unimpaired loans from the banks?' he said. 'If you look at the original report that formed the basis for the establishment of NAMA it was as much about restructuring the construction and property sector as repairing the banking system. I have no problem with the fact that the Irish construction and property sector should be restructured, but I do not see why it should be done at any cost to the taxpayer and at the expense of a speedy resolution of the banking crisis.' But Smith compiled his report at the request of the Construction Industry Federation. Therefore it was dismissed as tailored to the views of a vested interest when, in fact, it pretty well summed up the reality of the situation. When the government made its first formal announcement as to what it would buy and pay, it said that it would take on €77 billion in loans and pay €54 billion for them, a much deeper discount than had been expected. However, there was a twist. The government admitted that it had been estimated that those loans were worth only €47 billion at current market prices. It was overpaying by €7 billion on the basis that that's what they'd be worth in ten years' time.

The government could not act without consulting with Europe. The European Commission, preferring the theoretical to the practical, appeared more concerned that competition might be distorted than that things might go badly wrong in the Irish State. The European Central Bank was concerned about the use of its money, given that the bonds the Irish government gave to the banks in exchange for the loans would be presented to it as collateral for future borrowings. Both had an interest in what NAMA would pay for the loans it took from the banks and what it would do with the underlying assets afterwards.

The commission initially provided some flexibility in setting values, as it already had set parameters for dealing with situations such as the one Ireland was facing. (It had never anticipated anything on this scale, however.) Impaired assets could be judged on their 'economic value' or 'through-the-cycle' value – which meant that 'estimated average values' over NAMA's life could be used, rather than current market prices. But they could not be too far away from the market price, the commission instructed. That was fine, but how could anyone assign a market value to property assets when there was no active market, with normal borrowers and lenders bust and the demand for property almost non-existent?

This was a time-consuming process, as was putting together the necessary legislation. NAMA would not legally come into being until December 2009, but an interim body under Brendan McDonagh began preliminary work from May 2009. In the meantime many of the banks behaved badly. They knew they had a ready-made buyer for their worst property loans, in the form of the taxpayer, and chose to sit on their hands. Rather than moving swiftly against developers who were not making repayments – and who probably never would – they rolled up interest and just added it to the loans they intended to transfer. Sometimes they even added further money on to the loans, usually for working capital, in the expectation that they would subsequently be able to transfer it all to NAMA. Indeed, it was reported later by the *Sunday Tribune* that, in the build-up to NAMA, the banks tried to transfer €1 billion in loans given to developers as working capital at 100 per cent value, citing an agreement with the Central Bank. NAMA took only half of those loans, apparently because it was not happy that the paperwork was in order or that the loans were commercially justified. But further damage to the banks had still been done, even if NAMA refused to deal with those loans.

The suspicion that the banks were trying to take NAMA and the state for fools was pushed by a Fianna Fáil TD, of all people. Michael McGrath, as a member of the Dáil's Public Accounts Committee (PAC), took the highly unusual step of contacting the Garda Commissioner, the Financial Regulator and the Office of the Director of Corporate Enforcement, asking them to investigate the information provided by the banks to NAMA prior to the transfer of loans to the agency. He claimed that the banks had sought to dupe NAMA into paying €20 billion more for the loans than they were worth.

McGrath had raised the issue at a PAC meeting attended by NAMA and was encouraged to act by the answers he received. He learnt that NAMA had been informed by the banks that the average loan-to-value ratio across the property and development loan book was 77 per cent, when it was actually closer to 100 per cent, meaning there was less developer equity to wipe out and larger losses for the banks – and then NAMA – to cover than there should have been. He said that the banks had told NAMA that 40 per cent of their loans were 'performing'; NAMA concluded that payments were being made on only about 25 per cent of the loans. McGrath said there was a need to investigate how 'false, misleading information' had been provided to NAMA, because it could have led to a 'huge overpayment by the tax-payer' to the banks. He said the evidence was 'overwhelming'. McGrath was encouraged to make his formal complaints when Chief Executive Brendan McDonagh told the committee hearing he did not disagree with the points being made, and Chairman Frank Daly chimed in to say that 'the figures were certainly misleading. You can speculate as to what was behind it.' However, the investigation was short-lived: after NAMA told the fraud squad it had no evidence that banks had deliberately provided it with misleading information about their loan books.

It was an interesting decision by NAMA, because McGrath had not been talking about estimates as to recoverability of loans – which nobody seemed able to call correctly – but the provision of hard information on the status of loans. NAMA officials had long been appalled by what it had discovered about the practices of the Irish banks before the crash. These went beyond hopeless optimism about continued increases in property prices and the ability of borrowers to repay their debts. The government had decided that NAMA should value loans on the strength of the collateral – which made sense – but often the problem was not the value of the collateral but the bank's legal right over that collateral. Without proper, legally enforceable security on a loan, that loan might be worthless.

In the rush to lend money, some banks had not established or registered proper title to some properties. It was sheer carelessness motivated by greed; they feared that if they got bogged down in paperwork, the borrower might go to a rival for the deal instead. In most cases lending had been secured on the supposed capital value of a property, not on the cash flow that an asset or the business that it owns was able to generate. This was supposed to provide more certainty to the lender if the repayments stopped. Unfortunately, banks got caught up in the hype about the alleged value of property and diluted their own security by valuing it at inflated market rates, instead of looking at what the real value would have been in an emergency sale – particularly if large amounts of property were suddenly made available for sale at the same time.

But it got far more complex than that. Many developments were what came to be called 'multi-banked'. Instead of one bank taking on all of the risk, it was apparently shared out amongst a consortium of lenders. The paradox was that this actually managed to increase the risk to individual lenders in the consortia. Which banks had security over which assets acting as collateral?

Within this sort of structure, all banks have some form of security over the asset or a related asset. What, though, if more than one bank laid claim to a particular asset? Or, if there was a batch of assets, who would get first claim as creditor over the lot? Even though all of the loans were going to NAMA, this mattered to the discount that would be applied and to the bank's subsequent capital position after the loss was taken. And what if a foreign bank – foreign banks weren't part of NAMA – claimed a right to an asset also being claimed by an Irish bank?

Here's where things got really complicated. A developer might have borrowed from a bank but not just offered the land being purchased as collateral; he might have offered other land as well. But that land might have a charge against it by another bank for another loan. If the original bank hadn't checked, because it didn't want to upset a good customer, it was in trouble. Duplication of security became a major issue as NAMA went about its work.

It got worse again. Developers issued bonds secured on their future cash flow from rental properties or future sales, and used these as collateral. They indulged in things called cross-collateralized debt obligations. There were options, credit swaps, derivative contracts and other exotic financial instruments that not only confused the layperson but also on occasion those who were trading or investing in them.

Further complications arose when the banks had looked for additional security. Often borrowers provided what were called 'liens' or 'assignments' on other forms of assets. This meant that when NAMA and the banks went calling on developers for repayment of debts, they ended up with art collections and stallions as well as cash deposits and shares. The problem with shares was that they were frequently in bank stocks, and so now worthless, or nearly so. Personal guarantees, which the banks, almost uniquely in Europe, had as their fallback positions, were also called in, but the reality was that few borrowers had much left to cover these guarantees. And even if they had, they failed to sell these assets because there were no buyers.

NAMA needed to make sales, to put itself out of business, as it were. The state did not want to own unused development land, empty houses, apartments and office blocks, or commercial units, shops and hotels that were providing only a fraction of the rent that they should have been, and that were acting as unfair competition to private-sector businesses – which were paying higher rent or charging higher prices to customers because they needed the cash to pay their debts. But how could NAMA sell the vast portfolio of property that it had acquired, when to try to do so would swamp the market? And who would have the money or the desire to buy, especially with the banks not able to lend? In any case should banks use their limited supply of cash to lend for property speculation? Would they not be better off lending to productive businesses instead?

NAMA's aims had mutated after its establishment. Initially, its brief was to fix the banks. Then it was given an instruction by the government, worried about the mounting political criticism and intervention by the European Commission, not to make losses by overpaying for loans. Buying at market value satisfied the political directive that NAMA not make losses but it destroyed the banks. They had agreed to NAMA on the basis that it would pay somewhat over the odds, that the state would get its return over a ten-year period as the market recovered. What was happening now only damaged the market further.

Even if NAMA bought those loans at so-called market prices, it would be impossible for it to sell all the property over which it had taken control without causing enormous market distortion. Economist Ronan Lyons estimated that the loans in NAMA's portfolio were secured on Irish-based commercial property that had been valued at about €8 billion at its peak. Yet he cited how property services firm CBRE had estimated that the entire value of *all* commercial-property transactions in Ireland in the decade 2001 to 2010 was only about €11 billion, and the bulk of that was during 2005 to 2007, a time of vastly inflated prices. How, then, could NAMA sell that much property and to whom?

That was one problem; what to do with all the empty houses and apartments was another. Vacant units and estates lost further value if they were not maintained, even leaving aside the social problems for those in adjacent units. Having such a supply of empty stock created a dilemma for potential buyers: why pay more for a house in a full estate than was being quoted for a house in an empty or half-full estate near by? On the other hand, why take the risk of moving into a development that might never be finished and where many of the basic facilities might never be provided? Not surprisingly, many people chose to wait, which only served to send prices further downwards.

In a bid to deal with the problem, NAMA floated the idea of offering a form of insurance against negative equity to individuals and families who were willing to buy houses or apartments from its developer clients. It volunteered to absorb the first 20 per cent of any subsequent loss on the value of the property by deferring 20 per cent of the purchase price for a period of up to five years. If the market fell by 20 per cent in this period, the money need not be repaid. It seemed a good offer but it didn't necessarily deal with fears people had about jobs and income or make the location of many of these properties any better – some of the reasons they hadn't sold in the first place. NAMA said it would try to sell up to €1 billion of property in five pilot schemes to be launched by the end of 2011. In the first three months of 2011 the entire market for first-time buyer mortgages was

€239 million. But, as NAMA controlled €9 billion of loans secured on residential property and more than 25,000 homes, it had to try something.

By February 2011 NAMA had purchased 11,000 loans from 850 borrowers at five banks that had an original or face value of €71.2 billion. It paid just €30.2 billion, amounting to an average discount of 58 per cent, a much bigger 'haircut' than had been intended originally. The intention was to increase this to an €88 billion portfolio at a final cost of €37 billion approximately. The thirty most heavily indebted debtors had accounted for about €27 billion of the loans. The top three borrowers transferred to NAMA, who were not identified publicly, owed €8.3 billion between them. Detailed work had been done in drawing up the valuations: some 43 per cent of those debts had been valued on a loan-by-loan basis and had those values validated by the European Commission, while another 17 per cent had gone through full due diligence.

The argument in favour of NAMA remained that if it had not come into existence the banks would simply have held on to their bad loans, gradually written them down over the years and constantly sought new capital injections. They would have become like the Japanese 'zombie' banks of the 1990s, which had stumbled on with barely adequate capital and which did not have the money or the will to lend to the productive economy.

But NAMA didn't solve that problem. The long-delayed establishment of NAMA created paralysis in the market, drove down the estimated value of properties and sites as the valuation process was under way, and increased the scale of the bank's capital needs. The result was an enormous bill for bailing out the banks, which will lead to an enormous reduction in the standard of living for all Irish people over the next decade. With NAMA's help, Ireland became a classic example of a society that privatized profits but socialized losses.

23. The Carrot and the Stick

NAMA was our economic equivalent of Janus, the mythological Roman god of beginnings and transitions, with its two faces, one looking to the past and the other to the future simultaneously. NAMA was two-faced too, but not just because it had to deal with the past and look to the future, but because it had to confront both the banks that it was meant to rescue, and the property developers who had borrowed from those banks.

Dealing with the banks might have been tricky and troublesome, but it was only a taster of the difficulties NAMA would have to confront when it turned to the entrepreneurial class of once-wealthy property developers who faced potential penury. There were a great many of them, as opposed to just six banks. These property developers were cornered men who faced losing the luxurious homes and the lavish lifestyles they thought they'd secured for themselves for ever. (It was nearly always men who had borrowed heavily, albeit often with encouragement from wives and partners.) They were prepared to fight hard to keep as much as they could; some would be duplicitous. They had always resented intrusion into their affairs but now faced extensive engagement about both their ability to repay their loans and the real value of the assets they had provided as security for those loans, information that NAMA would need to help it assess the true value of the loans it was buying from the banks. They had become used to the banks being compliant in meeting their needs, but now they feared NAMA would enforce a style of relationship that was entirely alien to what they had become accustomed.

Some of the developers hoped that their long-standing cordial relationships with Fianna Fáil would help when it came to appointments at NAMA and how the agency would go about its business. They wondered whether, through NAMA, they would be able to escape part of their debts or even to finance their efforts at recovery.

The government's appointment of Frank Daly, the recently retired head of the Revenue Commissioners, as NAMA's chairman carried with it a statement of intent that was not necessarily good news for the developers, however.

Daly was Brian Cowen's choice for the job as chairman and agreed to take it after a personal phone call from the Taoiseach making the request. As a lifelong tax collector, it was part of Daly's career DNA to seek the payment of all money properly due to the state. Many of the developers with whom he would now have to deal had made a speciality of minimizing their payments to the taxman, mainly through legitimate tax avoidance but in some cases through evasion. Some would have had history with Daly, directly or through his officers, because of disputes about the full amount of tax owed. While the Revenue under his direction might have allowed a little wiggle-room on the timing of payments, especially if a taxpayer was having short-term difficulties in raising cash, it did not have a reputation for flexibility when it came to the size of the payments. For that very reason Daly suited the government's requirements when it came to the optics of appointing a suitable NAMA chairman: this man would do all he possibly could to get the state's money back. His short spell as a public-interest director on the board of Anglo Irish Bank would also have increased his understanding of the issues involved, or so it was hoped.

Defining NAMA's job and therefore Daly's suitability was not an easy task. In some respects his brief for dealing with the property developers seemed simple enough. Once NAMA purchased loans from the banks it had to ensure that it recovered all of the money that it had spent in buying those loans, and, if possible, make a profit. Initially, the government announced that NAMA would aim for an eventual profit of €4.8 billion. Not long afterwards it had to revise this to a hoped-for figure of €1 billion or, in a worst-case scenario, a loss of €800 million. Some cynics said it would be doing well if this was the worst it would do, especially as in its first full year of operations, 2010, it managed to lose €1.18 billion.

Daly had an additional task to undertake, one that was dictated by a political need to deal with public anger. NAMA was to be required to seek repayment not just of the money it had paid for the loan but of the balance of the money that the borrowers originally owed. The debt still existed in its entirety. Brian Lenihan had made it clear that developers would repay every cent they had borrowed, not just the discounted amount that NAMA had paid for the loans. The government was under enormous political pressure to prove that NAMA was not a bailout for builders, Fianna Fáil's friends from the infamous Galway Races fund-raising tent. Bailing out the banks looked bad enough without it being said that the same thing would be done for the developers. Lenihan promised that builders 'would be pursued to the ends of the earth' to repay all the money they owed. While it was a popular and noble sentiment it complicated matters somewhat. Effectively, NAMA was being asked to engage in a political process of punishment and retribution against errant borrowers, making an already tough job more difficult. There was a significant argument to be made that this might best have been left to the courts and regulators, leaving NAMA to organize more practical matters such as managing assets and collecting money.

There was a risk that taking an unduly aggressive approach to bankrupting developers would only exacerbate the crisis. An even greater oversupply of property because of foreclosures would drive prices down further, because few were willing to take the risk of buying in a falling market. Even those willing to do so could not get loans from the banks. Being tough with too many developers too quickly would create losses for NAMA when it tried to sell its assets, as well as damaging investment values for everyone else with property.

NAMA began by trying to engage with the developers on a positive basis, irrespective of how much criticism there might be from the public that doing so was 'soft'. It took the approach of giving each borrower a chance to prove that he could work his way out of trouble, emphasizing that it had no interest in 'knocking borrowers over for the sake of it'. Daly said that 'NAMA's preference is to work with the developer or borrower – they have expertise or experience, although maybe they haven't always used it wisely.' But the carrot was accompanied by a stick: 'Very often the threat of insolvency is enough to bring people to the table and get them to engage with us realistically.'

Everyone who had loans transferred to NAMA was asked to provide a business plan outlining how they would work out their debts. The business-plan documents given to developers required them to be completed 'in utmost good faith with full disclosure of all facts, assumptions and issues likely to influence NAMA in reaching a decision on a course of action regarding a debtor'. Daly told an Oireachtas committee in 2010 that 'they have to be evidence-based, they cannot be aspirational and we want them to answer all the questions that we have asked them.' The list of requirements was extensive and ran almost to the length of a book. Among many other things, NAMA wanted a full schedule of creditors and commentary on the relationship with them; full details of all sales or transactions with third parties and connected parties for over three years; historical details of all loans, personal income and tax affairs and projections for the next three years; and, finally, forecasts for what might happen if things went better than expected, but also, more importantly, if they went worse.

Daly made it clear early that 'viability is not a matter of survival on taxpayer life support until the good days come again.' However, he said the agency was only accepting plans that set out a target for significant debt reduction over a three-to-five-year period. 'This means submitting a list of assets which will be sold to raise cash and to repay debt,' he said.

The requirements of the business plan shocked many developers, who had become used to a very relaxed approach from their bankers in recent years. Seven of the first ten business plans submitted to NAMA were rejected and returned, a trend that was to continue. Some developers did not submit all of the required information; some made unrealistic assumptions about the repayments of their debts; some retained grandiose plans for development of green-field sites; some sought salaries that were unacceptable to NAMA; and some simply just wanted to wait in the hope that the market would correct itself.

NAMA emphasized that it would not emulate the banks by continuing to provide 'interest-only' facilities on loans without the repayment of principal. There would be exceptions, though, if it could be shown that there were 'viable development projects which will generate cash in the short- to medium-term'. If the plan was agreed, the borrowers could continue in business, albeit under strict new conditions. If the plan was not feasible, NAMA would take control of the assets and use them to raise the money to pay the loans, either by selling them or 'working them' under the control of a receiver.

It was an approach fraught with difficulty. Deciding at what time a loan should be repaid could have major implications for how much money NAMA would ultimately be able to collect. An early sale – particularly in the moribund Irish market, where finance was not available from the banks to assist in purchases, further depressing realizable prices – was likely to trigger a sizeable loss for the developer, who would then have no means of clearing his debts. The argument made by many developers, not always self-serving, was that a larger sale price might be achieved at a later date, benefiting everyone. NAMA did not wish to be seen to indulge in what Daly called 'wishful thinking' on the part of the developers: that a medium-term view about the timing of disposals would prove more financially beneficial. He was particularly aware that, while some had been unlucky in what had happened to them – having been conservative in their borrowing but still caught by the massive fall in property values – many had taken blue-sky optimism into orbit. This extraordinary optimism, built into their business DNA, was reflected in the presentation of some business plans; bordering on the delusional, such plans were rejected quickly. They believed that things would improve if they wanted them to improve badly enough.

Good arguments were, in certain instances, made to NAMA, which meant it had to make choices about who to support and who to ditch. The agency would have to decide when it would be a developer itself – in partnership with the original developer – when a liquidator, when a little bit of both. This would require a considerable degree of speculation on the part of NAMA regarding possible future levels of property prices. But Daly clearly did not have that type of expertise. His chief executive, Brendan McDonagh, had moved from his job at the National Treasury Management Agency, so he had the advantage of no connections to the property sector, which meant he was beholden to no one in it and could cast a cold eye over things; but he suffered the disadvantage of no practical experience of it either, having only hearsay knowledge of who could or could not be trusted among the developer classes.

NAMA recruited a team of senior managers to report to John Mulcahy, the agency's head of portfolio management. Mulcahy was an interesting appointment, having been one of the most prominent commercial real estate agents in the country and advised some of the richest developers and investors on sales and purchases. He had an incomparable knowledge of the system and of who was who in it.

Many of his appointments came from the same ranks. Kevin Nowlan is the son of Bill Nowlan, from asset-management firm W. K. Nowlan, who was one of the most provocative commentators on the market in a variety of newspapers. Nowlan had previously worked for Treasury Holdings and Anglo Irish Bank, where his clients included Treasury itself, Gannon Homes and Bovale Developments. The last, owned by the Bailey Brothers, had been at the heart of the first phase of the Planning Tribunal because of its extraordinary relationship with the corrupt politician Ray Burke.

Another member of Mulcahy's NAMA team was Mark Pollard, Treasury's former development director. He took Donal Kellegher and Michael Moriarty from the Savills estate agency: Kellegher was best known in the profession for leading Savills' development land division, acting for Dublin Port in its 2006 sale of the Irish Glass Bottle site in Ringsend. He helped get a good price for the seller – €412 million – but Bernard McNamara, Derek Quinlan and the Dublin Docklands Development Authority's loans on that disastrous transaction were transferred to NAMA at an 87 per cent discount, emphasizing just how insane the entire transaction had been in the first place.

Alison Rohan – daughter of Ken Rohan, one of the wealthiest builders in the Republic and the owner of Charleville House in Enniskerry, County Wicklow – also joined the NAMA team. Her father had benefited massively from an extraordinary tax break passed by Bertie Ahern during his time as minister for finance, when Rohan had been able legally to avoid millions in income tax by offsetting the cost of acquiring antique furniture against his bill. The builder had hosted a fund-raising dinner, attended by Ahern, in his home, at a time when he was in dispute with the Revenue Commissioners; shortly thereafter the Revenue's case against Rohan was torpedoed by Ahern's tax legislation. (In addition, Ahern's amendment to the 1994 Finance Act had applied retrospectively to Rohan's tax returns. Although, in theory, anyone could have availed themselves of this tax break, Rohan was the only one known to have done so.) Alison had been working at D2 Private, a property-investment firm founded by Deirdre Foley and David Arnold; some of its disastrous investment decisions would bring it within the NAMA remit, although Rohan was not held responsible for them. NAMA said that clear demarcation lines would be drawn for its employees: if they had ever any connection to a borrower or a piece of property, they would have to declare this and have no connection whatsoever with it on NAMA's behalf. Failure to do so would be an immediate sacking offence. There was no suggestion that any of these people did anything other than act in NAMA's best interests, but, given the small size of the country, the potential for conflict must have been huge. The lack of transparency about NAMA's operations – excused on the basis of commercial sensitivity – also gave rise to fears about the appropriateness of any actions NAMA might undertake.

24. Developers in Denial

Since the collapse of the property boom, some developers had sold their helicopters and private jets but others hadn't. Many were still living in their mansions, driving top-of-the-range cars, and jetting off to holiday homes or luxury hotels at destinations the rest of us, now indirectly funding it all, could only dream of visiting. The Construction Industry Federation had sent a circular to its members in June 2010 entitled 'Lifestyle of Borrowers Must Adjust to Reflect Business Realities', urging restraint, but many seemed to prefer to ignore the new realities.

Developer Johnny Ronan became the tabloid emblem for bad-boy property developers, his continued hedonistic excess posing NAMA with an unwanted dilemma. In early 2010 the 56-year-old Tipperary-born property developer made the front page of the tabloids when a row with his on-off girlfriend, Glenda Gilson, the TV3 *Xposé* presenter, former model and niece of the once-jailed, and since deceased, Fianna Fáil TD Liam Lawlor, erupted into violence outside a busy Dublin pub. He retreated to his €650,000 Maybach car at the end of a two-way foul-mouthed tirade that had spectators aghast. The next day he hooked up with former Miss World Rosanna Davison, daughter of crooner Chris de Burgh and a supposed rival to Gilson in the search for modelling work and publicity, and flew her on his private jet to Marrakesh in Morocco. Details of the luxury trip, estimated to cost €60,000, found their way into the tabloids. The matter was raised in the Dáil, which was surely a first.

Ronan's personal worth at the height of the boom had been estimated by the *Sunday Times* at over €400 million, made up of his investments in Treasury (which made him landlord to NAMA and co-owner of the Convention Centre Dublin), foreign-development companies REO and China REO, office blocks in France (which made him a landlord to BNP Paribas), twelve racehorses and a vast

vintage wine collection valued at €4 million. He had about €40 million in cash in the bank, according to published accounts. But he had
enormous debts, both corporately and personally, that combined ran
into billions of euro. They couldn't be repaid immediately and most
likely would never be repaid in full at all.

It didn't end there: his companies had massive overseas and domestic development plans that required substantial additional financial
support from NAMA (and other foreign lenders) to improve the
chances of the original loans being repaid. He was under instruction
from NAMA to stop making charity donations from his businesses.
He had been asked to consider reducing overheads and professional
fees at Treasury, 'in the context of meaningful debt repayment', and
to accept a new reduced salary, but his Marrakesh trip suggested he
wasn't really getting the message. NAMA was in a dilemma: it was
relatively happy about its dealings with other senior people in Treasury, such as his partner Richard Barrett and Managing Director John
Bruder, but Ronan's public behaviour made continued support hard
to justify. Ronan was instructed by Barrett to calm down and to keep
out of sight, at least until the official opening of the National Convention Centre later that year, when he was pictured embracing
former Taoiseach Bertie Ahern and overheard to say 'There's Bertie,
he always looked after us.'

Ronan featured in an RTÉ television documentary in 2010 that
outraged many who, their reading confined to the business pages,
may have failed to appreciate just how outrageously some developers
had been acting over the years. The others who featured may not
have been quite as prominent in the tabloids, but it didn't make them
any the less interesting.

Michael O'Flynn was the developer of the country's tallest and
most expensive apartment complex, the Elysian. Located in the heart
of Cork City, very near the City Hall, this eye-catching development –
71 metres in height and with 17 storeys – was Ireland's tallest building.
It had 211 residential units, including triplex penthouses that were
being offered for €2 million and single-bedroom apartments that
would cost €375,000. It was marketed as 'a beacon of light overlooking
a city striding with confidence into the 21st century'. It was launched just

two days after Lehman Brothers collapsed and less than a fortnight before the government guaranteed all deposits and bonds at the banks. Hardly any of the units sold, and O'Flynn refused to drop his prices.

Notwithstanding this blow to his business, O'Flynn took on a prominent role as spokesman for developers with the Construction Industry Federation. The *Primetime Investigates* special on RTÉ brought him to national prominence when he was shown boarding his chartered helicopter on the manicured rolling lawns outside his enormous, relatively recently built mansion at Ovens, to the west of Cork City, and then disembarking at a horse race meeting at Down-royal, where one of his horses proceeded to win.

O'Flynn did not keep his head down subsequently, even if he was more discreet in the use of his helicopter (he eventually got rid of it). A week after the RTÉ programme, when his horses Elysian Rock and Shane Rock competed in the Christmas racing festival at Leopardstown, O'Flynn issued a statement: 'my family and I, like many other people from all walks of life, have been supporters of the horse racing industry for many years and I am proud of my personal ongoing involvement in what is a very important industry in Ireland.'

He also got involved in an extraordinary row with Tom Parlon, the CIF director general (and former junior minister). Parlon's old political instincts had come to the fore during a radio interview in which he was under pressure to justify the continued luxury of some developers' lifestyles. He compared some developers' homes to 'headstones over their egos' and observed, correctly, that thousands of people in construction were struggling to make ends meet because they weren't being paid by the men who had contracted them (though he did not suggest that O'Flynn was one of those).

O'Flynn responded with an e-mail to members of the CIF board, in which he accused Parlon of displaying an 'obvious disdain' for some developers and of 'ridiculing' them. The fate of the family home was 'one of the most frequent concerns of members around the country', O'Flynn claimed. It was 'shocking' that Parlon should have 'initiated an attack in a most personal and offensive manner on myself and a number of specific CIF members'. 'If we must take abuse from other members of society, so be it; but for abuse to be self-inflicted by a man whose salary we pay is unforgivable.' O'Flynn told his colleagues that they should stand 'shoulder to shoulder' and be determined to 'defend our members' in very difficult times.

The display of continued enjoyment of wealth on the RTÉ documentary was controversial, and NAMA chairman Frank Daly was not slow to complain. He responded to the programme by saying that developers would have to curb their lifestyles and sell off their 'jets, their yachts, their Bentleys or whatever'. It wasn't just O'Flynn he had in mind: the appearance of developer Gerry Gannon was most probably more in his mind, especially as NAMA was in a serious dispute with him.

Having first informed viewers that Gannon owed NAMA more than €1 billion, RTÉ next presented clips of him depositing seven bags of shopping from Dublin's most expensive retailer, Brown Thomas, into the boot of his Range Rover, which was in its car park. He then got into the vehicle, removed his distinctive hat, without which he is rarely seen in public, and mopped his brow to restore himself after all the effort. Cue hoots of derision in hundreds of thousands of households throughout the country.

The documentary also featured the mansion Gannon was in the process of building for himself in a prime position on the Hill of Howth – before showing all the other domestic properties that he had owned. Intriguingly, land registry records indicated that Gannon had signed over as many as twenty-two properties, many in expensive parts of Dublin, to his wife not long before the establishment of NAMA. He had also signed over seventy-four hectares of land in Loughglynn, County Roscommon, including a former convent that had been considered for possible redevelopment as a hotel. All of the transfers were completed before NAMA officially came into being in December 2009. Margaret Gannon lodged applications for the first registration of eleven apartments – all located in Dublin – in her name on eight separate dates between 14 July and 3 November 2009.

Questions were then raised about the extent of NAMA's powers in such cases. Did a wife enjoy a privileged status that allowed her to take control of these assets and keep them even if her husband could not repay his debts? Was the NAMA law in itself enough to force the return of these assets or were there other laws relating to fraud, bankruptcy or reckless trading to which it could turn, as long as it could prove such serious charges against any developer? Had legal action been taken to force Margaret Gannon to hand over the assets? What happened if an asset was solely registered in the wife's or partner's name in the first place?

Many other leading developers had made similar moves. House builder Seamus Ross of Menolly Homes – developer of, among other things, the expensive enclave of Farmleigh Woods in Dublin's Phoenix Park, and owner of the five-star Dylan Hotel in the capital – transferred a three-storey over-basement Georgian property on Harrington Street in Dublin to his wife, Moira, on 13 July 2009, as well as two other Dublin properties. Joe O'Reilly – whose company Chartered Land is perhaps best known for building the massive Dundrum Town Centre – transferred the family home at Kerrymount Avenue in the upmarket suburb of Foxrock to his wife on 5 March 2009, according to filings from the Registry of Deeds; on 2 November 2009 a number of apartments at Riverhall in Castleknock were put into her name as well. Liam Carroll, once the busiest apartment builder in the country and said to be worth over €1 billion before his group collapsed under the weight of unsustainable debts, was also amongst those found to have transferred properties to his wife before the formal establishment of NAMA. Bernard McNamara – another former billionaire, who admitted that he was broke in early 2010 and who saw NAMA appoint receivers to his vast conglomerate of building companies and property investments later in the year – tried to transfer assets to his wife or had put them in her name originally.

There was widespread speculation that developers who transferred assets to their wives or other family members before NAMA was set up in November 2009 could not be forced to reverse them. As far as NAMA was concerned, however, it was not bound to honour transfers that its new customers had made before NAMA itself came into existence. It would do whatever it could to get its loans repaid, following the Lenihan dictum of 'we will chase them to the ends of the earth.' The 2009 NAMA Act had a specific provision to deal with developers who unjustly tried to place their assets beyond its reach;

there was no time limit on how far back NAMA could reach to ascertain if a borrower had unjustly transferred assets. And NAMA didn't have to prove insolvency at the time of the transfer or an intention to defraud: the Act allowed NAMA to set aside transfers where it was a court's opinion that it was 'just and equitable' to do so.

Whether that was possible when cash or title to assets was transferred to offshore tax havens has never been established properly. The fear was that NAMA had no powers to go after assets transferred to places like the Channel Islands or other offshore havens like the Cayman Islands before December 2009 and the enactment of the legislation. Public questioning of the extent of the wealth that remained with NAMA clients was prompted by the continued ostentatious lifestyles of the likes of builder Sean Dunne and investor Derek Quinlan, both of whom decamped for a time to Switzerland.

Dunne came a cropper when he failed to develop his plan for an Irish version of the plush London Knightsbridge district on land he had bought, expensively, in Ballsbridge, Dublin 4. By mid 2008 Dunne's company Mountbrook had bank borrowings of more than €763 million, including €218 million that was repayable on demand. His main bank, Ulster Bank, put together a new ownership structure that almost ended Dunne's shareholding in the company: his €125 million personal equity investment was eliminated. In August 2010 the *Sunday Times* reported that nearly €350 million in loans associated with Dunne had been transferred to NAMA at a discount of 42 per cent. He was not an Anglo client, but had borrowed from AIB, Bank of Ireland and INBS.

Dunne and his wife, Gayle, had owned two of the twenty-two houses on Shrewsbury Road in the heart of Dublin 4, once the most expensive address in Ireland. Ouragh, a faux-period home at 20A Shrewsbury Road, was their home but this was rented to the South African Embassy in late 2010. Despite repeated denials from the Dunnes, the *Sunday Times* had reported consistently that Gayle was the beneficiary of a trust fund that spent €57 million in 2006 to buy a house called Walford, at No. 24, a record for a single residence in the country. It was offered for rent in June 2011. The Dunnes were refused planning permission to make additional use of the land on which it stood; it has been vacant for years and its resale value has collapsed.

Yet somehow the couple lived in a suburb of Geneva from 2008 to 2010, having produced a sufficient statement of means to receive a residency permit (definite and proven statements of net worth have to be provided in Switzerland before residency is allowed). They then moved to the US in a manner that provided high drama but also raised legitimate questions as to what wealth the couple continued to possess despite their ongoing relationship with NAMA. Belle Haven – described as an exclusive Greenwich, Connecticut, enclave, with its own security force, home to singer Diana Ross, hedge-fund billionaire Paul Tudor Jones II and retired IBM executives – was where the Dunnes chose to relocate; they rented a Mediterranean-style villa on Field Point Avenue at a reported monthly cost of €17,500. For that they got a house with an indoor swimming pool, billiards room, several reception rooms, a grand piano in its own dedicated rooms, and extensive gardens, enough presumably to remind them and their three young children of their old home at Shrewsbury Road.

The Dunnes had plans to stay in the area permanently at a different 4,600-square-foot house but these went badly awry in episodes of high farce: a large sum of money – about $500,000 – they had given to the American lawyer hired to secure their residency went missing and they were embroiled in controversy over illegal demolition works at a residential property they denied owning. Gayle Dunne had applied for an investment visa in the United States on the basis of an unnamed property; if granted she, her husband and children would then have been able to remain in the US for as long as the visa continued. The typical life-span of such a visa is five years but can be renewed indefinitely. The applicant's spouse can also apply for authorization to work in the United States, which would have been of use to Sean. Unfortunately, it appears that the Dunnes picked the wrong lawyer to represent them. By March 2011 the Dunnes had moved out of the rented accommodation and headed for destinations unknown. Their problems were mounting. Gayle Dunne took a tough line with media queries, at one stage issuing a formal statement through her solicitors, declaring that her 'marital affairs, place of residence and finances are not legitimate matters of public interest'. 'She is not a public person and has no bank debts with any Irish bank covered by the Irish Government guarantee, and for absolute clarity is not the subject of any NAMA loans,' her spokesman declared.

By July 2011 Sean Dunne's relationship with NAMA had deteriorated to the point where the state agency decided to appoint receivers to the assets attached to its loans, removing him from any control over their future. Dunne claimed to be disappointed that a business plan hadn't been agreed with NAMA, saying in a statement: 'We proposed that NAMA send in a representative to work alongside and supervise our dedicated team, which would be more cost-effective than the appointment of receivers. Unfortunately, this proposal was declined.'

He also maintained the move came as a surprise to him: 'It was a shock, given that the progress made on our NAMA business plan to date was excellent, and well beyond expectations in very tough market conditions . . . There was no indication of any deterioration in our relationship with NAMA, and indeed they specifically complimented my team, and I, for our full cooperation.' Pointedly, NAMA refused to comment.

One of the Dunnes' neighbours on Shrewsbury Road, Derek Quinlan, had also left Ireland once it became clear that the crash would ruin him. He too headed to Switzerland, to Epalinges, a small town seven kilometres from Lausanne, where he soon set up his new home. This choice was somewhat surprising, given that he had spent €48 million in January 2006 to buy an extraordinary villa in Cap-Ferrat on the Riviera, just a few moments' walk from the landmark Grand Hotel. He had then borrowed another €8 million to renovate and furnish the mansion, as well as the one-storey housekeeper's residence, a garage with pigeon loft, a pavilion in which to greet guests, a greenhouse, a swimming pool, and extensive parklands and gardens stretching down to provide exclusive access to the sea, one of only about a dozen houses to enjoy that privilege, all on 8,000 square metres of land. The villa itself included a large entrance hall, dining room for ten, three bedrooms on the first floor and two on the second floor. The basement had a home cinema, a bar and wine cellar. But this house was to be put up for sale, as were others in California, New York and London.

NAMA had turned its attentions on Quinlan in particular from 2009, appalled not just by the size of his debts but by the use of this borrowed money to finance a vanity acquisition spree unlike anything they'd seen elsewhere. Many of Quinlan's purchases were of properties for personal use, which, even if rented, could not have financed the interest on the loans taken out to buy them. He was totally dependent on a continued rising property market to provide him with capital profits and in no position to cope when property values fell.

Quinlan had quit his company Quinlan Private in 2009 as he fought to protect his personal assets. A private equity group called Integral entered into talks with Quinlan about becoming an investor in his private investment projects. The *Sunday Times* reported that the private equity firm had offered more than €350 million to take over his assets and help him to repay a portion of his personal debts. It would have paid him €360,000 per annum for three years to work as a consultant in managing those assets. All his personal guarantees would have been lifted and he would have been able to keep his luxury family home. It seemed like a sweet deal and it was claimed that two of his major creditors, RBS and Barclays, were agreeable. NAMA was not. It felt that it had to be seen to take a hard stand in the face of excess. Quinlan was about to discover that he would be unable to escape the embrace of NAMA, no matter where he went.

25. The Walk of Shame

Almost every developer ended up doing the NAMA 'walk of shame'. This involved a visit to the NAMA offices at the Treasury Building in Dublin 4, beside the Grand Canal, and taking the lift to the third floor. As they looked out of the windows of the waiting room, they faced towards the Aviva Stadium at Lansdowne Road, where many had purchased corporate boxes or tickets that guaranteed seats for rugby and soccer internationals for the next ten years. These were among the type of minor assets that NAMA now wanted to take ownership of, or over which they wanted security in case loans weren't repaid. NAMA demanded to know everything from developers, often in humiliating detail, not just about their business but about their personal financial affairs, something that often revealed unwanted truths.

NAMA had good reason to be suspicious of the claims of many developers as to what they possessed. While the lifestyles of many had been well documented by the media, NAMA officials were still shocked by what they discovered about the assets purchased and the money borrowed to pay for them. Yet there was also an argument that NAMA's opinion of a developer's previous behaviour should be secondary to his ability to pay back what he owed. While bankrupting developers might be a popular action with an unsympathetic public, would it bring about the optimum financial return to the state? What if these developers actually had good business plans that could lead to recovery of the money? Would it be fair, or even moral, to bankrupt them to make a point – and would it result in the state clawing back more money?

Developers who went to the third floor had to agree a business plan with NAMA that included a schedule of debt repayments; otherwise, they'd be placed in receivership or liquidation. Many developers did not want to repay what they had borrowed; and many,

with assets that had collapsed in value, would have created even larger
deficits by selling to do so. Some did not feel responsible for the repayment of all of their debts. They had often borrowed on what was
called a non-recourse basis: the only security offered to the bank was
the value of the particular asset itself. And only the proceeds from the
sale of that asset could be used to repay the loan. If there was a shortfall, the bank was left to cover the balance. They felt that was good
planning on their part, so why should they have to pay retrospectively
for the weakness of the bank's security? If they had profitable assets
that could be sold, why should profits from those sales be used to
cover losses on other transactions, especially if they had lived up to the
terms of their deals with the banks?

But NAMA was determined that if a developer had made a profit
from any transaction he was not going to be able to shelter that
money: it would be used as compensation to the banks for losses on
other loans. The business plan was one way to do this, ensuring that a
developer's assets and liabilities could not be held separately from each
other; this was also cheaper than going the legal route. Some bankers –
particularly those who had refused to follow the trend to give banks
or investors personal guarantees on repayment – were deeply angered
by this, as it rendered redundant some of their very clever planning.

Michael O'Flynn was one of those determined not to be treated by
NAMA in this way. As one of the first ten developers in size to have
his loans – estimated at more than €1 billion – transferred to NAMA,
he should have had his business plan for the repayment of the debts
agreed and approved very early on. O'Flynn had set up his business
with unlimited corporate status: he was shielded from the requirement to file detailed financial statements in the Companies Office but
was apparently left, as owner, personally liable for any debts incurred
throughout the group. O'Flynn's corporate structure was not as simple as first believed, though, and ultimately he enjoyed all of the
benefits of limited liability, hindering NAMA's ability to put him on
the hook for the repayment of certain loans because he had not signed
any personal guarantees.

The widespread employment of a system of personal guarantees
had added an almost unique Irish dimension to the crisis. The per-

sonal guarantee idea was simple, and in the boom times it suited both sides of the arrangement, if only because neither bank nor borrower expected the personal guarantee to be called upon. Effectively, it meant that the lender did not need specific security over the asset that was being purchased or developed with the borrowed money (although that was often in place too, with the personal guarantee acting as an insurance policy). The personal guarantee meant that in the event, considered unlikely, that the loan could not be repaid through the sale of that asset, the borrower would meet the repayment by using his other assets, including his family home if necessary.

The vast majority of borrowers in other countries simply refused to sign them. Personal guarantees superseded the protection that should have been provided to company owners by the well-established international principle of limited liability. 'In other countries, it was simply assumed that there was a risk premium built into the interest rate on the loan,' said one developer. 'If banks abroad insisted on a personal guarantee, the client would simply walk away.' But with borrowers so keen to get finance, because of the apparent profits available, they fell victim to banks threatening to withdraw the offer of finance without the provision of the personal guarantee as security.

Now developers and company owners were facing not only the loss of their investments but also their personal assets, as they struggled to raise cash to repay loans. 'Previously, there was a big difference between personal borrowings and company borrowings. This was no longer the case,' said one developer. 'We should never have left them [personal guarantees] in.'

Anglo Irish Bank had set the trend, and the use of personal guarantees became the norm in Irish lending, whereas they should have been used only in exceptional situations. It wasn't just the banks who wanted them: investors started demanding personal guarantees from other investors or directors before putting cash into syndicate deals. Some lenders took large risks on the mistaken assumption that the provider of the personal guarantee had such a wealth of ready cash, or assets that could easily be converted to cash, that there would never be a problem in making payments.

Whereas limited liability provided a mechanism for discharging company debt – with the liability of shareholders limited to their investment – there was no get-out clause for personal debt. People remained lumbered with full repayment if they couldn't negotiate deals with the banks or NAMA, because that was exactly what the personal guarantee, by definition, involved – even if it was impossible to achieve.

The banks, in their own right or acting on behalf of NAMA, had a number of options open to them, including asking the county sheriff to seize assets, or even forcing through a bankruptcy petition. If the provider of the personal guarantee lost a court action and had a judgment issued against him, a nightmare ensued: not only would he lose the investment he had made in the business but also quite possibly any other investments, including his pension fund, other shareholdings, stock options, cash and the family home. But it wasn't easy for the lender either; even if a judgment in the High Court was obtained, trying to enforce it was difficult, to say the least. Unlike NAMA, which was to act relatively quickly when it got hold of loans, some of the banks gave customers time. There were two main reasons for this: one was that they did not want to confirm the extent of losses by seeking the repayment of debts that they knew they would never recover; the second was that there was little point in giving payments to lawyers out of an already small pool of money.

Nevertheless, the calling in of personal guarantees by banks, often on the instructions of NAMA and sometimes by banks without links to NAMA, became a major feature of Irish commercial life in the early years of this decade. Developers such as Paddy Kelly, Bernard McNamara, Niall McFadden, Hugh O'Regan, Michael Daly and Brendan Murtagh found themselves facing court judgments because of personal guarantees they had provided, running into tens or hundreds of millions of euro. And it didn't just end with guarantees over loans. Personal guarantees to meet rental payments on commercial properties caused more grief for borrower and lender alike.

The existence of personal guarantees also complicated efforts to replace borrowings with new equity from third parties, a system regularly used in other countries to re-establish the financial base of a company. 'Do you know what the foreign money-men call Ireland?'

one developer told me, smiling ruefully. 'PG-land. Do you know what that means? It means that everything is complicated by every bloody personal guarantee that the banks demanded from everyone before they gave them any cash for anything. Nobody can pay back what they owe but they're still on the hook for the PGs and nobody will deal with them until they know they're clear from them.'

NAMA's Brendan McDonagh revealed during one Oireachtas committee hearing that the so-called 'top-ten' developers in NAMA had given personal guarantees which covered 60 per cent of their total loans of €16 billion, which NAMA had acquired for €8.5 billion. That might have sounded all well and good for the taxpayer but it was almost certain that those personal guarantees could not be met. The developers' assets simply did not cover their loans. Would NAMA acknowledge this reality or fail to do so in case it met with public flak? Would it be better to do deals with developers for the repayment of a realistic portion of their debts instead of bankrupting them for not meeting their personal guarantees? Would these deals, if agreed, involve sharing the profits on the sale or the completion of the development of some assets, provided the developers exceeded certain targets?

McDonagh claimed that 'around twenty' of the first thirty developers, before their loans were transferred to NAMA, had signed their assets over to family members or third parties. NAMA said it had clawed back more than €130 million of assets from three unnamed developers alone who had tried to put them beyond the agency's reach. In one case NAMA seized jewellery worth €200,000 that a developer had given his partner and put it up for sale. Property developers were voluntarily transferring back their assets in return for getting their business plans approved by NAMA, said McDonagh, obviating the need to spend money on legal action.

NAMA's dealings with Gerry Gannon were a good example of its approach. It knew all about Gannon's efforts to transfer assets before the RTÉ documentary broadcast and had acted accordingly. The agency engaged in a strategy that it called 'persuasion'. It had a big stick with which it could hit any errant developer. Once a transfer of assets became known to it – usually by way of examining the full sworn statements of assets owned and previously owned (supplied as part of the business plan) – and having cross-checked these against land registry documents and mortgage registrations, it sought to have transfers reversed in a 'consensual' way. Developers were usually given about eight weeks to comply. If they didn't, they ran the risk of having their business plans rejected and their assets recovered through the courts.

Gannon featured in the RTÉ *Primetime* programme because of how he had tried to sign over assets to his wife, Margaret, just before his loans were transferred into NAMA. Gannon had had an estimated net worth of €180 million at the peak of the boom but now had debts estimated at over €1 billion.

Documents filed at the Companies Office emphasized the extent of Gannon's downturn and the extent of his denial. Accounts for one of his main companies, Gannon Homes, lodged in October 2010 revealed losses of more than €50 million for 2008, before things presumably got even worse in the following years. The company admitted that it was 'dependent on NAMA support to continue as a going concern', yet Gannon said he would not sell assets, believing that the market had undervalued them. This put him at odds with the expressed wishes of NAMA. He insisted that €33 million in asset write-downs put into the accounts was excessive, when arguably it was generous.

Gannon began the process of trying to sell assets to raise cash. In the middle of 2010 he offered his 49 per cent shareholding in the K Club, the internationally renowned County Kildare golf resort and 2006 Ryder Cup venue, for sale, subject to any deal being accepted by NAMA. Gannon had paired with Michael Smurfit to buy the club from the Jefferson Smurfit Group in May 2005 for €115 million. 'I cannot expect the taxpayer to fund an exclusive loss-making club in County Kildare,' he said.

It was what once would have been called a 'trophy asset'. A buyer of the K Club would get two golf courses designed by Arnold Palmer, a 64-bedroom luxury hotel, and Ryder Cup Village, which houses a second clubhouse and a ballroom. There was also planning permission for eighty-five one- and two-bedroom apartments alongside the hotel, a courtyard development of twenty-four town houses on the Ryder Cup course, and a further 250 homes throughout the 560-acre estate, although the attraction to a buyer might have been limited given the economic downturn. Bizarrely, despite the proposed sale of his share, Gannon wanted to retain all of those development rights at the K Club. In addition, Gannon offered a 74-acre parcel of land at Straffan, County Kildare, opposite the entrance to the K Club, for sale: he had ambitious plans to develop a new village on this, at a price of up to €25,000 an acre.

Gannon continued to seek and receive planning permission to use development land in his nominal control. In the summer of 2010 Fingal County Council provided permission for the development of 3,400 homes, on 270 acres in an area called Oldtown, about four kilometres beyond Swords on the road to Ashbourne in County Meath. The infrastructural facilities were to include three or four primary schools, as well as a secondary school. Gannon Developments has owned most of the land since before the turn of the century and Gannon was reported as describing the adoption of the local-area plan for his landholdings as 'a good decision for me and a good decision for NAMA'. Just how he intended to finance the plan and who would buy finished units was not made clear. He was already having enormous difficulties selling units at the arguably better located Clongriffin in north County Dublin.

Gannon had about 700 acres of undeveloped land at the time his €1 billion-plus loans were transferred to NAMA. One of his worst investments was made in early 2008, when it was clear to most people that the boom was over. He joined with the Dublin Airport Authority to buy twenty acres from the Parnell's GAA Club in Collinstown for €24 million; it was to be used for a new airport car park. But by May 2010 a new independent valuation put its value at just €8 million. The joint venture formed to purchase the land, called Gatland Property, had bank loans of €23.9 million and Gannon had provided personal guarantees against €17 million of the bank loans from AIB. DAA provided a guarantee for its share of 'any interest and default interest accruing pursuant to the company's loan agreement'. The loan was transferred to NAMA. But who now would want to buy the land? The need for a new car park, especially one so distant from the airport, had disappeared with the collapse of airport traffic.

This was typical of the type of problem NAMA faced: bad decisions that seemed insoluble, made in their hundreds by people indulging in grandiose plans. In 2004 Gannon had also bought the 215-acre Belcamp College site in North Dublin for €105 million, but most of it was still undeveloped. The plan had been to build a medical campus for the Royal College of Surgeons in Ireland (RCSI) on a sixty-acre portion of the site. He would construct a medical school for over 2,000 students, a 320-bed teaching hospital, a ninety-bed nursing home, research and development facilities, staff and student accommodation, and a hotel and leisure facilities. The construction costs were estimated at €756 million over ten years; and, while the college was expected to raise some of the money through the sale of long-term bonds in the US, and additional private investment was to be sought, much of the finance would be supplied by bank borrowings. This speculation would now be overseen by NAMA.

How would it regard Gannon's way of doing business? Gannon's initial strategy with NAMA involved looking for interest roll-up, where the interest on a debt is added to the principal instead of being repaid, simply increasing the overall size of the loan. It eased the pressure on the borrower in the short to medium term, but created problems if the property behind the loan did not recover its old value. While the Irish banks may have been generous with interest roll-up arrangements before NAMA was set up, helping some developers to avoid insolvency, NAMA was taking a tougher approach.

Gannon had done some of the things the agency required. He sold his private jet and his helicopter. He withdrew funding for the newly established Sporting Fingal soccer team, not long after its maiden FAI Cup victory in 2009, having contributed €1.25 million to it previously. Without him the club, for which he had planned to build a stadium at Lusk, collapsed.

Gannon had been in the habit of giving personal guarantees and indemnities, as the accounts for his much smaller but still significant UK interests showed. Getting proper title to assets covered by the loans, or to other assets where no loans applied, was important. It was also reported that Margaret Gannon had given personal guarantees to the banks for loans transferred to her by her husband. These personal guarantees were in turn acquired by NAMA and made its job of trying to recover other assets transferred to her or registered in her name much easier.

NAMA claimed it had four legal ways – some based on the 'clawback', or 'asset reversal', provisions found in family, divorce, company and bankruptcy cases – available to it to overturn property transfers that it believed were conducted with the intent of defrauding current or future creditors.

If a developer was bankrupt, transfers in the two years leading up to the bankruptcy could be set aside. So threatening to bankrupt a developer if he didn't reverse transfers was a tactic that could be used.

Problems arose when transfers had been made to spouses and families earlier – and when the developer was confident that family members would allow him to live off their incomes and assets. In those circumstances, transfers in the previous five years could also be set aside in a bankruptcy unless a developer could prove that he was solvent at the time he transferred or gifted the asset. As most of them could plausibly argue that they had a sizeable surplus of assets over liabilities, based on the circumstances of the time, the threat of bankruptcy in such cases was a riskier proposal for NAMA.

If property had been transferred before 2009, NAMA could use the 1634 Conveyancing Act (Ireland), which allowed property conveyances and other transactions to be declared void if they were made with the purpose of delaying, hindering or defrauding creditors. But, again, proving intent might be very difficult. If property was transferred after 1 December 2009, the 2009 Land and Conveyancing Law Reform Act allowed transfers to be set aside if the intention had been to defraud a creditor. Again, proof was required and additionally many transfers had been made prior to that date.

So when there were doubts as to whether the law was in NAMA's favour, it seemed sensible to use the other avenue open to it: refusing the business plan. Developers depended on these plans to keep them solvent, so if they refused to reverse transfers, even those going back five years or more, they would find themselves in deep trouble.

NAMA forced developers to sign sworn statements in which all their worldwide assets were disclosed in return for support, and NAMA was allowed to trawl back through five years of cash movements to ensure no money had been hidden or taken out of the company to avoid the payment of debts. They were also told to unwind trusts to make it easier for NAMA to seize assets, should they be needed to cover debts. And the usual well-funded retirement funds were to be unlocked as well.

This angered many developers, who felt that legally made transfers were being set aside so that NAMA could minimize its own legal problems. There were those who regarded it as close to legal and financial blackmail. Some argued that they had made transfers in good faith without ever anticipating that they would be in financial straits in the future; they had engaged in legitimate forward planning for their family members and, ironically, were being punished for not betting all of their wealth on new speculations.

However, Frank Daly said it would be possible for the courts to infer that a person had intended to defraud future creditors by the transfer of assets to their spouse. 'A person doesn't have to be insolvent,' he said. Reasons such as tax planning, providing for family and following the advice of professionals had all been given for the movement of assets, 'but I would be pretty sceptical', Brendan McDonagh said. 'A lot knew what was coming, especially if they had given personal guarantees.'

The issue got a political airing when Minister for Social Protection Éamon Ó Cuív claimed in late 2010 that developers and bankers who moved assets offshore or transferred them to their family members were not acting in a patriotic or an ethical way. He said there needed to be a debate about 'people's sense of duty' and the nature of society following the excesses of the Celtic Tiger era. 'There are many things that are legal but they are not in my view very ethical, very desirable or very patriotic,' he told *The Irish Times* in an interview.

NAMA took no developer at his word when it came to their asset disclosures. It used tax returns, forensic accountancy, spending records and other material to scrutinize sworn statements and wealth. To make matters worse for developers, the Revenue Commissioners disclosed in August 2010 that it was receiving information and documents from NAMA on the loans that were being transferred. This raised the possibility of unpaid tax being discovered and further financial distress for the developers.

Most developers simply didn't have one company; they had a maze of them. Sometimes this was because they brought partners in on projects. Sometimes it was to minimize tax by using what were called 'special-purpose vehicles', companies especially set up to borrow money and buy land, before later selling on the land and moving the profits back to the parent company. The difference between tax avoidance, which is legal, and tax evasion, which is not, was difficult to establish in some circumstances.

NAMA had to look out for everything. It emerged that some property developers with NAMA-bound loans had been exploiting a loophole that allowed them to claim tax deductions on interest payments to their lenders, even if they had not actually been making the payments. To make matters worse, some developers with rental income from commercial-property investment portfolios – such as office blocks and/or shopping centres – were understood to be retaining significant amounts of rent from tenants. They refused to pass this on to their banks, instead using the money to pay bills, including personal lifestyle ones. The use of offshore trusts for the transfer of properties and other assets, including cash, was particularly interesting to both NAMA and the Revenue. Given their lavish spending during the boom, some developers probably had reason to fear a large benefit-in-kind bill at the very least.

NAMA's relationship with many developers worsened during the negotiations about the salaries they were to receive for continuing to run their businesses. Daly confirmed, as reported in one newspaper, that an unnamed developer had demanded €1.5 million annually to work out the problems at his company on behalf of NAMA. Apparently he felt that he needed the income not just to cover his lifestyle but to repay debts to the same institution that would, he hoped, now be paying him handsomely. He ended up getting a salary that was a fraction of his initial demand, according to Daly.

Most settled on annual salaries of about €200,000 and the right to remain in their trophy homes for the next five years; the sum was still sufficiently large to outrage many in the general public, and the right to reside in luxury also grated. Why should the public, all paying higher taxes to cover the losses incurred by the banks in lending to these individuals, have to pay, via NAMA, such high salaries? Why should these people be allowed to continue to live in splendour? Again, there were pragmatic, if not popular, reasons.

Expensive family homes could not be sold; the only market for them was at massively reduced prices that might not reflect future value if and when the economy returned. But that was secondary to the main reason for NAMA's decision. Appointing a receiver to a company would cost at least €10,000 per week − €500,000 per year − according to reliable estimates (the price went up the bigger and more complex the work). Better, then, to keep the developer (and his financial controller at much the same cost) because at least they knew where all the bodies were buried − if, of course, they were prepared to disclose all relevant information. What focused the minds of many was the penalty for supplying false and misleading information about their assets: five years in jail and fines of up to €5 million.

But there had to be some incentive beyond just a salary, especially if it was insufficient to allow the developer to clear his debts. These people didn't just buy and hold assets; they created companies and, in some cases, had a genuine vision as to how to improve the stock of the country, both practically and aesthetically. This raised the thorny issue of the seemingly politically impossible: debt-forgiveness packages between NAMA and the developers. These provided an incentive for the latter to walk away from part of their debt if they met certain conditions: achieved an acceptable sale price for their assets; unwound transfers of privately held shares, properties, trusts, pension funds and cash; and cooperated with NAMA fully during the so-called 'work-out' process. Failure to do as required would lead to the bankruptcy of the developer.

When NAMA left developers in place, most usually with accountants in tow, it insisted that non-executive directors were appointed to the boards, not only to keep a watching brief but also to supply advice about keeping up the repayment of debts. NAMA has powers of approval of appointment. Sometimes there was an insistence that new senior management be introduced, especially if companies had been spared the attentions of an appointed receiver.

But much came down to the personnel at NAMA itself. Assessment of the business plans was often left to external experts, mainly from outside the country. Some of the relationship work with borrowers was outsourced to the banks themselves, ostensibly to keep costs down but also because NAMA simply didn't have the required number of people. This brought about its own problems because there was a danger of some bank personnel maintaining old friendships and relationships even if now under different instructions. Just as importantly, NAMA felt that some of the charges from the banks for providing these services were excessive, and major rows broke out between those who were supposed to be working together.

The tension between both sides only increased when proposals on working capital needs and money for new developments were forwarded to the agency. Requests for money required NAMA to have the attitude of a developer: it had to assess the likelihood of projects succeeding if it provided working capital to have them finished – and that could involve entrusting sizeable amounts – running into hundreds of millions of euro – to a developer who was highly indebted already. There were different classes of developer after all, and some were better to work with than others, even if more heavily indebted. If it went right then great, but if it went wrong . . .

There were still some developers who thought they had good prospects, particularly if they had assets overseas. Many felt they were being treated badly and vindictively, even if they weren't. It was inevitable that somebody would eventually kick back against NAMA, using the courts to do so.

26.   The Empire Strikes Back

It was only a matter of time before one of the big property speculators confronted NAMA in the courts, in an attempt to stop the
transfer of his bank loans to the new entity. The man who did so was
Paddy McKillen, originally from Belfast, who now moves between
Dublin, London, Los Angeles, Vietnam and France, and who is believed
to spend as few as twenty days a year in Ireland. In an extraordinary
irony, he was NAMA's landlord; he and Johnny Ronan were co-
owners of the Treasury Building where both NAMA and the NTMA
were tenants, paying €810,000 a year in rent.

McKillen has been dubbed 'reclusive' by the media – which con-
jures up images of a Howard Hughes-style billionaire holed up in a
hotel room – but he would be better described as low profile. The
most commonly used picture of McKillen is from 1989, when he
attended, in black-tie, a Construction Industry Federation dinner. A
more recent picture of him has appeared, but it is of relatively poor
quality: the noticeable difference is that his hair has greyed totally.
He has not hidden away, though. He is just not very high profile in
his socializing in Ireland, like many other business people, nor in the
country often enough to be recognized. His rarely used Dublin home
is in a small but upmarket modern development on Torquay Road in
Foxrock called The Birches. His neighbours once included Johnny
Ronan and Sean Dunne, who would also come to merit the attention
of NAMA.

McKillen – who made his original fortune in car maintenance –
was early to property development in Dublin, particularly with regard
to the Temple Bar area and the Treasury Building. His biggest success,
achieved in partnership with another low-profile businessman called
Padraig Drayne, was the development of the Jervis Street Shopping
Centre. This duo, with assistance from another Northern businessman Paschal Taggart, who acted as the public face of the project,

bought the old Jervis Street Hospital in 1995 for just £3.5 million. Within thirteen months they had spent another £30 million on building a 1.25 million-square-foot shopping centre, the biggest of its kind in the country at the time. They borrowed the money mainly from Anglo Irish Bank, although other banks chipped in too.

Many retail analysts thought they were mad in their choice of location; consumers apparently would not carry on down the highly popular Henry Street to shop in this new centre, having spent their money before they arrived anywhere near it. But the Irish economy was just starting to pick up speed and consumer spending was soaring. McKillen also had a knack for identifying good tenants, often international companies without an existing presence in Ireland, who would sell the type of goods that Irish consumers wanted. Among those he persuaded to enter the Irish market via Jervis were major UK retailers Boots, Debenhams, Currys and Argos. The centre got the required footfall. Quickly, Jervis was worth a multiple of what it had cost; even in 2010, after the crash in property values, McKillen was able to quote a valuation of €118 million on his half-share of it, although it had been valued once as high as €225 million at the height of the boom.

McKillen bought many other property assets, not just in Ireland but in Britain, France and Vietnam too. To do this McKillen borrowed enormously. The extent of his borrowing became clear in his High Court challenge to NAMA: he had debts of €2.1 billion, of which €900 million was owed to Anglo.

McKillen did not expect his loans to fall under NAMA's remit, however. He carried on regardless even after Anglo fell into state ownership, nor did he seek other banks to refinance the Anglo loans for him. Anglo, under new boss Mike Aynsley, regarded him as one of its best clients and said it wanted to keep his loans on its books because he was regarded as one of the better customers for making repayments. McKillen, in common with many other developers, seemed to misread NAMA's powers and intent. His understanding was that NAMA was to take control of loans provided by banks for the financing of land or for future developments, not loans that applied to existing commercial developments. McKillen did not regard himself as a speculative developer but as an investor, the holder of properties that had established incomes from safe tenants. Therefore he did not expect his loans to be moved to NAMA.

However, NAMA decided that it wanted McKillen's business in its fold – probably because his lucrative assets were of a kind that could be sold to meet the repayments on other loans on its books, or could generate rental income to cover the interest bill at least and some of the capital repayments. It felt entitled to do this on the basis that McKillen had borrowed some money for development purposes and any failure to meet repayments could constitute what was held to be a systemic risk to the state. Under the legislation, NAMA could lay claim to all of his loans. Much to McKillen's chagrin, NAMA did not even consult him about its decision to include him among the first ten developers whose loans would be transferred to its books. Despite his reported aversion to publicity, McKillen decided he had to make a legal challenge to the powers and authority of NAMA.

He did so in a tangential fashion. His legal action was taken to try to prevent the transfer of a portion of his loans from Bank of Ireland to NAMA, claiming that to enforce this transfer would be a 'total' invalidation of his rights. Somewhat confusingly, McKillen put the amount of these loans at €211 million, although NAMA calculated them at €297 million. The overall stakes were much higher. If this tranche of loans was transferred, there was nothing to stop the rest of the loans from other banks following. If he won, all the loans would stay with his banks. NAMA put a stay on all transfers while the case was being heard.

The case was to disclose enormous amounts of information – not otherwise available – as to how NAMA and its clients went about their business. But, more crucially, it was to be a landmark hearing with the potential to create all sorts of legal precedents. The implications for the state were huge; they were no less enormous for all large property developers, not just McKillen.

If McKillen won on his main arguments, the government's approach to dealing with the banking crisis could be ended almost as soon as it had begun.

The importance of the action that McKillen was taking was highlighted by the approach of the judiciary. High Court President Justice Nicholas Kearns decided to take the case himself but looked for help: he sat with two senior commercial judges, Justice Peter Kelly and Justice Frank Clarke, to hear the arguments. The government regarded the matter so seriously that it took the almost unprecedented step of sending its attorney general, Paul Gallagher, to publicly argue its case. Gallagher was regarded in legal circles as possibly the finest barrister of his generation. He had overseen the drafting of the NAMA legislation himself, so in a sense his own reputation was on the line, even if that was very much a secondary issue.

McKillen did not attend court, as his barrister, Michael Cush, presented the case. Cush's arguments were specific to the impact on McKillen of being moved into NAMA and did not touch on whether NAMA was a good idea or whether it would work. What Cush claimed was that the transfer of McKillen's loans to NAMA would be 'the cause of significant adverse effect on him and his companies, particularly on their financial well-being'. McKillen worried about NAMA's reputation, claiming that it was 'clearly perceived' by international financial institutions as a 'bad or toxic bank set up by the state to deal with distressed loans against properties which have failed'. He had 'grave concern' as to what it would do to his own reputation, Cush said. 'The borrowers of these loans are perceived, perhaps wrongly, as having engaged in reckless conduct over the past ten years in Ireland and as requiring the assistance of the state to bail them out from poor business decisions.'

McKillen insisted, through his senior counsel, that he had made a 'conscious and determined decision as far back as 2000 to steer clear' of what he called the 'lunacy' already evident in Irish property prices and to focus instead on investment in mature markets overseas. 'Whether through prudence, good business decisions or good fortune, I managed to stand back in amazement while this gross overpaying for property was going on and avoided acquiring development land in this market,' he stated.

McKillen claimed NAMA's actions were 'an unjust and disproportionate attack' on his property rights, as protected by the constitution, and a breach of his human rights. He argued that NAMA was a 'work-out vehicle', rather than a bank, and so would subsequently take a shorter-term view that would lead to assets being sold off quickly, often at less than what he believed to be their real long-term value. NAMA could demand more onerous repayment terms than the banks, while partnerships with other investors could also come under pressure. McKillen argued that it would not be good banking practice to demand the full repayment of a loan because of a 'temporary' loan-to-value issue (caused by a fall in the value of the property), particularly if repayments were being made, or to decline to renew a loan because it had reached maturity.

McKillen did not merely make his own arguments: he arranged for a variety of 'expert witnesses' to swear statements in his favour and against NAMA. Most notable was an affidavit from the Nobel Prize-winning economist Joseph Stiglitz, which was read in court, attracting a lot of publicity. The American captured the headlines when he argued that NAMA could damage the interests of the taxpayer by increasing the costs of recapitalizing the banks. 'NAMA is structured with incentives that go against the purported public interest in reviving the economy,' he claimed. Stiglitz said NAMA's structure gave it the incentive to 'underpay the banks, seize good assets in order to offset losses from riskier loans on their books and create short-term gain' for NAMA's institutional shareholders. Specifically in relation to McKillen, Stiglitz maintained that the NAMA transfers 'disrupted and may well continue to disrupt McKillen's core long-term real estate business'. Other international experts supported Stiglitz in doubting whether NAMA, without a bank licence, would be able to finance or understand the needs of its clients.

Extraordinarily, the state was to find that another of McKillen's most prominent supporters was an arm of the state itself. Anglo Irish Bank wanted to keep McKillen's loans on its books rather than transferring them to NAMA, and it gave evidence on his behalf against the state that had taken ownership of it. Aynsley described McKillen as someone who could 'actively participate in Ireland's recovery' and who offered it 'great future value'; he said he was disappointed that McKillen had become 'disillusioned, frustrated and alienated' because of the planned transfer of loans. It even turned out that Aynsley had written to NAMA in June 2010 asking it to meet with McKillen to explain its actions and listen to McKillen's concerns.

In making his arguments Cush had to provide full disclosure on the finances of his client's empire. Cush argued that, while McKillen had debts to the Irish banks amounting to €2.1 billion, he still had sizeable assets, estimated at between €1.7 billion and €2.8 billion, depending on when they would be sold. He said only a quarter of McKillen's sixty-two properties were located in Ireland, of which 96 per cent were let to 'blue-chip' tenants on 25-year leases, with an annual rent roll of €150 million. Just €89 million of this was needed to cover interest payments.

Some of McKillen's claims raised eyebrows, however. For example, while he had told the High Court that he had not invested speculatively in the Irish market since 1998, many had seen plenty of public evidence that it was not for want of trying. He and his friends from U2, Bono and The Edge, had hired 'starchitect' Norman Foster to draw up spectacular plans for the redevelopment of the Clarence Hotel: while the red-brick façade of the listed building would have been retained, the interior would have been gutted, and an elliptical flying-saucer-style roof added to the top. He also planned to become involved in the construction of the U2 Tower on Britain Street, at the confluence of the Liffey and the Dodder. This was to rise to 180 metres in height, and include a battery of vertical wind turbines and a huge solar panel. The band's egg-shaped recording studio at the top was to be suspended above an observation deck. Because work on neither project had taken place, McKillen felt able to tell the High Court that he was not a speculative borrower. He said that he and his partners had been wise enough to stop when the economic downturn became obvious, although the reality was that they had just been been lucky: the development was delayed by the planning process and by rows at the Dublin Docklands Development Authority over the competition – which they eventually won – to build the U2 Tower.

The state's response to McKillen's seeming impertinence in bringing his action was to make him aware that he was not going to be regarded as anything special and to emphasize that it would be ruthless in highlighting the failings of some of his business practices.

Gallagher made it clear that McKillen was going to be included in NAMA, just like everyone else, because NAMA was part of the government's 'unprecedented intervention' to support the financial system and economy, arising from the bank guarantee of September 2008, whether McKillen liked it or not. He insisted that McKillen was not entitled to any 'special' treatment, and that he and his experts did not appear to recognize that the banks could not have financed his loans without state support. If he proved unable to repay them, this represented, at €2.1 billion, a 'systemic risk' to the entire banking system itself.

He pointed out that McKillen had been given time to act between the announcement of NAMA and its legal establishment, but he had not repaid his loans at the NAMA banks with loans from other lenders. Gallagher argued that this failure to refinance was indicative of the true state of McKillen's position: other banks didn't want to touch him. Damningly, Gallagher argued that it was an 'inescapable fact' that McKillen's loans were impaired and non-performing, as he was unable to repay certain loans that had expired and could not give a date on which he would repay the full amount owed.

Gallagher alleged that there was an 'elephant in the room'. Even if experts had testified on McKillen's behalf that he was a good borrower with 'technical defects' in his loans, the law stated that there was an obligation to repay if a loan had expired. McKillen had failed in this, and just because banking practice in the past had been to extend such loans to a new repayment date, that did not mean the same procedures applied now or in the future. The fact that there had been so-called forbearance by banks towards McKillen, he argued, was not relevant, because the banks would be unwilling to admit they had impaired loans on their books that would damage their balance sheets. He said it was 'quite amazing' that the experts who had spoken for McKillen did not address that in their evidence.

Importantly, Gallagher also argued that McKillen was a speculator. While McKillen said he had not bought property or development land in Ireland since 1998, NAMA disclosed that he had 'released equity' on his half-share of Jervis. Crucially, he had secured borrowings of €200 million against that to use as a deposit for another loan:

one to finance the speculative development of student accommodation in the Dublin docklands, and for use in Belfast. A second loan had been taken out to finance the expansion of the Berkeley Hotel in London by way of the purchase of an adjacent property. And once it has been established that a single development loan exists, NAMA can take all the others.

McKillen denied this last claim, saying the purchased adjacent property had tenants who were paying enough rent to cover his loan repayments – which made it an investment rather than a development loan. But there had been plans to expand the Berkeley by changing the existing use of the adjacent property – adding twenty-seven new bedrooms in the 35,000 square feet of available space – and that was the basis on which the loan had been secured. The rent on the property adjoining the Berkeley was just £400,000 and the plans for the redevelopment could have cost £101 million if implemented.

Gallagher alleged that, in addition to the development loans, NAMA had grounds for its actions based on breaches of loan covenants and failures to refinance loans, the existence of which McKillen had withheld from the court. He said it was remarkable for McKillen to claim constitutional protection for loans that did not have legal contractual protection, either because they had reached their repayment date or because the loan-to-value requirements of the contract had been breached. And, while the rent might cover McKillen's interest repayments, it would not deal with the principal owed. He also argued that NAMA did not have the time to hear McKillen and everyone else as it went about its business.

The state had its own expert witnesses. Ann Nolan, the Department of Finance official responsible for the government's banking plan, swore that McKillen had benefited directly from the state's rescue of McKillen's Irish lenders. 'If the banks had not remained in business Mr McKillen would have been faced with urgent refinancing, transfer or enforcement of his loans by liquidators,' she argued. 'McKillen postulates a gulf between ordinary bank practices and the operation of NAMA that has no basis in reality,' said Matthew Webster of HSBC in London, who acted as a NAMA adviser.

The case had thrown up many interesting facts that would otherwise have been kept secret and were very revealing about the high-wire act that many leading developers performed. McKillen seemed to rely on a system whereby banks were happy if the interest was paid and content merely to roll over the principal, which might never get repaid, just to claim fees and have it run through the books. McKillen had provided personal guarantees of over €135 million on his loans with Anglo and had reason to be worried that these personal guarantees could be called in if NAMA enforced the sale of assets during depressed market conditions. His advisers estimated that the early sale of his property and investments could cause him a loss of €373 million in personal equity, leaving him unable to repay his debts. He wasn't prepared to trust NAMA when it said that it had no intention of causing such losses by forcing a fire-sale, or any sale, upon him.

Doubts were raised also about the true worth of McKillen's portfolio. The Liffey Valley Shopping Centre was to have been sold late in 2010 for €350 million, suggesting that there was international money available to make commercial property investments in Ireland, notwithstanding the depth of the recession (although the deal did fall through subsequently). The court was told that the yield (annual rent roll as a percentage of the purchase price) on the transaction was 9.4 per cent, whereas during the boom such yields had fallen to low, single-digit levels. The importance of the example was what it implied for McKillen's assets. A similar yield applied to McKillen's rent roll in its entirety would imply a capital value on his portfolio of €1.6 billion, not just €100 million less than his own lowest valuation as stated to the courts, but €500 million less than what he owed the Irish banks.

When the High Court ruled on 1 November 2010 it found in the state's favour. It emphasized that it had not made a judgment as to whether the creation of NAMA was good or bad policy, but had decided whether the government's action was permissible in its attempt to deal with the banking crisis. The legislation setting up NAMA was 'a proportionate response to the very grave financial situation in which the state finds itself', it said, and there was 'a rational basis' for the agency. NAMA had also received European Commission approval, which meant that it was not limited to acquiring just impaired loans or other loans connected with such loans.

As for McKillen's claim that he shouldn't be eligible for NAMA, the court decided that 'scale alone' within the property and development sector was sufficient to contribute to a systemic risk in the financial system. Loans were not going into NAMA to punish borrowers but to enable the government to take whatever measures were necessary to repair the banks.

Pertinently, the judges criticized McKillen's business model, pointing out that he funded long-term property investments with short-term bank loans. They said this left McKillen and other developers 'at the mercy of the banks'. The court described as 'fanciful' the idea that banking relationships could remain unchanged, given the scale of what had happened.

McKillen could not be excused on the basis that he hadn't been part of the original problem. 'Very many people will be paying both in money, in jobs and in other ways, for a very considerable period of time, to pay the price of solving the problems of Irish banks,' the judges said. 'The vast majority of those persons had nothing to do with creating the problem. Yet they will be required to play their part in its solution to their cost.'

It was a comprehensive victory for NAMA but not a total one. In one of the few criticisms in the 147-page judgment, the court found NAMA's response to McKillen's correspondence was 'less than open and transparent' and that 'institutions with significant power' should respond 'in a more open and forthright fashion'.

McKillen appealed the decision to the Supreme Court, leading to an expensive six-day hearing in December 2010. Lawyers acting on his behalf returned to many of his previous arguments and expanded upon them. They returned to the issue of fair procedure and the constitutional right to ownership of property and to earn a livelihood. Unlike many others going into NAMA, he was not a loan defaulter; most of his loans were performing, and only a tiny percentage was related to land and development. He was making his interest payments, even on expired loans, and his banks were happy to renegotiate rather than call in loans. He said banks would not transfer his loans to another lender without consulting him, even if it was their contractual right. He continued to demand the right to be heard. Just before Christmas 2010 the full seven-member Supreme Court reserved judgment. In February they returned with what seemed a sensational verdict.

McKillen won the unanimous support of the seven judges at the Supreme Court – much to NAMA's initial shock and discomfort – who decided that the agency had never at any stage made a legally valid decision to acquire McKillen's loans; its interim board had made the orders for transfer before the agency was legally set up on 21 December 2009 and no subsequent action by NAMA provided legal validity. NAMA had started working on the biggest borrower loans soon after the creation of the agency was unveiled in the April 2009 emergency budget. The only record of its decision to take over McKillen's loans was an agency spreadsheet on which the word 'disagree' had been added to the banks' view that his loans were not eligible for NAMA. The court rapped NAMA on the knuckles for this failure, saying this was 'fundamental to the functioning of a statutory body'.

However, it was soon being suggested that the victory was limited and indeed pyrrhic. All NAMA had to do was start again and make the decision formally this time. NAMA chairman Frank Daly was quick to issue a statement arguing that what had happened 'does not have implications for other acquisitions now completed by NAMA'.

The Supreme Court had dismissed McKillen's claim that NAMA's activities had breached the constitution and were tantamount to illegal state aid. There was no obligation on NAMA's part to acquire only impaired loans. Had the court ruled in favour of that particular argument, not only would NAMA have been put out of business but all of its work, including the transfer of loans, would have been unwound.

Ultimately, McKillen escaped the grip of NAMA, exactly as he had wanted. In July, NAMA suddenly announced that it had decided not to purchase McKillen's loans after all. It justified its shock decision by saying that McKillen had paid off some of the capital that had been due to the banks; and that a number of what NAMA had originally claimed were development projects should now be regarded as investment projects, just as McKillen himself had argued previously. This put the loans associated with those assets outside of NAMA's reach. Things had changed since December 2009, NAMA said.

It was an extraordinary decision, given the effort the state had made to force McKillen into NAMA. It also meant the state had to pay nearly €7 million in legal fees, as McKillen's costs were awarded to him by the Supreme Court. The agency seemed to fear that McKillen would take further legal action against any new attempt to force him into NAMA, and that he would succeed, again at the state's cost.

The only consolation for NAMA was that the McKillen case did not set a precedent that would allow other developers to evade its clutches. But it raised some very important questions as to the conduct and performance of the agency.

27. A Very Irish Monster

In October 2010 Tom Parlon and Hubert Fitzpatrick of CIF made a journey to the offices of NAMA on the third floor of the Treasury Building, the same one that so many of the developers they represented had made previously. They went to tell Brendan McDonagh and Frank Daly that NAMA wasn't working and almost certainly couldn't be made to work.

They argued that the NAMA process had 'decimated banks' balance sheets' through excessive write-downs and that it would do the same to those of borrowers/developers. Parlon and Fitzpatrick claimed that NAMA's plan for a 25 per cent reduction in the amount of assets it held over the coming three years would fuel a 'vicious cycle' and that planned fire-sales would further depress the market and result in more defaults.

They maintained that NAMA's short-term business strategy was 'inherently flawed' because the market simply wasn't there and that the agency was 'ill equipped' to manage the assets, or even 'bank supervise' them. This must be 'urgently addressed', they said.

They told the NAMA officials that they should 'optimize returns' in the medium term rather than in the short term. They demanded that 'viable projects' should be 'developed to completion as quickly as possible' but warned that NAMA's €5 billion working-capital facility would be 'inadequate' to 'manage [out] or improve' the €74 billion in distressed property assets that had been transferred from Irish-owned banks. They warned that NAMA was mistaken if it believed there should be no new building in Ireland for the next decade; the longer it took the agency to realize this, the greater would be the damage to the country.

Parlon and Fitzpatrick did not get a sympathetic response from the NAMA officials present.

Much of what the CIF had put forward was in a report that it had commissioned from the British-based Lombard Street Research; it released this publicly soon after the fruitless meeting with NAMA. This report also alleged that NAMA's 'implicit' objective was to restructure the construction industry. It condemned NAMA as 'a flawed idea and a failure' and recommended that the agency operate as a developer and not just as a liquidator. Its 22-page report claimed that by doing just the latter, NAMA was 'destroying value' rather than putting a floor under property prices.

'The current position undermines values and prolongs the uncertainty over the Irish real estate sector, thus exacerbating the losses that may ultimately be suffered by the Irish tax payer,' the report warned.

Lombard's research was critical of NAMA's policy of acquiring unimpaired loans: by taking good as well as bad loans, NAMA had undermined the banking system. It warned that if the agency rejected bids for assets that did not cover the full nominal loan value, it might later result in a 'fire-sale' at even worse prices. Lombard also recommended that NAMA should accept an element of debt restructuring and 'encourage the use of outside capital to help stabilize the construction industry'.

NAMA had held fire after the private meeting with the CIF in October 2010, but after publication of the Lombard report it shot back publicly. It rejected the report's analysis as 'flawed and one-sided' and accused the CIF of wanting NAMA to help developers deal with their problem loans at the taxpayers' expense while at the same time allowing them to siphon off profits from their performing loans.

NAMA said the CIF's regular criticisms of it had been 'grounded in a naive expectation that NAMA would protect the developers and the broader construction sector from the impact of the excesses of the property bubble and its subsequent collapse in which some members of the CIF played a significant role'.

'Self-serving reports like this suggest that the leaders of that industry are continuing to live in denial of the crisis,' NAMA stated. 'NAMA did not cause the problems in the construction sector or the banks but we are trying to find solutions and fix them in a way that does not penalize taxpayers.'

NAMA said it had been given a brief by the Oireachtas, approved by the EU Commission, to ensure that borrowers could not 'walk away from the consequences of their poor decision-making and continue to profit from those investments which are profitable or performing'.

It rejected criticisms that it had compounded problems in the banking and property markets by applying steep discounts to loans transferred to the agency, saying the EU had verified that it had adopted 'a prudent, consistent and fair valuation policy', as Daly put it.

NAMA insisted that it did not discourage external capital and had worked with borrowers to enable joint-venture projects to be pursued with third parties. 'The CIF . . . would be better off helping their members deal with that changed world and working constructively with NAMA rather than criticizing how it works . . . Our hope is, where possible, to work with developers to recover the loans. We have had very constructive dialogue with a number of developers. But where developers are not willing to work with us, we will move to enforcement,' it thundered.

One of the country's biggest developers, who spoke to me for this book on condition of anonymity, suggested that 'the NAMA people are insecure. They are focused on petty cash, rear-view mirror stuff, not looking at rescue. I thought NAMA would be commercial but it's not. It doesn't have the management structures to establish the relationship it needs with the borrowers.'

Any ambitions that NAMA might have had to be 'commercial' were constrained by Brian Lenihan's promise that the developers would be 'pursued to the ends of the earth'. But some developers had to be persuaded not to walk away, because they had skills that would enable them to recover sizeable amounts of money. An incentive, other than honour, had to be provided for them.

Speculation grew that NAMA would do deals in which developers who had repaid a certain amount of their debt would be released from the remainder of their obligations. By late 2010 it was reported in the *Sunday Tribune* that fourteen developers — identities undisclosed — had agreed debt-forgiveness packages with NAMA. The agency had decided to allow some developers to escape from part of their debt if they achieved a specified sale price for their assets; if they unwound family transfers; cooperated with NAMA during the work-out process; and satisfied the agency that they had exhausted all means of repaying their loans. In those circumstances developers got fresh funds to complete developments and other projects, but under the condition that these would be repaid in full before the debt-forgiveness agreements kicked in. If they failed with the new money, the chance of bankruptcy increased dramatically. It was all done quietly, though, so as to limit any controversy. The lack of transparency at NAMA was again an issue. Such decisions may have been pragmatic but they were also highly political.

NAMA had plenty of opportunity to move against developers, should it have wanted to. Most major loans contain what are known as 'on-demand' facilities that can trigger the immediate repayment of a loan. If a developer missed a few payments, or if the value of the equity in comparison with the size of the loan fell because of a downward valuation, the entire loan could be called in or NAMA could lay claim to the security on the loan by seeking a judgment. In such instances personal guarantees could be enforced, ruining developers and threatening the loss of the family home.

The temptation for NAMA must have been to sell apparently good assets immediately because it brought in some money now, even if those good assets might be worth far more in the future. Much depended on whether NAMA had staff suitably qualified to assess a development appraisal. There were agents and experts and people who had provided support to developers, but there weren't many who had direct experience of development. NAMA responded to criticism that it didn't possess the right people by saying that it couldn't possibly do a worse job than the banks had; for years they had made dreadful lending decisions based on no knowledge whatsoever of a development's prospects. And it could hardly repeat the madness of the developers.

For their part, developers believed that NAMA preferred the sale of properties to the provision of working capital – but, had they thought about it from NAMA and the state's point of view instead of their own, this would have made sense. NAMA had to raise money to repay debts. It was primarily a liquidator and provided banking facilities only if that improved the likely outcome of the eventual liquidation of the loans it had purchased. Many of its decisions simply came down to who would be forced to sell immediately and who would be supported until they too were forced to sell. Not all developers deserved to be treated in the same way but the irony was that sometimes it was the more highly indebted who were in possession of the skills that could get them out of trouble, or at least mitigate it.

Smaller operators were often amateurs who had come late to the party because they had spare cash they didn't want to leave in low-interest-rate bank accounts. They didn't necessarily understand the attractiveness or otherwise of the locations they had chosen, and, because they didn't understand the financing mechanisms properly either, got left with big land banks and debts. Indeed, it was the arrival of the johnny-come-latelies, particularly the professionals – accountants, solicitors, insurance brokers and auctioneers who wanted a piece of the action for themselves, and who got access to cheap finance from banks which should have known better – that ruined things for everyone else. Knowing little, they became involved in consortia and bid up the prices for land, design teams and construction contracts. The more professional operators were made to pay the price of their ignorance.

Having dealt with the first thirty developers with the biggest loans – €27 billion between them – NAMA moved on to the next batch without giving any indication as to how many were being provided with new finance, what incentives were being offered or how many it was going to put out of business. It did say, though, that it would be doing the next tranche with a slightly changed approach and introduced what it called, rather unimaginatively, 'Business Plan II', aimed at borrowers with twenty loans or fewer and a maximum of 300 assets.

NAMA's Kevin Nowlan told a meeting of the Chartered Accountants Ireland that there had been 'significant lessons learned on dealings with the first thirty debtor business plans' but unfortunately he was somewhat vague on what they were. He revealed that 'Business Plan II' gave 'increased prominence' to the 'sworn statement of affairs of the debtors and to the rights of non-NAMA lenders, their security and the repayment of these facilities'. More time would be spent on finding out how debtors intended to use 'unencumbered assets' as a way of reducing debts or ongoing running costs, with cash flow getting more priority too. Less prominence apparently would be given to 'historic financial information' and 'market analysis'.

Business Plan II allowed NAMA to argue that it was flexible and learning. Some wondered if this flexibility was actually an admission that it had made some awful mistakes and had been too slow to act because it had focused on the wrong things.

The implementation of the business plan would require the appointment of new board members to the borrowers' companies. NAMA's overseeing of the day-to-day running of the companies at board level was designed to ensure that there would be no deviations from the approved debt-repayment plans. The companies could nominate, but NAMA had to approve and in many cases it simply ordered appointments.

Although NAMA said no credit application had been forced to wait for more than a few weeks for a decision, this was disputed by many companies. Worse was the cost of new and additional money. A 2010 survey by Chartered Accountants Ireland disclosed that three quarters of developers claimed to have agreed, under pressure, to paying a higher margin on their loans on their transfer to NAMA, sometimes as much as 2 per cent extra.

There was also the involvement of the European Commission to be reckoned with. It had forced the government to give assurances that NAMA would not use a number of the powers contained in its enabling legislation, ostensibly to protect competition. It cited fears that NAMA's activities could distort property prices and the banking market for years to come. The answer to that should have been: 'But of course, any version of NAMA will do that because that's what it was set up to do.'

Importantly, though, NAMA was restricted in its ability to seize properties from defaulting borrowers if the properties had been part-financed by banks outside the NAMA scheme, unless agreement came from those (mainly foreign) banks. The commission placed strict limits on NAMA's use of compulsory-purchase orders and on its right to receive payments from an insolvent company ahead of other creditors. The government also agreed that NAMA would not request information on an individual borrower from the Revenue Commissioners, even though allowed to do so in principle in the legislation. This was not for reasons of confidentiality but so as not to 'create distortions of information and negatively affect the interests of third parties'.

How often did NAMA break or bend its own rules? Fianna Fáil Senator Mark Daly caused controversy when he accused NAMA of selling property through private sales, when under the agency's code of practice its assets had to be sold by way of auction or competitive tendering. It was often forgotten that NAMA bought *loans* from banks, not the properties that formed the security for those loans. When a borrower was required to repay part of his loan, he did this through selling his property, and of course he might choose to do this through a private sale. It was only when NAMA took control of the process and appointed a receiver that assets had to be sold by way of auction or competitive tendering.

Finding buyers in Ireland to participate in NAMA's ambitious sales was another massive challenge. McDonagh had given a firm commitment in September 2010 that NAMA would recoup loans worth €20 billion by way of asset sales by the end of 2013, both in Ireland and abroad. That was a tall order when so few transactions had taken place that year, and it was made more difficult within months by the arrival of the IMF. Who would want to buy Irish property in a market that, driven by further economic contraction, might be about to fall further? A number of sales of Irish portfolios planned for late 2010 – two to foreigners, one to Green Property, the biggest Irish property company to have escaped the clutches of NAMA because of its absence of development loans – fell through as uncertainty mounted.

The other published targets in NAMA's business plan added to its difficulties. Its cash-flow statement anticipated the entire NAMA €54 billion being repaid over ten years at the rate of €6.5 billion each year from 2013 onwards. That added to the pressure on NAMA's developers to come up with cash quickly: by selling assets, by getting a new banker or equity subscriber, or by somehow repaying their loans according to the terms of the original agreement.

As NAMA had been perceived as a distressed seller, potential buyers were looking to buy as cheaply as possible. It was very hard to find buyers who would pay an attractive price for Irish-located property, given that foreign property was easier to trade and more certain in the income it would produce. Even if some buyers, either domestic or foreign, found some Irish property that they liked – and had sufficient belief in the Irish economy – getting the money to complete a deal was a problem. The Irish banks were reluctant to commit their limited funds to property lending. What left every investor and banker nervous was the possibility that the market had even further to fall, due to a combination of continued distress in the national economy, reduced consumer spending and decreased confidence.

Because foreign banks regarded Ireland as so risky, buyers needed to offer collateral in addition to the property itself – probably not Irish-located property, given the difficulty in realizing liquidity from it – or stump up a much larger proportion of the purchase price as equity, reducing the amount needed from loans.

A fear that too much activity would force down prices even further seemed to prevent many foreign banks from taking the more hard-line, quick-sale, no-matter-what-the-price approach that might have been expected of them. This is perhaps just as well, because they could have undermined the price of future sales by doing so. Admittedly ACCBank (part of Rabobank since 2002) did go after the likes of John Fleming, a Cork property developer whose plan for a massive development at Sandyford, Dublin, flopped spectacularly, and who responded by going to Britain to declare personal bankruptcy; and Liam Carroll, once Dublin's biggest apartment builder. But its €6 billion exposure to Ireland made it one of the smaller investors among foreign international banks that had been active here. Bank of Scotland (Ireland) had a total loan book in Ireland of €33 billion, and Ulster Bank almost double that at €63 billion, so it was not in these banks' interests to bring about far larger property write-downs and subsequent loan losses. They knew that the more they offered for sale, the more likely it was that all prices would fall further, when the reality of how little money there was to spend on it all actually hit home.

Foreign venture capitalists – sometimes described as 'vultures' as they swept on to 'distressed' properties that they hoped to buy on the cheap for subsequent resale in just a few years' time – were also disinclined to get involved in the Irish market. Such activity could have provided an external injection of cash, but they didn't see Ireland as providing enough upside to take the risk. And there were other problems for NAMA in selling to such funds. They wanted extremely low prices, which often meant that NAMA had to accept a loss on the price it had paid for the loan. That might have been NAMA's own fault for getting the price wrong in the first place, but it was reluctant to take 'a haircut to the haircut'. These deals, if completed, would have left NAMA vulnerable to criticism of mismanagement.

The case of McInerney Properties showed that NAMA was rarely prepared to take the same approach as foreign banks, which were more willing to cut their losses and run when it came to writing off debts. The radical plan for rescuing the company – finding new investors and paying creditors only a fraction of what was owed as a way of stopping its fall into receivership – was prevented by two Irish banks acting on the instructions of NAMA and, it should be noted, by one of its foreign banks too.

McInerney had €236 million of borrowings in its overall group of companies, of which Lloyds and RBS held €125 million in the British operations. They were prepared to write off 30 per cent of those debts. That left the Irish operations and the remaining debt of €113 million, which McInerney hoped to write down enormously, to reflect the greater problems in Ireland.

At the height of the boom in 2007, McInerney reported sales of €221.54 million and its peak valuation on the stock market was €636 million. By March 2010 it had reported a pre-tax loss of €193 million, having to write down the value of its land holdings by €156 million. It also suffered from a collapse in revenue. In the previous six months it had sold just sixty-three houses, taking in just €10.5 million in doing so. Not only had demand collapsed but the prices it could charge had fallen by more than 50 per cent. The company's share price had dropped so low that the company was now valued at just €10 million.

An American private equity investor called Oaktree Capital Partners was induced to offer €40 million to help sort out the overall group balance sheet and give McInerney a chance of surviving. But, while McInerney found its British bankers to be accommodating, its Irish equivalents were willing but powerless. McInerney's overdraft was cancelled with immediate effect on the instructions of NAMA. The company was also told that it could no longer keep any proceeds of house sales, effectively the company's only Irish revenue stream, or any other money coming to it. This was known as a 'cash sweep' by the banks.

McInerney pitched its case for restructuring, and requested the return of its normal banking facilities, at a meeting with NAMA on 13 August 2010. Less than ten days later McInerney was met by Bank of Ireland, which had been appointed to represent the syndicate of bankers. Its pitch had been rejected. The deal to rescue McInerney was then put into the public domain. Oaktree had offered to buy McInerney's €113 million Irish debt from its banks – Anglo Irish Bank, Bank of Ireland and KBC – for just €25 million, a recognized loss of €88 million. Unsecured creditors would get 7 per cent of what they were owed, yet a majority agreed on the basis that something was better than nothing and that they would have a future relationship with a better-financed company.

NAMA was not going to take a loss now and it was not going to provide a publicly disclosed settlement, as would usually happen with a company of McInerney's stock-market status. The precedent might have been perceived as dangerous, and there was also the political danger of being seen to go too easy on a company in distress. The agency got support in the courts, when Justice Frank Clarke took the view that if Oaktree was willing to make an investment of €25 million in Ireland, it had to believe it had a reasonable prospect of making a return on that. In other words, it wouldn't be investing unless it believed its offer undervalued the real worth of the company. If the banks didn't want to take that and chose instead to pursue an extended receivership, it had to be assumed that they also believed that they would make a reasonable return on that sum.

'On the facts of this case, I am satisfied that the banking syndicate has a realistic prospect of doing better under the proposed receivership model than under the scheme of arrangement,' Mr Justice Clarke said. He added that the scheme was unfairly skewed against the banks, and he found against McInerney.

Separately, venture capitalists complained privately that Irish assets they were interested in buying were not for immediate sale. This was seen by some in the trade as a pity, as these investors did not need Irish bank financing or sometimes any loans at all. They blamed NAMA for distorting values in the market by failing to make decisions. Indeed, it seemed that NAMA had adopted the approach for which the banks had been criticized before moving the loans to NAMA: doing nothing. Rather than agreeing to a transaction that would establish a new value on the property and crystallize a loss, it would wait and hope that by the time the market recovered it might be able to profit on the sale of the properties attached to the loans, while drawing enough income off them in the meantime to justify all this.

It was alleged that decisions were not being made even when price was not an issue. Offers for commercial property were being made at levels commensurate with what the banks would have written them down to, but they were still not going through. It seemed that NAMA's fear in these situations was that venture capitalists would quickly resell, at a profit, to the one category of buyer with whom it did not want to deal: the developer seeking to buy his own assets back at a reduced price.

I've been told of examples of original developers wanting to buy back their assets at 25 cents in the euro. This may have been the price at which the loans were transferred to NAMA (but also may have been lower). Whatever the case, NAMA did not want to be seen to be endorsing that. But if a venture capitalist came in and offered to buy the assets at 20 cents in the euro, and NAMA accepted, what was to prevent the new owner from making a quick profit by selling on to the original owner at the 25 cents he had been prepared to pay NAMA? Why should the state forgo 5 cents in every euro merely to be able to say that it hadn't sold to an indebted developer?

There were claims that this was happening anyway. These got attention because they came from Fianna Fáil Senator Mark Daly, who was also an estate agent. The Kerry-based auctioneer accused other estate agents of flogging NAMA properties at 'bargain prices' instead of maximizing the possible price. He said that 'in the case I came across, the original loan was €12 million. The haircut was €6 million and the actual value of the property was €9 million.' He claimed the developer 'arranged for a buddy to buy the property at €6 million and turned it around and sold it for €9 million'. Which sounds sensational – too sensational, in fact. How did the indebted original owner manage to source €9 million when he must have had loans to clear with NAMA? There was no evidence to support the story but unfortunately new Taoiseach Enda Kenny repeated the bones of it some months after coming into office and was embarrassed into retracting it swiftly.

Frank Daly emphasized that NAMA 'had no tolerance' for properties being sold to the original lenders or to persons or entities associated with them. But in theory it was true that developers could set up 'shell' companies or other financial vehicles to buy back the same loss-making assets that they had transferred to NAMA. There was nothing in company law to stop any individual setting up a company to buy assets transferred to NAMA by debt-ridden developers. It was virtually impossible for NAMA to know the true identity of the purchaser involved – and it might not care as long as it got its money. The purchaser could then benefit from any subsequent upturn in the property market by selling later at a higher price.

Those profits presumably would still have to be used to settle outstanding debts to NAMA, however. It, like the Revenue Commissioners, reserved the right to recover arrears at any future stage. But what if the profits from such deals were not known to NAMA or the taxman and had been transferred to jurisdictions with which Ireland does not have reciprocal treaties such as the Channel Islands or the Cayman Islands? One possibility would be an 'attachment order', which would legally compel repayment if an individual came into money.

★

What all of these stories did underline was that NAMA was simply too big and unwieldy. The Swedish model upon which it had been based was just 3 per cent of the size of the Irish monster. The banks weren't rescued by it, and, despite the initial suspicions of the public, neither were the developers.

What was clear was this: virtually all private-enterprise development had come to a halt and, as state-funded investment stalled too, because of a lack of available capital, the construction sector went into meltdown, causing the loss of hundreds of thousands of jobs.

At the peak of the property boom in 2006, close to 90,000 new homes were built in the Republic. This was an unsustainable level, as many people said at the time, only to be shouted down; but, by the same token, the near-absence of any new building at all is also unsustainable for a real economy.

In June 2010 DKM Economic Consultants, an independent firm that regularly produces reports on the sector for the state, among other clients, predicted that the year's total of newly completed housing units could be as low as 7,500 and that 2011 might struggle to match even that. This had enormous employment consequences too, as the number with jobs in the sector had fallen by two thirds over three years to under 100,000 people.

The knock-on effects are huge. The sector's massive tax contribution has almost entirely gone and instead the social-welfare costs have soared. Suppliers of materials as well as labour have suffered. The providers of legal, accountancy, engineering, architectural and other professional services have had their income decimated (although some have been compensated by involvement in the NAMA process). The development contributions to the local authorities have disappeared, creating a funding crisis that is being lumped on to struggling businesses in the form of extra rates at a time when they have reduced income from customers and problems in paying the rent.

Many subcontractors have been left unpaid for work done, meaning that more jobs have been lost, many companies have gone out of business and lots of people have been left seriously out of pocket. Particularly scandalous has been the treatment of subcontractors – subbies, as they're known – not just by the main contractors but by the actions of the state, which gave large contracts to contractors without ascertaining their financial security or without insisting on prompt and full staged payment to their creditors as work was being done.

The construction industry's value to the economy slumped from €40 billion at its peak in 2007 to just €17 billion in 2010. In 2011 this is expected to shrink to €11 billion as a bust state cannot afford to fund capital-expenditure projects. NAMA was let loose upon a near-derelict sector and set about vandalizing what remained of it. Its failure to rescue the banks contributed to a credit famine: there was no money for development, no money for bridging finance, no money available for mortgages to potential buyers.

The consequences of all of this were potentially ruinous. How, for example, would Ireland attract new multinational investment if there was a shortage of proper accommodation for businesses? One of the rare examples of NAMA providing funds to complete a job was at Treasury's Montevetro Building, adjacent to its own offices. Would Google have moved such a major part of its operations to Ireland had such a building not been ready and available? It is true that there is a massive supply of unused commercial stock in Ireland; it's estimated that nearly 25 per cent of office space in Dublin alone is vacant, about seven years of supply, with demand at its lowest in fifteen years and rental income down a quarter. Much of this vacant space is unlikely to ever be of use again and much of it will need considerable investment to bring it back to commercial use. Outside of Dublin (and possibly Cork) the supply of zoned and serviced land – much of it with planning permission in place for things that will never be needed or built – is more than sufficient, probably for at least a decade.

The lack of demand for this stock of available office and industrial space emphasized the perilous state of our economic future. Confidence had departed: few, even if they had the money, were brave enough to buy, in case it would be worth less almost immediately afterwards, continue to fall in value and never recover. Some of the few sales going on were at or below build cost, even reckoning land values at zero, just so sellers could get some cash. Due to the fall in values it was not economically viable to build new commercial buildings or houses. 'You can't build any more, even in what should be good locations,' one major construction figure told me ruefully. He highlighted how the problem of dramatically falling values went beyond the difficulty it caused for borrowers in recovering the value of a loan taken before the sale of the asset. 'The value of a property has to be sufficiently high to allow you to cover the costs of construction, the purchase of the land and all other costs that have to be covered. There were places previously that went undeveloped because there was no profit to be made when final sales values were so low. We're going back to that. Even if the land was for nothing the costs of building cannot be recouped in the sale price, let alone give you a profit, so there's no point,' he said.

It is considered unlikely that we'll see apartment blocks built in this country for many years, other than some in city-centre locations in Dublin. The construction costs of apartments are too high. It is expected that the days of speculative house building are over and that builders will return to the old method of building show houses, taking booking deposits and building them in small numbers of about twenty units a time. Once the sales have been completed, they'll open a new show house and start the process again.

Even more interesting will be what happens in the commercial market, where it is likely that offices or industrial units will be built only when they have been pre-sold or pre-let, with insurance companies and pension funds targeted as the likely buyers. Getting the finance for such developments will be a task, as banks will not be willing to provide the bulk of finance.

But there were still some who wanted not just to trade in property but to build. Michael O'Flynn wanted to be ready to build houses, despite the massive overhang in the market. This may have seemed somewhat counter-intuitive, given the oversupply of vacant houses in the country, but he believed the market would pick up eventually. Many of the constructed houses throughout the country, he thought, would never be inhabited because of their locations, but, in time, houses and apartments would be needed in major cities, or on their outskirts, and that holding land in the Cork area would eventually be seen as a good investment, even if few saw that now. He wanted to be in a position to proceed with a €400 million development of 1,200 houses at a 235-acre site near Dunkettle House outside Cork City. O'Flynn pushed the idea that there was a class of developer who deserved another chance because they had 'skills' that many others – such as part-timers – didn't have. He claimed that 'Saturday-night property developers', who had decided over a pint or at a dinner party to become investors, had ruined things for those who knew what they were doing.

O'Flynn publicly claimed many times that there needed to be a functioning property market if NAMA were to be a success and that a 'more sophisticated' development sector had to be created to attract future foreign investment into Ireland. He said he agreed with correcting mistakes, but that if Ireland didn't plan for the future properly during the slump it was in danger of repeating the mistakes that had been made during the boom.

In a series of articles he wrote for the *Irish Examiner*, O'Flynn said construction and property activity had fallen to below 6 per cent of GDP in 2010 but needed to normalize at around 12 per cent for there to be 'a functioning market'. He warned that NAMA should not be used as an excuse for rejecting or restricting planning permission for projects that could help the construction sector recover.

'You have to have a market where people can construct and make some development profit. If you cannot make a development profit, you won't get funding and if you don't get funding, you will have a dormant market,' he said. 'Developers have the financial motivation to make the most of their sites and to pay back their borrowings. They are part of the solution with NAMA and the taxpayer,' he said. 'The last thing that NAMA should do is to reduce that motivation.' He claimed that many of the country's main developers wanted to restructure their companies and accept equity investment from new investors, often foreign, but were prevented from doing so by NAMA; this was because the agency wanted payment on previous personal guarantees given to banks before it would allow any new investors to become involved in their businesses and take part of any subsequent profits.

★

Even when new investment and approval were forthcoming from NAMA, the problem remained of how to value land, vacant buildings and occupied residential and commercial property. One of the arguments was that the market had to be rigged, doing what Sweden had during its 1990s crisis, when it established a National Valuation Board to set economic values as a base for the market. That is what Brian Cowen seemingly meant in one of his earliest comments on NAMA (before the EC demanded that NAMA was to pay the current perceived price for transfers) when he used the phrase 'economic value based on underlying cash flows and broad-time horizons' to explain why the government was prepared to pay over the market price for loans. Unfortunately, he didn't outline his reasoning well enough and critics of NAMA excoriated the 'long-term economic value approach' as a way of overpaying banks for loans that were in reality worth a lot less.

But the European Commission should bear a major responsibility for this disaster too. The 'match-to-market' price, upon which the EC had insisted, was determined by the circumstances of the time and in Ireland's case the downward slide in prices drove values down even further. Although there were substantial arguments that the original prices were so insanely high that it made the size of the eventual correction inevitable, it is also true that other countries did not engage in such an aggressive attempt to 'correctly' measure the new values of properties and to take losses accordingly. This approach, which had been forced upon us by the commission, was taken in few other places, and few other places suffered as much as we did as a result.

28.   A Country Rent Apart

In the run-up to the 2011 general election, Fine Gael and Labour made promises to change the laws relating to the commercial rents paid to landlords. It seemed like a sensible move: retailers in particular were complaining that excessive rents were putting them out of business and costing jobs, that greedy landlords were looking for increases rather than offering reductions at a time of economic crisis. The announced programme for government copper-fastened their promise to bring about change.

But the consequences for NAMA threatened to be catastrophic. Reduced rents meant lower capital values and immediate losses on the prices NAMA had paid for loans secured on commercial property; this is because properties producing lower rents fall dramatically in resale value.

The law as it currently stood helped NAMA and other commercial-property owners in one crucial regard: almost uniquely to Ireland and the UK, existing rental contracts between landlords and tenants built in 'upward-only' rent reviews. Once a rent had been increased, it could never be lowered again, no matter what the financial circumstances of the company paying it (or of the individual behind the company, who might have been induced to sign a personal guarantee on the payment of rent, sometimes for bizarrely long periods of thirty-five years). This provided NAMA and foreign investors with enormous financial protection, assuming of course that their properties remained let and tenants paid what was due, which was not always the case.

However, by the end of 2010, 23 per cent of all commercial space in Dublin was empty (some of it admittedly new stock that had never been let). All over the country, empty buildings and units in shopping centres could be seen, as retailers and other businesses shut, often citing the prohibitively high cost of paying the rent as the reason for closure. The capital values of some property, if honestly assessed by the auditors, were just a fraction of what they had been when previously assessed. Even so, bankers and developers alike anticipated that they would be worth more again in the future, even if less than in the past, especially when new tenants moved in, albeit at lower rents. Those tenants who remained in business wanted rents cut to reflect the market reality of the availability of this cheap and surplus stock; and they wanted help in reducing their own excessive running costs at a time when incomes were crashing for many, which led to a big drop in retail spending. But this rarely happened and there were even landlords who insisted on hiking the rent, sometimes, despite the woes of the tenants, dramatically.

Developer Joe O'Reilly was one of the first ten developers to be drawn into the NAMA web, with demands put on him to produce income to meet the repayments on debts of more than €1 billion, particularly if he didn't want his assets immediately sold at what might prove to be overly low prices. He particularly wanted to hold his prized Dundrum Town Centre, a shopping centre that at its peak had annual customer numbers of about 20 million. Even as its popularity ebbed slightly, and spending there cooled (admittedly not as much as at other less well located and less busy venues), his Chartered Land company sought massive rent increases from tenants. O'Reilly claimed that high retailer demand for units justified rent increases of between 40 and 100 per cent, as laid out in a range of negotiations and arbitrations during 2010. A company that itself pleaded for mercy from NAMA itself showed little tolerance towards its own customers when they were in financial difficulties: one tenant told the story of approaching centre management about a rent reduction but being hit shortly afterwards with a bill for a 70 per cent increase.

Whatever about Dundrum, the focus of public attention turned upon the Grafton Street area of Dublin, where property prices had soared during the boom. In 2007 Dublin City Council had outlined an ambitious plan for Grafton Street, designed to make Dublin's seemingly most attractive shopping street rival the exclusive shopping districts of Paris and Milan. The council wanted restrictions on the type of traders allowed to open on the pedestrianized street: it wanted only attractively fronted shops where people would be induced to spend loads of money.

But the plan couldn't be implemented because the prices paid for properties on the street soared and rents reflected those prices paid by investors, often overseas pension and investment funds that had outbid the Irish. International retailers, as seduced by the bubble as the Irish, were eager to take up tenancies. As recently as 2008 clothing retailer Karen Millen had paid 'key money' of €1.4 million on top of the annual rent to secure prominent premises on the street. However, much more prominent on the street were high-turnover convenience stores and a plethora of mobile-phone operators: they seemed the ones best able to generate the cash to pay the high rents. It couldn't last, especially not when consumer spending collapsed.

Within a year of the bank guarantee being put into place, empty units were visible all over the street (and most particularly on side streets running on to it); this trend continued into 2010 and 2011. Few retailers were interested in taking up vacant or available space, not even when the phenomenon of 'reverse premiums' came into play from those keen to exit existing arrangements.

A 'reverse premium' was when a tenant offered a financial inducement to another company to take over its lease. John Corcoran, the owner of the Korky's shoe chain, who became the prominent spokesman for the Grafton Street Tenants' Association, was so keen to close his outlet that he offered €300,000 to anyone who would take over his lease for a 900-square-foot shop near the Stephen's Green end. It cost him €445,000 a year in rent to Canada Life Assurance. There were no takers and Corcoran said he was losing €1,000 per day by staying open. The lack of interest was no surprise to him. Why would a new owner take on the lease of an outlet where the incumbent, an established name, had seen his rent quadruple in a decade and where rent was now 40 per cent of his new turnover?

Corcoran was an articulate advocate and a doughty fighter, as his refusal to pay all of his rent to Canada Life showed. He may have been pushing his own position but he saw a bigger picture: 'If landlords continue to close down trading companies, there'll be no jobs, there'll be no rates for the local council and eventually there will be no country . . . it will be a waste land.' The restaurateur and pub and nightclub owner Jay Bourke said he had given up his interest in Bewley's on Grafton Street, where he'd run a Café Bar Deli, because the rent had been increased from €750,000 to €1.4 million. 'If the rent had stayed at the old level, it would have made a profit,' he complained.

Bobby Kerr had started his Insomnia coffee-shop chain on Grafton Street in the late 1990s, growing it to thirty-two outlets, all leased, and all on 'upward-only rent reviews'. Kerr said that his main business task during 2009 to 2010 was to renegotiate rents with unwilling landlords and that he was not always successful. He couldn't believe the way institutional landlords were prepared to let tenants go out of business, as any replacement would pay a smaller rent, sometimes less than half. Most eventually gave in to him.

Kerr was not the only tenant to call the bluff of landlords. The Irish franchise of the Italian café/restaurant Carluccio's, on the corner of Dublin's Dawson and Duke streets, hit the headlines in early February 2010 when it closed its business, saying it would not reopen unless a rent reduction could be agreed with its landlord, the Duke Co-Ownership Partnership. The venue had opened in March 2008, but within a year had implemented what it called 'a pause in rental payments'. It claimed that while it had done what it could to reduce its operating costs, it could not cope with an annual rent of €680,000.

Carluccio's got plenty of publicity because it turned out that its landlords included the likes of Sean FitzPatrick's family and former AIB chairman Dermot Gleeson. They would hardly relish a drop in rental income, but any money coming in was better than nothing: had Carluccio's gone, it is unlikely that any other restaurant would have been brave enough to take the space. It reopened once the landlords were forced to accept a deal.

Others were not so fortunate, however, particularly when their landlords were overseas financial institutions. Sasha, the Irish fashion chain, and O'Brien's Irish Sandwich Bars were among businesses that suffered insolvency during 2009. Both cited impossible rents as the biggest single issue they could not resolve as they sought to cut costs. Four Star Pizza was rescued from receivership in 2010 but only after the new owner secured much reduced rents for its outlets. Many other companies went out of business in a similar fashion. Hope was provided by a Supreme Court ruling in December 2009 that the leases of Linen Supply of Ireland could be discarded in an effort to aid its rescue by way of examinership, but few others were successful in that way.

Businesses looked to government intervention to change the existing legislation, pointing out that only Ireland and Britain operated 'upward-only rent reviews'. Corcoran was characteristically colourful when he described it as 'a pernicious form of landlordism that would not be acceptable in most European countries'. In the majority of EU countries rent is adjusted annually and indexed to some measure of inflation. As some experts argued, that was just a different form of upward-only rent review: consumer-price deflation is very rare. 'In Europe they have a 3-6-9 approach, where the rent is changed every three years in accordance with inflation,' one accountant told me. 'If those rules were here in Ireland then it would depend on what measure of inflation was used, but rents would not have gone down.' But nor, he conceded, would they have gone up as fast as they did over the previous decade, way ahead of inflation and with the result that ridiculous new bases were established for subsequent increases.

All sorts of ideas were provided to government: state compensation to retailers who couldn't get out of the leases; state compensation to landlords who allowed the conversion of upward-only leases to market-rent leases; similar state compensation if the landlord would agree that rent could be based on a percentage of the business's turnover, as is popular in some parts of Europe, and as some retail chains, such as Zara and H&M, were able to demand when they arrived in Ireland.

But, while Corcoran and his allies may have been correct in their assertion that the old leases drawn up in the boom years were no longer workable, some landlords had good reason to hang on to the old charges for as long as possible, or to leave a unit vacant in the hope of finding a replacement, instead of admitting to a fall in rental income. As previously mentioned, a fall in the rent implied a fall in the capital value, against which the owner might have taken large borrowings to fund the original purchase. And a write-down in the capital value might have significant implications for the published worth of the fund that had bought it.

A property expert in Dublin provided me with this real example of a late 2010 dispute involving a fast-food restaurant in the Grafton Street area. The retailer had been paying about €460,000 per annum in rent up until November 2009. A dispute arose with the landlord, a foreign blue-chip pension fund. The tenant offered a new annual income of €320,000 and said that if it was rejected he would go to legal arbitration. This was rejected by the landlord, which expected to win the case. However, to the shock of both sides, a High Court judge ordered the rent be set at €205,000 per annum to take account of new market realities.

This had enormous consequences for the landlord, as it implied a massive fall in the capital value of his property. The building might once have been valued at about €23 million, when investors in the area were accepting a yield (or return on money invested) of as low as 2 per cent. Should the property still be producing a 2 per cent yield, the implied value would be €10.5 million, a fall of half in the worth of the building. However, by late 2010 yields on property weren't anything like 2 per cent: they were commonly regarded as being around 10 per cent, the higher return reflecting the risks involved in holding property and its lack of attractiveness in comparison with other investments. This suggested that, on a rent of €205,000, the property was worth just €2.05 million. Even if a generous assumption of a 7 per cent yield was applied, the capital value would still be just €2.9 million. The capital values in the area would have fallen, therefore, by 87 per cent, although some properties, better located and with high-turnover tenants, would not have suffered that large a fall. In some cases, however, the landlords would be in almost as bad a position as the retailers should the bankers demand repayments of the loans on the grounds that the underlying property values were no longer as promised.

Many of the institutions and pension funds that owned these properties – and that had often paid as much as developer speculators – had projected specific returns from their investments for many years to come and attracted investment on that basis. Accepting a reduction in value on one property might trigger reductions across their entire portfolio – if one property had fallen so greatly in value, others must have done so as well. If a mortgage was attached to a property, a fall in value of a property could activate a change in banking covenants, or increase the cost of borrowing, or bring about a demand for immediate repayment. Clearly, this was as much an issue for NAMA as for institutional investors who were not involved with the state agency. NAMA had good reason to want to let things sit.

The Fianna Fáil/Green government acted but only to a limited extent. Former Minister for Justice Dermot Ahern decided to ban the automatic entitlement for upward-rent reviews on all new lease contracts. A ministerial order for the 2009 Land and Conveyancing Law Reform Act was brought into force in February 2010. The ban was not to be applied retrospectively, following advice from the attorney general that to do so would impinge on existing constitutional protections to property ownership: the law could not be changed to remove protections on income that had been in place when investments were made.

Few were happy with the outcome. It did not help those retailers with existing leases, while ironically it could assist new tenants taking cheaply units that had become vacant because existing tenants had gone bust in trying to make payments. It also eliminated the opportunity to sell on leases at existing rental prices to new tenants, even with the incentive of so-called reverse premiums. Why take on someone else's expensive deal when a cheaper, better one was now available?

Property investors and their agents weren't happy either. They claimed that the absence of income security in the future would result in the banks insisting on lower loan-to-value ratios for commercial-property funding, higher profit margins and loans of shorter-term duration. While it would not be an immediate issue for most, they argued that the absence of certainty about future rent levels would impact on the pre-funding for the construction of developments. They claimed foreign investors would be less interested in Ireland if guaranteed returns were not available, ignoring that this was standard in most other countries. They also predicted, correctly, that fewer tenants would want to take over older leases tied to upward-only clauses, bringing down the attached capital values of their properties even further.

Their fury increased during the 2011 general election campaign, when both Fine Gael and Labour launched their proposals to effect retrospective changes to the upward-only rent reviews.

Bill Nowlan, a chartered surveyor and town planner, managing partner of property-asset management company W. K. Nowlan Associates, and father of Kevin Nowlan, one of NAMA's most senior executives, wrote regularly in the *Sunday Tribune* before it closed and on the commercial-property pages of *The Irish Times* attacking the proposals.

He was appalled in particular by Fine Gael's election proposal that it would give all tenants, without exception and irrespective of their existing review clauses, the right to have their commercial rents reviewed in 2011, notwithstanding the legal and constitutional issues it knew would arise. He claimed that nobody, domestic or foreign, would 'invest in a banana republic that doesn't respect long-term contracts'. He forecast 'Armageddon' in the property and banking industries, estimating that up to 20 per cent of the remaining value of investment portfolios would be written off by the implementation of such a measure. He argued that landlords 'should not be expected to suffer cuts simply to put extra cash into a retailer's pocket. That rent is a mortgage payment or the income of some pensioner.' He argued that the landlord might be under the same sort of stress as the tenant, possibly from the bank. And if all the tenants in Ireland submitted claims seeking relief, any assessment system would be overwhelmed. He claimed no other 'advanced country' had ever introduced retrospective legislation to reduce contracted rents. 'This is like changing the 12.5 per cent corporation tax retrospectively,' he said.

Nowlan had a second point of attack: the possible implications for NAMA and the banks. How would NAMA cope with a fall in its rents, which were being used to help cover its costs, and a fall in the value of the property acting as security for the loans it had taken on at particular prices? The projected contracted rental income, among other things, had been a factor when calculating the price it had paid for its Irish loans. Would it now be able to sell these properties at a price that would cover repayment of the loans?

NAMA seemed to agree, because its board sent a formal letter to Lenihan and the Department of Finance saying it was 'very concerned' about the implications of changing the law. Doing so would mean 'NAMA would have effectively overpaid . . . the various participating institutions for assets that NAMA acquired and will acquire from them.' It argued that a retrospective change to rent provisions would reduce the value of Irish investment property by 20 per cent to 25 per cent, resulting in a write-down of up to €2.25 billion in the value of its Irish loans.

Others looked at the NAMA situation differently. Economist Colm McCarthy asked how NAMA would dispel the 'widespread perception' that it was exploiting its dominant market position as the biggest commercial landlord in Ireland, keeping rents and property values at artificially high levels. McCarthy had been hired by lobby group Retail Excellence Ireland to provide a report supporting its position. He argued that radical intervention by the government in the commercial-property market was justified and that 'upward-only rent reviews' hindered that market from returning to normal levels. 'Keeping prices and rents artificially high depresses demand and activity, and ensures the prolonged survival of high vacancy rates,' he argued on its behalf.

The reality was that things had changed. Landlords had to adapt because of the new economic circumstances for consumers. When new rental agreements were reached, they were increasingly turnover-based, that is, rent was linked to how well the business was performing. Break clauses, allowing a retailer to leave the premises after a period of time, such as a year or up to three years, became more common. Landlords offered to share the cost of fitting out a new tenant's store. Fewer personal guarantees were offered and fewer were sought because it had become clear they were unenforceable.

The arrival of the IMF and ECB had gutted whatever confidence was emerging: how could any investor believe that domestic consumer spending would recover now that a regime of much higher taxes and lower wages was looming? While 2010 saw an improvement – with estimated sales of €270 million in commercial-property transactions compared to just over half of that in 2009 – it paled by comparison with the €3.6 billion of Irish transactions achieved in the heady days of 2006.

One of the first large transactions to be abandoned was the proposed sale by Royal Liver Assurance of a Dublin retail portfolio of nineteen properties, worth €120 million, to Green Property (owner of the Blanchardstown Shopping Centre and a company that had stayed out of NAMA because it had been too cautious to have any development properties at all) and its American associate, TPG Capital.

Worse was to come in February 2011 when it emerged that two British investment funds, F&C Reit Asset Management and Area Property Partners, had withdrawn a firm €350 million offer for the Liffey Valley Shopping Centre in Dublin, owned by Grosvenor Estates (controlled by the Duke of Westminster) and Aviva Investors (who had bought it from Cork developer Owen O'Callaghan). The decision was blamed on the doubts raised about future rental flow. Apparently, the banks that had agreed to fund the deal had been unwilling to approve a loan because of the possibility of the value of prime property suddenly dropping. The owners had badly mistimed the sale of the shopping centre and an adjoining site of more than seventeen acres. They had made their intention to sell known in July 2008, when the downturn was already becoming evident, even before the introduction of the bank guarantee. Back then they invited offers of between €300 million and €400 million for a 50 per cent stake, but now they couldn't sell the whole thing for that amount, even though the centre was producing a rent roll of €30 million from 46,400 square metres of retail and leisure space. The refusal by An Bord Pleanála in October 2010 of permission for a major extension to the centre, including a large food store for Tesco, didn't help either in securing what would have been the biggest commercial-property investment transaction in Dublin for a decade.

The new Fine Gael–Labour coalition's programme for government committed it to the introduction of legislative change with a view to rent reductions. 'I'll be interested to see what priority that gets and how, when they realize the implications for NAMA, they'll look to see how they can change that,' one of the country's most important financial figures told me the week after the government took office.

The CIF was quick to seek a meeting with Alan Shatter, the new justice minister, to warn him that abolishing upward-only rent reviews could depress the property market by another 20 per cent and further damage the banking, pension and insurance sectors. It warned that institutional investors would be 'obliged' to make constitutional challenges to any such legislation. It added that rent-review legislation could increase the banks' capital impairment and dramatically reduce the value of NAMA's assets.

In June 2011 the *Sunday Times* reported that an attempt by Treasury Holdings to transfer €2 billion of its debt from NAMA to new bankers – known in the business as a 'refinancing' – had failed because of dual concerns about the lack of economic recovery and the new government's ambitions on rent reviews. Treasury had worked on the deal for months with CIM Group, one of America's biggest commercial property funds, with NAMA's approval and involvement. The proposed deal would have included a large portion of its Irish property and some overseas assets, but CIM apparently pulled out for fear that the government's likely change to the upward-only rent reviews would wipe hundreds of millions of euro off the value of Treasury's Irish commercial property portfolio.

The retail industry, represented by Retail Excellence Ireland, responded with full-page newspaper advertisements in which it accused NAMA of causing job losses and business failures. 'By supporting upward-only rents NAMA will into the medium term undermine asset yields because more businesses will fail and more jobs will be lost, and then everyone pays,' it claimed. It said a 'competitive retail environment where market rents apply will enjoy: lower prices for Irish consumers; significant job stability and creation; the re-attainment of overall national competitiveness.'

The government waited, but even that was a cause of anger to NAMA and corporate financiers, who argued that making no decision was still expensive and cowardly. It had cost not just the Treasury deal but potentially many others too. At the time of writing the government, despite its promise on election, has not brought forward new legislation. It continued to promise that it was being drafted and would be introduced by the end of 2011.

29.   Carry On Regardless

The new Fine Gael–Labour coalition that came into power in March 2011 looked at NAMA with a jaundiced eye. The governing partners had not created it and argued often about its implementation. They couldn't see much of what was going on because of the deliberate lack of transparency, although they could see that it had not contributed to fixing the problem of the banks. They were horrified by its ineffectiveness and by its inefficiencies, its creation of a quasi-dole system for lawyers, accountants and estate agents. They wondered how it was that NAMA seemingly moved so slowly against the friends of Fianna Fáil in the developer classes, at least until it became obvious that movement against them could not be avoided.

The new government's first step with regard to NAMA was to block the intended transfer of all land and development loans worth less than €20 million that had not already taken place. The programme for government proclaimed: 'We will end further asset transfers to NAMA, which are unlikely to improve market confidence in either the banks or the state.'

This was a brave attempt because the transfer of these smaller loans to NAMA – not part of the previous government's original plan – had been a specific condition of the deal signed with the IMF, the EU and the ECB. But it was entirely logical: had it immediately made the transfers from the banks to NAMA, it would automatically have created further sizeable losses for the banks. They could not have afforded these and would therefore have required even more compensating capital from the state, which it, in turn, could not afford. If those loans were kept at the banks, they could be written off over a number of years, instead of in one go, spreading the new capital requirements over time, much as banks all over Europe were doing in dealing with their bad loans.

There was also a fear that dealing with the last and smaller of the loans would be an even greater administrative nightmare than dealing with the complexities of the big borrowers – which could now be avoided by ignoring the IMF/EU/ECB dictate. It was believed that many of the smaller loans had even more complex or questionable security attached to them. A good number belonged to smaller-scale investors who were ruined financially by their investments and who didn't know what to do about them. Dealing with such loans would be a bonanza for professionals, and many would probably be handed back, for a fee, to the banks to deal with. Transferring anything under €20 million simply made no sense.

To many, the damage had been done long before. Professor Morgan Kelly summed things up like this in a May 2010 *Irish Times* article: 'It is hard to think of any institution since the League of Nations that has become so irrelevant so fast as NAMA. Instead of the resurrection of the Irish banking system we were promised, we now have one semi-state body (NAMA) buying assets from other semi-states (Anglo) and soon-to-be semi-states (AIB and Bank of Ireland), while funnelling €60 million a year in fees to lawyers, valuers and associated parasites.'

It is arguable that NAMA should have been abandoned not long after it had been announced, once the critics had put forward the many good reasons why it couldn't work. It might have been abandoned at the point the European Commission interfered with the proposed valuation process and enforced an alternative system that undermined the banks. But, having committed itself to the project, the government was never going to turn back. It felt it couldn't without losing all face. An announcement that NAMA was being abandoned – even had that been the right thing to do – would have caused an immediate general election, such would the impact have been. The lengthy delays in setting it up – and it took far longer than expected – gave the government an opportunity to reverse its decision; but it failed to use this opportunity, and during that time matters became far worse. By the time NAMA had been established and made its transfers, the property market had collapsed to new lows and the banks had even less money to lend to those buyers prepared to take properties from NAMA. By the time it was up and running, reversal was almost irrelevant. Too much damage had been done.

The evidence was visible throughout the country. There were the so-called 'ghost estates', where people lived alongside empty houses with unfinished facilities; the largely empty retail centres in rural towns; and the half-empty hotels and leisure centres that had been constructed to take advantage of tax incentives, rather than filling a market need, and which few could afford to visit now.

NAMA and other state agencies seemed paralysed by the issue of what to do with these properties. One idea was for the agency to lease units at very low rents or effectively to give them away for use as social housing, by the Health Service Executive or by community and social initiatives. However, hardly anyone had the money to take on properties that might be given to them for small rents or even for free. Another idea was for NAMA to create an investment fund out of a portfolio of property assets, using the foreign properties as part of the bundle instead of selling them individually. If the port-folio could be assembled in such a way as to have a guaranteed income stream, including perhaps guaranteed government rents, it might be possible to sell for a very large amount of cash. It would also help NAMA to lessen its market dominance in Ireland.

NAMA did try to work with some of its clients and formed one of its best working relationships with its landlord, Treasury Hold-ings, despite the behaviour of Johnny Ronan, one of its main shareholders. Treasury had reason to be nice to NAMA. It was the majority shareholder in a stock-market-quoted development com-pany called Real Estate Opportunities (REO). In 2006 REO paid €600 million to buy Battersea Power Station in London, with ambi-tious plans for redeveloping the forty acres into a major residential and commercial centre at a cost of up to £5.5 billion.

The proposals included the construction of more than 3,400 new homes, office space, hotels, shopping and leisure facilities, on about 8 million square feet in total. REO talked up the potential of the location, near the enormous landmark new US Embassy at Nine Elms due to open in 2017. But by the time NAMA took over €815 million of loans provided by AIB, Bank of Ireland, Anglo and Irish Nation-wide, REO still had not obtained planning permission, losses on the project were mounting and the company had no way of making pay-ments on loans and bonds that were falling due.

The REO business plan given to NAMA in May 2010 forecast that it would be able to repay all of its £815 million debt to NAMA within eight years. It wanted the debt renewed on its original terms, the deferral of interest payments and the provision of fresh working capital. Even if NAMA felt that was all unduly optimistic, it had two good reasons to hold off on the enforced repayment by REO of what it was owed. If REO could get planning permission for Battersea, it would be in a much better position to raise finance elsewhere, either through a sale of more shares or through new loans – be it from sovereign-wealth funds, private-equity groups, well-financed property developers or wealthy family investors – to pay off NAMA. In addition, EU rules meant that NAMA could not act in a fashion that prejudiced the interests of a lender from another state, in this case Lloyds, the owner of Bank of Scotland (Ireland). NAMA had to support REO for as long as Lloyds did.

REO also drove a hard bargain. By late October 2010, when its debts stood at £1.66 billion, it warned publicly that without help from its bankers and creditors it might not be able to keep going. Everyone blinked, knowing that immediate receivership or liquidation was likely to produce a far less satisfactory outcome than a trade-off on debt, at least until such time as planning permission was obtained. Bankers such as NAMA didn't just defer the receipt of interest; they increased their exposure in the hope that they would get back more of the original loans.

In July 2011 NAMA issued its first audited annual report. Although an operating profit of €305 million had been made, it had, unfortunately, overpaid for its loans by €1.485 billion. The 'haircut' on the loans had been calculated at the market prices of September 2009, but it now conceded that those valuations had been too optimistic.

The agency confirmed that it had bought about 11,500 loans from 850 debtors from the five participating institutions. It had paid €30.2 billion for nominal loan balances of €71.2 billion, a 58 per cent discount; and then, in February 2011, it had paid AIB €300 million for loans with an original face value of €1.1 billion. That brought the value of the entire original loan portfolio to €72.3 billion, for which NAMA had paid €30.5 billion. It reported that three developers had debts of over €2 billion outstanding and that twelve owed more than €1 billion. By mid 2011 it had reviewed the business plans of 91 of the top 180 borrowers, who accounted for 77 per cent, or €55 billion, of the face-value loans on its books, and said that the reviewing process would be finished by the end of 2011. It described about 59 per cent of the assets it had acquired as investment properties, with the balance regarded as land or property 'under development'.

What it called 'enforcement action' had been taken against twenty-seven borrowers; the receivers had been sent in because NAMA was not happy with the performance of the borrowers in paying down their debts. The agency did not do this lightly; it preferred to put pressure on borrowers to sell the properties themselves and to repay loans from the proceeds, rather than seizing assets. But persuading borrowers to follow orders was not always easy.

The highest concentration of sales had been in the UK, where the market had lifted by 7 per cent on average during 2010, and good sales prices had been achieved, with €3.9 billion raised; but trade in the Irish market – in the light of a lack of finance from banks and an uncertainty about future rents – had proved almost impossible. When an asset was sold in Ireland, it tended to be at below the price at which the loan had been acquired by NAMA. This was described as being 'reflective of the market'.

The scale of the problem was emphasized by NAMA becoming by far the country's biggest golf course operator, with over 30 premium courses. It owned the loans to 83 Irish hotels (and another 60 abroad), and was reasonably confident of selling the 8 five-star and the 33 four-star hotels; but selling the 32 three-star hotels and the one two-star hotel (for which 'all offers will be considered') would prove considerably more difficult, almost at any price. 'We are not in the business of supporting any hotel that is not commercially viable,' said Daly.

The task facing NAMA was enormous, however. It had a target of reducing its debt by 25 per cent by 2013, which would require selling assets for about €7.5 billion in just under a year and a half. This would require the type of luck that Ireland had not enjoyed for some considerable time.

Daly said the property market needed to be kick-started, even if that meant selling property at below what the agency had paid. Most of its early disposals were overseas, but as 2011 began NAMA had undertaken to 'tease the market here' to find out what the floor was. The idea was that the disposal of property would then 'accelerate very quickly'. But the arrival of the IMF and plans by the new government to change the rental market meant, not surprisingly, that its best-laid plans were set back. By the end of the first quarter of 2011 it had approved just €3.1 billion of sales.

Daly claimed progress, however. 'The opening months of 2011 have been exceptionally busy as NAMA has moved from a period of intensive analysis of the position of the largest individual debtors to the next phase of the project,' he said in May 2011. 'The focus now is on identifying those we believe we can work with and moving others into the enforcement process.'

Daly said the agency had two objectives for the coming two years: to act as a source of liquidity to buyers and to contribute to a reactivation of the property market. Subsequently he announced a €1 billion initiative to try to restart sales of home properties. NAMA would sell properties to first-time buyers and would offer a refund of losses to buyers if the price dropped by up to 20 per cent over the first five years after the sale. It seemed that NAMA came to the conclusion that nobody could call the bottom of the market until lending was available to buyers, but that raised dangers that Daly would create a false market using his incentives and nothing else. After all, previous government interventions had not just distorted the property market but inflated the bubble. There was little to suggest that the state would do better this time.

NAMA had started to work together with some of what it regarded as its better clients, providing them with incentives for cooperation. Quietly and confidentially it began to enter into agreements to share the profits on the sale or work-out of some assets, provided that developers met or exceeded certain performance targets. Whereas receivers were sent into Bernard McNamara's floundering empire, and were already in place for Liam Carroll's, a number of the other top-ten borrowers, including Sean Mulryan, Joe O'Reilly and Treasury, appeared to develop tolerable relationships with NAMA. The business plans did include such things as first charges on family homes and the surrender of pensions, which were often worth millions still. But they would be allowed to stay in and keep the family home if they performed to target. The approved retirement-fund money could be used as working capital, but the holiday homes, artworks, racehorses and helicopters had to go. All the developers had to reduce their office overheads, including personal salaries, by between 50 and 75 per cent.

The tougher line was emphasized by what happened to Derek Quinlan, one of that top ten. Quinlan surrendered in his efforts to escape NAMA's clutches in April 2010 and a fire-sale of his assets commenced.

The Dublin accountancy practice KPMG got the job of itemizing Quinlan's assets and personal debts for use by NAMA and other creditors. It estimated that Quinlan had personal borrowings of more than €700 million, having borrowed €300 million from Anglo Irish Bank and about €250 million from Bank of Scotland (Ireland). AIB, Bank of Ireland, Barclays and RBS were owed an average of more than €40 million each, and a final group of banks, Citi, Lombard and First Active, were each owed less than €11 million. If debts owed by Quinlan in partnership or via companies were included in the total, his total borrowings held with NAMA and with British banks were more than €1.5 billion. The extraordinary collection of expensive houses that he had assembled, both in Dublin and abroad, was sold at NAMA's instructions.

Gerry Murphy, an adviser to Quinlan, said in a statement: 'The business plan we presented to NAMA was simple – we would sell all assets as quickly as possible, taking guidance from NAMA in this regard at all times. We were realistic from the very first meeting with NAMA and never pretended that we could repay all debts. In that sense our business plan was inadequate. We apologize for the losses for which we are responsible.' Quinlan's wife and daughter Caroline Brooks were also forced to sell assets. Quinlan's daughter put her Sandymount, Dublin 4, house up for sale in the summer of 2011 at a price of just under €2 million. She had bought it five years earlier for a price of €9.5 million. It was just one of many spectacular examples of crashing property prices and of massive debts that might never be covered.

PART FOUR

The Blame Game

30. A Comfortable Bankruptcy

Whoever it was who coined the phrase 'the wheels of justice grind slowly' may have had Ireland's dealings with financial malpractice in mind. As the country struggled to cope with the financial and social consequences of going bust, the legal system, both criminal and civil, had its problems in dealing speedily with the issues and the people that most held responsible for that bust.

More than anything else it was dealing with the legacy of Anglo Irish Bank, which exemplified these issues and shortcomings. It was not on its own in this, however: Justice Peter Kelly in May 2011 strongly criticized the DPP's failure to mount any prosecutions following commercial court cases involving judgments for millions of euro, despite what he called 'prima facie evidence' and even admissions of criminal wrongdoing, with papers to that effect having been sent by him to the authorities years ago. 'This is not a desirable state of affairs,' he said. 'An apparent failure to investigate thoroughly yet efficiently and expeditiously possible criminal wrongdoing in the commercial/corporate sectors does nothing to instil confidence in the criminal justice system.'

More than anything else the public seemed to demand action in the case of Anglo. At the time of writing no one has been convicted or jailed; no criminal prosecutions have even been initiated. To the ordinary person it may have seemed that there was obvious evidence of wrongdoing but the law works to a much higher standard of proof. Laws to cover what had happened were not necessarily on the statute books at the time. When suitable laws did exist, obtaining and collating the necessary information for a successful prosecution was often very difficult, especially in the absence of whistleblowers or confessions, and where there was a lack of cooperation from those under investigation.

The public also became somewhat sceptical about the ability and even the will of the necessary authorities to push cases. There was considerable drama in March 2010 when Sean FitzPatrick was arrested at his home in Greystones, County Wicklow, and brought to Bray Garda Station for a lengthy series of interviews. FitzPatrick was not given prior notification or asked to attend the station; yet the media was present at his home to see him taken away. His house was searched and documents removed, but sceptics maintained he would have destroyed or removed any incriminating evidence, if there was any, given the time that had elapsed since FitzPatrick left Anglo. If nothing else, it made for sensational pictures. Some observers wondered if it was a coincidence that this much publicized event occurred just weeks before the government was due to make its latest statement on giving Anglo more money to cover its losses, although there is no suggestion that the gardaí colluded with anyone else to convey this impression. Many wondered how quickly prosecution would follow, if at all.

The public frustration may have been summed up best by Justice Peter Kelly in May 2011 when twice he complained publicly about the slow pace of the investigation into the carry-on at Anglo Irish Bank. Kelly was furious that the Office of the Director of Corporate Enforcement had asked him for a six-month extension to the investigation, noting that this had already been granted five times previously. The ODCE sought further orders that allowed it to retain and deal with material seized in February 2009 under an 'extended power of seizure', given by way of search warrants.

Under the Companies Act, the court, when considering whether to grant such orders, was obliged to 'have regard to the progress' of any investigation. Kelly accepted that the investigation was complex and that some people wouldn't attend interview or had delayed in making witness statements, and could not be compelled to do so. But he complained that, more than two years later, he had not obtained 'anything like a firm estimate' of when the investigation would end: 'every effort' was being made to complete it by the end of 2011 but nothing more precise was on offer.

He insisted he was not a 'rubber stamp' and asked if the investigation 'was ever going to come to an end'. The judge said the collapse of Anglo 'has had profound and serious consequences for the economic well-being of this state and its citizens'. It had 'caused hardship to many small shareholders who invested in it in good faith' and he emphasized that it had played 'no small part in seriously damaging Ireland's business reputation throughout the world'. Kelly extended the inquiry only to 28 July and said he expected 'much progress' to have been achieved by that deadline. And on that date he granted a further extension, even though he was told it would be early 2012 before decisions on prosecutions could be made.

Four issues were being investigated to ascertain if possible breaches of the Companies Acts and/or common law should lead to prosecution. The first was the circumstances surrounding the loans of €451 million provided by Anglo in 2008 to the so-called 'Maple Ten'; these loans allowed ten men to purchase shares that had been acquired by Sean Quinn in the form of CFDs and that Anglo wanted placed with other investors (as described in previous chapters).

The second was Anglo's loans to its former directors and the regular 'warehousing' in Irish Nationwide of some of those loans at the end of Anglo's financial year by FitzPatrick, apparently without the knowledge of the auditors, before they were moved back on to Anglo's books (see Chapter 15).

The third subject of investigation was the so-called 'back-to-back' deposit arrangement between Anglo and Irish Life and Permanent Group at the end of the latter's financial year in September 2008, apparently to give Anglo the appearance of having a stronger balance sheet than it actually had, thereby misleading investors and possibly the Central Bank.

The fourth probe related to an €8 million loan to former Anglo finance director Willie McAteer.

Also considered for investigation was whether the four issues just outlined constituted breaches of European regulations, as well as of Irish law. Any investigation of this kind could not get under way until the investigations into the other four issues had first been concluded.

Not surprisingly, given the length of time it was all taking, many questions were asked about the competence of the authorities chasing down these inquiries. The ODCE had about fifty people working in it, including members of the Garda Síochána, lawyers, accountants and a small number of civil servants who provided administrative support. Only about a third of them were said to be working on the Anglo investigation. Paul Appleby, the director of the ODCE, responded publicly; he insisted that 'substantial' progress had been made in a 'complex' case. He said that more than 200 people had willingly provided witness statements to Garda officers but that 'obtaining statements from reluctant witnesses can be a difficult and time-consuming task'. He claimed that even with cooperation similar investigations by the UK Serious Fraud Office had taken between four and six years. 'In my view, the Anglo operation is well ahead of this benchmark and I'm satisfied that it's progressing with all possible speed,' he said.

Garda Commissioner Martin Callinan told his officers in a public speech in April 2011 that he had 'absolute confidence' in the investigation team and the resources available to them and that the length of time the whole thing was taking should not be regarded as indicating a 'lack of commitment'. He said the job was 90 per cent complete at that time. The DPP, James Hamilton, insisted that there was nothing untoward or unusual in the length of time that was being taken, and that he'd been given all the resources he'd requested. The DPP had acted to stop Chartered Accountants Ireland, the professional body of which some of the key figures from the Anglo debacle were members, from going ahead with disciplinary action against four of them: FitzPatrick, McAteer, David Drumm (Anglo's chief executive) and Irish Life & Permanent's former finance director, Peter Fitzpatrick (no relation to Sean). There were fears that evidence given to, and findings made at, a tribunal held by the Chartered Accountants Regulatory Board might prejudice the outcome of any future criminal cases. That body had hired the former comptroller and auditor general (effectively the public-sector auditor), John Purcell, who found that all had cases to answer.

An indication of the most relevant issues arose in a civil action in the United States. After his December 2008 resignation, David Drumm and his family moved to Cape Cod in Massachusetts, where they owned two very expensive houses, purchased in 2007 and 2008.

Drumm had worked in the US for Anglo for years and, according to Drumm, was advised to return there by Donal O'Connor, who said he could then avoid the 'blame culture' in Ireland.

He could not hide from Anglo's efforts to secure repayment of €8.3 million in loans that had been made to him. Drumm retorted that Anglo owed him €2.62 million in salary, pension and a deferred bonus payment, and he demanded damages for the loss of his job, including money for the mental distress the bank had allegedly caused him.

Drumm attempted to negotiate a settlement with Anglo but simultaneously worked on Plan B: availing of the US's less onerous bankruptcy laws. His lawyers claim that he made an offer on 24 September to give Anglo all of his assets, apart from his clothes and jewellery, but this was rejected on 8 October by Anglo. Days later Drumm filed for Chapter 7 bankruptcy proceedings in a Massachusetts court, having done all the preparatory work while negotiations with Anglo were ongoing.

There were benefits from the US bankruptcy law that were not on offer in Ireland, including the chance to exit its restrictions far more quickly. There was a chance that he would be able to keep his share of the equity of the US family home and part of his pension too. Had he succeeded in obtaining an American declaration of bankruptcy, his court-appointed assignee would have had the power to apply to the Irish courts for recognition of his US bankruptcy and then sought to use those Irish assets to the benefit of creditors.

Anglo had to react to protect its interests. It informed the Boston court that it would pursue a claim against Drumm for alleged breach of fiduciary duty – in other words, the behaviour that would be expected of Drumm in the discharge of his responsibilities to Anglo – arising from alleged misconduct and deception.

At the end of March, Drumm faced two days of private questioning by Anglo lawyers, having been compelled to attend by a US bankruptcy judge. Although the session was closed to the media, a list of the issues to be investigated was made known. These included: Drumm's role in the loans made to FitzPatrick and their 'warehousing' with Irish Nationwide at the end of each financial year; Drumm's non-disclosure of the loans to FitzPatrick in Anglo's annual financial statements; Drumm's role in relation to the transfer of billions of euro in deposits between Anglo and Irish Life & Permanent in 2008 to give the impression that Anglo's asset base was bigger than it actually was; Drumm's role in changing the terms of loans to ten property developers who had been provided with the finance to buy shares in Anglo itself that had belonged to Sean Quinn; and Drumm's role in changing the terms of loans to five executives at Anglo, including himself and McAteer. The McAteer loan was for €8 million and was secured only on the value of the shares themselves, even though their value was falling fast and the money was being used to clear McAteer's loans with Bank of Ireland.

Drumm's behaviour in the US caused consternation back in Ireland, and sometimes moments of unintended humour. On one occasion he shouted out of the letterbox at the front door of his house as RTÉ reporter Charlie Bird flapped about excitedly, yelling that he had found Drumm at home. Drumm demanded that his family be left alone. Drumm was certainly interested in providing for them, as evidenced by regular updates from the courts, where his undiminished expensive tastes were outlined on a regular basis in minute detail. He also engaged in large cash transfers to his wife, Lorraine, the pattern of which became clearer when the court insisted that he provide them with all the details.

Among Drumm's many claims was that his move to the US was motivated not by a desire to avoid his responsibilities, but by the fact he had 'little prospect of securing employment in Ireland or Britain after Anglo'. But he was tardy in producing documents for the civil proceedings, which led to justifiable speculation as to how cooperative he was being with the authorities in Ireland over matters that could come to be judged as criminal.

One of the things that could be said in FitzPatrick's favour was that he stayed in Ireland to face the music – apart from some apparently regular trips to Spain to play golf. He was declared bankrupt on Monday, 12 July 2010 and would retain that status for twelve years.

'I can't repay all of the liabilities that I owe [but] I didn't run and steal the money,' he said in an interview for the book *The FitzPatrick Tapes*, published in January 2011. 'When people talk about ruin and losses, I am one of the biggest victims of it. I have to say that very carefully, because people would pillory me. They would say they have lost so much money. I have lost money as well. My commitment was there in pounds, shillings and pence.' He spoke of 'the stress' and 'the humiliation' and how his 'whole social circle has diminished', although he said some of his friends had remained loyal to him.

When he went bust FitzPatrick's debts exceeded his assets by more than €95 million. According to documents supplied to the courts for his bankruptcy hearings, he received €3,693 net of tax per month from an Irish Life annuity. However, he was also making a net loss of €3,505 per month on three properties he jointly owned and rented out. As a result, his net income was just €188 per month.

It became apparent that easy access to credit had turned FitzPatrick into a greedy speculator, something he had in common with many other people. But, with the exception of the most high-profile developers, they hadn't had the opportunity to borrow on the same scale. He had so-called secured debts – because he had offered to pass over ownership of certain assets to lenders if unable to repay his loans – of just over €84 million. Of that, all but €11 million had been borrowed from Anglo but Ulster Bank, AIB, Bank of Scotland (Ireland), Friends First and Haven Mortgages were all owed money too. His unsecured debts, for €61 million, included contingent liabilities of €9.3 million for personal guarantees made in respect of his adult children and €46.65 million for personal guarantees he made in respect of various investments. To add to his woes the Revenue Commissioners wanted €3.5 million.

He had assets but they were worth only a fraction of what they had been. His wealth was overly dependent on bank shares and property investments. The report compiled by his court assignee estimated a loss of at least €46 million on investments made as far back as September 1998. His 4.9 million Anglo shares, worth €80 million at their peak and €50 million as recently as June 2008, had been rendered worthless by nationalization. He had used his pension to invest €16 million in AIB and Bank of Ireland shares and most of that too was lost.

Unravelling his finances was going to be an enormously hard job for the court's official assignee, as would managing and selling assets on behalf of creditors. FitzPatrick seems to have been a relatively easy mark for those who marketed consortium investments, grouping people together so they could pool 'their' cash for bigger deals. He invested in four overseas property deals put together by Derek Quinlan, and one with Quinlan's arch rival, Kevin Warren. He invested in another in London's West End with David Arnold's D2 Private concern. These didn't suffer the same sort of drop as Irish property, but many fell by a significant enough amount to trigger problems with loan agreements. In one bitter irony FitzPatrick found out that his old bank was putting the squeeze on friends of his at the projects in which he was a co-investor and demanding immediate sale and loan repayment. He had used his 'best judgement' in making investments, he said. One of his problems, however, was that he had walked into a number of unwise deals with his friends; an example of this was involvement in Nigerian oil-fields with Lar Bradshaw, the independent director at Anglo who had also shared a boardroom with FitzPatrick at the Dublin Docklands Development Authority.

FitzPatrick had tried to cut a deal with Anglo and the state before he opted for bankruptcy. He turned to veteran accountant Bernard Somers (brother of former NTMA boss Michael), adviser to millionaires such as Tony O'Reilly. Somers told FitzPatrick's creditors they should accept a private 'scheme of arrangement', because it would return more money, and sooner than bankruptcy would, especially as FitzPatrick had assets of €1 million that were not subject to any security and were available for dispersal.

According to a report in the *Sunday Times*, Somers estimated that unsecured creditors faced a shortfall of €47 million and could expect a return of 20 cents in the euro based on an asset pool worth €12 million. Creditors could expect a payout within three years. These unsecured creditors were warned that they would face a shortfall of €57 million if a bankruptcy proceeded. Assets available to be dispersed would fall by another €2 million, because of additional taxes, meaning creditors would get 15 cents in the euro. It would take four to seven years before a payout was made.

This might have provided the state with an additional €10 million, but it was not a risk Brian Lenihan was prepared to take. The desire to assuage public anger appears to have been central to his and Anglo's decision not to do a 'private' deal that would have prevented Fitz-Patrick from going bankrupt. In political terms it was impossible for Lenihan to be seen to reach an arrangement with FitzPatrick, even if it meant the state would have ultimately been better off. Imagine the rows, not to mention the conspiracy theories, if a 'deal' had been cut. The effect of FitzPatrick's bankruptcy was that he was forced to sur-render all of his personal assets, was barred from serving as a company director, and would have his future income seized by the court-appointed assignee.

But none of that meant FitzPatrick was destined for the poor-house, at least for as long as his wife Catriona stood by him, as she did loyally from the moment his troubles became visible. His wife has a half-share in their €1.5 million family home, and FitzPatrick will have that roof over his head for the remainder of his days, unless the assignee decides to sell the house (and give her half the proceeds).

There are other properties too. There is one in Spain in which FitzPatrick's wife owns a half-share that is worth an estimated €1.3 million (but that has a mortgage attached). She obtained a half-share in her husband's pension pot after he left Anglo, which is worth €3.4 million to her and from which she can draw a sizeable monthly income. She had €1.6 million in cash in the bank. So, while the Fitz-Patricks would have difficulty living in the fashion that they previously enjoyed, they have a lot more available to them in cash and assets than most people. Questions remain, however, as to whether she earned this wealth independently of FitzPatrick.

Despite the ignominy, bankruptcy has an upside. FitzPatrick can probably sleep a little more soundly now that he no longer has to worry about repaying the €150 million he owed. That has become the responsibility of the court-appointed assignee. FitzPatrick's main concerns at the moment are ensuring that he doesn't breach the rules about accepting gifts from family or friends and finding golf courses where he isn't blackballed. The possibility of criminal proceedings still looms, but presumably a bankrupt is eligible for free legal aid should they come to anything. In public, he seemed at some peace with himself, telling his creditors that he accepted 'full responsibility for my own ruin'. He shocked many when he cooperated fully for *The FitzPatrick Tapes*, although he had no control over the final editorial product and the book did not cast him in anywhere near as good a light as he might have expected.

In April 2011 an American lawyer called Byron Georgiou visited Dublin. He had been one of the ten members of the Financial Crisis Inquiry Commission in the US, which had investigated the causes of that country's massive banking crisis. It had held a public inquiry that everyone of relevance was forced to attend – and if they refused to give testimony they were compelled to do so by subpoena; the proceedings appeared in the form of an authoritative report published as a paperback book. When I met him he was incredulous that we had not had a similar public commission in this country that would have forced politicians, regulators, public servants, bankers and their advisers to give evidence about their roles in our crisis. Instead he agreed that we had indulged our elite by allowing them to be the subject of privately conducted inquiries, followed by reports in which individuals are not even named and blame is spread in general terms rather than being aimed at guilty parties. He admitted that many of those who had been interviewed in the US remained in denial – and he was angry that in the US too so few have faced prosecution – but at least they had been forced to confront their failures publicly.

But he had a surprising degree of sympathy for the Office of the Director of Corporate Enforcement and the slowness with which it had advanced its investigation into Anglo. He pointed out that in the US Bernie Madoff, often cited here as an example of how the Americans deal with crooks, was almost the exception rather than the rule. Less than a dozen people had gone to jail in the US as a result of the most recent financial scandals, compared to hundreds after the American Savings and Loans scandals of twenty years earlier. An international culture of not punishing those responsible for what might be called 'crimes against capitalism' had emerged.

31. Wright and Wrong

Sean Quinn might have finally received his public comeuppance (financially, at least, because there was no suggestion that he had done anything that deserved legal retribution) and Sean FitzPatrick might have been declared bankrupt, but there were many others who seemed to have escaped the blame for their roles in contributing to the country going bust.

Many of the guilty parties might have argued otherwise: NAMA's belated crackdown on the builders who could not repay their debts meant that, eventually, many were facing radically changed lifestyles; some of the top bankers had gone from their jobs; the personnel in the most senior positions at the regulators had been changed; most notably, the Fianna Fáil government had been comprehensively cloven.

But there remained a perception that not enough had been done, especially when consideration was given to the formal punishments meted to those who had been held responsible for the mess, beyond the loss of reputation and financial inconvenience. NAMA builders were still seen to be living beyond their means, and suspicions remained that some had managed to put assets beyond the reach of the authorities. The departed bankers had received extraordinarily generous pensions, often guaranteeing them six-figure annual incomes that, for legal reasons, continued to be paid (although it was not clear if the pension income of some was being diverted to help meet unpaid borrowings). The bankruptcy of former Anglo Irish Bank boss Sean FitzPatrick was the exception rather than the norm. The departed regulators also received generous state-funded compensation and pensions, and many of those directly beneath them – names unknown in most cases to the public – remained in place, continuing to draw state salaries. Even the politicians who were rejected by the people had received generous redundancy payments and massive pensions funded out of borrowed money to cushion their falls.

Others seemed to be escaping their fair share of the blame. The professional classes maintained their anonymity to a large degree. The auditing profession in particular and the advisers in the Department of Finance largely escaped blame and retribution for their particular failures during the boom years, and indeed afterwards for their roles in the disastrous attempts at recovery.

We got expensive state-sponsored investigations into what went wrong and their attendant reports, but they were unsatisfactory to put it mildly. There was a failure to attribute blame, to name names; instead, as the cynics had predicted at the time the terms of reference were published, they had produced unsatisfactory outcomes because their briefs had been too wide and too vague, allowing the establishment to get off the hook. One report, by Peter Nyberg, went so far as to blame almost the entire country for what had happened – echoing the contentious claim of Brian Lenihan in November 2010 that 'we all partied too much' – rather than any individuals. This must have delighted the guilty. Worse, we had criminal investigations, but, at the time of writing in July 2011, we have not had a single prosecution, let alone a conviction for wrongdoing, and the indications are that we will have to wait until 2012 at least.

Some investigations were prepared to allocate blame. John Purcell, the former comptroller and auditor general, who had been hired by the Chartered Accountants Regulatory Board to investigate the behaviour of some of its members, found that Ernst & Young, Anglo Irish Bank's former auditors, had a case to answer. This raised questions as to how he was able to act so quickly, when the state, with all of its resources, could not, although presumably the burden of proof for a criminal prosecution was somewhat higher.

The inclusion of E&Y in the regulatory proceedings brought long-overdue attention to the role of the accounting profession: in highlighting poor practices and mistakes at the banks as late as they did, they let down the shareholders in whose interests they supposedly acted. As auditors E&Y collected €6.4 million from Anglo from 2005 to 2008, including €4 million for audits, the balance for other advice. It gave Anglo a clean bill of health for the original version of the 2008 accounts, failing to notice the €7.2 billion in secret short-term deposits from Irish Life & Permanent. Less than three months later, E&Y reissued the 2008 accounts with a health warning before resigning. It was not on its own in missing things of great relevance about the financial performance of the bank it was auditing while still collecting its fees.

For example, during the same four-year period, Pricewaterhouse-Coopers received €41.7 million in fees from Bank of Ireland, more than half for extra services beyond the statutory financial audit, such as providing 'letters of comfort' about the bank's financial health. After the bank guarantee was introduced, it was hired by the Department of Finance to work on restoring the banks to good health and got €5.5 million in fees for that, the bulk of this earned between September 2008 and January 2009.

In mid 2010 NAMA's Frank Daly publicly told a convention of accountants and auditors that they needed to look in the mirror before 'absolving themselves of responsibility'. 'We cannot go back to a situation whereby an audit firm can complete its audit and then claim either that it did not spot the elephant in the room or that it was not its job to point out that four-legged hunk with the trunk in the corner.'

Accountants for their part denied that their profession had performed poorly, suggesting that outsiders did not understand their role. They said that they were 'watchdogs, not bloodhounds' and that, in any event, warning banks about dangers in their lending practices was not part of their brief; nor was it their place to comment on a strategy or a way of doing business that had been implemented by management with approval of the board. Their job was merely to report on whether the accounts gave a factual 'true and fair' view of the financial position. They were also required to establish if a company remained a going concern, and, although again this was based on historical data, the necessity for a bank to show it had provided against possible future losses is an important part of the accounts that an auditor must sign.

The payment of lucrative audit fees and additional fees for other non-audit pieces of work acted as an incentive for accountancy firms to find themselves in agreement with the companies. Unless very careful, they could become lapdogs. But there was one very good reason for the auditors to stress their competence. Had any been found to be negligent, shareholders would have been able to sue for damages.

The rewarding of failure was not restricted to auditors. The awarding of large redundancy cheques and large pensions to bankers and regulators scandalized the country in late 2008 and early 2009, but reassurances were offered that everything had changed and it would never happen again. The story of Colm Doherty, appointed as boss of AIB in 2009, and then forced to resign in September 2010 as a condition of further state investment in his bank (see Chapter 18), illustrated perfectly the point that little had seemingly changed.

It wasn't until late April 2011 that it emerged that Doherty's 2010 salary of €432,000, paid up until his departure on 10 November 2010, was only a fraction of the money he had received from AIB in that year. He got €1.966 million instead of pension benefits payable and €50,000 in taxable benefits. He received a payment of €953,000 in lieu of twelve months' notice: this covered his salary and taxable benefits as well as unclaimed holidays and a pension allowance for the year-long notice period. The bank also made a one-off contribution of €1.043 million as compensation for a reduction in his annual entitlement at normal retirement date from €303,000 to €203,000 (something that had saved the bank €1.75 million in future pension commitments). He was to receive an annual pension of €203,000 starting at an unspecified future date, but before he reached sixty-five.

The payment was made by AIB with the approval of the Department of Finance, as ordered by Lenihan, in accordance with Doherty's 'contractual entitlements'. The fact that AIB had failed to raise enough capital to cover its losses, and now had to be rescued by the state, was incidental, apparently. The new minister for justice, Alan Shatter, said bankers had legally enforceable contractual positions and an expectation that they should receive financial rewards if their employment was terminated. However, he acknowledged that employment contracts were a 'two-way process', and some bankers had run their banks so badly that it amounted to a 'fundamental breach of contract'. It remained to be seen what would be done about it. There had been major rows too with Bank of Ireland over the extraordinarily generous pension arrangements for its chief executive, Richie Boucher, and the continued payment of bonuses to highly placed staff.

The Department of Finance had its own questions to answer. Governments rarely want to have fights with their civil servants because they depend so much on them. The advisers are permanent and know that the politicians are just passing through before being replaced by other politicians. So it would have caused ructions had the department officials been blamed soundly for failing to do their jobs properly, for failing to spot what was going wrong, or, if they had, for not doing anything about it. It would have required a comprehensive change of personnel that would have been almost impossible to implement.

So the department got very lucky when a Canadian civil servant called Rob Wright answered the call to investigate its performance. Controversially, Wright came to the conclusion that Department of Finance officials had provided repeated warnings to the government about the risks involved in running a so-called pro-cyclical budgetary policy – spending the proceeds of the boom and therefore inflating the bubble further instead of dampening rampant growth by saving the money for a rainy day – during the Celtic Tiger years. He claimed that 'the department's assessments of the risks from the Irish housing bubble were at least as strong as any public analysis over the period.'

Unfortunately, Wright had little in writing to back up this contention. Instead he referred to 'oral reports' that he'd been told about. This didn't stop RTÉ from broadcasting that 'an independent review of the performance of the Department of Finance over the past decade has found that the department did warn the government about the dangers of the economic policy it was following, but that its advice was overruled by the cabinet.'

One of the criticisms Wright did offer was that finance officials should have altered 'the tone' of their warnings, because they were ignored in each successive budget. Even though the decisions on tax were government policy, an analysis of the risks involved 'should have been provided and communicated forcefully to the minister for finance and the government'. Failures 'to pay sufficient attention to the broader macroeconomic risks during the period may, in part, have been due to a shortage of highly trained economists and financial market experts', it was claimed, although this did not explain why there had been a shortage of such experts in the requisite disciplines. The department, Wright said, had had neither the time nor the resources to conduct in-depth investigations of the issues, which meant that it was ill-equipped to deal with what was demanded of it.

Vested interests seized upon Wright's report. Lenihan, still in office, described it as a 'very fair and thoughtful assessment' of the Department of Finance's performance over the past decade. The Association of Higher Civil and Public Servants claimed the report vindicated the advice given, and the decisions taken, by its members in the department. 'This report clearly states that the actions of politicians, rather than civil servants, were the primary factors behind the crisis,' said its general secretary, David Thomas, who insisted that his members had been scapegoated by some for the economic collapse.

One aspect of the report was received with great anger by the Irish Congress of Trade Unions: its criticism that the government's budget process had been 'completely overwhelmed' by the programmes for government and the partnership deals agreed during the period, with too little emphasis having been placed on public-sector reform.

ICTU's general secretary, David Begg, described the ascribing of blame for the economic crisis to the social-partnership process as 'a facile exercise in scapegoating, designed to obscure the true cause of the collapse: banks, builders and toxic government policy'. He said politicians adopting short-term policies had ignored repeated warnings of an impending downturn and failed to respond appropriately when it hit. Begg had been a member of the governing board of the Central Bank, which had itself failed grievously in its duties during the same period.

One of the most worrying recommendations of Wright's report was his suggestion that budget advice provided to the minister should be outside the scope of the Freedom of Information Act for five years after it was given. Wright claimed that knowledge of the public's access to information was 'limiting the creation of non-consensual advice in the department'. As excuses for inaction go – transparency in the performance of public duty is somehow inadvisable – it was novel and also potentially very damaging. But it was manna for an establishment that could now spread the blame for everything by citing an official report.

However, in a delicious irony it was the disclosure of presentations that had been made to Wright – and discovered by the *Sunday Times* because of a Freedom of Information application – that brought about far more serious criticisms of his report.

It emerged that Donal de Buitleir – a former assistant secretary with the Revenue Commissioners who had become general manager in the office of the chief executive of AIB Group – had claimed there had been a serious failure in the department's accounting standards, one that largely ignored future liabilities, did not meet modern standards and gave misleading signals. He said that, because heads of finance functions were not required to have any financial management qualifications, there was an 'important skills deficit' in the civil service. His credibility may have been questionable due to his role at AIB, but his previous insider status at the Revenue gave him some grounds for making his claim.

Edmund Honohan, master of the High Court and brother of the Central Bank governor, said the commission needed to investigate whether 'healthy debate' had been encouraged in the department and to what extent its briefings had been ignored by the last government. He said the issue of 'passing the buck', by blaming the Financial Regulator or hiving off decisions to quangos, also needed to be examined.

But the most pertinent material came from Robert Pye, a highly respected retired assistant principal in the department, who said in a written submission to Wright that he had circulated seven papers within the department in 2004 and 2005, warning a 'major global shock could have a devastating impact on both our fiscal position and our banking system'.

Pye said he'd had a meeting with three assistant secretaries of the department in October 2004 to discuss his fears. He suggested the exchequer should run a large budget surplus for several years to build up a stockpile of cash for use if the economy ever crashed or slowed unexpectedly. He said he'd been told his concerns were 'legitimate', but 'simply untenable on political grounds'. A number of senior civil servants confided in him that they broadly agreed with his analysis, but none was prepared to voice their support openly.

Pye told Wright about an environment of 'unquestioning obedience' to politicians, which was reinforced by senior managers who rebuked staff for questioning government policy. 'We might advise the government that white was white, but if the government decided that white was black, then the department was deemed "legally" to preach the same message to all and sundry – without question,' Pye claimed.

Pye tried to 'do a Morgan Kelly' in January 2007. He sent an article to *The Irish Times* for publication, setting out what he feared would happen to Ireland if there was a sudden outside shock from the global economy. He received an official written warning from the department telling him not to submit his article, which he withdrew.

Importantly, he claimed that department civil servants actually had the required skills to recognize the property bubble, and the mistakes it made were due to an 'appalling' inability to inform the government of the 'sheer recklessness of its policies'.

Pye finally wrote for *The Irish Times* in May 2011, elaborating upon his presentation to Wright. He revealed that his papers to his superiors had included one in November 2005 called 'Eight Reasons Why a Global Economic Shock is Inevitable by end-2008'. 'At a meeting with three senior managers I was told that, while the risk factors which I had identified were plausible, there was not the slightest possibility that they would receive a hearing at a political level . . . Most managers appeared to expect a gradual tightening of credit on the international markets and a manageable levelling off in Irish property prices. No one seemed willing to entertain the possibility that the alternative, the sudden onset of a major international credit crisis, would have catastrophic implications for the Irish economy.'

He revealed that in his submission to Wright he had said: 'The government had no incentive whatever to take corrective action. It was reaping a colossal revenue windfall, most of which it then channelled into current expenditure. As an egregious violation of the most basic principles of economics, this is probably impossible to beat. Many commentators bleat about the need for greater specialist skills in economics and financial management in the department, but this is nonsense. The mistakes that were made had nothing to do with skills. They were due rather to the appalling inability of the department to impress upon the government the sheer recklessness of its policies.'

He had recommended that the state run a large budgetary surplus for up to six years and build up a substantial sinking fund to reinflate the economy after the inevitable tsunami struck; that the availability of credit to domestic borrowers be greatly curtailed; that the National Pension Reserve Fund (NPRF) switch heavily into commodities and precious metals; that a far greater proportion of the national debt be denominated in dollars to take advantage of its inevitable significant fall in value; and that the major financial institutions be urged to reduce their exposures to the markets that would suffer most when the crisis hit. He had been ignored.

'Regarding its statutory role, the department traditionally saw itself as the last line of defence against the predations and venality of a self-serving political caste. In the course of the 1990s, however, as the public coffers expanded, a polar shift occurred and the department began to see itself merely as a provider of "advice" to the government. Its defensive role was forgotten,' he claimed.

'It is probably fair to say that, thereafter, whatever the politicians wanted, the politicians got. The department had no vision of its own for Ireland, nor any sense of the dangers lurking in deep waters. It had ceased to stand as a bulwark between the people and the politicians and had become instead an obedient arm of government, with no mind of its own,' he alleged.

Wright wasn't the only outside expert hired at great expense who critics might say pulled his punches. In April the sequel to the Honohan and Regling–Watson reports, authored by a Finn called Peter Nyberg and provided after six months' work at a cost of €1.3 million, was published.

The report may have run to 156 pages and been based on 200,000 documents and 140 interviews – with whom he did not say, other than to indicate that some limited their participation by the use of legal advisers – but it disappointed and infuriated many in equal measure, telling us almost nothing new and, worse, pointedly refusing to pin blame on individuals. It was difficult to assign blame, Nyberg said, because there were just too many people to blame; he indulged in the controversial charge that hundreds of thousands of people had jumped on the bandwagon and participated in a 'national speculative mania'. He came worryingly close to parroting Lenihan's much derided 'we all partied' line. It was not useful to name individuals, he said, and it was his decision not to. Instead he blamed all sectors of Irish life, saying that property buyers and banks had made bad decisions, while the Central Bank, the Financial Regulator, the government and politicians hadn't understood or cared about the risks. Had one of those parties shouted stop, the country would not have found itself in the depth of the crisis it was in, he claimed, contradicting himself somewhat: clearly just one voice would not have done the trick such was the 'collective mania' he had identified.

Contrarians within banking faced 'sanctions, loss of independence, loss of job or loss of credibility', said Nyberg, but he refused to provide evidence of how many such people he had found or what had happened to them. He said that the bankers he'd met were in denial about the scale of the risks that they had taken on. Asked about whether interviewees differed widely in their explanations as to what had happened and how, he said that some were 'devastated' by the damage to their reputations and their financial well-being, while some still blamed Lehman Brothers and others for the crisis. He referred to what he called 'disaster myopia' within the banks: the expectation of a 'soft landing' in the property market, which meant there was little or no planning for something more serious and most certainly not a crash. 'It appears now, with hindsight, to be almost unbelievable that intelligent professionals in the banking sector appear not to have been aware of the size of the risks they were taking.'

Nyberg also observed that external auditors were 'silent observers'; that there was 'no evidence' the department was particularly worried about 'prudential matters' in any bank; and that non-executive board members at the banks were out of the depth of their expertise. Without the names of individuals, this was not dissimilar from what the opinion columns of the newspapers had been saying for two years. Nyberg could have cited names without the fear of libel actions that restricted newspapers.

Instead, we indulged our elite by allowing them to be the subject of privately conducted inquiries, followed by reports in which blame was spread in general terms and guilty individuals once again escaped identification.

32. Taking the Pain

What had happened to the country was not the fault of the vast majority of ordinary people, be they public- or private-sector workers, the unemployed or students, the elderly or children. The crisis resulted from the reckless actions of the wealthy elite, greedy bankers and their property-developer mates, the incompetent regulators and the inept government up to 2008; and it had been compounded by the disastrous error involved in guaranteeing non-essential banks such as Anglo Irish and Irish Nationwide and the invention of NAMA. But, regardless of that fact, there was now a massive mismatch between the government's spending commitments and what money it could take in to pay for it all. There was nothing fair or moral about those without responsibility for the crisis being landed with the bill, but that's where it landed.

Nobody was able to escape the financial consequences of the economic collapse. This was the first fully fledged economic depression in a generation, recalling the miserable days of the 1980s. It was arguably far worse because there was a major increase in privately held debt and because the size of the fall and its suddenness were more severe.

By 2011 every taxpayer had to pay more in taxes to try to fill the gap in the public finances. Public services were reduced or in some cases cancelled to bring down the exchequer's costs. Pay rates fell in most jobs, both public and private. Unemployment soared, reaching 14.5 per cent of the workforce, nearly 450,000 people by the end of April, particularly among those who had worked in construction and those who were just finishing their education and looking for a job. Forced emigration returned after it had seemingly been banished. Most people with assets, be they property, shares or pensions, found they were worth a lot less. More people dropped below the poverty line. Little of this would have happened if those people running the banks hadn't gone mad, swept along in a frenzy of greed and encouraging everyone else to join in with them. It wouldn't have happened if the regulators had done their jobs, if senior politicians hadn't been so impressed by the apparent wealth of donors in the property classes and so seduced by the tax revenues being generated.

But the consequences had to be dealt with, regardless. The loss of over 100,000 jobs in the construction sector represented a double blow to the economy. All of the employment and related taxes from employees was gone, as was the VAT on the sale of finished output, let alone the taxes from developers, which had been substantial. The state now had to contend with a massively higher social-welfare bill.

The collapse in tax revenues was extraordinary – €47.25 billion in 2007, €40.7 billion in 2008, €33.1 billion in 2009 and €31.75 billion in 2010. It simply wasn't possible to drop expenditure at such a quick rate. But the problem was that there was a gap of €14.65 billion between the government's day-to-day spending and its income for 2010, and that was before the cost of that year's contribution to the bank bailout had increased the annual deficit to €18.7 billion.

Imagine that a household had income each year of €32,000 but outgoings of €47,000. It would be near impossible to organize ongoing loans with the bank to cover the gap, especially if there was a large amount of debt that already had to be repaid. To get more money from the bank, the householder would have to demonstrate that he was engaged in a considerable effort to close that gap and indeed eliminate it. If his chance of earning extra income was limited – as would be most likely during a recession – an immediate and severe curtailment of spending would be demanded by the lender. The same would apply to a company taking revenues of €32 million annually but with costs of €47 million. Requests to the banks for more finance would not be entertained unless massive cost reductions were undertaken first. Any arguments that the company needed to receive more money than it could spend, in an effort to stimulate a hoped-for improved incoming of cash, might get short shrift.

Governments are different, of course. A government can argue, plausibly, that it simply cannot eliminate the deficit in quick time. Just look at where that €47 billion is spent: nearly €20 billion is on social-welfare supports and not much less is spent on health services. But what was affordable during times of plenty, when tax revenues exceeded spending, simply wasn't possible any more. It didn't really matter how much people had become used to the services and employment the money provided, or how much they'd liked what they received. Cuts were inevitable, no matter how unfair they were and no matter how much hurt was caused, because the money was no longer there.

What is often forgotten is that the public finances problem had become apparent even before the September 2008 bank crisis struck. Brian Lenihan had already started public spending cuts and had brought forward the December 2008 budget to October so as to get an early benefit from some tax increases and further spending cuts.

What happened had a major impact on much of what was to follow. One of Lenihan's measures was to remove the automatic entitlement of a medical card for those aged seventy and over, which they got irrespective of their wealth and income. Pensioners protested on the streets and, remarkably, occupied a church near Dáil Éireann to hold an impromptu rally. Had any group of younger age done that, there would have been outrage about their behaviour; instead the elderly were treated like they were heroes. Independent TDs and backbench Fianna Fáil TDs reared up and the measure was abandoned. The memory of its experience with the elderly was to handicap the government in future decision-making.

It did introduce an emergency budget in April 2009, however. It added extra taxes, doubling the special income levy and the health levy that many people didn't even realize that they'd been paying. Mortgage-interest relief was cut, as was some of the early child supplement. Lenihan reduced the threshold at which the higher levy for tax was set. A decade's tax improvements for workers were removed in one fell swoop.

It was a sign of how bad things were getting. Lenihan had insisted for months that he would not have a supplementary budget in the spring of that year because the economy could not bear the burden of additional taxes. He had said that it would be counterproductive. Yet the government decided that it would deal with falling tax revenues by increasing tax rates rather than by making politically sensitive cuts. It was a big risk. Imagine a company with dramatically falling sales trying to make up the loss in revenue that it had suffered by massively hiking all of its prices.

The government's excuse that it was too late in the year to cut its spending was bizarre. There were eight and a half months left in the year. It is hard to imagine a company in financial trouble of the same scale saying it was unable to introduce major spending cuts for such a long period of time, and that it would wait because to do otherwise would be too hard. But the government seemed to fear anarchy and a damaging loss of public services due to strikes if it tried to cut the public-service jobs or wages. Such strikes – and the trade unions were adopting war footings – might have done serious damage to both the economy and our international image. It did not want a fight with the trade unions, especially with an eye towards the rerun of the Lisbon Treaty referendum or the looming European and local elections.

But Lenihan was opposed to increasing the tax burden – although he had a controversially nuanced view on that, believing that many were not paying their fair share, amongst the lower paid as well as the higher. He also feared that imposing a further tax burden would do even more damage to an already struggling economy, particularly when it came to consumer spending and business investment. He believed that the increase in the rate of VAT announced in October 2008 was a mistake that had made the decline in retail sales worse. Lenihan was of the belief that history as much as theory showed that additional taxes, especially during a recession, did not create wealth; rather, tax increases could prolong and exacerbate the economic downturn, especially if even less money in the pocket dampened consumer demand further and brought about increased unemployment. Investment, both local and international, might be driven out of the country in a high-tax environment. He thought that by pitching rates too high, the actual take would fall instead of rise.

Even before the savage budget of December 2010 put up taxes further, the top marginal tax rate – when various income levies are taken into account – had hit 52 per cent under Lenihan's direction, the highest it had been since 1992. Although there were many legitimate arguments that the rich were not paying their fair share because they had various legal means of sheltering their wealth from tax, Lenihan highlighted that 50 per cent of workers had been outside the tax net and that only 11 per cent had paid at the highest rate. That was why he introduced an income levy on all – although it was then removed for those on the minimum wage – before finally bringing in the Universal Social Charge in December 2010 – a combination of all levies that was paid by all irrespective of income. It was a philosophical decision on Lenihan's part as much as anything else. He did not believe that those who contributed nothing in direct taxes appreciated what they were getting from the state.

But the government did avoid introducing some taxes because of the political damage they believed they would cause. It deferred the introduction of property taxes, for example, even though most economists regarded them not just as a reliable and consistent source of income but as an equitable one too. It floated, but then rejected, the idea of a 'home services levy', a flat charge of something like €200 per year applied to every house, seemingly regardless of the income of the occupant, in advance of a properly worked-out property tax (Fine Gael's new environment minister, Phil Hogan, was to embrace the idea after the 2011 general election and announced in July that for two years from January 2012 an annual household charge of €100 per annum would be introduced, almost without exception. Property taxes would then be introduced from 2014). Nor were water charges introduced, although a commitment was made that the following government had to honour. It managed to avoid the reintroduction of third-level education fees too, again leaving that to its successor.

All of these extra taxes and charges were required because of an unwillingness or an inability to reduce spending on politically sensitive areas. Softer targets emerged. It was easier not to spend on something that had been planned for the future, even if it was necessary, than it was to not spend on something already there.

Many of the capital spending plans were abandoned, even though economic studies showed that such spending has present and long-term benefits, providing immediate employment and permanent facilities that will be of productive benefit to the economy for years to come. Indeed, a country that abandons capital spending, or even one that does not replenish its physical stock as it depreciates, is going to face serious economic problems in the future.

But the government was more concerned with meeting payments to public servants, past and present. The public pay and pensions bill almost tripled in less than a decade to €19 billion. Fianna Fáil had inflated the size of the public sector, by adding massively to the numbers employed without insisting on value for money, and by increasing payments by way of 'benchmarking' against allegedly similar jobs in the private sector. It had done this to win favour with the tens of thousands who got those jobs, and to create the impression that it was providing a better service. Public-service numbers were frozen in March 2009, but there were still 278,000 full-time public servants who had to be paid. The number of pensioners hit 103,000 in 2010, compared with 72,000 in 2005. Early retirement merely moved people from one payroll to another and the money came directly from annual revenues or borrowing: there were no pension fund reserves to be drawn upon. There was also the extraordinarily expensive burden that had arisen from benchmarking, the process that had delivered the big pay increases. And, finally, public-service pensions were now linked to the pay that currently applied to the equivalent grade a person had been on when he retired, rather than to what a person had actually been earning when he retired. Some people were earning more now in retirement than when they had worked and they were not required to pay the hated pension levy.

This levy, which averaged at around 7 per cent, was Lenihan's one major attack on the public-service pay rates. He began by describing it as a contribution towards a defined benefit pension that would cost the state way more than the employees were paying for it. Eventually it came to be described as a pay cut, but, compared to what was happening in the private sector, it was regarded by many outside of the public sector as a relatively small sacrifice. Public-sector workers did not see it that way and things got worse when Lenihan came back again in December 2009 and announced pay cuts that ranged between 5 per cent and 10 per cent from January. All this had the desired effect:

the net public pay bill of €17.4 billion in 2010 was a drop of 6.2 per cent on the previous year. This was the budget where Lenihan had declared boldly: 'We can now see the first signs of recovery . . . our strategy is on track.' He said the budget was 'the last big push of this crisis . . . our plan is working, we have turned the corner.'

However, what the government wasn't going to do was implement many, if any, of the proposed cutbacks in public spending suggested in a special review group chaired by the economist Colm McCarthy. The gruff-speaking Dublin economist – who had been through all of this before in the 1980s when involved in an expenditure-cutting group called An Bord Snip – now put together a report that got the nickname An Bord Snip Nua. It had big ideas that would have involved savings of €5.3 billion per annum and the loss of 17,500 jobs.

Government and unions reacted with horror, even though the cuts proposed involved about 7 per cent of existing annual government spending at the time (when capital expenditure was included) and less than 5 per cent of public-sector jobs. In private enterprise, such cuts would have been made almost without debate, but not in the public sector. That gave rise to the suspicion that McCarthy had thrown in the kitchen sink when making his recommendations, knowing that there was no point in going soft because the eventual compromise would do too little of what was required.

McCarthy was prepared to battle a widespread assumption – at least among trade unionists – that all of the government's day-to-day spending – about €55 billion in 2009 at the time of his study – was somehow money well spent and that any reduction in that amount was going to lead to a noticeable and dangerous reduction in the quality of services provided. One of the criticisms made of McCarthy was that he had not given enough consideration to the damage to services and people that would be done by his cuts, that he was interested only in finding ways to save money. This argument was rather facile, and it could equally be said that during the boom years successive governments threw money at the public sector, both through increased wages and through the creation of new bodies and positions, without looking at what benefits would be created.

The greatest example of this is the Health Service Executive, where McCarthy recommended cuts of less than €400 million. A multiple of this has been added to its budget each year since the organization's creation with little or no improvement in services. What should have provided an opportunity for organizational rationalization has instead been turned into the creation of an administrative monster. Indeed there was a strong argument that, McCarthy's recommendation notwithstanding, the government should have been looking to take back much of the money that had been given to the HSE on the basis that it was misspent. Yet taking back what had been given because it was misused, let alone because it could not be afforded, rarely featured on the agenda. McCarthy was not allowed to address the major issue of public-sector pay. The benign interpretation of this was that it ensured he focused on finding structural waste without being distracted by the easier option of recommending pay cuts.

The failure to implement many of the An Bord Snip Nua recommendations – especially the abolition of unnecessary, highly paid, jobs-for-the-boys quangos – because the consequences would seemingly have been too horrific or unfair, did not provide encouragement that a sufficient number of tough decisions would be taken, irrespective of the seriousness of the circumstances. Few people appeared willing to discuss the need for these hard decisions, apparently for fear of being labelled right-wing. While it was the banking crisis that ultimately brought about the arrival of the IMF and the EU, it is possible that outcome might have been averted had enough been done to cut even more public spending, either on top of all of the budget adjustments or instead of the tax increases.

The government decided, however, that it could not take more pay from public servants, not after the combination of the pension levy and the pay cuts. Yet it was still paying, at €20 billion per annum, more than it could afford. It entered into negotiations with the public-sector unions, looking for ways to find savings through non-replacement of staff, lower wage rates and pensions for new entrants to the service, and productivity increases at no extra cost. In return it promised no wage cuts for a number of years. There was some uncertainty, though, as to what these measures might actually be;

and there were major criticisms subsequently, even from the trade unions, of a lack of urgency by public-sector management to implement the deal. A significant get-out clause had been inserted into the Croke Park Agreement between the government and public-sector trade unions, signed in early 2010: if economic circumstances changed dramatically, the government was entitled to renege. But even the arrival of the IMF – which was a good deal more than dramatic, seismic in fact – failed to trigger the clause and the outgoing government stuck resolutely to the terms of the deal. Seemingly, the IMF had not put them under any pressure on this issue. The new coalition stuck by Croke Park too, although various Labour Party ministers set a September 2011 deadline for measuring real and substantive financial benefits.

But there were other reasons for not chasing further public-sector pay cuts. No matter how enormous the scale of the gap in the public finances, it was hard to see how cutting current spending and increasing taxes further would do anything except send the economy into another tailspin. The hope had to be that the amount to be borrowed would reduce over time, assuming the economy recovered somewhat and extra tax revenues arose from exports and higher domestic spending. And in any event it was going to be hard to demand even more from people when many of those to blame for the bust continued to enjoy very luxurious lifestyles indeed.

PART FIVE

Brave New World

33. No Free Lunches

The general election had been completed, and Fine Gael and Labour were conducting their coalition-government negotiations, when Central Bank Governor Patrick Honohan decided he'd better tell them publicly what was what.

It was 1 March 2011, and Honohan contacted RTÉ and offered to appear on the television current-affairs programme *Primetime*. To Honohan's evident frustration, the interview became bogged down at the start with questions about the responsibility for the decision to introduce the bank guarantee in September 2008; he had more pressing and immediate issues to address. Honohan wanted to talk about the new government's need, as he saw it, to commit itself to implementing the terms of the IMF/EU/ECB deal, especially in relation to the banks, for which he had responsibility as Ireland's ECB representative.

During the election campaign Brian Lenihan had taken a remarkable decision. The terms of the IMF/EU/ECB deal demanded that the Irish government invest €10 billion in the recapitalization of the banks under its control and do so by the end of February. It was one of the most contentious elements of an agreement drawn up in haste but almost certainly the one the ECB saw as the most important. At Europe's instruction, our Central Bank hired international consultants to conduct yet another round of stress tests at the Irish banks. This was the latest effort to estimate what the losses might be and how much extra capital would be required to cover these on top of this €10 billion and the €40 billion that had been injected previously. The ECB was determined to provide such a comfort level of capital at the Irish banks that other depositors would feel confident enough to provide cash, so that it didn't have to do so. But Lenihan decided that it didn't seem to make much sense to commit the capital in advance of those 'stress-test' findings, not due until 31 March; he had serious worries that Ireland was going to be asked to provide more money than was actually needed. Privately Noonan understood what Lenihan was doing even if it didn't suit to say so publicly during an election campaign.

The announcement that he was deferring the payment, leaving it to the next administration to decide upon, was judged in some quarters as an old-fashioned Irish election campaign political stroke. There had been some 'no more money for the banks' talk during the election campaign from Fine Gael and Labour. It appeared now that Lenihan was forcing them to suffer public anger for doing, once in power, what they had said they wouldn't, at the demand of our foreign creditors.

It was hardly an issue about which to play politics. The immediate recapitalization of the banks – and factors associated with that – was the central element of the entire deal, and it was what the ECB in particular wanted dealt with first. To not do it seemingly put the whole agreement in jeopardy. Lenihan reassured the public that this wasn't the case. 'They conveyed to us they understood the government's decision,' Lenihan said about the troika's attitude. The money for the Irish government to meet its bills and for the banks to continue supplying cash was not under threat, apparently.

Honohan had a different view on that but felt that he could not comment publicly during the election campaign: it would be inappropriate for an official to become involved in such debate, as he might be accused of trying to influence the outcome of the election in favour of whichever party agreed with his position. (Equally, he laughed heartily when he heard about Fine Gael's briefly spun campaign idea of raising a €50 billion loan from the US Federal Reserve, even if he made no comment about it publicly.) Instead he waited for the election to be played out and then used the TV interview as an opportunity to emphasize how important the state's investment in the banks was to the deal.

Apparently Lenihan's decision, which the minister said had been endorsed by the outgoing government, had caused considerable angst at the ECB. It 'had to be convinced' that this was appropriate behaviour during an election campaign and that the new government would not renege on what it had regarded as an agreement set in stone. Honohan said that the decision to miss what he described as 'an important deadline' had been greeted with 'alarm'. Honohan's line with his European counterparts was that the new government would have more authority to make the payment and that there would be greater 'buy-in' from the Irish public if the new government said it was the right thing to do. Now, though, he was in the position of having to convince the new government to honour the commitment made by its predecessor.

Honohan went further when he firmly ruled out default on bank or sovereign debt as an option, saying he did not know of any country where such a decision had worked out well. He held out the hope that the government would be able to renegotiate parts of the €85 billion bailout package, including the high rate of interest on these loans, and said that this would be an ongoing negotiation that would take place continuously over the years rather than in one event. But, as far as he was concerned, this would be possible only once the new government had started doing the big things to which the Fianna Fáil-led government had agreed. Reading between the lines, this was another warning to the new government that it should go easy on promises that it would be able to get major changes to the deal at such an early stage.

If Lenihan's actions during the election campaign had spooked the ECB, policies from some of the likely new government's leading figures also caused worry. Fine Gael had released a banking-policy document entitled 'Credit Where Credit is Due' in early February, and in it Noonan raised the idea of asking Europe to help to pay the repair bill for 'systemically important' banks such as Bank of Ireland and AIB. 'If other European countries have set their face against a default by Irish banks on reckless loans from banks regulated in their own jurisdictions, then they should be willing to contribute directly to the recapitalization of Irish banks,' the document read. Fine Gael modified its position somewhat during the campaign after Leo Varadkar had claimed that 'not another cent' would be put into any of the banks. This line was changed to one of 'no more cash for Anglo'. Inflammatory expressions such as 'burning bondholders' were replaced by phrases like 'burden-sharing'. The difference was important: the first implied unilateral action; the second required negotiation.

The Labour leader, Eamon Gilmore, delivered what was probably the election campaign's most memorable and notable soundbite when he declared 'it's Frankfurt's way or Labour's way' in relation to the banks. However, it rebounded on him somewhat, as most engaged voters realized that was a battle he was always going to lose, even if they liked the sentiment.

If anything, such claims gave the election campaign an air of unreality. Much of it was dominated by the desire to punish the outgoing government for its failings, and this, rather than substantive measures for dealing with the future, framed many of the public debates. Some individual politicians and smaller parties prospered by promising things in relation to the IMF/EU/ECB deal that they would never be able to deliver in power, but knew they could offer because they'd never realistically be in a position to implement them. None the less, a portion of the electorate was persuaded of their ability to do things they couldn't and voted accordingly.

The EU, the ECB and the IMF were experienced enough to disregard much of the noise as electoral posturing, expecting a new government to engage with reality quickly enough. The problem was that some voters were likely to be bitterly disappointed when they found, inevitably, that the new government would have to slip into the strait-jacket that the outgoing administration had already prepared for it. Elections give hope about change and, after the battering the Irish psyche had taken in previous years, few wanted to rain yet on the new parade.

Part of Enda Kenny's campaign involved the claim that he had a personal friendship with the German chancellor that he'd be able to exploit to Ireland's advantage. To prove it to the sceptics, he took a flight to Berlin during the campaign and secured a short meeting with Merkel at her Christian Democratic Union Party headquarters. It culminated in the photo opportunity that Fine Gael wanted, even if a somewhat uncomfortable-looking Merkel, perhaps distracted by Kenny's hand behind her back, failed to match her visitor's beaming smile.

It was already becoming clear that Ireland would be required to give if it was going to receive. Our problem was that any new government had little of worth to bring to the table. The corporation-tax issue, which the outgoing government had said was protected in the troika agreement, was raising its head again among foreign politicians. In his press conference after the meeting with Merkel, Kenny said he had emphasized that Ireland would not surrender its corporation-tax rate as part of eurozone reform in a discussion about the 'possibility of movement on an interest rate on the IMF/EU deal'. He was also asked about a perceived growing anti-German tone in sections of the Irish media. 'The problem in Ireland was not caused by Europe but a lack of regulation, a lack of oversight and government incompetence,' he said. 'This problem was caused at home first. I know about exposure of German banks, obviously we've got problems, some of which we can deal with ourselves, some in a European context.'

Kenny went on his travels again after the election – in which Fine Gael fell seven seats short of a majority – but before the programme for government with Labour was finalized. He headed to Helsinki in Finland and a meeting of leaders attached to the European People's Party, the group with which Fine Gael is affiliated in the European Parliament. These included Merkel. 'What we are looking for here is a reduction in the cost of the package and that's in the two priorities we identified: the interest rate and the cost of the banking element of it,' Kenny said. 'Ireland wants to pay its way and Ireland wants to play its part but it can only do so in a programme that is sustainable, that allows for Ireland to pay its way and at the same time grow our economy, create jobs and bring about recovery and the current situation is not going to allow that to happen.'

Though it was becoming clear that Merkel had done Kenny a favour by saying nothing after their meeting in Berlin, this would change now that her 'friend' had been elected. On her way to Helsinki for this meeting she questioned if there was any need to change the conditions of Ireland's €85 billion package, saying interest rates could not be cut 'artificially'.

The Finnish finance minister, Jyrki Katainen, who hosted the meeting, was even blunter. 'There are no free lunches,' he said. 'Of course we have to take care that the Irish package really works, because it is in all our interests to ensure that Ireland will recover . . . Therefore we have to look at the debt sustainability. I don't know exactly what will be the outcome because we have to at the same time look at the Irish sustainability development and be very strict. We don't loosen the package.'

It was against this background that the negotiating teams from both Fine Gael and Labour – in the absence of Kenny and Gilmore – set about forming a workable programme for government that would include as much of each party's election manifesto as possible, while conceding ground on issues where there was divergence. But that wasn't the only constraint: the programme had to be written with the requirements of the IMF/EU/ECB deal foremost. That put enormous limitations on what could be promised to the electorate and by the parties to each other.

What was remarkable about the programme for government was that it promised, nonetheless, to confront some of the things in the troika deal to which the previous administration had committed its successor.

Fine Gael's manifesto had promised to cut the budget deficit to below 3 per cent of GDP by 2014, but Labour's had wanted 2016. Not surprisingly they settled on 2015, as Rehn had said already could happen, but significantly agreed that the budget adjustments for 2012 and 2013, as set out in the IMF deal, would be implemented, contrary to what Labour in particular had stated the previous November. This concession would make it almost impossible for Labour to meet its commitment of reducing the size of the budget adjustments in 2012, 2013 and 2014 by just €7 billion instead of the €9 billion originally planned. Now no figure was being mentioned.

The programme for government also promised no further changes in income tax beyond those already introduced for 2011, a statement that could come back to haunt it. It undertook to examine the introduction of a site-valuation tax but there was no indication of how and where it would raise the €1.5 billion in additional taxes that the IMF/EU/ECB deal required for 2012, a figure to which it remained committed (along with a further €2.1 billion in spending cuts). Adherence to that plan would necessitate a lowering of personal income-tax bands and credits, a reduction in pension-tax relief and other reliefs, a new property tax, a higher carbon tax and a reform of capital taxes. A decision was taken to leave such difficult discussions until nearer the December 2011 budget announcement: there was no point in major rows before the government got down to business. Neither was there much merit in announcing such bad news to the public straight after the election or committing to too many things that might not be implemented.

The new government also decided to reverse the €1 per hour reduction in the minimum wage (to €7.65) that its predecessor had introduced at the IMF's insistence. The inclusion of this requirement in the deal had seemed odd to some: it had no direct impact on the government's finances and offered no help in dealing with the banking crisis. However, it did allow the outgoing government to justify further cuts in social-welfare entitlements: a situation could not be allowed to develop whereby a person could make more money on the dole than by working. Now the government was reducing its own flexibility, in the name of social fairness.

Fundamentally, the IMF and the EU believed that Irish people were overpaid compared with their European counterparts and that this went from the bottom up, with Ireland's minimum wage being second only to tiny Luxembourg's in the EU. At the other end of the scale the troika had ordered a review of legal and other professional fees, believing these to be grossly expensive, but it was the change to the minimum wage with which the new government chose to take issue.

The most significant issues arose in relation to the banks, particularly in the light of Honohan's warnings of just a week earlier. The new government made it clear it would follow Lenihan by not putting new capital into the banks as yet but would wait until the stress-test results were available at the end of March.

It also decided upon a new approach for NAMA. The IMF/EU/ECB programme had ordered that all property-development loans had to be transferred from the Irish banks to NAMA, whereas previously NAMA took loans from banks only if the developers' accumulated debts were more than €20 million in size. Many critics thought that this idea of a so-called NAMA 2, even bigger than before and dealing with many small loans that would create enormous bureaucracy relative to their size, was insane. It would also force the banks to take an immediate loss on the transfer of the loans, which amounted to about €16 billion in nominal total but might now be worth far less than this – mainly at AIB and Bank of Ireland, thereby increasing their need for further capital. The incoming government said the plans for NAMA 2 were 'unlikely to improve market confidence in either the banks or the state', but this decision was not as brave or as controversial as might have seemed. Apparently, the troika of lenders – with the IMF, increasingly frustrated by its partners and sympathetic to the Irish, in the vanguard – had conceded that the idea of valuing assets to existing market values, when there was no market to speak of, was one that would greatly increase losses at the banks unnecessarily and had started to back off. The new government would try to take advantage of this.

Linked to this was a debate about how quickly the Irish banks could be 'downsized', one of the major considerations of the IMF/EU/ECB plan, indeed probably the most important one to the ECB. The first problem was that the Irish banks had too many loans relative to the size of their deposits, a legacy of the mad property lending of the boom. For example, Bank of Ireland's loan-to-deposit ratio had been 160 per cent in November and the ratio at AIB stood at 159 per cent. It was decided that the size of a bank's loans should not exceed 122.5 per cent of its deposits. The total loans at the six domestic banks at the end of December 2010 amounted to €282 billion but as deposits amounted to just €157 billion this gave an unfeasible ratio of 179 per cent.

However, the number of loans on the balance sheets of the banks was actually falling because of the contraction of economic activity. For example, the total of outstanding residential mortgage loans in Ireland to be repaid fell below €100 billion in December 2010 for the first time since early 2006. Compared to the all-time peak, reached in May 2008, the banks' aggregate mortgage loan book had shrunk by 22 per cent. Lending for consumer purchases had also declined sharply, standing at €18.5 billion in February 2011. At its peak in January 2009 this had amounted to €29 billion.

Unfortunately deposits were fleeing the system at an even faster rate. Deposits in Irish banks had shrunk by 40 per cent from the time of the introduction of the guarantee: from €250 billion in 2008 to €150 billion in December 2010. It wasn't just foreigners who were removing their money; prudent Irish businesses were putting theirs in foreign banks as well. This was exactly what the bank guarantee had been designed to prevent, but the flight of deposits, as much as soaring bond yields, was a firm indication that investors did not believe in the ability of the Irish government to live up to its promise that all depositors would always get their money back. The fact that both trends continued after the IMF/EU/ECB deal was also a sure sign that many people thought it was a bad and unworkable one.

This meant that the ECB's position was now getting worse. It had provided about €100 billion in loans to keep the system going, about €70 billion of this through a scheme called exceptional liquidity assistance, because the collateral being provided by the Irish banks would not normally have been of the standard required. Another €87 billion or so came from the Irish Central Bank but ultimately the ECB would be responsible for that too.

As the ECB was heavily involved in providing money to replace deposits, it tried to force the pace of the sale by the banks of more of their assets, their non-NAMA loans. But there was something of a catch-22 at play again: the arrival of the IMF had caused the ratings agencies to downgrade Irish debt, both sovereign and at the banks, further prompting more outflows of bank deposits and, in turn, even greater reliance on ECB funding. The problem was getting worse and there was no sign that it would get better.

The new government agreed with the idea of shrinking the size of the banks to bring their loans closer in line with deposits, but it worried about the speed with which the operation could be conducted. Offloading about €65 billion to €70 billion in loans, in addition to the €88 billion in loans that had gone or were going to NAMA, was one thing, but the price obtained was crucial. The new programme for government rightly argued that this 'must be paced to match the return of more normal market conditions and demand for bank assets'. Noonan, like Lenihan, felt that too quick a sale, on top of the NAMA losses, would further increase the capital needs of the banks to an unsustainable level; the continuing outflow of deposits emphasized that.

One of Noonan's main pleas to Trichet was to change the nature of the ECB's emergency support for Ireland's financial system. He thought it would be better if the banks did not have to renew their money from the ECB on a fortnightly basis – because it made investors anxious that the ECB might suddenly stop supplying the money – but rather had medium-term loans at similar rates of interest instead.

The IMF/EU/ECB deal had included a €25 billion contingency fund for use on the banks – the initial €10 billion, plus another possible €15 billion to provide for extra capital when assets were sold at a discount. The idea was that the banks would then be able to raise operational money as required on the financial markets without the need for ECB intervention. They would be able to do so because they would have enough capital to be regarded as sufficiently safe and reliable to attract deposits again.

However, the cost of borrowing that €25 billion contingency would be enormous to the Irish State – on top of all its existing and committed borrowing – and had been conceived just to get the ECB off the hook. Not only did the new government need a cheaper interest rate but also time to reduce the size of the banks – so that they weren't forced into further losses – and a concurrent commitment from the ECB to continue its funding over that period. The government believed the banks could not secure the deposits they needed, no matter how well capitalized, if they had to borrow the balance of their requirements every fortnight. Noonan tried to convince the ECB to provide a long-term loan of €60 billion for this purpose of restoring confidence.

Whatever its hopes of getting that loan, the new government, despite the bursts of rhetoric by both member parties during the campaign, must have known it was on more than doubtful ground when it came to the idea of 'burden-sharing' with senior bondholders. What it suggested in its programme for government was miles removed from what the parties had championed during the election campaign, and its chances of achieving even that were slim.

The aspiration for 'burden-sharing' was now described in the programme for government as 'may be necessary', the type of language that suggested wriggle-room. While the programme hinted at legislation to allow the burning of those senior bank bonds that were neither guaranteed by the state nor secured against specific assets – such bonds amounted to about €16.4 billion, less than one third of the total value of all senior bank bonds – few thought the ECB would agree to this.

Within weeks Noonan, as the new finance minister, was to discover the extent to which the ECB opposed the idea of writing off part of the money it was owed or of allowing foreign banks that had bought Irish bank bonds to suffer any losses on their investments. Whatever about Irish banks suffering losses that would require the state to supply new capital, the same was not going to be required of Continental banks. Proponents of such a move pointed out how bondholders in a Danish bank in financial trouble had recently been required to take such a haircut, a decision that didn't result in other Danish banks being shut out of the debt markets. That Denmark was not a member of the euro was held by the EU to be the key factor in preventing contagion.

When Noonan told the Dáil in March that 'government consideration as to the approach to burden-sharing will be further informed by the important capital assessment currently being undertaken by the Central Bank, as well as international developments on burden-sharing', few believed that he would be able to have his way. The planned discount on junior subordinated bonds – as put forward by the previous government anyway – would be helpful but it wouldn't deliver much in the way of savings: only €6.9 billion of these were left to be redeemed, so just a few billion euro could be 'saved' in this way.

The hope developed that by not pressing for the burning of bondholders Ireland would receive other things in return. 'We should now get a quid pro quo in respect of two items. The first is a reduction in the interest rate and the second is a renegotiated long-term debt package,' the minister for social protection, Joan Burton, argued. Again, there was no joy: it was claimed in Europe that the principle of senior debt remaining free from government-imposed write-downs was central to the whole funding system for banks worldwide.

But much more relevant was the position of the German and the French banks, and why they were far more concerned about our banks defaulting than the possibility of our state doing so. It turned out that German and French banks held only about €10 billion of our sovereign debt, a very small amount. But, as German banks were owed €99 billion by Irish banks, and French banks owed €30 billion, it was no wonder that they were so keen to stop Ireland defaulting on even part of the bank debt.

Indeed, according to figures from the Bank of International Settlements, French and German banks between them were owed €763.8 billion by Ireland, Greece, Portugal and Spain. Their fear of the effects of contagion was obvious. A bank default in Ireland might set a precedent for these other countries. The German and French governments did not want to have to compensate their own banks or to bring about circumstances in which they might lose money from bank defaults in any of these countries. Instead, the Irish people were left to carry the can for the reckless borrowing of privately owned banks, notwithstanding the reckless lending to them by privately owned foreign banks which were now being protected by their governments.

Too few people were making this point to Enda Kenny as he set about trying to change the sentence imposed by the IMF/EU/ECB on our country – too few, in fact, for him to listen to with any seriousness.

34. A Gallic Spat

After his long wait – thirty-six years a member of Dáil Éireann, just two and a half years as a government minister a decade and a half earlier, and eight and a half years as leader of the opposition – there was a spring in Enda Kenny's step now that he had finally made it to the top.

On the night that Fine Gael won its seventy-six Dáil seats – its largest ever tally, guaranteeing that Kenny would lead the next government – the incoming Taoiseach promised a new government 'of responsibility, not privilege, a government of public duty, not personal entitlement, a government looking with confidence and courage to the future, not with guilt and regret at the past'.

'We stand on the brink of fundamental change in how we regard ourselves, in how we regard our economy and in how we regard our society,' he said. 'We have to close the gap between government and the people, between politics and the people, because it is in that gap that the rot started and the rot flourished.

'We cannot have another generation of Irish building the futures of other countries,' he said. 'For the next four years, let us be mindful of our duty and our responsibility during the period of the next government, and above all, in the midst of what is for many a national heartbreak, let us be mindful of each other . . . On this spring day let us begin again to bring new life, new clarity, new shared purpose to Irish life, to Irish politics, and to the Irish future . . . So let's lift our hearts up, and let's lift our chins up, because now we've been given a responsibility and a mandate and let us not shirk in our duty to our people.'

It was fine talk, and its confidence and ambition were what people wanted to hear after the misery of previous years. However, many wondered how realistic it was for anyone to promise substantial re-negotiation of the previous government's deal with the IMF/EU/ECB, to concentrate on cuts rather than tax rises for the rebalancing of the public finances, to create 100,000 jobs over the following five years and to promise that young people would no longer have to go abroad to seek work unless it was their own choice. After all, the IMF/EU/ECB called the shots now and the austerity was due to intensify.

For Kenny to make such promises raised even more concerns. Nobody doubted Kenny's affability, decency or dedication – he had done a considerable job in rebuilding Fine Gael after its electoral disaster of 2002, when it appeared to be heading for political irrelevancy. However, there were serious and legitimate questions about his intellectual ability, economic knowledge and suitability to cut it at the highest level, especially as he would have to deal with heavyweight leaders at meetings such as those of the Council of the European Union. There he would be on his own, without any advisers to rely upon. If some people in Ireland found it hard to take him seriously, what would others think?

He had come to power more because of the shortcomings of others than because of his own strengths – not forgetting the electorate's preference for almost anyone of a conservative ilk other than Fianna Fáil. He'd had a mixed general election campaign. The polls guaranteed him the position of Taoiseach almost from the outset because Fine Gael was always going to be the biggest party, barring a disaster. Whereas in previous elections the personality of Bertie Ahern had drawn floating voters to Fianna Fáil, Fine Gael worried that Kenny might actually cost them votes because of his mistakes. His handlers kept him away from sections of the media, where his weaknesses, as someone who sometimes struggled to think on his feet, might be exposed. His failure to appear for interview with certain broadcasters – and poor performances with others when he did – raised doubts as to his ability to take part in difficult negotiations on serious issues. It may have hindered Fine Gael's appeal in the last week of the campaign and cost the party its best ever chance of an overall majority.

Victory clearly gave him self-confidence, and he handled the first day of the new Dáil's proceedings very appropriately. Some of the

media coverage was hysterical: it was as if a Barack Obama-style figure had suddenly emerged.

The praise, hype and hope may have gotten to him at the wrong
time. Within days of his confirmation as Taoiseach he'd had to go to
Brussels for a crucial meeting of the Council of the European Union.
Kenny walked into his first meeting with his European counterparts
with what some perceived to be something of a strut. There had been
a certain amount of encouragement from the European Commission: 'I can see that there is a case to reduce the interest rates paid by
Greece and Ireland,' Olli Rehn had said. Kenny was under pressure at
home to show himself to be different from Cowen, to be ready to
stand up on behalf of Ireland. But, for all of his talk of rebuilding
relationships with Europe, it appears that Kenny may have slightly
misjudged the mood of the room. Ireland was supposed to remain
humble, especially as it was looking for something. According to
some, Kenny was too firm in his approach. The UK Channel 4's economic editor, Faisal Islam, later reported that a number of other
leaders had been shocked to find Kenny so 'cocky'.

Whatever the truth of that, he ended up in a full-scale row with
the French president, Nicolas Sarkozy, just as Cowen had five weeks
earlier. More than anything, Kenny wanted a reduction, from 3 per
cent to 2 per cent, in the surcharge interest rate being charged on
Ireland's loans – saving no more than a few hundred million euro per
year – and possibly more time for the loans to be repaid. He ignored
the evidence that 5.8 per cent was actually a pretty standard rate at
the time for economies in deep trouble. Nor did many think Ireland's
offer to bring in new curbs on annual spending, known as the 'debt
brake', would persuade the European powerhouses to temper their
demands on this country.

Kenny also wanted a commitment that the ECB would continue
to provide liquidity funding for the banks on a more sustainable basis
should the sale of bank assets go more slowly than expected. He
wanted the loans to be made available on an annual or bi-annual basis
and was not persuaded to accept promises that it would continue
fortnightly without any problem or need for guarantee. He wanted a
lot, but he was not prepared to trade what he did have in return.

Most particularly he did not want to give up the 12.5 per cent corporation-tax rate or to contemplate the introduction of the so-called 'Common Consolidated Corporate Tax Base' (CCCTB), which he described as a 'back-door' route to tax harmonization. The CCCTB would involve the introduction of a single set of rules for companies operating within the EU when calculating their taxable profits. This taxable income would then be divided up between all the countries in which the company operated, to be taxed at the local rates. Many feared that it would be almost impossible to standardize twenty-seven individual national sets of laws pertaining to the taxation of corporate profits, and to ascertain in which location the profit should be taxed. The tactic of the 'optional' CCCTB as an alternative, as suggested by Germany, had the worrying look of a Trojan horse about it.

Kenny introduced himself by telling his colleagues that the election of his government represented a 'fresh start' for Ireland, including in its relations with Europe, and that the people of Ireland expected to be treated differently because they had a new government that they had elected. He then went on to push the case that the terms of the deal his predecessor had struck were too onerous.

Sarkozy was quick to intervene and to question Kenny as to why he was looking for a lower interest rate when he could raise more money by increasing the 12.5 per cent corporation-tax rate. When Kenny said that was impossible politically and counterproductive economically, Sarkozy in turn told him that Ireland was receiving many billions of euro from its partners and that it should be showing more gratitude for that. The exchange reportedly became heated, although, as is usual in such situations, the participants played things down in on-the-record comments afterwards.

'In respect of a good vigorous and vibrant discussion that I had with the French president – I'm not sure whether you'd call it a Gallic spat or not – obviously the French president has had very clear views about the corporation-tax rate for quite a long time, but then so have I,' Kenny stated afterwards, somewhat diplomatically. Sarkozy said he understood corporation tax was 'a very touchy subject' for Ireland, but said euro countries must move towards convergence. 'No one is asking Ireland to have an average rate which is comparable to Europe, but it's also difficult to ask other countries to bail out Ireland when Ireland is determined to keep the lowest tax on profit in Europe,' Sarkozy said.

Kenny fared little better with his friend Merkel, even if she did not handbag him as obviously as Sarkozy had. She wanted to concentrate on the bigger picture – which was the objective of the summit as she saw it – of a more permanent solution for future problems of this kind. She was not in the mood to review something that had been agreed only four months previously. Germany was not as exercised as France in wanting an increase in the corporation-tax base, but it wanted something else akin to that: Ireland's entry into a CCCTB in exchange for German support for a cut in the interest rate on our bailout. A reduction of 1 per cent was available to Greece; it was also granted an extension of its loans from three years to seven and a half when it agreed to an enormous privatization deal worth over €50 billion – not, as was to be shown subsequently and very quickly, that it did much good.

'We weren't satisfied with what Ireland agreed to today, so the question of lowering interest rates has only been addressed for Greece,' Merkel said. 'It is simply fair to say we can only give our commitment when we get something in return.' She saved her wrath about Ireland for her return to Germany. 'No one in Europe will be left alone. No one will be allowed to fall, because Europe can only succeed together. But this requires, of course . . . a sensible mix of self-exertion and solidarity,' Merkel told the Bundestag. 'I can tell you, we're not that far in the talks with Ireland . . . I'll be perfectly honest with you. I'd rather take care of Europe's growing competitiveness than continually spend my time taking care of rescue programmes for other countries.'

There seemed little understanding of just how important the 12.5 per cent corporation-tax rate was to most of the Irish as a way of attracting foreign investment and keeping it. It has been estimated, for example, that US firms operating in Ireland contribute up to €5 billion in taxes annually, more than what is received from excise duties and VAT. About half comes from corporation tax, the rest from employment taxes contributed by their 100,000 or so workers. Ireland argued that it wasn't the only reason why these firms located in Ireland – the common first language of English was significant – but it was implicit that the tax had to provide some sort of advantage to the country. On the other hand, there was no guarantee that investment would move to Continental Europe if EU tax rates were harmonized or near-equalized. Ireland tended to compete with countries like Israel, Singapore, Switzerland and Puerto Rico for major technology and pharmaceutical projects.

The French and the Germans seemed to have little memory of how the Irish rerun of the Lisbon Treaty referendum – which provided the required endorsement – had had to be helped along by the addition of a legally binding codicil that recognized our sovereign right to select our own rate of corporation tax. Or it may be that they did remember and were now attempting to punish us for our 'disobedience' at the time of the first referendum vote and our 'arrogance' in insisting on things such as the corporation-tax rate at the second time of asking. Nor did they seem to grasp that they would fatally wound Kenny if, as his first major act as leader of the Irish people, he was forced to roll over and surrender to their demands.

European Council President Herman Van Rompuy was trying to be diplomatic when he said eurozone leaders were asking for 'constructive engagement' from Ireland on tax coordination. 'They [the Irish] haven't met all the conditions, so can't have reduced interest rates,' he said. Kenny was fortunate to escape from the fray and to avoid being lynched at home because of the outcome. He had failed in his oft-stated objective of getting any change to the troika's deal with Ireland, despite making many promises. That it was his first meeting, and had taken place only two days after he had been installed, helped him enormously. So did the understanding among the Irish electorate that he had little to offer – and was being asked to give too much. He was also aided by the fact that it was known he would get another opportunity to pitch later in the month.

There would be more opportunities but they were rarely prioritized by the EU because Ireland was only a small issue in the bigger scheme of things; as far as the EU was concerned, we'd been sorted in November, even if Ireland had somehow failed to realize or to appreciate that. Germany and France were trying to put together a new fund to deal with EU sovereign crises, one with well over €500 billion available to it. Germany's aim was to enforce stronger disciplines upon all euro-member states, to make them behave more like Germany did, and it was doing so with strong French support. It wanted member states to agree that they would write firm rules constraining the size of their absolute debt and government deficits – specifically the terms of the existing Stability and Growth Pact, which limited budget deficits to 3 per cent of GDP and overall debt to no more than 60 per cent of GDP. It wanted to establish firm guidelines or benchmarks on wages and pensions, with Ireland particularly in mind, such was the distaste for what were regarded as our excessively high levels of pay, particularly in the public sector. It was very detailed and intrusive stuff, albeit not quite a surrender of self-determination on the scale of the IMF/EU/ECB deal, yet sufficiently serious to raise the question of whether a new European treaty would be required and, by extension, a referendum in Ireland to endorse it, as is demanded by our constitution. Perhaps with Ireland in mind again, Germany somehow decided that it would not be a full treaty issue because the measures would not be enforced uniformly across all member states. Running the risk of losing another referendum in Ireland – which would have held up the whole thing or derailed it – was not to be done. (There would be a certain irony in Kenny's government denying the people the chance to vote on such a fundamental issue relating to our own powers, when his party in opposition had derided Fianna Fáil for not putting the IMF/EU/ECB deal to a referendum.) And Germany continued to harp on and on about the trouble Ireland tended to cause everyone else.

Kenny knew that he had to return to another meeting of the Council of the European Union in less than a fortnight. Much of the work of negotiating with the ECB, in particular, and with the IMF and EU, was left to government ministers. The troika was invited to talk with Noonan and Brendan Howlin, the new minister in charge of the public sector, in Dublin on 18 March. But the dynamic was shifting. Whereas Kenny had gone into office confident that he could change the deal, he now found he was coming under pressure to sur-render on corporation tax, to pay a big price in return for a relatively small concession. And the argument that Ireland could be over-whelmed by the demands of the November 2010 deal was not being heard favourably either, especially by the ECB.

Noonan was trying to compensate for the EU's refusal to allow defaulting on bank bonds by requesting help in other ways. 'We are not actively pursuing burden-sharing but we are explaining to our European colleagues that there's a certain point where a combination of the sovereign debt is manageable and [with] the bank debt put on top of it we reach a point where the sustainability of the situation becomes doubtful,' Noonan said. 'Unless the bailout package is made more affordable, there is a high risk, without anybody taking a policy decision, a bank will run into a default position.'

The line from the government was there would come a point when the burden on the Irish State caused by the financial drain from the banks would become unbearable. This implied that the govern-ment would be forced into a choice between a bank default and a sovereign one.

The new government had reason to fear that the amount of cash provided by the troika deal simply was not enough. If it managed to meet the budget targets set for it by its predecessor, it would still have used €42 billion of the €85 billion that had been made available to it by 2014. That left just €8 billion in reserve, as another €35 billion was earmarked for the banks. What nobody seemed to take account of was the cost of redeeming existing government bonds as they fell due, which would normally be done by raising new, replacement loans on the bond markets. The NTMA had an estimated €28 billion of such stock that had to be repaid between 2011 and 2014. Where would it get the money to do that and also honour existing senior and guaranteed bank bonds during the same period? It was estimated that this would involve another €41 billion, with a further €20 billion to follow at later dates. The cost of having failed to keep the banks separate from the state was now proving all too expensive.

Meanwhile, money drained out of bank deposits but it seemed that the ECB would continue to provide funding for this hole. What was really worrying for it, however, was that the November solution had not taken account of this particular issue. In January 2011 alone some €17 billion of deposits had been withdrawn.

The 18 March meeting hosted by Noonan and Howlin did not go particularly well. Ireland got little of what it wanted and precious little public support from the troika afterwards. EU Commissioner Olli Rehn, who had previously shown some inclination towards a reduction in the rate of interest being charged on Ireland's new loans, said, 'No, I don't,' when asked if he shared the view that the bank rescue was in danger of becoming unsustainable. ECB President Jean-Claude Trichet told the European Parliament that Ireland could carry both its government debt and its bank debt. 'Ireland can do it, Ireland will do it,' he said. The German finance minister, Wolfgang Schäuble, said that Ireland would have to make 'proposals' if it wanted a reduction on the interest rates. 'When someone wants to change a contract which he has just agreed to, then he has to think not only about what the other party to the contract should change, but he must also come up with suggestions about what he can change himself,' he said.

But Noonan persisted in refusing to budge on corporation tax, calling it 'a red line issue'. 'We have no axe to grind about the effective tax rates available in other countries but merely wish to point out that the effective rates are more material to the debate on tax competition than headline rates,' Noonan said. He sought to shift attention from our headline tax rate of 12.5 per cent to the effective rate, which is what companies actually paid once they had made all the legally allowed deductions. He claimed that the effective corporation tax rate in Ireland was about 11.9 per cent and that the French, who allowed a massive range of deductions before applying a much higher headline rate, had an effective rate that was not much higher. He stopped just short of accusing the French of hypocrisy. 'If the debate is to continue I will be pushing that it takes into account the effective rates rather than the nominal rates because nobody pays the nominal rates as far as I see,' said Noonan.

There were rumours that Ireland might offer a compromise that involved taking part in the setting up of CCCTB. This provided

Fianna Fáil with a rare opportunity to seize the high ground. 'The government cannot leave the door open for participation in CCCTB. Two weeks ago, Taoiseach Enda Kenny himself said he opposed plans to establish a CCCTB and described this proposal as "the harmonization of tax rates by the back door", and not up for discussion,' Brian Lenihan said. 'Fianna Fáil believes this is a Trojan horse and will ultimately lead to tax harmonization. We have vehemently opposed the introduction of CCCTB over many years on the basis that we believe it would have very serious consequences for foreign and direct investment, a cornerstone of our economic policy.'

Kenny headed back to his second summit knowing that EU finance ministers, including Noonan, had agreed to support a permanent new €700 billion bailout fund that would have the power to introduce debt restructuring from 2013. While the European Financial Stability Facility did not have the power to buy the bonds of a bailout recipient at a discount to their issue value – which would be a backdoor mechanism for achieving debt write-down – the prospect of its 2013 successor, the European Stability Mechanism (ESM), having this power was live now, which would create a situation in which sovereign default, to the detriment of private investors, could happen.

It was claimed that this would be for debt issued after 2013, but the markets none the less took it as a sign that there could be default on existing debt from countries like Ireland. On 23 March the yield on existing Irish two-year bonds – government bonds, not bank bonds – reached 10.7 per cent. This level was an indication that many traders feared that Irish government bonds would not be repaid and they sought this high rate of interest to compensate for the risk of Irish default.

The summit was meant to resolve all this. Tougher budget discipline rules, structural economic reforms and a strengthened bailout mechanism were supposed to end the crisis for the euro and provide the political cover that Merkel needed in Germany. Unfortunately, it was dominated by a new economic and political crisis in Portugal. Contagion had taken hold before the medicine could be administered. It followed Ireland in applying to the IMF and EFSF for financial help, as its bond yields made borrowing on the markets impossible.

This all meant that Kenny had a much quieter summit than he had anticipated. Ireland was not regarded as an issue of concern at this time. This suited him. He knew that he wasn't going to get anything so he was spared the political embarrassment of rejection. He also knew that a week later another crisis would have to be dealt with: the results of those stress tests on the banks would be known and finally the cost to the Irish State and its citizens of rescuing its bust private-sector banks might become clear.

35. Pillars of Society

Six months after Brian Lenihan announced what he said would be absolutely the final bill for sorting out the banking sector, his successor Michael Noonan had to do so again, making it the fifth 'final bill' that had been presented.

With a combination of sorrow and anger, on 31 March 2011, Noonan revealed that another €24 billion of state money would be required in new capital for four of the six institutions covered by the bank guarantee. It had been known from the time of the November deal with the troika that at least another €10 billion would be required – and that no more money was to be given to Anglo Irish Bank or Irish Nationwide – but this was still €14 billion more than had been expected. This would bring the total bill to the state in new capital for the banks to over €70 billion. For a country already running a deficit of nearly €20 billion per annum this additional requirement threatened to be ruinous.

A shamefaced Patrick Honohan had to admit that Ireland had suffered the most expensive banking rescue in history. 'This is the best way forward, but there are no good ways forward,' the Central Bank boss said. He admitted that it 'doesn't score high on fairness' but that not attempting to achieve this 'would be biting off nose to spite face'.

The outgoing government had admitted in a formal letter to its lenders the previous November what it had already been told by them, particularly by the ECB: that we didn't need a domestic banking system which, at its peak, had been five times the size of the overall economy.

In admitting that a 'fundamental downsizing and reorganization of our banking system is essential', the outgoing government promised that it would raise the capital standards that were currently in place to protect against losses as quickly as possible, recognize those losses for what they really were and get on with investing the new capital to meet the new standards.

The Central Bank called in expensive outside consultants – led by an American firm called BlackRock – to run the rule over all the loans on the books of the banks. They concentrated on the likelihood of individual mortgage holders being able to meet their repayments on homes and investments. At last, the elephant in the room was being addressed.

In addition to the disastrous loans to developers and speculators, the banks had lent recklessly to the purchasers of houses and apartments. There were two main problems. One was that borrowers did not have the means to repay once interest rates went up or, as unfortunately had happened to many, their incomes had fallen, either by way of losing a job or having pay reduced at a time when taxes went up. The second was that in a number of cases the banks had guaranteed their own losses by offering long-term loans at rates that had been attractive enough to win custom; however, once the method that banks had used to borrow money was no longer affordable to them, they found themselves locked into ongoing losses. The banks had been hoist by their own petard, in the form of the once highly popular and ubiquitous tracker mortgages. These guaranteed that the borrower would pay only a set margin over the prevailing ECB base interest rate, even though the banks themselves were funding these loans on a short-term basis on the money markets, and were thus subject to higher money-market rates. Now that the price of such finance to the banks had become prohibitive, their losses were inevitable. How the Central Bank and the ECB had ever allowed such a model to develop in the first place was not a question that was answered.

BlackRock assessed about 700,000 mortgages, both for residential and investment properties, looking at the likelihood of loans being repaid if the economy deteriorated further. It calculated how many of the loans would be repaid and how many were locked into what were unprofitable interest rates for the lender. BlackRock then used this information to work out how much money the banks should put away in capital to cover these eventualities. Next it looked at how much more money the banks would need to enable them to resume lending to businesses and consumers for everyday activities, which, after all, was the reason why they had been rescued in the first place.

The consultants estimated that Irish house prices had fallen by an average of 38 per cent from their peak at the end of 2006, although clearly regional variations and other factors meant that some property values had fallen by far more. It was assumed that the fall in prices had not concluded and would continue apace until the end of 2012 at least, culminating in an average fall of 55 per cent to 60 per cent in what it called a worst-case scenario, where unemployment would peak at 15.8 per cent (compared to the 14.7 per cent it was at already). Likely losses over the life of the mortgages were estimated to be €16.9 billion under this scenario, and the banks would need new capital to cover those losses. But they would need even more to cover losses by the banks on the sale of overseas assets – one of the demands that had been made by the ECB to reduce their size – and to be able to function as normal lenders in the Irish market again. A decision was taken that our remaining banks – not including Anglo Irish and Irish Nationwide, which were to be shut – required €24 billion in fresh capital. The Irish banks would be among the best-capitalized in Europe, even higher than some of the Swiss banks, all at the expense of the Irish citizen. It would sort out our banks once and for all and stop speculation about their future, or at least so we were told.

But the plan for the banks went further than just finding the new capital. They all had to 'downsize', which meant selling assets such as overseas businesses and profitable loans – which would, in theory, make it easier for them to secure a level of deposits that was more in keeping with the aggregate size of the loans they had made. The regulators had looked at the loans-to-deposits ratios at the banks and resolved to reduce them. Selling under such pressure would almost certainly lead to additional losses and increase the banks' massive capital requirements. It didn't seem to make much sense. But the ECB was determined to reduce the size of the Irish banks, so as to limit their financing needs and – most importantly of all from the ECB's point of view – decrease their dependency on it for day-to-day cash.

Possibly the most interesting example of the new discipline was to be found at Irish Life & Permanent, a company that had not lent to property developers, avoided taking any state money up until now and retained its place on the Irish stock-market. Its Permanent TSB (PTSB) subsidiary was the biggest mortgage lender during the boom, issuing about one in five of all mortgages. It had aggressively targeted not just first-time buyers but those who wanted to 'invest' in the establishment of property portfolios, houses and apartments that would be rented to those who couldn't afford to buy, the so-called 'buy-to-let' market.

However, it had done this at a pace that was well beyond its own resources, giving itself a loans-to-deposits ratio of a whopping 200 per cent: in other words, it had lent €200 for every €100 it had on deposit and had had to borrow the balance. This did not compare favourably with the industry average of about 165 per cent and the new requirement of 122.5 per cent for the overall Irish banking sector.

If that wasn't bad enough, PTSB's financing structure was a mess. Nearly two thirds of all of the mortgages it had advanced were trackers, with many pegged at 1 per cent above the European Central Bank rate. That meant that those borrowers were paying 2 per cent at a time when the bank was paying about 5 per cent on the money it had borrowed to finance these loans. The loss to the bank would be around €400 million a year, with little or nothing it could do about it unless borrowers could somehow be persuaded to give up their trackers. Suddenly, it was decided that IL&P needed €4 billion in new capital. Some of this could be raised by the sale of Irish Life, the assurance business that accounted for 30 per cent of the life and pensions market, by way of a stock-market flotation or trade sale, although that was unlikely to cover the entire bill. IL&P was also told to reduce the size of the loans it had made to customers by €15.7 billion. The future existence of PTSB itself was now a subject for debate.

Indeed, it was decided that €72.6 billion of loans had to be removed from the books of the Irish banks by the end of 2013. Bank of Ireland was told to remove €32.6 billion and AIB €19.4 billion. The Central Bank assumed the banks would make losses of €13.2 billion in selling these so-called non-core assets. This determined the amount of capital that each institution had to raise: Bank of Ireland was told that it now needed €5.2 billion in new capital, AIB €13.3 billion and EBS €1.5 billion.

There was more. The government endorsed the 'consolidation' of the banking sector. Where there had been six there would now be two. Anglo and Irish Nationwide would close; EBS would be merged with AIB to form a second banking 'pillar' to rival Bank of Ireland. A decision had yet to be made about what to do with PTBS after Irish Life was sold. This came as a complete shock to EBS. It had spent ten months negotiating with a group of private-equity investors, led by Dublin's Cardinal Group and including American investment funds Carlyle and W. L. Ross, before persuading the NTMA to get involved on behalf of the state. Suddenly EBS was told not just that the NTMA had withdrawn from the negotiations but that the government had ordered that it was to become a subsidiary of AIB.

In addition, the two remaining 'standing pillars' of AIB and Bank of Ireland were themselves to be split into core and non-core banks. The core banks would focus on lending to businesses and consumers in Ireland only. The so-called 'non-core' would have three years to sell or close their international businesses.

The Central Bank's recommendations on the required capital injections into the four lenders were based on 'expediency' and delivering the best possible 'net gain' for Ireland, Honohan said. 'I don't want to end up saying it's a fantastic investment for the government,' he admitted. He said that the 'two-pillar approach' would mean that the banks could actually start lending into the economy again. Having only two banks and both of those in public ownership wasn't ideal, he said, but the system had to restart somewhere.

The only crumb of comfort that Honohan offered was that at least €3 billion of the €24 billion in new capital would come back to the state over the short term and that the government might get other returns in the long run. But he had to admit that almost all of the extra capital would have to come out of the state's coffers, even if Bank of Ireland engaged in an immediate and frantic exercise to attract private investment to avoid the same fate as AIB: nationalization. 'I don't want to prevent anybody from raising capital in the market,' Honohan said. 'But at this scale of capital we will see major-ity state ownership of all institutions. I suppose that's only realistic.'

Part of the thinking was that the recapitalized banks would be suf-ficiently attractive to allow for subsequent resale, possibly to foreign owners. But such investors would have to be confident about the prospects for the Irish economy for that to happen. The Department of Finance put in place targets for lending to different sectors of the economy based on Central Bank estimates that the demand for credit up to 2014 would be €16.5 billion. The idea was that the two pillars would have nearly double that amount available to them for new loans.

It seemed like a case of back to the future: the old AIB–Bank of Ireland duopoly would be re-established. Borrowers would have few choices and face higher prices for loans and services: domestic bank-ing would contract, and many foreign lenders had already either abandoned Ireland or slimmed down their businesses enormously. The irony was that, while frenetic competition had been bad for the economy – because it led to reckless lending – we would now have not enough of it. The hope was that Ulster Bank – owned by Royal Bank of Scotland – would fill the gap now that it had decided not to abandon the Republic of Ireland (as had seemed possible in 2009 and 2010). It had stayed but its lending was exceptionally cautious.

Noonan needed to focus on the ability of the new banks to lend into the economy, because his announcement had been humiliating for the new government, within just weeks of its establishment. It had failed to burn the bondholders and, just like its predecessor, this new government was committing Ireland to meeting the full cost of repaying the bank creditors. The election promises had been empty, as most observers had suspected: Noonan could do no better than Lenihan in that regard.

It was a dreadful moment for the new government. The former Fianna Fáil-led coalition was punished for many things but chief among them was its refusal to reduce the excessive cost of the bank rescue by forcing bondholders to accept the repayment of only a por-tion of what they were owed. Fine Gael and Labour had inflated the likelihood that they would succeed where the outgoing government had failed. The new government learnt an early and painful lesson about the extent of its powerlessness, that it was not able to re-establish Irish sovereignty at will.

The only contribution that the bondholders would make was the €5 billion that had already been taken from the junior bondholders at Anglo Irish Bank and Irish Nationwide, and possibly some more from junior bondholders at the other four banks. Noonan admitted that all he was left with in relation to the senior bondholders was the hope that the ECB's policy might change when it came to the senior unguaranteed debt of €7 billion left in Anglo and Irish Nationwide.

His claim that a minority of the ECB's governing council had come around to the idea of allowing Ireland to impose haircuts on some of the senior bank debt, and that he'd received public support for that from Axel Weber, the outgoing governor of the German Bundesbank, didn't matter a damn. Pragmatism ruled Noonan now. 'We would like to burden-share on senior unguaranteed bonds but the ECB, at present, will not change their policy,' he said. It was no longer 'reasonable nor logical' to go after senior bondholders in AIB and Bank of Ireland, because those banks would need more credit from the bond markets in the years to come. The minister for public expenditure, Brendan Howlin, illustrated the changed Labour position when he admitted that burning the bondholders in AIB and Bank of Ireland would 'be invidious' to their securing further capital.

There had been other failures on the new government's part. It had been a long shot but its attempt to persuade its eurozone partners to allow the EFSF bailout fund to become an investor in bank recapitalizations, by way of providing capital when it was not available on the market, had not succeeded either.

Nor had its campaign to get the ECB to switch from a system of financing the Irish banks on a fortnightly basis to a much longer-term basis. On the last weekend of March, before the announcement of the results of the stress tests and the latest recapitalization of the banks, there had been reports in the newspapers, based on leaks from 'informed sources', that the ECB was working on an emergency plan to provide Ireland with €60 billion in liquidity loans, which would be announced in conjunction with the new bank rescue plan. It simply didn't happen. This failure was seized upon by Lenihan, now Fianna Fáil's finance spokesman in opposition. He said it was very important to realize in dealings with the ECB that 'this is an autonomous institution', not one that is 'subject to direction or megaphone diplomacy from national governments'.

Taoiseach Enda Kenny was forced to respond and began a trend of sucking up to ECB boss Jean-Claude Trichet that would intensify in the coming months. He said that Trichet was aware that medium-term funding of the banks by the ECB was of great importance. 'Mr Trichet understands that very well. He cannot give a direction that this will happen. He is subject to the direction of the board. We have made a case that Ireland does want to deal with this problem and we want to see a solution come as soon as possible,' he said.

The *Financial Times*, consistently on the side of those who said that Ireland could not and should not be required to cover the repayment of all senior bondholders at the banks, suggested that the new Irish government had probably pushed too hard – and too publicly – for the special ECB liquidity facility. While it emphasized that Ireland needed an alternative to the way money from the ECB was being delivered, it also pointed out that the ECB did not want to be seen to be responding to political pressure; there were legal and technical issues too.

The ECB did do something for Ireland, though. It confirmed that even if the status of Irish debt and government-guaranteed bank debt was downgraded by the ratings agencies, as would happen in the days that followed, the ECB would still accept it as collateral for loans to Irish banks. That was an important concession, but the essential point remained the same: many outside forces controlled Ireland but none had the power of the ECB.

36.   The More Things Change . . .

'Tuesday, 30 September 2008, will go down as the blackest day in Ireland since the Civil War broke out,' Finance Minister Michael Noonan declared on 31 March 2011, the day he was left to announce the latest clearing-up exercise arising from the decision to guarantee that the state would pay everything that the banks couldn't.

Noonan wanted to lay blame before accepting responsibility for what he was about to do now as a result. His predecessor, Brian Lenihan, tried to dismiss Noonan's analysis as a 'rhetorical flourish', but the substance of what was offered by Noonan was correct. The decision made in the dead of night two and a half years earlier had defined and shaped almost everything that was to follow. The generous may have described the initiative as a gamble made in good faith, but it was a failed punt that had succeeded only in making an already grave situation far worse. It had brought about the surrender of Ireland's sovereignty, which would define and restrain the country for at least a generation and possibly longer.

It was a world away from Lenihan's much quoted boast to the Leinster Society of Chartered Accountants lunch in Dublin, on 23 October 2008, that the guarantee was 'the cheapest bailout in the world . . . so far'. Now his lame defence of that statement was his inclusion of the words 'so far'. Just as pertinent was another quote he had delivered after the introduction of the guarantee: 'I do not see a hazard or an exposure to the decision that I have arrived at.'

Noonan said things now that were at odds with his own previous declarations, especially those that had been offered the previous November. 'I want to be clear for the benefit of our people and of market participants, that we are committed to the EU–IMF programme . . . We will respect the overall fiscal parameters of the programme and where adjustments to the programme affect these, we will make appropriate offsetting adjustments, and it is clear from contacts to date that there is already a good level of understanding between us and the funding parties in this regard.'

Lenihan scoffed at the fact that Noonan had 'fully supported the IMF/EU/ECB agreement and the whole text of the speech was the same speech I would have delivered in the same circumstances'. But he did not offer unequivocal support himself. 'The standard used in the stress tests was a very severe one . . . I don't believe the economy is in for as rough a ride as that. If we are, God help us all,' he said. 'The big question is: is it right that we pay all the debts of these banks? And the second question is, and we've moved definitely into this territory: can the state stay afloat if we do so?' He did not appear to appreciate the irony of his asking these questions, but as he offered them the yields on government debts were rising, just as those on bank bonds were falling. The markets showed where investors thought things were heading: the banks were being protected at the expense of the state.

United Left Alliance and Socialist Party TD Joe Higgins said Noonan was repeating the policy of the previous government, whereby 'the taxpayers, the working people and the poor in this country are going to continue to pay the bad gambling debts of the major European banks'.

The new government seemed somewhat disconcerted that the size of its mandate – and the rejection of Fianna Fáil – had not brought about a major change in European attitudes towards Ireland. They hardly seemed to notice or, if they did, care. The decision of the Irish people to reject the Lisbon Treaty, in effect a quasi-constitution for the European Union, during the first referendum vote in 2008 had had a significant and lasting effect, as was feared at the time by many Irish Europhiles in positions of administrative influence and in the media. 'How can we be stupid?' was the refrain of those who believed that all things European were good for Ireland, that our engagement with the European Union had transformed us economically, socially and culturally. Our economic straits, however, strengthened the arguments of those who believed that, even if much of that was true, we should not bow to Europe automatically.

Enda Kenny's stated desire to rebuild Ireland's relationship with the EU may have been prompted by the type of comments made by Irish woman Catherine Day, the European Commission's secretary general at the end of March 2011. 'The perception in Brussels was that the more prosperous Ireland became, the more arrogant Ireland became and the less it felt it needed to invest in all of these things,' said Day, the EU's most powerful civil servant. 'Now Ireland needs Europe and Europe is there for Ireland. But people also expect just a little bit of personal investment in the whole thing,' she continued, as if Irish people had not already experienced a dramatic and sudden contraction in their living standards because of being forced to endure the cost of the banking rescue.

Day also predicted that if Ireland insisted on keeping its corporation-tax rate unchanged, it would have to find other sources of tax revenue instead. 'Every country can decide its own tax policy, but that is not the end of the story,' she said. 'So if Ireland decides it wants to keep a low corporation tax, it has to deal with the deficit in some other way and we will be saying: "Okay, that's your choice. If you don't deal with it that way, how are you going to do it?"'

Asked whether the commission can force a state to change its policy, Day said, 'No, we can't and we wouldn't . . . We can't make Ireland change that, but . . . perhaps public spending will have to be slashed even more severely. But those are national choices that we will not make . . . But what we will do, because it is our job to ensure that the euro remains strong, is to say that Ireland and every other member state has to have a credible path to putting its deficit back under control . . . It is for us to say what would work in a European context if a government doesn't get its public finances under control.'

However, Day may have been as guilty as other senior European figures when it came to misreading what was going on. Ireland's crisis may have been exacerbated by the public-finances problems, but it wasn't caused by them – and the only solution lay in fixing the banks. Day said the European financial crisis was 'a crisis of individual countries in the euro but not the euro', which was a highly debatable interpretation too, to put it mildly. She might have been playing politics, but if she believed that genuinely – and if it was indicative of the dominant thinking in Europe – the euro's problems, and those of the European Union, including Ireland, were even greater than had been thought. She also said that the issue of burden-sharing with bondholders was down to the ECB to decide; again, this was true technically, given the independence of the ECB, but only up to a point. It ignored the political realities of what had gone on over the previous year.

Máire Geoghegan-Quinn, the Irish EU commissioner, who had been appointed by Brian Cowen, was another Brussels insider who came forward to defend the institutions that now paid her wages. She claimed the commission was not 'dictating the pace' to the government on its approach to the public finances, and she also insisted that all taxation rates were for the government to decide. 'There is this view abroad, I don't know where it's coming from, that the commission is dictating to Ireland as to what it should do. Nothing could be further from the truth. There is a very, very open transparent cooperation and working relationship on both sides which is absolutely essential. It's essential from the eurozone point of view, it's working very well. It's very important to re-emphasize that any decision in relation to taxation is a sovereign decision of the member state and Ireland will decide what policy it's going to pursue in relation to taxation.' While this was true, it ignored the fact that enormous pressure could be placed on a country to make a decision it didn't want – as had happened to Ireland over the IMF/EU/ECB deal. Any change would be portrayed as being of a country's own choosing even if in reality it had been browbeaten into it.

Figures from outside the elected Irish system became engaged in the public debate. Former Taoiseach John Bruton had championed Ireland's adoption of the euro – memorably at one stage enthusing that it would give us the benefit of 'permanently lower interest rates', as though that would necessarily always be a good thing – and enjoyed a long spell as the EU ambassador to Washington. At a speech he made at the London School of Economics shortly after Fine Gael returned to power, he said, 'As Irish people we should think once, twice, three times, a hundred times before breaking our word. We have got to be realistic. We have to recognize who we are. We depend on other people. We must not let them down, even though it is hard,'

However, subtly Bruton seemed to indicate a shift of position by the Irish government; even if he did not represent it, his position as a former leader of the party now in government, with his brother Richard a member of that cabinet, meant that Europe would take note of what he said. He hinted that Europe owed Ireland more than it was giving in return, just as Patrick Honohan implied in another interview that Ireland had 'taken a bullet' for the stability of the euro.

'Irish taxpayers, in taking on in 2008 the private liabilities of the Irish banks to other European banks, are now helping to stabilize the situation of European banks, and of the European banking system,' said Bruton. 'If the central bank of a country was allowing its banking sector to grow to 300 per cent of its GDP, surely the ECB would have seen the dangers in that and used its powers? From 2000 on, British, German, Belgian, French banks, and banks of other EU countries lent irresponsibly to the Irish banks in the hope that they too could profit from the then obtaining Irish construction bubble.' He pointed out that these lenders 'were supervised by their home central banks, and by the ECB', which 'seemingly raised no objection to this lending'.

Bruton said, diplomatically, that the ECB had failed completely in its oversight role of its Irish subsidiary and had watched as French and German banks pumped loans towards our Irish banks. So, while our banks were punished for making bad loans, which was fair enough, the ECB ensured that the bigger banks from powerful countries remained unscathed despite their stupidity. It is undoubtedly true that we elected the governments that pump-primed the housing bubble, failed to regulate their own banks and gave the calamitous bank guarantee itself. And, in consequence, we listened to lots of posturing about moral hazard and how the borrowers in Ireland would have to repay every cent of what they'd received in loans. But that didn't hold for the French and German banks: they were being shielded from their own bad investment decisions. The hypocrisy of this was staggering, yet we were supposed to take lectures from the French and Germans about our corporation-tax rate.

Bruton used his argument to bolster Ireland's claim to retain its own corporation-tax rate. He said Ireland was the second-most open economy in the world and trusted by international investors because it had 'kept its word' on corporation taxes and other issues. According to the government, Bruton was speaking in a personal capacity and not on its behalf, but it must have been pleased, and other smaller countries had some sympathy with us for the way we were being bullied.

What those countries had less tolerance for was the way we spent the money we borrowed, especially on social-welfare and public services. Our citizens may need the welfare payments they receive in what remains a very expensive country in which to live, but our neighbours compared those payments to what they got themselves, without taking account of the relatively limited purchasing power of that money in Ireland. Many other countries that felt they had much lower standards of living than we did, particularly in Eastern Europe, were inclined to demand that we address these payments before things were made easier for us through a change in the terms of our loans.

The same went for public-sector pay rates: the Europeans didn't care that many of our young nurses, gardaí, teachers and doctors may have massive mortgages that had to be repaid out of already seriously lowered income. They just compared the rates of pay across Europe, regarded ours as out of kilter, even after the savage cuts imposed in recent budgets upon public servants, and said they were not going to help us any further until we dealt with that. It became very difficult for our officials and politicians to argue that we had exhausted all means of closing the gap between revenues and expenditure – and that we needed to borrow massively as a result – when we still appeared to be looking after ourselves rather well in comparison with other countries.

But the issue of massive private-sector debt often was overlooked in this discourse. Many politicians were past the age where that was a major issue for them, as their mortgages had been paid and their pensions were coming to them from the public pot. But it was the present generation that was bearing the costs of the bust banks as well as their own excessive loans. Nobody was interested in talking about bailing out the people who'd been most affected by all of this. The state had no money to do so and knew it was pointless talking to the ECB with that end in view.

Nobody in Frankfurt seemed keen to share Bruton's views about the partial responsibility of the ECB for creating our mess. Nor was the ECB impressed by, or concerned about, claims that it had to bear some responsibility for its own failings when it came to Ireland – for not properly overseeing the German, French and other banks that had lent recklessly to Irish banks. For example, in 2007 German and Austrian banks bought 37 per cent of the five-year bonds issued by Anglo Irish Bank. Ironically the entire bond issue was sold into the market on Anglo's behalf by French banking giant BNP Paribas. None of that mattered now.

A senior Irish official dealing with the ECB told me during interviews for this book that 'Nobody in Brussels likes us any more and nobody respects us either.' He regarded this as a deadly combination for a small peripheral region that has traded politically for years on its reputation as a convinced and able servant of the European project. Although it was not really an issue for the ECB, the first Lisbon Treaty referendum rejection had done enormous damage to Ireland's reputation at all of the institutions in Europe. Its passing of the referendum on the second go did not repair that.

The only way in which Ireland was of interest to the ECB was in what it would cost it, and it was taking on that debt only because ignoring it might affect the bigger economies within the ECB's remit. Ireland itself was expendable. It was to be used as a fire-break, devastated if need be to stop the financial fires crossing to Continental Europe, particularly Spain.

Spain was the ninth largest economy in the world – which meant much of its wealth was real – but it had a property bubble. Because of that wealth, the losses arising from the bubble were easier to hide, whereas with Ireland 60 per cent of all bank lending was property related, which was impossible to hide.

To the ECB the potential financial consequences of a run on the Spanish banks were frightening, given the costs that had already been incurred in propping up the much smaller Irish system. Indeed, analysts such as Professor Morgan Kelly offered the opinion that the sole purpose of the Irish deal was to provide a warning for the Spanish of the horrors that faced that country if it should reach the point of needing an IMF/EU/ECB rescue. Evidence from the Irish situation showed that the deal made no provision for Ireland to repair its public finances sufficiently for borrowing to resume on the bond markets at reasonable rates.

If anything, it seemed as if a dose of punishment was being meted to put the Irish back in their place. The profit margin on the money to be lent to Ireland was 2.9 percentage points: this was the gap between the price Ireland was being charged and the actual cost to the lenders of the money, which meant a really good profit. There was a double benefit to the EU in this: its members profited on the finance they were providing and they ensured that their favoured banks were bailed out.

Not everyone on the ECB governing council agreed that this was fair or workable. German Axel Weber said it was a mistake to make taxpayers liable for all bank risks, rather than obliging private investors to shoulder some losses. But he was in the minority, and it probably cost him his chance to succeed Trichet as the ECB chairman.

All of this raised questions as to why Ireland did not leave the euro, to re-establish its old currency, the pound. An independent country would be able to devalue its currency, making holdings of it less attractive, but giving the country, particularly an exporter, the opportunity to pitch export prices at a much more attractive rate – assuming of course that angry creditor countries did not boycott its goods and services. If a country could operate a balance of payments – in other words keep its now more expensive imports lower than its exports – the benefits could be enormous. It was something that we had done in the past – most recently in 1993 – and in some respects it set the template for the initial boom years of the Celtic Tiger. Exiting the euro would give the country an immediate boost, or so it would appear.

Indeed, Lombard Street Research, the London-based economic consultancy, issued a policy paper in early 2011 setting out the advantages of leaving the euro. It highlighted what it described as a combination of 'mismatched interest-rate policy, lack of structural reform, misaligned labour markets and divergent tax regimes – not to mention rich-country resentment of bailouts' that could make leaving the euro more attractive to some countries than staying in. All that was necessary, the report's author said, was for the 'pain of EMU membership to exceed either the benefits or at least the pain of leaving'.

Leaving a currency union is an exceptionally difficult thing to do. It has to be accomplished suddenly and completely by surprise. If a hint has been given prior to the announcement, bond prices will soar and there will be a massive withdrawal of deposits from banks earlier than would be desirable (and the aim would be to somehow prevent any flight at all). Yet there must also be a plan to mint a new currency – its design, manufacture and distribution. How the government would supply enough new money to the banks would be a moot point. The cost of our debts, unless we refused to repay them, would soar upon devaluation. Not repaying them would probably mean not being able to borrow from anywhere. Inflation would also surge after a devaluation, and interest rates on new and existing loans would rocket.

The possible trick for Ireland would be to honour its sovereign debt but renege on the stupidly acquired bank debt and hope that lenders would accept that, even if they didn't like it. The problem was that defaulting economies usually go to the IMF for help in such circumstances. We would hardly be able to do that, after having borrowed from the IMF along with the EU and the ECB. A default involving non-payment of existing debt to our lenders of last resort – now that they had replaced our original lenders – would be unprecedented.

But the ECB was screwing Ireland in other ways: putting up interest rates, just a quarter of one per cent at a time but enough to cause major problems. Early in 2011 Lombard Street Research noted the build-up of inflationary pressures in the eurozone, but warned that if the ECB chose to fight that inflation with higher rates, the whole Mediterranean fringe of the euro area, including Italy, would be condemned to depression. The same would be true of Ireland.

This had the potential to be catastrophic to Ireland's efforts to rebuild its economy, with more expensive money dampening consumer demand further and, more importantly, tightening whatever profit margins companies enjoyed. Whereas Ireland had suffered during the early part of the century when rates were often as much as 4 per cent lower than where we needed them to be, the last thing its banks needed now was a higher cost for the money it had to borrow and lend. It was further grist to the mill for those who believed that the ECB was indifferent to the creation of Irish banks that were fit for purpose and that could lend to Irish households and small- and medium-sized enterprises. Who among the big foreign banks would buy into AIB and Bank of Ireland if their chances of returning to profit were further undermined by such ECB actions? A sale of AIB and Bank of Ireland to international rivals clearly would remove the need for the ECB to provide emergency liquidity and for the state to invest in further share capital, and yet the ECB was making this harder to achieve.

Nouriel Roubini – the Nobel Prize-winning professor of economics at New York University who had been nicknamed Doctor Doom two years before the crash he had regularly predicted – was unimpressed by what was being done to Ireland. 'I'm not sure that it's going to be enough and putting all the losses of the banks on the balance sheet of the government and eventually breaking the back of the government . . . it's not the right solution.'

Roubini said that a better option would be to take the senior secured and unsecured debt of the banks and swap it into shares, 'reduce it, convert it into equity so you recapitalize the banks that way and you're not adding further losses to the balance sheet of the government. Otherwise, you're going to have not only a banking crisis, but also a sovereign debt crisis.

'At some point, we need to recognize that these are not liquidity problems of government or banks, but solvency issues, and where there are solvency issues, all the market-orientated but coercive restructurings of public and private financial debt is necessary to avoid this insolvency.'

Back in Ireland even economists who were regarded as being on the right of the economic debate – and who would have recommended austerity to bring the public finances towards balance – had come to condemn the ECB and the November deal. Colm McCarthy had drawn up both the plans for the downsizing of the public sector, to save over €5 billion annually, and the strategy for selling state assets to raise cash. He advocated reducing the exchequer deficit swiftly by way of spending cuts and he did not favour bailing out homeowners who had excessive mortgages. Yet, writing in the *Sunday Independent* in early April 2011, McCarthy said the IMF/EU/ECB deal 'has failed to resolve the banking crisis and has continued the policy of favouring bond investors in failed banks. It has also created a widespread perception that the ECB is not greatly concerned about the prospect of sovereign default in eurozone member states including Greece, Ireland and Portugal, all of whom are currently excluded from sovereign debt markets and with no visible re-entry strategy.'

He admitted that by November 2010 Ireland had already been shut out from the markets, and that as a deal with the IMF/EU/ECB was coming anyway, 'no damage was done by precipitating the inevitable.' He said that this made it look as if our government 'was in denial about the scale of the liquidity crisis and a few sharp prods helped to encourage a more realistic course'.

'But hasty entry into an unfavourable and unimplementable deal is a different matter and the behaviour of the ECB has created resentment in Ireland. It appears that policy is being dictated to an elected government by a remote and unaccountable financial authority and that the policy is not self-evidently a good one.'

He said it was being assumed by Europe that the Irish financial situation could be resolved solely through a further tightening of budgetary policy. 'This in turn assumes that there is no risk of sovereign default and that all debts can be paid, which implies that the markets have got it wrong,' he said. 'Alternatively, if the markets are right and there is a sovereign default, then that's just too bad.'

Writing about Greece and Portugal as much as Ireland, McCarthy argued that the 'absence of a visible exit strategy places their governments in an impossible position. They cannot fashion a credible political message for their electorates, offering a credible probability of success in exchange for more fiscal pain. It is not politically viable to tell people that further large tax increases are coming, along with more big cuts in expenditure and no bank credit, with no prospect of economic recovery and no end in sight. The "rescue" package cannot be sold as a kind of economic black hole from which there is no escape.'

McCarthy said the original obligation to repay the bank bond-holders was undertaken imprudently by our government 'in the belief that the banking problems were much smaller than they actually are. The result is that Irish taxpayers have already transferred substantial sums to investors who made losing bets on Irish bank bonds and they are expected to make further transfers in the future. The perception that the costs of the European banking crisis are being borne disproportionately by Ireland is corrosive of public support for desirable policy reform.'

But it was to get worse. The simple dynamics of debt require growth if a country is to break out of this debt trap. It becomes more difficult to grow if the government is sucking money out of the economy. The new government decided to implement and endorse, to all intents and purposes, the plan its predecessor had been forced to put into place, to reduce the deficit by €15 billion over four budgets, sort out the banks according to the ECB dictate, and, if possible, help to restore business competitiveness through the imposition of cost cuts where possible.

Yet it was faced with a dilemma, in that it thought the plan unworkable. Worse, it feared that it would drag the economy into deeper contraction and deflation, and would not create the circumstances in which the state, or its dependent banks, could return to the bond markets to borrow at affordable rates. This was a damning indictment of the haste with which we were forced into the deal and put the IMF in particular in an awkward position: it had disagreed fundamentally with much of the deal and itself been forced into something that could fail. That wasn't supposed to be how the IMF did its business.

In April the new government published two important documents. The first, entitled *Ireland Stability Programme Update April 2011*, set out revised forecasts for the economy and public finances. It predicted growth of 0.8 per cent for 2011, annual growth of 3 per cent a year from 2013 to 2015, and gross government debt peaking at 118 per cent of GDP in 2013. The growth estimates were lower than those in the original document of November 2010. The April 2011 update estimated that our total tax take would return to €40 billion per annum but that one fifth of that would go in annual interest payments.

The second document, which had been signed by Noonan and Honohan, was sent to Trichet at the ECB; Juncker at ECOFIN; Strauss-Kahn at the IMF; and Rehn and a Hungarian, György Matolcsy, who had been assigned a particularly important role in monitoring us, at the European Commission. It undertook to give legal effect to the austerity measures that had been forced upon us, and was thus another stage of the surrender: confirming the dramatic downsizing of the banking system in a way that diminished its ability to help the Irish economy grow, and prioritizing the use of money to repay European creditors. NAMA was also given just over two and a half years to get rid of 25 per cent of its toxic loan book, a boon for buyers. There was a promise that a Fiscal Responsibility Bill would be introduced in 2011 to ensure that the externally imposed targets would be met. This meant that from 2012 onwards, there would be 'binding multiannual spending ceilings', copper-fastening the removal of our own ability to decide on fiscal measures that might help the economy.

These developments prompted the return of Morgan Kelly, with a near-3,000-word missive in *The Irish Times* on 7 May 2011 that dominated public discourse for many days afterwards.

Kelly claimed that the government was now 'on track to owe a quarter of a trillion euro by 2014' and that as a result 'a prolonged and chaotic national bankruptcy is becoming inevitable . . . Ireland is facing economic ruin.' Describing the November deal as an 'abject failure', Kelly argued that 'Ireland is so far into the red zone that marginal changes in the bailout terms can make no difference: we are going to be in the Hudson.'

Worse, he predicted that a bankruptcy would not purge or repair Ireland's finances. 'Given the other commitments of the Irish State [to the banks, NAMA, EU, ECB and IMF], for a bankruptcy to return government debt to a sustainable level, the holders of regular government bonds will have to be more or less wiped out.

Unfortunately, most Irish government bonds are held by Irish banks and insurance companies.'

Kelly also made a claim that kicked directly at the credibility of Honohan, accusing him of making the 'costliest mistake ever made by an Irish person' in underestimating the size of the bank losses and allowing the repayment of all bondholders, even those not under guarantee. He said, 'the real error was in sticking with the guarantee long after it had become clear that the bank losses were insupportable. Brian Lenihan's original decision to guarantee most of the bonds of Irish banks was a mistake, but a mistake so obvious and so ridiculous that it could easily have been reversed.'

Kelly continued that 'as a respected academic expert on banking crises, Honohan commanded the international authority to have announced that the guarantee had been made in haste and with poor information, and would be replaced by a restructuring where bonds in the banks would be swapped for shares.'

Kelly argued that, while the ECB did not want to rescue the Irish banks, 'it cannot let them collapse either and start a wave of panic that sweeps across Europe. This allows Ireland to walk away from the banking system by returning the NAMA assets to the banks, and withdrawing its promissory notes in the banks. The ECB can then learn the basic economic truth that if you lend €160 billion to insolvent banks backed by an insolvent state, you are no longer a creditor: you are the owner. At a stroke, the Irish Government can halve its debt to a survivable €110 billion. The ECB can do nothing to the Irish banks in retaliation without triggering a catastrophic panic in Spain and across the rest of Europe. The only way Europe can respond is by cutting off funding to the Irish Government.'

Kelly's answer to that dilemma was for the government to bring the budget immediately into balance, in other words raise taxes and cut spending by about €18 billion per annum immediately.

Honohan responded almost at once, going on the following day's RTÉ Radio *This Week* programme. Honohan had some regard for Kelly – much more so than for those whom he regarded as 'celebrity economists', who were addicted to the publicity their statements drew – and conceded that a lot of Kelly's analysis was 'absolutely spot on'. But he defended himself too and said there was no way that the bank guarantee could have been reversed. 'I took a lot of legal advice on this. There was no way of the government walking away from that very formal guarantee, endorsed by the Oireachtas,' he said. 'The government would have been treated as a bankrupt right away.'

Honohan also moved to deny the charge, previously stated implicitly by Brian Cowen, that there was a conflict of interest between heading the Central Bank and having a role on the governing council of the European Central Bank. 'Everything that was done here by me and by colleagues was on behalf of Ireland – I was playing for Ireland,' he said.

Honohan said the deal struck with the IMF and the European authorities last November was agreed in a hurry and designed to be altered. 'It was not a final solution,' he said. 'I would regard it as a holding operation, something to offer a window of time in which to get what could be sorted out within our own competence in Ireland sorted out. It's not the end of the story. Negotiations, discussions will continue with Europe for a long time to come as we know there are already discussions about the interest rate and so forth.'

He also said he was aware that our ability to keep trying to repay our debts depended on growth prospects. 'If things don't go well in terms of economic growth it will be much more difficult . . . in that case there will be a problem and in order to cope with that situation we need to think of better financial arrangements with Europe. The fact of the heavy debt and the growth of that debt is a serious problem and needs to be managed in discussion and in negotiation with our European partners. We need to think of risk-sharing arrangements that would ensure that the growth will come right.'

Honohan was not on his own in conducting the establishment retort to Kelly. John Bruton waded in again, using *The Irish Times* as a vehicle for the claim that if Ireland did as Kelly suggested, the European Central Bank itself might go bust and the euro could collapse. He claimed that Kelly had not considered the impact of what he was suggesting on other countries, and how they might react. 'If Ireland were to walk away from the EU–IMF deal, that would leave the European Central Bank itself with a huge shortfall. In fact the ECB might be insolvent. It might have to go to the member states to look for more capital. Emulating Ireland's example, they might refuse, and then the euro would collapse. If they even hesitated about recapitalizing the ECB, the resultant uncertainty could have a devastating effect on the world economy; an economy on which Ireland is more dependent for sales than most.'

There are those in Ireland who might not have cared about that or about Bruton's other major fear: 'In walking away from the EU–IMF deal, Ireland would be reneging on freely contracted debts to an EU institution and to other EU members, so we would also presumably be excluded from the benefits of EU membership.' He pointed out the many possible repercussions. 'For Ireland, the Common Agricultural Policy would disappear overnight, as might its access to EU markets for other products, at least until the debts it owed had been collected by other means. Professor Kelly, who is an economic historian, should look up what happened when we last walked away from international financial obligations. We refused to pay land annuities to the UK in the 1930s, and found some of our critical exports excluded from the UK market, with devastating effects in what came to be remembered as the Economic War.'

Bruton claimed that Ireland retained some influence and that it could be used 'to move the EU towards a more credible long-term strategy, one that allows countries such as Ireland time to restore their finances, and allows surplus countries such as Germany time to rebalance their economies towards consumption.

'But trying to achieve all that overnight, by holding a gun to everyone else's head as well as to our own, as the professor urges, seems to me to be needlessly reckless. But, like the advocates of default, I am afraid that the course he favours would destroy our international credibility instantly. It would involve immediate shock therapy for our economy, which could do much more harm than good. It would undermine trust.'

Trust was the currency with which Enda Kenny continued to try to trade with Europe. It was 'Europe Day' in a specially convened Dáil Éireann on the Monday after Kelly's latest missive. Ireland's fundamental interests would be damaged 'if we stand on the margins or allow ourselves to be isolated', Kenny announced. He said he was 'greatly saddened' that the 'shine' had gone off Ireland 'and that we are not regarded as good team players any more by some of our European colleagues'. There was more hopeful talk about the interest rate on the EU portion of the loan deal being reduced and, in time, an amendment of the overall deal.

Asked about Kelly's suggestion that the budget deficit be reduced immediately, Kenny said he had 'no intention of delivering a lethal injection to the Irish economy by trying to bridge that extent of the deficit in one year'. All was not necessarily as bad as had been painted either. While 440,000 were out of work by April, there were still 1.7 million in jobs, nearly double what it had been two decades earlier. If one in seven was out of a job, six of seven still had one, albeit they were probably paid less than previously and levied with higher taxes. If one in ten could not pay the mortgage, at least nine in ten could, again, albeit with much difficulty. Some people were able to save or to pay off debt, with the savings rate reaching 12 per cent, the real problem with this being that money was not being invested.

Kelly began to find himself isolated, even among his peers. Trying to get the government budget back into balance immediately would be a near impossibility – and trying to do so would have such a negative impact on the economy that the deficit would actually increase dramatically. A halving of social welfare and pensions would have massive social repercussions. Slashing wages – by at least a third and possibly half in the public sector – and raising taxes would leave many people without money to spend, wrecking the domestic economy and making things worse. A €15 billion deficit could quickly become a €30 billion one, resulting in more self-defeating tax increases and wage cuts – in fact, a destructive spiral. Our dependency on international trade meant that isolationism appeared a daft idea. The risk of losing foreign investment, upon which we were so dependent for jobs as well as income, was too dangerous to contemplate. A return to protectionism and a dependence on the UK hardly seemed wise.

What was useful, though, about Kelly's intervention was how it brought into focus the point that a reduction of 1 per cent in the interest rate charged by the EU for its share of our 'bailout', while useful, would save only about €400 million per annum and, as time went on, even less. It would be sizeable and important but not a game changer. The deal needed far more radical surgery than a fraction shaved off its cost.

That is where Patrick Honohan's reaction to Kelly was most interesting perhaps. He had held out the possibility of restructuring the deal over time. Our hope had to be that by constructive engagement with the EU, a partial default on money owed to the ECB on behalf of our banks – but not state debt – would be allowed within a couple of years, to reduce our overall debt burden – our reward for taking a few bullets to save the euro. It was not the type of thing that could be said by any of the interested parties in advance, but waiting for that, even if it didn't work eventually, seemed a better strategy than immediately engaging in even more self-harm. We'd done enough of that.

The secret fear of the government – not to be expressed in public – was that it would be unable to return to the bond markets to borrow money at the end of the term of the troika deal. An extension of the existing deal or a new arrangement with the troika would be required, for which it, and not the previous government, would then have to take responsibility. Minister for Transport Leo Varadkar gave the game away in a *Sunday Times* interview in June 2011 when he admitted that Ireland was 'very unlikely' to be able to return to the bond markets to borrow money. The possibility of a second bailout from the IMF and EU existed, he said. His analysis was spot on and shared by many economists, who looked at the facts dispassionately, unlike the politicians, who looked at them in hope. Reputable economists such as Professor Karl Whelan of University College Dublin had warned that the economy's prospects continued to dim, largely because of the unsustainable repayment burden of our state debts and continuing fears about a further deterioration in the banking system. He predicted that a further IMF/EU/ECB deal for Ireland was likely and would involve the European Stability Mechanism, which would have 'preferred creditor status', meaning it would have to be repaid ahead of anyone else. This status, combined with the existing preferred status of IMF loans, would cause private investors to become even more wary about buying Irish bonds, Whelan argued. The absence of private investors would make it very difficult for Ireland to return to the bond markets on normal terms.

Even more worryingly, the IMF's Ajai Chopra summarized a number of negative developments that had taken place in Ireland since the deal was signed, including lower-than-expected economic growth, worsening unemployment, further downgrades to the state's credit rating and the continued crisis in the eurozone. He suggested that the European Union would have to give more funding to bailed-out countries if the eurozone crisis was to be contained. Chopra praised the Irish authorities for their 'decisive' actions, but warned that, even if all the bailout terms were implemented, they might not be sufficient to allow the state to return to the bond markets.

Varadkar was castigated for effectively doing little more than agreeing with these experts. A ludicrously over-the-top editorial in *The Irish Times* a few days after the *Sunday Times* story thundered that 'in wartime, careless talk costs lives. In peacetime, careless talk by government ministers on fiscal policy at a time when the state's very solvency is at stake can prove extremely damaging. It creates doubt and uncertainty in financial markets among those that most matter, the bond investors from whom the state hopes to borrow again next year.'

It accused Varadkar of 'not simply speaking out of turn' but of undermining government efforts to reassure bond markets that it would meet the targets set in the IMF/EU/ECB rescue plan 'and, above all, to distance and to differentiate Ireland from Greece. Because Greece has failed to achieve the targets set for it, a second bailout seems likely – and sooner rather than later – if a debt default is to be avoided.'

Varadkar had said nothing about our government reneging on the undertakings given to the IMF and EU, even if they were so onerous that it should; indeed he was one of the ministers most in favour of reducing the deficit at speed.

Ireland's credit rating was just a touch above junk status long before Varadkar spoke. The yield on existing traded ten-year bonds stood at 11 per cent, the budget deficit remained enormous, and the banks continued to be dependent on the European Central Bank for funds. Official silence or delusional optimism was not going to change any of that.

Indeed, when Varadkar said that there would probably be 'either an extension of the existing programme or a second programme', he was talking of something that might even have been desirable, if introduced on different, and more favourable, terms from the first deal.

All that Varadkar was guilty of doing was failing to toe the official party line. Taoiseach Enda Kenny – former scourge of Brian Cowen – declared in early June that 'we will repay our loans. We will not restructure our debt. We're not looking for any further time. We are going to meet this challenge as we are already meeting the conditions set up under the EU–IMF deal.'

If anything, comments made by Minister for Finance Michael Noonan in New York in mid June may have been more provocative and potentially damaging than anything his colleague – less than half his age – had said. Noonan told an interviewer that the government would seek to burn bonds that had been issued by Anglo Irish Bank and Irish Nationwide Building Society, worth about €5 billion-plus. The reasoning was absolutely sound and logical. These financial institutions were being killed off. They were so bust that the idea of lenders escaping scot-free was nonsense. The bonds had been issued outside of the guarantee period. This was exactly what the previous government had wanted to do and been prevented from doing. The reaction from the ECB was firm: Ireland would repay all the bond-holders, no matter what the circumstances.

Noonan had been discovering what a rotten job he'd been landed with. He was faced with the horrible task of delivering a budget in December 2011 that would take yet another €3.5 billion out of the economy, through a combination of new tax measures and further public spending cuts.

In December 2011 the previous government had agreed to tax increases worth €1.5 billion as part of its surrender to the IMF/EU/ECB. As the household charge proposed by the environment minister, Phil Hogan, would account for little more than 10 per cent of that – and as the corporation tax was untouchable and further VAT increases could diminish spending even more – it seemed that income-tax rises would most likely be required. But to mark a hundred days in power, Kenny pledged that no rise in the income-tax rate would be announced in 2011. The Taoiseach was determined to protect his and his party's continued popularity – which was based in some part on scarcely disguised contempt for Fianna Fáil – and soon after an *Irish Times* opinion poll gave him a 53 per cent personal approval rating, the highest he had ever achieved. But how long would the honeymoon last?

The introduction of the household tax from January 2012, even at an initial low €100 per household, the promise of its replacement by a far bigger property tax in two years' time, and the installation of meters in preparation for the introduction of water charges in 2014 – all this was bound to do damage at some stage to the standing of Kenny and his government. It had been elected to do something different, not implement the policies of the previous administration to the letter, which was what it was doing, by and large. And it had added some controversial initiatives of its own: for example, it had placed a special levy of 0.6 per cent per annum on pension funds, the first time such a tax on the capital of people's retirement savings had ever been introduced.

Noonan had some sympathy from one of his government colleagues, Minister for Education Ruairi Quinn of the Labour Party, who had served as an acclaimed finance minister a decade and a half earlier. Quinn told the Dáil that Michael Collins, the state's first minister for finance, had had more room for manoeuvre than Noonan possessed today. Noonan was being asked to do the near-impossible in acting as a quasi-receiver, rather than as a minister.

Noonan, bane of the latter part of Lenihan's tenure as minister, struggled when it was pointed out that he had failed to live up to many of his promises. He began to lash out at the opposition and told the Dáil in June that 'I prefer to try and encourage people to be a bit confident to get back to work, to all pull together in the interests of this country.' When he went on with 'you can keep knocking, you can keep talking it down as much as you like, but what we're going to do on this side of the House is to try and rescue the country', it could have all come from the mouth of Lenihan. 'If you want to scaremonger and frighten the children and talk about the bogeyman coming down the chimney in two years' time, go right ahead and do it,' he told Pearse Doherty, the Sinn Féin finance spokesman.

Noonan took the occasional lash at outside forces too. During the same New York trip on which he raised the bond issues, he told Bloomberg business news agency that France and Germany were looking for security over Irish state-owned assets in return for loans. He said that they could sing for it. Nor would he be 'waltzed around' by any state impertinent enough to try to force a change in our corporation-tax rate.

Noonan also threatened jokingly to get into the T-shirt manufacturing business. He wanted to print 'Ireland is not Greece' garments, he said, and sell them. He was speaking in June 2011, just as the Greek crisis exploded again, in an even more serious way than the one that had hit in April and May of the previous year – when his predecessor Brian Lenihan had insisted we would not need the type of help required by Greece.

Our problems, while sizeable, are nothing like those being endured by the Greeks. Even most of our sternest critics, both internal and external, say we should not be regarded and treated by others in the same way. The almost amusing thing about all of this is that back in November 2010 the Greeks were insisting that they shouldn't be compared to Ireland, that they were somehow a better credit risk than we were, notwithstanding the fact that they had been forced into the arms of an IMF/EU/ECB rescue six months before we had. The Greeks said they did not have a banking crisis like ours, which was true. But their public-finances deficit trumped ours hands down and they clearly did not have the same will to confront it through austerity measures as Ireland.

Appalling vistas were opening up everywhere. One was the prospect of the government being unable to repay its debts to its creditors. We need a Plan B to cope with the circumstances that would arise from a default on our debts, either sovereign or bank related (although the distinction has become marginal). We need a Plan C to cope with a failure to re-enter the bond markets when our current IMF/EU/ECB deal expires. Plans B and C need not be too different, because the circumstances outlined above would be quite similar, but few have confidence that any plans are in place, as the government is continuously fire-fighting instead of engaging in strategic planning.

A Plan D to cope with the consequences of a break-up of the euro or our eviction from the single currency is another necessity. Fears for the survival of the euro continued all throughout the summer of 2011, even as patched-up deals to tide Greece over were hatched. In the absence of full fiscal union, which would require a degree of political agreement almost impossible to achieve, the survival of monetary union looked equally difficult – although the European establishment did not want to concede this. If the worst were to happen, somebody would have to organize the printing presses for a return of the punt, look to new sources of borrowing (maybe in the US, or possibly China) and put together a plan to help individuals renounce full repayment of debts, just as the state would have to do.

It might never come to that, of course, and our new government and officials are clinging to the belief that everything will work itself out somehow – because if Europe fails and if everything goes askew, others would have to help sort out Ireland as part of the process. After all, the European Union is going to significant lengths to ensure that the euro survives; and finally, in July 2011, a more serious and concerted effort to find a solution to Europe's economic ills had the side-effect of sizeable benefits for Ireland, albeit not quite as significant as was claimed politically at the time.

In mid July the European Union decided that Greece had to be sorted again, because the original bailout was not having the desired effect. This wasn't for Greece's sake but to prevent so-called contagion from affecting Spain's and Italy's ability both to borrow and to repay what they owed already – sums that dwarfed those that had caused the problems in Greece, Portugal and Ireland. A second rescue for Greece was decided upon, and again it was at a bilateral meeting of Merkel and Sarkozy, a day before an EU summit, at which the key decisions were made.

What Germany, in particular, and France rejected was almost as significant as what they agreed upon. Germany baulked at the idea of the EU issuing bonds in its own right, instead of individual countries continuing to do so independently. Such common borrowing, with the proceeds then to be shared across the twenty-seven member states, would have meant cheaper money for the riskier economies, or for those which were regarded as such a bad credit risk that they couldn't get any money at all. The flipside would have been more expensive borrowing for those who could get money cheaply at present. For Germany it was reckoned that money costing it 3 per cent annually would, as part of an overall EU solution, then cost it 4.8 per cent, or about €44 billion annually. Germany would not wear that, particularly as it was continuing to subsidize the old East Germany with which it had been reunited in 1990. Nor did it believe it would be politically possible to persuade its own people to engage with the concept of a more closely united Europe – which the issue of common bonds would have brought a step closer – when its fury at the profligacy of the Greeks, Portuguese and Irish was palpable.

The solutions debated for Greece were interesting in so far as they might be applied to Ireland's situation. The first proposal was that Greece should be given €30 billion or so by the EU to use for the purchase of Greek debt as it became due for repayment, but at a significant discount. This was rejected, as it was de facto default. The second idea was that all banks, even our Irish ones, should pay a new bank levy of 0.25 per cent of assets annually for five years, and the €50 billion or so raised would be used to refinance Greece. This too was regarded as impossible, as banks that had not lent to Greece would be involved in bailing out those that had.

The proposal decided upon was a new €109 billion bailout for Greece, to which private investors – those now infamous bondholders – would have to contribute up to €50 billion. And the issue of so-called 'burden-sharing' was finally taken on board and would be implemented before 2013. (In the months that followed, the Irish government would use this precedent in its attempts to renege on the final payments to bondholders in Anglo Irish Bank and Irish Nationwide.)

Just as importantly, there was an admission that the austerity measures being enforced upon Greece as part of its rescue simply weren't working and were contributing to a steeper decline in the

Greek economy. Greece is expected to have a national debt of €350 billion by 2014, amounting to 170 per cent of its GDP. While it remains doubtful that Greece will ever be able to escape from that burden without a major default, it is also clear that it cannot be expected to pay sky-high interest rates on its loans as part of that recovery. So when Greece had the interest rate on its EFSF loans cut to 3.5 per cent, and was told that it had far longer to repay its loans, Ireland was in a position to say 'Well, if that's true for Greece, then what about us?'

Michael Noonan should not go without credit for putting Ireland in a position to benefit from the Greek misfortune. Weeks earlier he had cleverly changed tack when he saw that the interest-rate argument – that it was unfair to us – was getting nowhere. Emphasizing that the original Greek deal could not work and would have to be changed – as indeed occurred – he insisted that the same thing should happen to Ireland, because our burden was unsustainable too. When the terms and conditions of Greece's loans changed, so should Ireland's.

Ireland would benefit in two ways. The interest rate on our EU loans would be reduced from 5.8 per cent to between 3.5 and 4 per cent, although the exact details were to be worked out over the coming months. This could reduce Ireland's annual interest bill by up to €800 million from 2013 (once all the loans had been drawn down), and some estimates suggested that the savings could reach €1.2 billion per annum if the IMF followed suit by reducing the price of its loans. The repayment period was extended as well, doubled from seven and a half years to fifteen.

Given its claims on entering office as to what it would do, the Irish government, surprisingly, was relatively muted in taking credit for the changed situation. In the preceding months it had played down the likely benefits of an interest-rate cut, as the prospect of this actually happening receded; it would therefore be difficult, though not impossible, to assert now that it was a great triumph. It was also clear that the Irish windfall, if it was that, was the result of Greece's bad fortune, as much as anything else. But such things rarely stop politicians from taking credit for achievements. The problem was that the new arrangements, while welcome, were little more than a consolation that the government could use as a political fig-leaf.

The most salient facts remained unchanged. There would be no immediate benefit to the public from the government's having to pay less interest on its loans in 2012 than previously would have been the case. It did not free up any money for investment or reduce the necessity to raise more taxes and cut spending. The austerity in the budget for 2012, when delivered in December or earlier, would be the same as if nothing had happened in July 2011. Taxes would go up every bit as much and spending would come down.

The terms of the IMF/EU/ECB deal would be implemented to the letter over the three remaining budgets of the four-year plan. The July breakthrough meant nothing in that regard. There was still a projected deficit of some €15 billion between the taxes raised to run the country and the amount being spent; and the priority was to face that. Things had changed, but not by much.

Indeed, there was an unintended negative consequence. The EU's Greek solution meant that there was no longer a guarantee that private investors would be paid all the money they were owed by European states, which would cause them to look warily at those with problems in covering their repayments. Ireland might hope to re-enter the debt markets in 2013 to escape the troika's clutches, but, should it have failed to do what the markets would consider a 'good job' in reducing the deficit by that time, it would not be considered a safe recipient of loans. The paradox remained: too much austerity would reinforce the depression; while a failure to reduce the deficit by a large amount would necessitate another package of loans from the troika, rather than a return to conventional borrowing on the markets. We remain caught in our dilemma, knowing that, however it turns out, one thing has been confirmed: Ireland really has gone bust and is now dependent on the kindness of strangers.

Acknowledgements

Many people helped in providing information for this book, most on an off-the-record basis at my suggestion, and I owe them great thanks for their time and thoughts. I had decided that people might open up more if they felt they were not going to be quoted directly; it was up to me, then, to test their factual recollection or views against those of others and also for me to make decisions as to the legitimacy and veracity of their claims. That often involved my making judgements that may be disputed, but I hope that my interpretation has been fair and accurate, and that I have been able to provide you with a roadmap as to what happened in the most extraordinary period of Ireland's economic and political history.

I have to acknowledge and thank my family for their indulgence as I researched, wrote and edited, and spent time away from them. My love to Andie, Aimee, Millie, Zach and Harry, and their mother and my wife, Aileen, as ever. I also have to thank my production team at *The Last Word* on Today FM – Patrick Haughey, Mary O'Hagan, Killian Murray, Mary Carroll and Ronan Lawlor – for their understanding of my occasional absences and dark moods as the workload intensified. My thanks also to Willie O'Reilly, John McColgan and the rest of the ever supportive people at Today FM. My work with Ciaran O'Eadradh on GAA, rugby and other sports for TV3 remains a great pleasure for us and my thanks go again to David McRedmond at TV3 for his constant encouragement. Frank Fitzgibbon and John Burns at the *Sunday Times* are great editors to work for, and discussions as to the content of the weekly column helped inform and shape much of this book. My thanks too to Tim Vaughan at the *Irish Examiner* and Jack Power for their understanding of my occasional late delivery of copy.

But most importantly I have to thank the people without whom I would never have started or completed this book. Michael

McLoughlin at Penguin continued to have faith in me, even as I delayed things, which is very necessary for a busy author, and Patricia Deevy was again a wonderful editor to have, stern when necessary but always encouraging and focused. A small upside of the sad and untimely demise of my old newspaper, the *Sunday Tribune*, even if only a personal and selfish one, was that the insightful Diarmuid Doyle was available to play a very important role in helping me to shape and structure the book. Donna Poppy did her usual thorough and essential job of cleaning up my often poorly written sentences, and I am greatly indebted to her. I also relied upon the great support of my literary agent, Faith O'Grady.

Some perhaps unusual acknowledgements with which to finish: trainer Paul Byrne has transformed my fitness over the last nine months, helping me to feel better than I have done in over twenty years, with the result that this book and its associated workload didn't drain me anywhere near as much as its predecessor had. And here's the bizarre one: a bad habit I developed as a student was always having music on as I worked, something I was told I should never do because it would impact on my concentration. This habit has continued into adulthood and I always have a CD or an iPod on as I work, usually listening to a Canadian rock band called Rush that I've followed for over thirty years. Rush finally got to Dublin for a concert this year, and I got to meet them before seeing them live in action – the lift I got from that was equal to a series of those hard training sessions I both hate and love. It's such strange and personal things as this that keep me going and allow me to get things done. The book is now done, and I hope you have found it worth while.

Index